C0-AVN-896

THE
PSEUDO-GREGORIAN
DIALOGUES
II

STUDIES IN THE HISTORY
OF
CHRISTIAN THOUGHT

EDITED BY

HEIKO A. OBERMAN, Tucson, Arizona

IN COOPERATION WITH

HENRY CHADWICK, Cambridge
JAROSLAV PELIKAN, New Haven, Connecticut
BRIAN TIERNEY, Ithaca, New York
E. DAVID WILLIS, Princeton, New Jersey

VOLUME XXXVIII

FRANCIS CLARK

THE
PSEUDO-GREGORIAN
DIALOGUES
II

LEIDEN
E. J. BRILL
1987

THE
PSEUDO-GREGORIAN
DIALOGUES

BY

FRANCIS CLARK

VOLUME II

LEIDEN
E. J. BRILL
1987

BR
65
.G56
C55
1987
v.2

ISSN   0081-8607
ISBN   90 04 07773 1
       90 04 07776 6

Copyright 1987 by E. J. Brill, Leiden, The Netherlands

All rights reserved. No part of this book may be reproduced or translated in any form, by print, photoprint, microfilm, microfiche, or any other means without written permission from the publisher

PRINTED IN THE NETHERLANDS BY E. J. BRILL

CONTENTS OF VOLUME II

Part Three: The Internal Evidence

Part Four: The Dialogist and his Legacy

PART THREE

THE INTERNAL EVIDENCE

CHAPTER TWELVE

A KEY TO THE ANALYSIS OF THE *DIALOGUES*: THE "STORE" OF GREGORIAN LITERARY REMAINS IN THE LATERAN *SCRINIUM*

I have already made mention of what I call the "store" of genuine Gregorian remains and fragments which can be shown to have remained in the archives in Rome after the death of St Gregory. In this chapter I shall explain more fully how the existence of this deposit of Gregorian literary remains, still accessible in the Lateran *scrinium* during the seventh century, provides a key to the analysis of the *Dialogues* and to the dispute about the authenticity of the work. Even those who have been disconcerted by the apparently unGregorian character of so much of the *Dialogues* have still felt constrained to concede Pope Gregory's authorship of the work because of the presence in it of many exegetical, doctrinal and moral passages which bear the unmistakable stamp of his thought and style. To resolve the stylistic paradox presented by the *Dialogues* I show, first, that there was a considerable fund of unpublished Gregorian texts which the Dialogist could have utilized, in order to give his pseudonymous work an appearance of authenticity; and, secondly, that the convergence of evidence demonstrates that he did in fact utilize such texts. In Chapters 14-17 I shall deal individually with the "Eighty Inserted Gregorian Passages", pointing out signs of incongruity which betray his design and methods. In order to appreciate how the store of Gregorian remains originated and to identify the kind of material which it contained, we must study the history of Pope Gregory's literary activity and his method of composition and revision. We must also see what is known about the operation of the papal *scrinium* itself.

Like other authors, Gregory knew the labour of painstaking composition, pen in hand. However, most of the Gregorian corpus of writings as we have them were not physically written by the pontiff's own hand. Some of them were composed by careful reflection in his study and dictated to amanuenses; others originated by a less structured process, being spoken as extempore commentaries or homilies and taken down by reporters, to be edited later by their author for publication. It must be remembered that the fourteen years of Gregory's pontificate were years of intense application and concern, during which he was incessantly weighed down by the burden of pastoral cares and responsibilities. Prolonged application to literary composition in the peaceful retirement of a cell or study was no longer possible for him, much as he might long for such opportunity. As well as being overburdened with the cares of his office, Gregory was increasingly enfeebled by ill health and racked by agonizing gout.

The *Regula Pastoralis*, a work written at the beginning of his pontificate, was evidently carefully composed in library and study. In Chapter 10 I mentioned the fortunate survival of a 156-folio manuscript of the *Regula Pastoralis* clearly originating from Gregory's own secretariate and probably under his direct supervision. This Troyes manuscript testifies to his practice of making successive revisions and redactions of his works before he was sufficiently satisfied with the text to authorize its publication. Although the MS is already a "fair copy", carefully inscribed in fine Roman majuscule, it is authoritatively emended, as E. A. Lowe observes: "There are numerous alterations, corrections over erasure and marginal insertions—all by a contemporary hand—which suggest that our manuscript represents the author's revision of a preliminary edition of his work; the corrected version is closer to the text as we have it today ... Written in Italy and probably in Rome, as suggested by the paleography of the manuscript and the manner in which the text is manipulated: obviously it bears the marks of a book revised under the author's immediate supervision".[1]

However, it was rare for Gregory to have time and peace for careful literary composition of the kind he devoted to the text of the *Regula Pastoralis*. Already in previous years, when he was papal representative at Constantinople, he had adopted the method of composition which he was to use for practically all the works composed during his pontificate. In his letter to Leander, prefaced to his great *Commentary on Job*, he recalled how he had undertaken that work at the urging of his Spanish friend and of the monks who were with him at Constantinople. He described the manner in which he had composed and later revised the text:

> As you remember, the brethren thought fit to press me with importunate pleading (and you too added your urging), to expound the book of the blessed Job ... Whereupon, with the brethren assembled to hear me and with the book open before my eyes, I spoke my commentary on the earlier chapters straight out. For the later chapters, finding that I had somewhat more time at my disposal, I dictated the text reflectively. Finally when considerably more time was available, I went through the whole text, which had been taken down as I uttered it, correcting it and arranging it into books. I added many things, omitted a few, and left others as they were. When I was dictating the last part of the work I gave careful attention to

---

[1] *Codices latini antiquiores*, VI, p. 40.

the style in which I had orally delivered the earlier parts. Thus I ensured that, by going through the sections which I had delivered by word of mouth and carefully correcting them, I should bring them into fair consistency with the sections I had composed for dictation; and conversely I ensured that those sections which I had dictated to scribes should not be notably different from the language I had used when speaking to the brethren. That is, by expanding the material here, and by contracting it there, I sought to mould into a harmonious whole what had been produced by different manners of composition. However I have left the third section of this work almost as I uttered it by word of mouth, since the brethren, by drawing me away to other tasks, have not allowed me to emend it in more detail.[2]

Although the *Commentary on Job* had been undertaken while Gregory was *apocrisiarius* of Pope Pelagius II at Constantinople, more than ten years elapsed before he was able to send to Leander an edited copy of the work. In April 591 he explained why there had already been several years' delay: "You write asking me to send you the commentary which I gave on the blessed Job. Since I had spoken this in the form of colloquies, imperfect both in expression and in sense, I have devoted what care I could to casting it into book form. It is now being transcribed by the copyists."[3] Notwithstanding Gregory's expectation, stated in the same letter, that the whole work would soon be ready for despatch, it was to be another four years before the finally-edited text was sent to Leander. (Even then it was incomplete, for transcripts of two sections were not available.) In an accompanying note Gregory bewailed the harsh pressure of affairs which prevented him from writing more than those brief lines to his best friend.[4]

The method of composition which Gregory described in some detail in the case of the *Moralia* he also used, for the most part, when composing his other works. When he could find time and strength amidst the arduous affairs of his pontificate, his preferred method of composition was to prepare his material mentally, with prayer and reflection, and then to dictate the text to secretaries. He would afterwards carefully supervise the correction and improvement of the text they had taken down. When shortage of time or ill health did not permit him to prepare his homiletic discourses in this way, he simply spoke extempore with the page of sacred Scripture open before him. Stenographers (clerics or monks) took notes of his discourses, and later reproduced them—in at least one case even without the authorization of the pontiff. Gregory was very particular that these *reportata*, written out from shorthand records of his spoken words, should not be disseminated without his express sanction. This he would

---

[2] Ep. V.53a; Ewald-Hartmann, I, pp. 354-5.
[3] Ep. I.41; Ewald-Hartmann, I, p. 58, lines 2-5. See also the note on p. 353.
[4] Cf. Chapter 5 above, footnote 70.

not give until he had carefully corrected, improved and edited the text.
His account of how his *Homilies on the Gospels* came to be published is
revealing in this regard. When eventually he was able to complete the
editing he sent to Bishop Secundinus of Taormina an authorized copy of
the work. In an accompanying letter he explained how it had been
brought into this final form:

> During the sacred solemnities of the Mass I expounded 40 readings from
> the holy Gospel, from those which it is the traditional custom in this Church
> to read on fixed days. In some cases the exposition which I had dictated was
> read out to the assembled people by a notary; in others, I myself made a
> spoken explanation while the people listened, and as my words were uttered
> so they were taken down in writing. But some of the brethren, fervent with
> zeal for the sacred word, reproduced what I had said before I could revise
> it by careful correction in the manner I intended. These I would rightly
> liken to starving men who rush to eat their food before the dish is properly
> cooked. For instance there is my commentary on the text: "Jesus was led
> by the Spirit into the desert to be tempted by the devil". My first exposition
> of this text was somewhat ambiguous, but afterwards I corrected that am-
> biguity by a clear annotation. I have arranged these homilies in two codices
> in the order in which they were delivered. The first 20 homilies, which were
> composed by dictation, and the remaining 20 which were spoken with the
> Bible open before my eyes, are thus placed in two distinct groups. Your
> Fraternity need not be surprised that in the earlier part are found some
> homilies of which the relevant readings occur later in the Gospel, and that
> some texts which were written by the evangelist in earlier chapters are com-
> mented on later in my work. The reason is that just as these homilies were
> delivered by me at different times of the year, so they were also transcribed
> by the note-takers into the codices at different times. If Your Fraternity,
> always so diligent in sacred reading, should come across a transcript in
> which the aforesaid text of the Gospel is expounded in an ambiguous man-
> ner, or if you should find these homilies not arranged in the way which I
> have described, you must realize that the transcripts in question have re-
> mained uncorrected. In that case you should correct them according to the
> text which I have taken care to send to you by the present bearer, and on
> no account allow them to remain without such emendation. The edited text
> is preserved here in the *scrinium* of our holy Church, so that if there are some
> readers who are at a distance from Your Fraternity, let them find here, in
> our codices which have been duly emended, an exemplar from which they
> can resolve any uncertainty.[5]

In the case of the *Moralia* Gregory had delivered the first part of his
commentary by extempore colloquy, and had composed the subsequent
part by reflective dictation in his study; but it is clear from this letter to
Bishop Secundinus that in the case of the *Homilies on the Gospels* these pro-
cesses were reversed. Whereas the first 20 sermons were composed by

---

[5] Ep. IV.17a; Ewald-Hartmann, I, pp. 251-2.

dictation in his study, the last 20 were delivered extempore from the pulpit. At the beginning of the 21st homily Gregory explained to the people why he had decided thus to change the manner in which his sermons were communicated to them:

> For many of my discourses, beloved brethren, it was my custom to speak to you by word of mouth what I had already prepared by dictation. However, because of my intestinal malady I have not been able to read out personally what I have prepared by dictation, and I see that some of you in the congregation are less well pleased on this account. Wherefore I have decided to set aside my previous practice, and to demand from myself the effort to expound the readings from the holy Gospel during the celebration of Mass, not by reading a sermon which I have dictated, but by speaking to you familiarly. Thus while I am speaking the homily, it may be taken down. For the voice of one speaking in familiar colloquy avails more to arouse torpid hearts than a sermon which is read out ...[6]

The letter to Bishop Secundinus well illustrates the meticulousness—some might even call it fussiness—with which Pope Gregory supervised the editing and authorization of his books. He took a close interest in the work of the *scrinium* of the Roman See. There, as we shall see, he had at his service a filing system that enabled him to retrieve and adapt passages or fragments which he had composed at an earlier time, and which for one reason or another had not been included in any of his published writings. From his constant pruning, revision and recasting of his works, and from the stenographers' records of his Scriptural homilies and lectures, there remained in the Lateran archives a considerable number of such passages and fragments, intended to be reworked and reused if the author so desired.

We gain further insight into the methods by which Gregory's expository writings were produced from what he says about his composition of the *Homilies on Ezekiel*. In the dark days of 593-4, when the army of the Lombard king Agilulf was menacing Rome, he delivered his series of 22 spoken discourses on the prophecy of Ezekiel. I recalled in Chapter 5 how, ill, tense and overworked, Gregory could not prepare his commentary by careful forethought and dictation in his study. He spoke extempore from an anguished heart while the notaries took down his words. Distracted by his daily cares and the horrors of the siege, he found it increasingly difficult to bring his mind and will to bear upon the task. Eventually he could preach no longer, but broke off with a cry of affliction.[7]

The *Homilies on Ezekiel*, dramatically interrupted by the worsening crisis of the Lombard siege of Rome, were left unrevised for eight years.

---

[6] *PL* 76.1169.
[7] *Homilies on Ezekiel* II.10.24.

The *schedae* or notebooks of the reporters who had taken down the Pope's impassioned words as he spoke them in the Lateran basilica lay gathering dust in the papal *scrinium*. In all that time Gregory was unable to find opportunity to edit them for publication. At length, at the renewed request of the monks and others around him, he brought himself to work on those notebooks and to supervise the preparation of the text for publication. In a dedicatory letter written in 601-2, to Marinianus, Bishop of Ravenna, Gregory recalled: "Oppressed by a multitude of cares, I had left in oblivion the homilies on the prophet Ezekiel, which had been taken down in writing just as I spoke them to the assembled people. But after eight years, at the urging of the brethren, I took pains to send for the *schedae* of the notaries, and with the help of God I revised them. As far as the pressure of my afflictions permitted, I have corrected the text."[8]

The editing of the *Homilies on Ezekiel* not only illustrates the various stages through which his writings passed before he authorized them for publication, but also provide us with a valuable glimpse into the workings of the Roman *scrinium*. Here is one more indication of the existence of earlier drafts and redactions of Gregory's works, which were preserved in the *scrinium* awaiting eventual revision when the pontiff could find time. Indeed we have positive evidence of the survival after Gregory's death of pericopes which he had excised from earlier recensions of his works. In Chapter 6 I mentioned the presence of some "lost" passages, said to have come from the *Homilies on Ezekiel*, which are found embedded in the seventh-century anthology of Gregorian Scriptural exposition known as the *Liber Testimoniorum* of Paterius. Others are ascribed in early MSS to the *Moralia* and to the *Regula Pastoralis*. It is time to look more closely at the implications of the survival in the collection of Paterius of these otherwise unknown Gregorian passages.

The existence of several "lost" passages from the *Homilies on Ezekiel* has long been recognized. The Maurists alluded to them, and in his edition of Gregory's works,[9] J. B. Galicciolli later printed an (incomplete) series of the additional passages which were not to be found in any manuscript of those Gregorian homilies. R. Étaix completed the list in an article of 1958,[10] and M. Adriaen reprinted the full series in his critical edition of the *Homilies on Ezekiel*.[11] Asking where those additional

---

[8] Ep. XII.16a; Ewald-Hartmann II pp. 362-3.

[9] Vol. VI, Venice 1769, pp. 263-71. The Maurists had already signalled the existence of such passages in their edition of the work of Paterius.

[10] "Le *Liber Testimoniorum de Paterius*", in *RSR* 32, 1958, pp. 66-78. Étaix noted that the passages cited by Paterius were, in the early MSS, referred to Homilies VIII, IX, X, XI of Book I.

[11] *CCL* 142, 1971. Adriaen remarks of these passages: "...*haec tamen fragmenta nec in codicibus (ni fallimur) nec in editionibus harum homiliarum invenies*" (p. 400).

passages came from, Étaix suggested that they were copied from the *schedae* of the notaries who took down Gregory's words as he preached the homilies in 593-594. Adriaen considered this a "shrewd hypothesis", and agreed that "there can be no possible doubt about the Gregorian origin of these fragments."[12] Étaix also made the pertinent suggestion that some of the Paterian excerpts were derived from "a first edition of the *Moralia*".[13]

Adriaen brought out the interesting fact that several of those "lost" Gregorian passages are also used, usually in fragmentary or abbreviated form, by Tajo of Saragossa in his *Libri Sententiarum*.[14] It cannot be inferred with any certainty that Tajo took them from the compilation of Paterius. His use and arrangement of them differs in some particulars from that of Paterius; and there are a few instances elsewhere in which Tajo reproduces unknown Gregorian fragments which Paterius does not.

We saw in Chapter 6 that there is no proof that the ascriptions of the Paterian extracts to particular Gregorian works, as given in the eighth-ninth century manuscripts, were originally written by Paterius himself. Rather, from the fact that they are not consistent in different early MSS, one may infer the contrary. It may be, then, that some at least of the excerpts which are stated in those MSS to have been taken from the *Homilies on Ezekiel* were not after all drawn from the *schedae* of those discourses, but from unedited Gregorian expositions of other books of the Bible.

Drawing up his list of 28 such "lost" passages cited by Paterius, R. Étaix commented on the fact that such a considerable body of Gregorian texts should be known to exist and yet be in practice unnoticed and ignored:

> It may well appear astonishing that authentic texts of St Gregory, published under his name in the Latin Patrology, should never be utilized. Now these texts are found in the *Liber Testimoniorum*, and they seem to have hardly ever been noticed, although the Maurists conscientiously noted that a certain number of extracts cited by Paterius are not to be found in the known works of St Gregory the Great. From both external and internal criticism we are obliged to consider these pieces as being fully Gregorian.[15]

Étaix concluded his article on the "lost" Gregorian texts which survive in the work of Paterius by raising an interesting question: "It would be

---

[12] *Loc. cit.*, p. 400.

[13] He further surmised, however, that Paterius, being himself a notary in Gregory's secretariate, took his extracts from the unrevised notes in the *schedae* before Gregory edited them for publication in 601-602. I find this surmise implausible. It seems clear that the Paterian compilation was made after Gregory's death.

[14] *Op. cit.*, pp. 401 ff. He lists 19 such fragments. See Chapter 6 above.

[15] *Op. cit.*, p. 76.

useful to study these texts, with the purpose of discovering the reasons for their suppression in the ''official'' editions published by St Gregory. Was it in order to correct certain assertions which seemed inadequate or ambiguous, or simply to lighten the weight of his composition?''[16] This question put by Étaix with reference to the unknown Gregorian passages which he lists from the pages of Paterius may be relevantly adapted to our own context, when in the following chapters we discuss the provenance of what I call the ''IGPs'' (Inserted Gregorian Passages) which are to be found embedded in the *Dialogues*. I shall argue that just as Paterius—and Tajo—were able to draw on a store of authentic but unpublished Gregorian pericopes, so also was the Dialogist able to do the same. In a number of cases Paterius, Tajo and the Dialogist all utilized the same unpublished items. As with Paterius and Tajo, so with the Dialogist, it will be relevant to ask why each of the Gregorian gems which he found unused in the Roman *scrinium* had been omitted from the ''official'' editions of the saint's works. We shall find that in some cases we may reasonably conclude that Gregory omitted items because they duplicated what he had said elsewhere.[17] The other motives suggested by Étaix seem also to have been operative: namely, desire for brevity or scholarly caution about assertions made in earlier drafts.

So far, in our discussion of the contents of the store of Gregorian remains in the Lateran *scrinium*, we have considered only ''snippets'' or excised passages which for one reason or another had been omitted from the definitive texts of Gregory's writings as he had authorized them for publication. But we know that there was also a very considerable body of unpublished Gregorian texts still preserved in his secretariate at the end of his life, which were not merely separate fragments but continuous and substantial treatises. The known *corpus* of Gregory's writings reproduces only a part of his work of Scriptural, doctrinal and homiletic exposition. His expository activity was spread over a period of nearly 30 years, from the time that he retired from political office about 574 to live in the monastery of St Andrew, which he had established in his family mansion on the Coelian Hill. Both before and after his elevation to the papacy the monks were assiduous in taking down in their notebooks the spiritual discourses of their illustrious protector.

The quantity of Scriptural expositions thus recorded in the *schedae* was considerably more extensive than our *corpus* of Gregory's known works. Although he had it in mind eventually to edit those additional materials

---

[16] *Ibid.* p. 78.

[17] This reason must be qualified. Gregory was inclined to be repetitious, and he certainly did not eliminate all ''doublets'' and reiteration when he revised his works for publication.

for publication, the cares of his pontificate and his illnesses prevented him. Nevertheless the monks and scribes treasured their unofficial records of the oral teaching which he had delivered to them. One monk in particular, named Claudius, is mentioned in this connection. He took notes of the commentaries which Gregory delivered "*sub oculis*", that is, with the book of the Scriptures open before him. As we recalled in Chapter 11 (E), he was not very competent either in shorthand or in comprehension. When he became abbot[18] of the monastery of SS John and Stephen at Classis, near Ravenna, he took with him his precious transcripts of Gregory's lectures. When Claudius died they were left there, evidently exposed to unauthorized usage. Gregory's indignation about this was forcefully expressed in a letter written two years before his death to his representative at Ravenna, John the Subdeacon, ordering him to go to the monastery forthwith to take possession of the manuscripts and to send them back to Rome:

> My beloved son, the late abbot Claudius, was a listener when I delivered some discourses on *Proverbs*, on the *Canticle of Canticles*, on the Prophets, on the *Books of Kings*, and on the Heptateuch. Because of my infirmity, I could not commit those discourses to writing; wherefore he had transcripts made of them according to his own interpretation, lest they should perish in oblivion. The intention was that when opportunity occurred he would bring his transcripts to me so that I might correct them for publication. But when he read them to me, I found that the sense of my words had been changed in a very unsatisfactory manner. Wherefore it is necessary that without any excuse or delay you should go at once to his monastery, call the brethren together and order them, with the strictest precept, to bring out into the open whatever manuscripts, on those different parts of Scripture, that Claudius took there. Take possession of them and send them to me as speedily as possible.[19]

Assuming that John the Subdeacon carried out this trenchant command (and Pope Gregory expected and exacted faithful obedience from his subordinates, most of all from those to whom he delegated his authority in the papal patrimonies), then we know of a considerable augmentation of the store of unrevised Gregorian works in the Roman *scrinium* at the close of his life. A collection of transcripts of his lectures on *Proverbs*, on the *Canticle of Canticles*, on the Prophets, on the *Books of Kings* and on the Heptateuch would indeed constitute a large sheaf of folios. The Heptateuch, or first seven books of the Old Testament, comprised the Pentateuch (the Five Books of Moses—*Genesis*, *Exodus*, *Leviticus*, *Numbers* and *Deuteronomy*) and the two additional books of *Joshua* and *Judges*, which were considered to form a unity with them. In fact, we

---

[18] Some time before July 592; see Gregory's Ep.II.45; Ewald-Hartmann I, pp. 143-4.
[19] Ep.XII.6; Ewald-Hartmann, II, p. 352.

find that some of the unknown Gregorian passages cited by Paterius are comments on texts from those books. We shall see that the Dialogist likewise inserts into his work genuine Gregorian exposition of texts from the Heptateuch, especially from *Genesis, Leviticus* and *Deuteronomy*.

An indication that John the Subdeacon did carry out the task enjoined on him, and duly returned Claudius's transcripts to the papal secretariate, may be seen in the survival of the truncated commentaries on the *Canticle of Canticles* and on the *First Book of Kings*. As we saw in the previous chapter, these texts, though substantially authentic, were not published in Gregory's age or for long afterwards. Among the commentaries mentioned in his letter to John the Subdeacon as having been taken down by Claudius and as being in the monastery at Classis, were expositions of those particular books of the Bible. P. Verbraken, the editor of those two incomplete commentaries in the *Corpus Christianorum* series, draws attention to a remarkable phrase in the *incipit* of the oldest MSS of the short commentary on the *Canticle*, stating that it had been taken ''from the *exceda* of the Lord Gregory, Pope of the City of Rome''.[20] Verbraken notes that *exceda* is a variant form of *scheda*, the term used for a notebook or loose folio. Hence the text of the *Canticle* commentary was reproduced from those *schedae*, which, as we have already seen, were the notebooks in which the notaries took down Gregory's extempore commentaries and conferences.[21] Verbraken comments: ''This work, then, was drawn from the archives of the pope'', and he considers that the phrase in the ancient *incipit* ''offers all the guarantees of an origin contemporary with Gregory''.[22]

There can, then, be no doubt about the existence of a store of unpublished Gregorian texts preserved in the Roman *scrinium*. The excerpts of Paterius and Tajo show that it was still there during the seventh century, and John the Deacon attests even in the ninth century that undivulged writings of Gregory were still preserved in Rome.[23] When in the following chapters I point to it, to explain how the Dialogist was able to find and to insert into his book some eighty genuine Gregorian fragments

---

[20] ''*In nomine domini incipit expositio in canticis canticorum a capite de exceda relevata domni Gregorii papae urbis Romae*''. (*CCL* 144, p. 3.)

[21] The term *schedae* was used by Gregory himself to refer to the notaries' scripts of his spoken commentary on *Job* (Ep.XII.16a).

[22] *Op. cit.*, p. VIII. We have a letter from St Columban to Gregory, written some time between 595 and 600, in which the Irish monk requested the Pope to send him his exposition of the *Canticle of Canticles*, referring especially to a verse in Chapter IV. This suggests that there did exist a longer form of the work, extending beyond the commentary on the first eight verses of Chapter 1, which is all that has survived.

[23] '' ... *reliqua ipsius opera nunc in sancta Romana Ecclesia retinentur adhuc sub custodia, ne penitus vulgarentur.*'' (*PL* 75.223).

and thus to give exceptional verisimilitude to his pseudonymous work, I shall be pointing to a source that is not a mere hypothesis but an established fact.

It is more and more apparent that the Roman *scrinium*, in the papal residence which adjoined the Lateran basilica in Rome, has a special significance for our study of the riddle of the *Dialogues*. In the course of our investigation I note many indications that the author of the *Dialogues* was involved in the work of that office, and that his writing betrays clerkish characteristics and interests. It is my submission, to be justified further in later chapters, that he was himself a functionary of the papal secretariate who was active in the second half of the seventh century. He would thus be familiar with its archives and traditions. Because of this significance of the *scrinium* for our following of the trail of the Dialogist, it is pertinent to summarize here what is known of its organization and work in the late sixth and seventh centuries. From a valuable (but neglected) monograph by J. B. De Rossi, "On the Origin and History of the *scrinium* and Library of the Apostolic See"[24] the salient facts can be gleaned.[25]

The papal *scrinium*, as it originated in the early centuries, was an ecclesiastical parallel of the civil archives which were kept in the *scrinium memoriae* of the Roman imperial court. There is record that as early as 338 Pope Julius I gave organized status to the *sanctum scrinium*. From at least the fifth century not only the pope's letters, sent and received, but also other official papers—legal, fiscal, administrative as well as literary and theological—were kept in what St Jerome had called the *chartarium ecclesiae romanae* and what was now ordinarily called the *scrinium* or *scrinia sedis apostolicae*. In classical usage the term *scrinium* originally referred to a chest or press in which documents and books were kept. In the Late Latin of the age we are studying it had a wider connotation, and can be taken to refer to the office or secretariate in which the scribes and librarians worked. (It is in this wider sense that the Dialogist uses the word, when he tells the story of Anastasius, the notary of the holy Roman Church, who, wishing to devote himself wholly to God, "deserted the *scrinium*" and entered a monastery.[26]) The *scrinium* was thus at the same

---

[24] Prefaced to his monumental work, *Codices palatini latini bibliothecae Vaticanae*, Rome 1886. I follow De Rossi for many of the details given below.

[25] There is also a short account in R. L. Poole's *Lectures on the History of the Papal Chancery down to the Time of Innocent III*, Cambridge 1915, pp. 13-25. J. Richards has a useful account of Gregory's aides in his chapter on "The Gregorian Court Circle" (*Consul of God*, pp. 70-84).

[26] "*Qui soli Deo vacare desiderans, scrinium deseruit, monasterium elegit ...*"; *Dialogues* I.8.1.

time the secretariate of the reigning pontiff, the archives in which present and past records were housed, and the papal library.[27] It was also a kind of official "publishing house" where multiple copies of books were transcribed. Others were copied in monasteries. Evidently Gregory I had many copies of his own works made, for there are several references in his letters to his sending codices of his writings as presents to bishops, monks and others. Doubtless the scribes in the papal *scrinium* also replicated copies of the Scriptures and patristic writings. When Gregory sent a *copia librorum* to Augustine of Canterbury he must have had recourse to a stock of books already transcribed and available for such a purpose, as B. Bischoff observes.[28]

The senior officials of the *scrinium* were the *notarii*. According to the sixth-century redaction of the *Liber Pontificalis* there were in the administration of the Roman Church (as well as seven deacons and seven subdeacons) seven notaries. The latter were considered to be subordinate to the subdeacons. The Roman *notarii* were, however, no mere pen-pushers. They formed an influential guild, known by Gregory's time as the "*Schola* of the Seven Notaries of the Regions". They belonged to the ranks of the clergy, and were usually in minor orders. At the head of the guild of the seven notaries was the *primicerius notariorum*. "It is established that, at least in the seventh century, the *primicerius notariorum* had reached such a height of dignity that when the papal See fell vacant he shared with the archpriest and the archdeacon the responsibility for governing the Roman church."[29] Next in dignity among the notaries was the *secundicerius*.

We know the names of some of the guild of notaries at Pope Gregory's court. The *primicerius* in 593 was Gaudiosus, who was consulted by the Pope on a question of episcopal privilege.[30] The *secundicerius* about that time was Exhilaratus, whom the Dialogist makes a character in one of his stories.[31] After Exhilaratus the next *secundicerius* was Paterius, who was appointed to the post at a date between 597 and 599. He had served loyally in the *scrinium* for some years before his promotion. His name is mentioned in several of Gregory's letters, and as J. Richards comments, "He clearly occupied the position of a favoured private secretary".[32] This is the Paterius who is credited with the compilation of the *Liber*

---

[27] Other local churches had their *venerabilia scrinia* too: cf. Ewald-Hartmann, I, p. 229, lines 37-8. Gregory refers to the *regalia scrinia* of the Frankish kingdom: Ep.XIII.7; *ibid.* Vol. II, p. 373, line 21.

[28] *Mittelalterliche Studien*, Stuttgart 1966-7, Vol. II, p. 319.

[29] De Rossi, *op. cit.* p. XXXI.

[30] Ep.III.54; Ewald-Hartmann, I, p. 213.

[31] *Dialogues* II.18.

[32] *Op. cit.* p. 76.

Testimoniorum. Not only the two chief officers but also the other members of the guild of notaries were used as papal agents and envoys in matters of moment. We see this in the case of another of Gregory's notaries, Pantaleo. Among the missions on which he was sent by the Pope between 593 and 603 were the tasks of supervising the election of a new Archbishop of Milan, of investigating the seduction of a deacon's daughter by a nephew of the Bishop of Sipontum, and of probing financial abuses in the papal patrimony in Sicily.[33] On the supposition that the Dialogist himself was employed in the Roman *scrinium* in the second half of the seventh century, he may have had the opportunity of accompanying those senior envoys on papal business in the Italian provinces, especially in Central Italy, with which region so many of the stories in the *Dialogues* are connected. I will return to these possibilities in Chapter 22.

We know the names of other notaries in Gregory's pontificate. One was Benenatus, whom Gregory appointed as rector of a sub-division of the papal patrimony in Sicily, based on Palermo. Two others with responsible tasks were Hadrian and Eugenius.[34] Then there was Aemilianus, who is mentioned in a papal rescript of 600 as a "notary of the holy Roman Church" who recorded a petition concerning an abbot's testament.[35] John the Deacon, writing his *Life of Gregory* in the ninth century, adds the information that it was Aemilianus the notary who, with his companions, took down in writing Gregory's *Homilies on the Gospels* as he delivered them.[36] Although many details in John's "*Life*" are historically dubious, it is quite possible that on this point he had reliable documentary record to go on. He had access to a surviving archival collection, including Gregory's subsidy-roll, which in his own day was still to be seen "*in hoc sacratissimo Lateranensis palatii scrinio*".[37]

For the more humdrum tasks of writing at dictation and of taking down reports of discourses and official proceedings the notaries had *exceptores* to serve them. These were stenographers trained in shorthand from youth. If some *exceptores* aspired to become *notarii* in their turn, clearly only a very few could attain membership of the select guild of the seven notaries. There were several other grades in the pontifical *scrinium*, again paralleling those in the imperial civil administration. We read of the titles of *scriba*, *regerendarius*, *scriniarius* and *chartularius*. The term *notarius* was sometimes applied to secretaries who were not members of the *Schola*.

---

[33] Ep.III.40, 41; IX.19, 112; XI.6, 14; XII.37, etc. cf. J. Richards *op. cit.*, pp. 77-8.
[34] Ep.III.27 and IX.110.
[35] Ep.XI.15.
[36] *Vita Gregorii* II.11. *PL* 75.92.
[37] *Ibid.* II.30; *PL* 75.98.

The picture we have seen so far shows us the Roman *scrinium* about the time of St Gregory the Great. We have noted the organization of that office, and the standing and duties of those who were employed there. This background helps us to understand how the store of unpublished Gregorian literary remains was available in the following century for use by Paterius, Tajo and the Dialogist. But it will also be relevant for the further stages of our inquiry to follow the subsequent history of the *scrinium* and the *scriniarii* through the seventh century. In probing the riddle of the authorship of the *Dialogues* converging clues repeatedly lead us back to the Lateran *scrinium*. It is as one of the lesser or middle-ranking functionaries in that bureau that I visualize the Dialogist. What then do we know of the history of the *scrinium* in the century following the pontificate of Gregory I?

During that period its organization and functions remained basically the same as those we have observed in Gregory's time.[38] The *scrinium* continued to be at one and the same time the papal secretariate, the administrative archives of the Roman See, and the papal library where books and manuscripts were not only stored but were copied for despatch to other places. "In the seventh century", writes De Rossi, "the *scrinium* and the library of the Apostolic See, over which the *primicerius notariorum* presided, was certainly in the patriarchal palace of the Lateran. In the formulae which were used in that century and are recorded in the *Liber Diurnus*, the '*archivum* of the Roman Church' and the 'sacred Lateran *scrinium*' were one and the same".[39] An impressive illustration of the complexity and efficiency of the organization of the *scrinium* in the middle of the seventh century comes from the Acts of the Council of Rome held under Pope Martin I in 649. The *primicerius notariorum* at the time, Theophylactus, was called upon to provide for the use of the assembled Fathers a large number of documents, including acts of councils, patristic and heretical writings, charters and other records. That he was able to comply with their requests, promptly and repeatedly, testifies both to the library resources of the *scrinium* and to the competence of its staff.[40]

The importance of the Roman *scrinium* as a principal centre for the transcription and provision of manuscripts increased with the ever-growing demand for books from the bishops, clergy and monks of the new regions of Christendom. When a northern bishop asked Pope Mar-

---

[38] De Rossi devotes a chapter of his monograph to this period: "*De scrinio et bibliotheca sedis apostolicae saeculo septimo*". cf. also O. Bertolini, *Roma di fronte a Bisanzio e ai Longobardi*, Rome 1941, pp. 372-3.

[39] *Op. cit.* p. LXVI. It appears that there was also an archive and a bureau for book production attached to St Peter's basilica.

[40] De Rossi, *ibid.* pp. LXVI-LXX.

tin I for a copy of a codex, the Pope had regretfully to reply that the stock of that particular work was exhausted, and that it would not be possible to have a copy transcribed as speedily as required.[41] The Lateran library was, as De Rossi observes, "an abundant source from which codices could be copied for those who requested them. Thus at this time the library of the Apostolic See was, as it were, the centre from which sacred books were disseminated throughout Europe, especially northern Europe".[42]

I recalled in Chapter 9 how eagerly scholars from the newly converted Anglo-Saxon kingdoms sought books in Rome. Some they bought, some were gifts from the popes.[43] The fruit of the prolific book-copying industry in the City can be seen in the "*magna copia voluminum sacrorum*" which Benedict Biscop brought back to England from his fifth visit to Rome in 684. The process of transcribing books and supplying them to the clergy and monasteries of Europe must have required a considerable employment of scribes and a suitably commodious area for them to work in. Moreover the enterprise must have brought some not inconsiderable economic benefit to the Roman *curia*. In the sixth century the main source of revenue for the Church and City of Rome had been provided by the estates of the papal patrimonies. Those revenues, however, had been much reduced by Lombard depredations, imperial confiscations and the general disorder of the age. Now with the rise of the new Christian nations to the north there came the first signs that Rome could look farther afield for new sources of revenue. The position which the Apostolic See occupied in the loyalty, esteem and religious needs of those nations assured Rome of sources of material support which would in time make all parts of Christendom tributaries to the coffers of the papal *curia*. The Roman book-production industry, especially valued in an age when new monasteries and centres of scholarship were springing up in England, France and Germany, was one of the earliest Roman enterprises to offer these wider financial opportunities.

It seems probable that it was this great expansion of the work of book transcription that led to the enhanced importance of the library department of the Roman *scrinium*, and to its eventual distinction from the notarial department which performed the work of the papal secretariate as such.[44] When did this separation of the two departments occur? A precise answer to this question can be given from the surviving records; and it is an answer which may help to illuminate the circle in which the

---

[41] *Ibid.* p. LXXIII.
[42] *Ibid.* LXXXIII.
[43] *Ibid.* p. LXXIV.
[44] *Ibid.* pp. LXXXIX-LXXX.

elusive Dialogist worked. We learn from the *Liber Pontificalis*[45] that is was in the pontificate of Pope Sergius I (687-701) that the division of the Lateran *scrinium* into two departments occurred. Pope Sergius committed the care of the library to a rising official named Gregory, whom he also made one of the seven subdeacons and *sacellarius*, or treasurer, of the Roman Church. This Gregory had been brought up and trained from an early age in the papal establishment in the Lateran palace.[46] His appointment to the new post of curator of the library supposes that he was well acquainted with the work of the *scrinium*, and his path to advancement would naturally have included service in the post of *notarius*. In the year 715, on the death of Pope Constantine I, he was elected pope as Gregory II. From his desk in the *scrinium* he had risen to the highest office of all. He was enterprising, energetic and had a fluent command of language— *facundus loquela* is how he is described in the *Liber Pontificalis*. It was about the time that he became curator of the Lateran library that the *Dialogues* were first emerging into the light, and it was during his subsequent pontificate that their influence became generally apparent. As we have seen in Chapter 1, Pope Gregory II was a principal promoter of Benedictine monasticism, which from that time onwards expanded rapidly and triumphantly, drawing special authority from Book II of the *Dialogues*.

I would draw attention to a remarkable passage in Adalbert de Vogüé's introduction to the *Dialogues*,[47] which is relevant to our discussion of features of the Dialogist's writing which link him with the Roman *scrinium* and the work of its clerks. Fr de Vogüé far surpasses all previous editors in his critical analysis of the structure and antecedents of the book, and in his penetrating observations on its characteristics. Most striking in our present context is his detection and description of what he himself aptly calls ''*un style de notaire*''. Under this heading he draws attention to a distinctive and strange feature of the whole composition. The style is that of a writer who is trained to draw up documents with stilted and lawyer-like precision, in order to make clear at every point who or what is being spoken of. The author of the *Dialogues* does this, as Vogüé observes, by ''the use and the abuse of adjectives or phrases of ''reference back'' (*renvoi*) every time a person or a thing already named reappears in the text.'' Constantly we find these adjectives and phrases: ''the same'', ''the said'', ''the aforesaid'', ''the one I have referred to'',

---

[45] Ed. Duchesne, Tome I; Paris reprint 1955, p. 396.
[46] ''... *a parva aetate in patriarchico nutritus* ...'' (*ibid.*)
[47] *SC* 251, pp. 81-2.

"whom I have mentioned above", etc.[48] It is the phraseology of a clerk versed in juridical formulae, of a curial official accustomed to drafting rescripts and recording depositions. At times we find a sentence so overloaded by the repetition of "the selfsame" or "the aforementioned" that it reads like a clause of legal jargon. Here is an example, from the story of a pious servant of an advocate ("the aforesaid Valerian"): "When the household of the same advocate was afflicted by the same plague the same servant was stricken".[49] Again, a venerable priest who is cited as witness of a spectral apparition in the baths at Centumcellae is at once re-identified as "*isdem presbyter in eodem loco*"—"the said priest in the said place".[50] Fr de Vogüé makes the following trenchant observations on the "*style de notaire*" which pervades the text of the *Dialogues*—observations which, even by themselves, should surely raise a serious question whether the author whose work betrays this peculiar trait can plausibly be supposed to be Pope Gregory the Great:

> Even in a short narration, these phrases—such as "the same", "the aforesaid", "whom I have mentioned above"—are multiplied with singular wearisomeness. There are cases in which three references of this kind are found in succession in the same phrase, or in which one such *idem* follows immediately after another. This literary *tic* springs from the juridical style, in which it is important not to leave the slightest occasion for ambiguity. By linking every new mention of an object back to antecedent mentions of the same, it overburdens the discourse with interconnections. In this it relates to another characteristic of the style of the *Dialogues*: namely, the abundance of connecting relative pronouns, which are also multiplied, often in monotonous sequence. The same concern with precise reference and with verbal linkings shows itself in the frequent use of the adverbs *nimirum, scilicet, videlicet*, which generally have little or no real function there.

This clerkish and legalistic style is distinctive of the *Dialogues*; it is not similarly pervasive in the works personally composed by Pope Gregory. Fr de Vogüé does indeed claim that this trait is likewise marked in Gregory's correspondence.[51] When comparing these usage-patterns in

---

[48] Among these recurring expressions of *renvoi* in the Latin text are *praedictus, quem praedixi, quem praefatus sum, cuius memoriam feci,* and the innumerable reduplications of *idem* in all its cases. (Vogüé, *ibid.* p. 82, footnote 162.)

[49] "*Cum veru eiusdem advocati domus eadem clade vasteretur, isdem puer percusses est*" (*Dialogues* IV.27.10; Vogüé, *loc. cit.* footnote 163.)

[50] *Dialogues* IV.57.3. Out of several similar examples cited by Vogüé is: "*Nocte autem eadem eiusdem ecclesiae custos ...*" (IV.53.2).

[51] *SC* 251, p. 81. Vogüé also points out (on pp. 80-1) a striking contrast between the manner in which the various states of life in the Church are referred to in the *Dialogues*, on the one hand, and in Gregory's Scriptural commentaries and the *Regula Pastoralis*, on the other. Vogüé considers that although the direct vocabulary of the *Dialogues* contrasts with the veiled and "functional" appellations habitually used by Gregory in those other

the *Dialogues* with those in the other works of the Gregorian corpus, however, we must remember that among the latter the *Registrum* is a special case. In Chapter 21, discussing discrepancies of vocabulary and style between the *Dialogues* and the other works, I shall take further account of the difference, highlighted by the work of Professor D. Norberg, between the style of the relatively small number of letters that Gregory evidently composed personally, and that of the majority of the letters, betraying a more formal and consciously mannered style, which were drafted by secretaries for his approval. In the latter category we do indeed find a greater incidence of clerkish *phrases de renvoi*—though still not equalling the heavy overloading of such phrases in the *Dialogues*, where in places they recur in rapid and uncouth succession. But in the letters in which we can hear Gregory's own accents dictating the words, this clerkish trait is not similarly apparent.[52]

The *Registrum* apart, the contrast between Gregory's style in his other works and the Dialogist's crabbed over-use of *phrases de renvoi* can hardly be gainsaid. In Chapter 21, when discussing discrepancies in vocabulary and style, I shall note statistics indicating that such usages are proportionately far more frequent in the *Dialogues* narrative than in Gregory's six pastoral and theological works. For instance, the referential adjective *praedictus*—"the aforesaid"—is found in the main narrative of the *Dialogues* in a frequency of one occurrence per 807 words; but in Gregory's pastoral and theological works the frequency is one occurrence per 33,546 words. Thus in the *Dialogues*, it is used, *pro rata*, 41 times more frequently than in those other six works taken together. Again, a numerical survey of the cases of *idem* reveals that the Dialogist's use of

---

writings, it nevertheless parallels Gregory's style in his letters. But, as D. Norberg has shown, and I will now recall, only a minor part of the *Registrum* can be taken to reflect Gregory's own literary style; the major part reflects the more formal style of the chancery.

[52] A personal letter in which such phrases are more frequent than usual is that sent by Gregory to the noble lady Rusticiana in Constantinople. (XI.26; Ewald-Hartmann II, pp. 287-9.) We note that they occur especially in the second part of the letter. There, after expressing his warm solicitude for his old friend, Gregory thanks her for alms sent to his monastery of St Andrew. Then he appends four stories of preternatural events concerning that monastery, so that Rusticiana may see how Providence guards the monks whom she had aided. It may be remarked that when introducing these stories Gregory explains that he had them "from the narration of the abbot and prior of the monastery"—"*quae abbate ac praeposito monasterii narrantibus agnovi*". When the Pope passed on Rusticiana's alms to the superiors of St Andrews, did he ask them to provide some edifying *exempla* of preternatural protection of the monks, which he could send with his personal greetings and thanks to their benefactress? If the four stories, doubtless of a kind which would appeal to the piety of Rusticiana, were added to Gregory's letter in the written narrative form supplied by the abbot and prior, then the last part of this letter would not reflect Gregory's own literary style but that of the monastic relators, as edited by the papal secretary responsible for the despatch of the letter.

them is in the order of approximately five times more frequent than in Gregory's pastoral and theological works.

The "abundance of connecting relative pronouns", which A. de Vogüé points out as a feature of the *Dialogues*,[53] is likewise not so obtrusive in the other works. To be sure, Gregory himself does use relative pronouns fairly frequently to maintain continuity in his discourses.[54] But his usage is notably less than the Dialogist's multiplication of such connecting pronouns, "often in monotonous sequence".

In the same passage in which he brings into relief the legalistic *phrases de renvoi* in the *Dialogues*, Vogüé also draws attention to an associated trait of the author. As a further unattractive aspect of the writing, he remarks, "we must note the heaviness and the monotony of the titles accorded to sacred personages, even when they are simply introduced as informants. One cannot count the number of occurrences of phrases such as *vir venerabilis, vir vitae venerabilis, vir venerandus*". Acceptance of the demands of social etiquette here involves "a heavy tribute paid to courtesy and to convention. The strictly hierarchized society of the Low Empire is reflected in the Church, both triumphant and militant. Each personage has a right to his proper title, in which "veneration" must be punctiliously observed."[55] I submit that in this obtrusively obsequious style we may discern once again the stamp of the curial official, schooled by long and daily practice to pen such fulsome epithets. His usage of them did not conform to Gregory's own usage, nor even to that of his secretaries, who in drafting his administrative letters would have to be mindful of his love of simplicity and his distaste for clerical ostentation. His principle, "*me vana superfluitas non delectat*",[56] may be reflected in the moderation with which the *consiliarii*[57] who prepared his official letters refrained from hyperbolic descriptions of ecclesiastical persons. Although in the Gregorian epistolarium there is careful observance of the customary titles of respect which protocol demanded, according to the dignity in Church or State of the personages addressed, this is a different tone from the ubiquitous epithets of veneration in the *Dialogues*, applied to any monk, priest or pious person, even though, as Vogüé remarks, he be mentioned only as a source of information. The characteristic expressions of veneration which recur countless times in the *Dialogues* are not similarly obtrusive in Gregory's letters (or in his Gospel homilies). The

---

[53] He cites two telling examples in *SC* 251, p. 82, footnote 165.
[54] An example of such frequency, pointed out by Fr de Vogüé, can be studied in *Homilies on the Gospels* 37.8-9.
[55] *SC* 251, p. 82.
[56] *Ep.* I.39a.
[57] Cf. *Ep.* VI.63; Ewald-Hartmann I, p. 440, line 13.

appellation *vir venerandus* does not appear at all in the *Index verborum* of Ewald-Hartmann's edition of the *Registrum*. The phrase *veneratione vitae*, applied to ordinands, appears twice in what was evidently one of the standardized curial formulae.[58] *Vir venerabilis* appears in three letters: once applied to a deceased priest whose merits were known to Gregory personally, once to an abbot wronged by a bishop, and once, in a letter to the Emperor, to a priest and a deacon who were not permitted to remain in Rome.[59] In a Gospel homily[60] Gregory, relating the testimony of an unnamed deacon, describes him as *"vitae venerabilis"*.

In fine, the *"style de notaire"* is distinctive of the *Dialogues*, in contrast to the undisputed writings of Gregory the Great. It is not Gregory's own style; and it is also significantly absent from those 80 pericopes in the *Dialogues* themselves which I designate as the "IGPs", and which I shall discuss in detail in subsequent chapters.

While the seven *notarii* of the Roman Church were normally clerics in minor orders, it is probable that there were monks among the scribes and stenographers in the *scrinium* in Pope Gregory's time. Gregory seems to have favoured monks and employed them in the papal administration. After his death there was an anti-monastic reaction, it seems, and a reassertion of the traditional prerogatives of the clergy in the Roman establishment. During several pontificates in the seventh century, with an occasional swing of the pendulum of papal favour, monks were excluded from official posts, and the clergy resumed their usual place in the administration of the Roman Church. I shall argue more fully in later pages that the Dialogist, whose sympathies and interests are recognizably pro-monastic, lived and wrote in a period when the prejudice against monks was no longer operative, and they could be once more involved in the work of the secretariate. These conditions were verified in some pontificates during the seventh century. In particular, Pope Vitalian (657-672) and Pope Adeodatus II (672-676) were favourable to monks and chose them for important offices. In Chapter 22 I will return to the subject of the papal *scrinium* in that period and the Dialogist's probable connection with it.

---

[58] Ep.I.15 and I.51.

[59] Ep.XIII.28; I.12; VII.6.

[60] 38.9

THE EIGHTY GREGORIAN PASSAGES APPROPRIATED BY THE DIALOGIST FOR INSERTION INTO HIS BOOK

It is, then, firmly established that a store of unpublished Gregorian passages and fragments remained in the Roman *scrinium* as a legacy from Pope Gregory's prolific literary activity. Some of these remains were pericopes excised by the Pope in his repeated revisions of his texts in preparation for publication; some were unrevised or unapproved *reportata* taken down by stenographers from his oral discourses, especially from Scriptural expositions delivered from the pulpit.

We have considered probable reasons for the excision or non-publication of these remains. In some cases a pericope was excised because it duplicated a similar pericope elsewhere. Such an explanation is particularly applicable in the case of excerpts from the long and diffuse *Commentary on Job*, the *Magna Moralia*. This work was composed over a considerable period of time, partly by extempore colloquy from the pulpit or conference chair, partly by reflective dictation at the desk. Despite its title, it is not restricted to the exposition of the *Book of Job* but draws on the Bible as a whole, commenting on a multitude of texts taken from the other books of Old and New Testaments. Naturally, when like themes evoked like comments, Gregory tended to repeat himself in his protracted discourses. In his work of revision and redaction he was able to remove some of these repetitions. In other cases, as we have seen, the reason he did not authorize publication of certain texts and commentaries was that he was dissatisfied with the wording as the *exceptores* had taken it down in their notebooks, and that he did not have time or inclination to correct and edit their transcripts. In a few other cases, as we shall see, we may surmise that Gregory prudently withheld from publication certain doctrinal passages (in particular, those concerning the lot of the separated soul after death) because they went beyond the hitherto accepted patristic teaching, and he may have wished to avoid the appearance of any innovation in doctrine.

With the existence of the store of *Gregoriana* firmly demonstrated, we may now turn to discuss the use which the Dialogist in his turn made of that quarry of unpublished materials. It was a considerable and ingenious use. I have already remarked that it is his frequent introduction of passages of Gregorian moral and doctrinal teaching, interspersed in his main narrative text, that gives his work its special character and its patristic authority. It is this quality of the writing that for centuries has powerfully persuaded scholars to accept the *Dialogues* as the indubitably authentic work of St Gregory. In most cases those moral and doctrinal pericopes are such as would appropriately be found in a Scriptural exposition, and often we can infer the nature of the context in which they were originally written by Gregory. The insertion of those theological passages into the *Dialogues* is often awkward or artificial, or at least strangely digressive. (A. de Vogüé called them "*excursus*".[1]) Time and again we find that they are introduced abruptly or gratuitously, and are not fitted to the Dialogist's own context. The passages which I am going to list and discuss are not all in the category of unpublished Gregorian remains. A number of them are taken from the saint's known and published works. Gregory himself did occasionally reuse passages that he had already written for another work—a notable example is his inclusion of long paragraphs from his recently composed *Regula Pastoralis* in the Synodical Letter which he sent to other patriarchs and bishops soon after his elevation to the papacy.[2] But the Dialogist's reuse of passages from Gregory's published work will be seen to be of a different order. He betrays himself even as he reproduces passages from Gregory's known works, especially in the way he adapts and embroiders them.

The investigator who examines the structure of the *Dialogues* with this key in his hand will make some interesting discoveries. He will observe how, following a picturesque tale in less than elegant Latin, there comes a leading question from Peter the Deacon, which often has only a forced connection with what has just been said. Its point is to provide a cue for the Dialogist to bring in a Gregorian passage which he has ready for use. Sometimes Peter's question leads straight into the Gregorian text, but at other times the Dialogist puts into Gregory's mouth some sentences or phrases of his own to link the question with the authentic Gregorian passage which is to come. After this preparation, there follows a pericope in the unmistakable language and style of St Gregory himself, giving some moral or spiritual teaching based on Scriptural exposition. The opening phrase of the pericope may be adapted by the Dialogist to make it seem relevant—often with the interposition of the vocative "*Petre*". Very occasionally he also inserts some words of his own into the text of a Gregorian excerpt, but generally he reproduces Gregory's words without adulteration. At the end of the borrowed pericope of elevated teaching, there is often a remark by Peter the Deacon in praise of what

---

[1] *SC* 251, p. 108.

[2] The first and larger part of the *Epistola Synodica* is taken almost verbatim from the *Regula Pastoralis*, I.10 and II.1-7; cf. Ewald-Hartmann, I, p. 29, footnote.

has been said, and the narrative then returns to the Dialogist's own level. At one point, after digressing in order to deploy an IGP, the Dialogist explicitly marks the return to his own hagiographical narrative: "*Sed quaeso ut ... ad narrationis ordinem redeas*" (II.3.12).

In most cases the original source of the "IGPs" can no longer be traced. Yet we are still able to discern the starting and concluding points of the Gregorian excerpts, to mark their linguistic difference from the surrounding text and to note the awkwardness in their appropriation by the Dialogist. We do not have open to our inspection the larger quarry of unedited and unpublished Gregorian remains which the Dialogist was able to exploit. Nevertheless, we have enough, both in Gregory's published works and in the unpublished fragments preserved by other scribes, to identify the sources from which some of the Dialogist's borrowings were taken, and we are able to make shrewd conjectures about the sources from which he made other borrowings that cannot now be directly identified.

In Chapters 14-17 I identify and delimit the 80 IGPs. There I present and discuss the evidence relating to each of them in turn, and point out their frequent incongruity with the main text in which they are embedded. I fear that some readers will be daunted by the intricacy and the length of the arguments in those chapters, which demand close attention to the Latin phraseology, style and division of the pericopes. Apart from scrutiny of the structure of the Latin text, there is required familiarity with Gregory's own sonorous style and vocabulary, in order to recognize the contrast between the inserted passages and the Dialogist's distinctively different and less elegant Latin in the main body of his narrative. Nevertheless I wish to make my main argument accessible to the general reader, and not to overlay it from the start with technical minutiae. In the present chapter I will take a single preliminary example to discuss in depth, in order to illustrate how the many other IGPs may be fruitfully subjected to the same kind of detailed criticism. The passage that I propose to discuss now as a typical example of the Dialogist's methods is taken from *Dialogues* II.38. I give here an English translation to compare with the Latin text in the Appendix. The chapter in question occurs at the very end of Book II, just after the account of the death of St Benedict and the ascension of his soul to heaven. After recounting the burial of the saint in the oratory at Montecassino, the Dialogist makes Gregory relate that St Benedict continues to work miracles in the cave at Subiaco. In this chapter one may observe all the four elements involved in the Dialogist's use of IGPs. First, there is the hagiographical narrative, with its miracle stories, into which the doctrinal digression is to be implanted; secondly, there is the leading question of Peter the Deacon, intended to provide the cue; thirdly, there is an explanatory passage, put into Gregory's mouth by the Dialogist, to link Peter's question with the Gregorian gem which is shortly to follow; and fourthly, there is the inserted Gregorian pericope itself, which I have here italicized. (This pericope I list in Chapter 15 as IGP 27.)

Dialogues II.38

(GREGORY) Even in the cave at Subiaco in which he first dwelt, he still to this day works glorious miracles, if importuned by the faith of those who seek his help. I now relate an event that occurred there recently. A certain mentally affected woman, who had completely lost her senses, wandered day and night through mountains and valleys, woods and fields, only resting where weariness forced her to take some repose. One day, when she had strayed far afield, she came to the cave of this blessed man the abbot Benedict, and without knowing what it was she entered and stayed there. When morning came she emerged in full possession of her senses, just as if no insanity had ever affected her. She continued the whole remainder of her life in that same sanity which had been bestowed upon her.

(PETER) What reason can we give that often we find it is like this, with the patronage of the martyrs likewise, that they do not bestow such great benefits through their bodies as they do through objects associated with them, and they perform greater wonders in those places where they do not corporally rest?

(GREGORY) There is no doubt, Peter, that in those places where the holy martyrs rest corporally, they are both able to show forth many wonders and actually do so, exhibiting countless miracles to those who seek with a pure mind. But since weak souls can doubt whether the martyrs are present to listen favourably to their prayers in those places where it is known that they are not corporally present, therefore it is necessary to show forth greater wonders in those places where the weak can doubt about their presence. But for those whose mind is fixed in God it has so much the more merit of faith, inasmuch as it realizes that they do not lie there in the body, and yet are present there to listen favourably to prayers.

Wherefore Truth himself, in order to increase the faith of his disciples, said: "If I go not away, the Paraclete will not come to you". Now since it is certain that the Paraclete Spirit is always proceeding from the Father and the Son, why does the Son say that he is going to withdraw, in order that he [the Holy Spirit] should come who never withdraws from the Son? It was because the disciples, beholding the Lord in the flesh, eagerly desired to see him always with their bodily eyes, that he well said to them: "Unless I go away, the Paraclete will not come". It is as if he clearly said: "If I do not withdraw my body, I do not show you what the love of the Spirit is, and unless you cease to behold me corporally, you will never learn to love me spiritually".

(PETER) Well pleasing are your words.

We observe two contrasting features in this sequence: first, the clearly Gregorian character of the concluding theological pericope, and secondly, the unGregorian character of the reasoning by which that pericope is made to seem relevant to what has preceded it. That elevated pericope does indeed bear the hallmarks of Gregory's phraseology and expository style. It is a comment on a text from St John's Gospel (16.7) which Gregory expounds in his familiar heuristic fashion of exegesis. The text says that the divine Son must depart in order for the divine Spirit to become present; but how can this be, since in the eternal procession of the Holy Spirit from the Father and the Son one divine Person is never separated from another? In the original context Gregory solved this theological objection by explaining that Christ was drawing his disciples' understanding to a deeper spiritual level. They were attached to his bodily presence, which they could see with their eyes, and they were to be weaned from this kind of attachment in order that they should know the true spiritual love that comes from the Holy Spirit, and that they should love Jesus himself with that love.

The Dialogist has cobbled this paragraph of typically Gregorian exegesis into his text as if it were an apt Scriptural illustration of what has just preceded; but the manner in which he uses it and attempts to make it relevant to his own context betrays a writer who cannot match the master whose literary mantle he has borrowed. In comparison with the lofty thought and spiritual sensitivity of St Gregory, the Dialogist appears as naive in his reasoning and as insensitive in his spiritual judgement. He has at his elbow a rich hoard of Gregorian texts which he seeks to insert at intervals throughout his homespun narrative. How does he find a niche for the Gregorian exposition of *John* 16.7, which explains the necessary connection between the departure of the divine Son from the Apostles and the coming to them of the Paraclete Spirit? The cue which he puts into the mouth of Peter the Deacon is intended to link it with what he had just recounted about St Benedict's miracles. He has no word of miracles worked at Montecassino, where St Benedict's body is buried, but he does relate that miracles are still worked by St Benedict in the cave in which he once dwelt at Subiaco. As an instance of this, he narrates the impressive story of the cure of a madwoman who spent the night in that cave. This would suggest the query: how is it that, whereas St Benedict still works miracles in the cave where he dwelt long ago, nothing similar is related about miracles at the tomb at Montecassino in which his holy body rests? Peter the Deacon's question implies this query. Commenting on the story of the madwoman's cure, he asks: Why do the saints (Peter mentions "the martyrs" also) bestow greater boons through objects associated with them rather than through their own bodily remains? Why do they work greater miracles in places were they are not buried (in this case at Subiaco) than they do at the tombs in which they rest (i.e. at Montecassino)?

The Dialogist has framed Peter's question as a cue to enable him to deploy his genuine Gregorian pericope about the divine Son and the Paraclete Spirit. He develops his answer to it in a way that will lead directly on to that pericope. He first makes Gregory explain that of course in those places where the bodies of the holy martyrs are buried there is no doubt that they can and do work many miracles for those who ask aright. Then comes a curious piece of theological reasoning: because those of weak faith or spiritual understanding may doubt whether the saints are present and ready to answer prayers in places where their holy bodies are not present, it is necessary for the saints to show forth greater miracles in such places—that is, in order to instruct and reassure such doubters. Truly devout believers, however, are aware that the martyrs are at hand to grant their prayers in places other than their place of burial, and this increases the merit of their faith.

It is as a corroboration of this quaint explanation that the Dialogist introduces his Gregorian exposition of *John* 16.7. His application of it to his own context may fairly be described as bathos. According to the real Gregory, when originally composing that pericope, Jesus intended to teach his disciples a profound lesson when he spoke the words, "If I go not away, the Paraclete will not come to you". The Holy Spirit cannot be separated from the Son, since he eternally proceeds from the Father and the Son; nevertheless Jesus in his human nature must withdraw from their bodily company, in order that they should experience divine love, and learn to love him spiritually. But what a crass application of this sublime lesson it is to make the Gregory of the *Dialogues* use it as an illustration of his preceding assertion—namely, that the martyrs had of necessity to work greater miracles at places other than their tombs because the weaker brethren had difficulty in understanding a distinction between the bodily and spiritual presence of the saints, and might otherwise suppose that their thaumaturgic power was restricted to their burial places![3]

The inserted Gregorian passage we have been considering (IGP 27) has a significant similarity to a shorter passage which is found in the *Moralia*.[4] There Gregory cites the same text from *John* 16.7 and gives a similar exegesis, though even more briefly. He has just been explaining

---

[3] A. Dufourcq comments that this is "a curious passage" (*Étude sur les Gesta Martyrum Romains*, Vol. I, Paris 1900, p. 383 footnote 1.)

[4] 8.41. In this *Moralia* passage the context concerns intellectual contemplation of divine things; IGP 27 is about attaining to divine love.

that in order to attain divine contemplation the soul must withdraw from all corporeal imagination. In support of this doctrine he then adds the Johannine text as a Scriptural illustration. In this quotation from the *Moralia* I italicize the phrases in which there is identity of wording with our pericope in the *Dialogues* (IGP 27):

Unde et eisdem suis dilectoribus *Veritas dicit*: "Regnum Dei intra vos est". Et rursum: "*Si ego non abiero, Paraclitus non veniet*". Ac si aperte diceret: Si ab intentionis vestrae oculis *corpus non subtraho*, ad intellectum vos invisibilem per consolatorem Spiritum non perduco.

Wherefore he who is *Truth says* to those who love him: "The Kingdom of God is within you". And again: "*If I go not away, the Paraclete will not come*". It is as if he clearly said: "*If I do not withdraw my body* from the sight of your eyes, I shall not bring you, by means of the comforting Spirit, to understand what cannot be seen.

The original context of IGP 27 was doubtless the same as the elevated theological discussion in which this *Moralia* passage is set. In the Dialogist's context, following on from his tale of the madwoman in St Benedict's cave, this gem of Gregorian exegetical wisdom is crassly misused. It is a false note to make Gregory's reflection on *John* 16.7 seem to apply to the bizarre notion put forward in *Dialogues* II.38.3—namely, that the saints in heaven have to disregard the expected pattern and *locus* of their miracle-working on earth in order to correct the misapprehensions of those of weaker understanding. The real Gregory, so profoundly reverent to the inspired word of Scripture, above all to the very words of Christ, *ipsa Veritas*, would not have made such a gauche application of the Gospel text.

It is quite likely that Gregory originally pronounced both of these two similar passages in the course of his spoken commentaries on Scripture. Every preacher tends to repeat his own phrases when he deals repeatedly with the same themes and the same texts. It may well be that IGP 27 was also originally uttered in the course of Gregory's long-drawn-out exposition of the *Moralia*. In the successive stages of editing the text for permanent publication, he would naturally note that there were "doublets", or places where he had repeated himself when alluding to the same text in different places. Where he realized this, it would be natural to excise one of the duplicated passages,[5] and the excised paragraph would thus be preserved with the other Gregorian remains in the papal *scrinium*. R. Étaix, when discussing the possible provenance of the otherwise unknown Gregorian passages preserved by Paterius, expressly suggests that "some of them could have come from a first edition of the *Moralia*", and he gives references to a number of Paterian excerpts where this seems likely.[6]

---

[5] I have noted above that some "doublets" of this kind do, however, survive in the existing text of the *Moralia*.

[6] *Revue des sciences religieuses* 1958, p. 78. R. Wasselynck accepts the same supposition. There were two redactions of the *Moralia*, he thinks; Paterius used the first redaction

I have examined at some length this case of misappropriation by the Dialogist of an unpublished Gregorian fragment, in order to illustrate his methods and to provide a typical example out of the eighty similar borrowings which can be detected in the pages of the *Dialogues*.

In the next four chapters I offer an annotated register of the genuine Gregorian excerpts which can be recognized in the four books of the *Dialogues*. I analyse each in turn, under introductory headings in which I use the following reference system. The IGPs are numbered in accordance with the order of their occurrence. Where a Gregorian pericope has been separated by the Dialogist into two or more parts which seem to be taken from the same original context, I number these as subdivisions of the same item, distinguished by small letters after the number: thus, IGP 8a, IGP 8b, etc. I then give in each case the numbers of the book and chapter of the *Dialogues* in which the passages occurs, and also its paragraph numbers within the chapter. I next quote the opening words of the passage and the number of the line in which it begins, followed by the closing words of the passage and the number of the line in which it ends. Where I judge that a word or phrase in a passage does not belong to the original Gregorian excerpt I note this afterwards in brackets.

In my discussion of each of the IGPs I shall assume that the reader is following the argument by concomitant reference to the Latin text of the *Dialogues*, which is printed as an appendix to my first volume. This text is reproduced, by kind permission, from the edition of A. de Vogüé (*Sources Chrétiennes*, nos. 260 & 265), which has superseded all previous editions in usefulness.[7] It should be noted that I adopt Fr de Vogüé's paragraph numbering within the chapters of the *Dialogues*, which is not found in previous editions. I also cite individual lines according to the line numbering printed in his edition, which I reproduce in the printing of the text in my appendix to Volume I. In that text I distinguish the 80 inserted Gregorian passages by means of marks in the margin and text, designating each by the reference number assigned to it in Chapters 14-17.[8] It is not always possible to mark out the exact word with which an inserted pericope starts. The Dialogist sometimes adapts the opening

---

which Gregory had brought back with him from Constantinople in 584. (*"Les compilations des 'Moralia in Job' du VIIe au XIIe siècle"*, in *Recherches de théologie ancienne et médiévale*, XXIX, 1962, p. 6.) Though Paterius compiled his anthology after Gregory's lifetime, he may still have used a codex of the *Moralia* containing the earlier redaction.

[7] A new critical edition is promised for the future in the *CCL* series.

[8] To observe the actual words with which the IGPs begin and end, and the Dialogist's occasional interpolation of individual words and phrases into the genuine Gregorian passages, it will be useful for the reader also to refer to the precise indications given for each IGP in Chapters 14-17.

phrases of his borrowed passages in order to fit them into his context, and to make them immediately relevant to what has just preceded. Thus his adapted opening phrases may include words from the Gregorian original intermingled with words of his own. In the following chapters, when delimiting the IGPs, I will indicate the beginning of each passage from the point at which I judge that he is reproducing the Gregorian pericope verbatim, even though that point may not be the beginning of a sentence.

The IGPs from Book I of the *Dialogues*, numbered 1-15, are analysed in Chapter 14; those from Book II, IGPs 16-27, in Chapter 15; those from Book III, IGPs 28-42, in Chapter 16; and those from Book IV, IGPs 43-80, in Chapter 17. In the first three books taken together the IGPs constitute close on 15% of the wordage of the text; but they make up around 40% of the fourth book. Taking the four books as a whole, the IGPs account for about 24% of the total wordage. Thus the main non-IGP narrative, the Dialogist's own composition, constitutes about 76% of the total wordage. Although the IGPs are studded into his narrative on a variety of pretexts, it will be seen that they are adventitious there. As more than one commentator has observed, these elevated but digressive passages dislocate rather than integrate the flow of the narrative. In Chapter 21, when discussing the stylistic peculiarities of the *Dialogues*, I will return to this aspect of the work.

Although I would claim that my register of the IGPs is substantially complete, and that the pericopes I have marked out are adequately distinct from the rest of the text, I do not propose the number 80 as necessarily exact. It would vary if my subdivisions of the IGPs were listed differently. Moreover, it would be possible to suggest some minor additions to that number if one included certain isolated Gregorian expressions found in the Dialogist's narrative. For although the 80 IGPs marked out in my register are recognizably self-contained pericopes of Gregorian doctrine, there are also to be found, scattered in the Dialogist's own less felicitous Latin, some other occasional phrases or clauses which have the veritable ring of Gregory's style and teaching. From his familiarity with the great pope's writings, the Dialogist was able to add those sporadic Gregorian touches, in order to give further verisimilitude to his pseudepigraphal work. I give here some examples of such isolated turns of Gregorian phraseology discernible even in the Dialogist's own narrative.

The Prologue of Book II contains a phrase used as least three times by Gregory: "*soli Deo placere desiderans*". (Line 13, cf. Vogüé, *SC* 260, notes on pp. 127, 438). In the next sentence the pithy oxymoron, "*scienter nescius et sapienter indoctus*" also has a Gregorian ring.

Dial. II.8.10: "*tanto ... graviora praelia pertulit, quanto contra se aperte pugnantem ipsum magistrum malitiae invenit*". The thought and the stylistic balance here are Gregorian. (cf. Epistola IX.147; Ewald-Hartmann II, p. 143, lines 16-7, *SC* 260, p. 440).

Dial. III.4.2: the rebuke to the devil here put into the mouth of Datius by the Dialogist seems to reflect a genuine Gregorian snippet. The quotation from *Isaias* is abbreviated by Gregory in just this fashion elsewhere. (cf. *SC* 260, p. 272, footnote.)

Dial. III.15.5; Surely Gregorian is the sonorous antithesis: "*quia antiquus hostis, unde bonos cernit enitiscere ad gloriam, inde perversos per indiviam rapit ad poenam*".

Dial. III.16.4: "*in quo mentis vertice stetit*" is paralleled by several similar turns of phrase in Gregory's writings. The very same words occur in his *Homilies on Ezekiel* II.6.9. But whereas Gregory used them there to praise the humility of St Peter, the Dialogist applies them here to a holy hermit Martin, whose spiritual eminence was such that for three years he was able to live unharmed with a sinister serpent in his cell.

Dial. III.17.6: "*Quid alii sentiant, ignoro. Ego autem ...*" There is a very similar remark in *Moralia* 27.77.

Dial. III.22.4 the reference to the divine "*dulcedo*" towards men shown in works of miraculous power echoes similar phrases in *Moralia* 16.33 and *Homilies on the Gospels* 26.3. But whereas in the two latter instances the real Gregory is referring to kindly miracles worked by the Lord Jesus, as related in Scripture, the Dialogist sees the divine "sweetness" displayed in such prodigies as the one he has just related, by which a thief stealing a sheep belonging to a church was struck into immobility as he passed a saint's grave.

After those examples of Gregorian allusions scattered here and there in the Dialogist's own prose, it is time to turn to the IGPs themselves. My criteria for discerning those genuine Gregorian passages, and for distinguishing them from the Dialogist's main narrative text in which they are set, are based on considerations of vocabulary, style, text-structure and linkages, thought-content and religious character. While the exact points of demarcation between the two disparate strata in the text are occasionally uncertain, I submit that the IGPs, as I delimit them in the following four chapters, are recognizably different in origin from the main narrative text, the unGregorian character of which I will demonstrate more fully in Chapters 18-21.

CHAPTER FOURTEEN

THE INSERTED GREGORIAN PASSAGES IN BOOK I
OF THE *DIALOGUES*

The Prologue of Book I begins with a brief setting of the scene of the colloquy between Gregory and Peter the Deacon. The first thirteen lines, which contain some echoes of known Gregorian phrases, serve to introduce a pericope of genuine Gregorian prose in which the pontiff poignantly bewails the spiritual loss he suffers amidst the cares of his public office. This elevated and fairly lengthy passage provides a distinguished exordium for the *Dialogues*.

IGP 1: Book I, Prologue, paragraphs 3-6. Gregory laments his lost contemplative peace. From line 14, "*... moerorem ... quem cotidie patior ...*", to line 53, "*... laboribus noluit occupari*". (Omit "*Petre*" in line 14.)

As we shall find very frequently throughout the *Dialogues*, Peter the Deacon is made to ask a leading question which includes a verbal link with the Gregorian pericope about to be introduced. In this case the cue is the word "*novus*", in Gregory's remark that his sadness "is always old because of long continuance and always *new* because of daily increase". In the immediately preceding line the Dialogist has put a corresponding cue into Peter's mouth with the question: "Has anything *new* happened, that sadness has hold of you more than usual?" IGP 1 follows as the sequel to this question. Into the opening words the Dialogist inserts the vocative *Petre*, to make it seem that the pericope was written for his context. As we shall see, he inserts the same vocative at the beginning of many of the other IGPs which will follow throughout the *Dialogues*.

Both the language and the thought of IGP 1 are authentically Gregorian. In his commentary on these lines, A. de Vogüé points out several parallels to passages in other Gregorian writings. In particular, the sentiments expressed—and in places even the phrases used—are very similar to those found in three letters written by Gregory in October 590, the month following his reluctant acceptance of the burden of the papacy, and in another written to Leander six months later. (Epistolae I.5-7, 41; Ewald-Hartmann I, pp. 5-10, 56-7.) The graphic nautical metaphor of IGP 1, in which Gregory likens himself to a storm-tossed sailor overwhelmed by the waves of secular cares, with the lost shore of spiritual contemplation receding out of sight and mind, is closely akin both in imagery and in verbal expression to the ship-and-storm analogies in those

letters. The same nautical allusion is found in Gregory's introductory letter to Leander which he prefaced to the *Moralia* (Ewald-Hartmann I, p.
354). Although there are one or two places in Gregory's later works (e.g.
Homilies on Ezekiel I.11.5-6) in which he renews his lament for his
vanished contemplative peace, the psychological climate of IGP 1 seems
to belong to the same earlier period as the four poignant letters to sympathetic friends at the beginning of his pontificate. It may well be that
IGP 1 was taken from another letter written by Gregory about the same
time as those four, which was either not sent or at least not copied into
the archive register of his correspondence. One may even surmise that
it was a letter written by Gregory to his beloved brethren in his "own
monastery" of St Andrew *ad Clivum Scauri*; the final paragraph of IGP
1 would thus have a special application to them.

The last paragraph of IGP 1 (lines 46-53) proved especially apt for the
Dialogist's purpose. It offered him a logical link between the lament of
the real Gregory for his lost peace and the resolve of the Gregory of the
Dialogues, now to be declared, to write a narrative of the miracles of holy
men. Yet after IGP 1, with its elevated expression of Gregory's spiritual
yearning, there is a disconcerting change of style. The Dialogist puts in
what one may describe as an abrupt editorial rubric, to explain how he
is going to present his narrative: that is, in the form of a dialogue, with
the names of the two participants prefixed to their parts, in order to
distinguish the questions and answers in the dialogue.

The first of these dialogical passages, spoken by Peter the Deacon
(lines 57-62) is particularly revealing. In IGP 1 Gregory has just recalled
with yearning those who, unlike himself, have been able to shun the cares
of the world and to live holy lives in godly seclusion. To this Peter the
Deacon responds with a simple (an unGregorian) equation between holy
life and miracle-working. He assumes—quite unwarrantedly—that in
IGP 1 Gregory has asserted that his devotion is kindled by the example
of Italian thaumaturges who performed miracles and works of power
(*signa atque virtutes*). In IGP 1 it was not said that the holy recluses there
referred to were miracle-workers; in fact there was no mention of
miracles at all, but only of saintly withdrawal from the world and of contemplative peace. Likewise there was no mention of Italy, which Peter
brings into his remark. The switch of thought here, and Peter's implied
assumption, does not escape A. de Vogüé's eye: "*Pierre passe de la vie sainte
aux miracles qui en sont le signe*" (*SC* 260, p. 15, footnote 7). No doubt for
the Dialogist miracle-working is so much the sign of holy life that the two
can be virtually equated; but that is not a Gregorian equaton.[1] As Vogüé

---

[1] Nevertheless it was doubtless this passage in the *Dialogues* that Adolf Harnack had
in mind when he scornfully declared that for St Gregory "miracle is the distinguishing

points out, Gregory says in his *Moralia* 27.36-7 and *Homilies on the Gospels* 29.4 that miracles are rare in his time, in contrast to the Apostolic age. Yet here (lines 63-6) the Gregory of the *Dialogues* replies to Peter, when the latter disclaims knowledge of any signs and wonders worked by Italian holy men, that if he were to relate all that he knew on this subject the day itself would not be long enough for his narrative.

There is another tell-tale phrase in Peter's first dialogical utterance which throws a light on the Dialogist's method of constructing his text. It is the phrase *"Ex quorum igitur comparatione accenderis ignoro"* (lines 58-9). We shall see now, when considering IGP 2, that the placing of this phrase here is awkward and inconsequential. It would appear that it was originally intended by the Dialogist to follow IGP 2, to which it has verbal reference. By leaving it here he unwittingly left a trace of his literary cobbling.

IGP 2: Book I, Prologue, paragraph 9. On the "examples of the fathers" and their spiritual value. From line 70, *"in expositione quippe ..."*, to line 79, *"... cognoverit, humiliatur"*. (Instead of "signorum" in line 72 read *exemplorum* or an equivalent expression.)

IGP 2 is one of the rare instances in which a substantial paragraph of Gregorian prose is put by the Dialogist not into the mouth of Gregory himself, but into that of Peter the Deacon. It is indeed somewhat incongruous to find this magisterial teaching pronounced by Peter, who in the rest of the *Dialogues* is presented as a docile but not very percipient disciple seeking but not giving enlightenment. The language and thought of IGP 2 is unmistakably Gregorian; in my judgement, the genuine Gregorian pericope begins only at line 70. The previous sentence excusing the "interruption of the work of exposition" has the character of an introductory plea by the Dialogist himself.

The teaching of IGP 2 about the value of the *exempla patrum*, that is, the models of godly living provided by the saintly fathers of old, is a familiar Gregorian theme. A. de Vogüé cites parallels: *Moralia* 30.37; *Homilies on the Gospels* 38.15 and 39.10; *Homilies on Ezekiel* II.7.3. To these passages many other parallels may be added. (e.g. *Moralia* 9.88-9; 22.13-4; 24.15-21; 25.15, 17; 27.16-8; 28.26-7; 30.36. *Homilies on the Gospels* 20.13; 25.10; 28.4. *Homilies on Ezekiel* I.7.22-4; I.8.1; II.3.18-19; II.10.18.) The phrase *exempla patrum* and equivalent phrases are found repeatedly in those parallel passages from the Gregorian writings. Variant terms I have noted in them are: *exempla sanctorum, exempla*

---

mark of the religious". See my discussion of IGP 15 below, where I cite Gregorian testimonies to the contrary, and the further discussion in Chapter 19.

maiorum, exempla iustorum, exempla praecedentium, exempla fidelium. There is also occasional mention of the bad example of unworthy superiors or of the wicked: e.g. *exempla pravitatis* in *Homilies on the Gospels* 17.14, and *deteriorum exempla* in *Moralia* 24.21.

Gregory's concern in those parallel passages is always to stress the value of the *exempla* of the patriarchs, apostles, saints and true servants of God as incentives to imitate and draw profit from their virtuous deeds. *"Antiquorum patrum nos exempla confortant, et ex eorum comparatione facere nos posse praesumimus, quod ex nostra imbecillitate formidamus"* (*Moralia* 27.17). When he thus constantly points to the Scriptural examples of the fathers and saints his lesson to his hearers and readers is not that they should marvel at the prodigious powers of those holy men, but that they should aspire to a more perfect way of life, and humble themselves by contrasting their own sinfulness and imperfection with the righteous deeds and lives of those heroes of the faith. This same teaching, reiterated again and again in Gregory's expository and homiletic works, is exactly what he says in lines 73-79 of IGP 2.

Although in later mediaeval usage *exemplum* came to mean any kind of anecdote, often a miraculous event, brought into a sermon by a preacher to keep the attention of his hearers, it is important to observe that in Gregory's usage the *exempla patrum* are always invoked as patterns for emulation and for moral exhortation, not as supernatural phenomena to marvel at. In all the instances that Vogüé cites it is so, as also in the many other parallel passages I have noted above. Thus in Gregory's terminology the *exempla patrum* or *exempla sanctorum*, so profitable to Christians as patterns of virtue, are never equated with *signa*, or miraculous signs. Where he refers to the *signa*, *mira* or *miracula* wrought by the Apostles and others he never calls them *exempla*. Those persuasive signs of divine power served to attest God's presence in his saints, and to convert or convict unbelievers (e.g. *Homilies on the Gospels* 30.10; *Moralia* 27.20; 31.2); but such miracles and preternatural powers could not be *exempla patrum* in Gregory's sense, since they could not be proposed to the faithful as examples to imitate. Indeed in a passage in his *Homilies on Ezekiel* (written in the same year that the *Dialogues* were ostensibly composed) Gregory expressly says that miracles must *not* be put forward as examples for right conduct, and that knowledge about miracles is different in kind from the spiritual formation that we acquire from doctrine and discipline: *"... miracula in exemplum operationis non sunt trahenda ... Sed aliud est quod nos de doctrinae usu atque disciplina discimus, aliud quod de miraculo scimus"* (I.2.4).

Now in spite of this clear and consistent teaching of Pope Gregory about the value and function of the *exempla patrum*, the Dialogist, by manipulation of the text, contrives in the Prologue of his work to change the sense of the phrase, so that the Gregory of the *Dialogues* makes it mean what the real Gregory excluded. First (in lines 57-62) Peter the Deacon baselessly assumes that in IGP 1 Gregory has asserted both that many "fathers of Italy" had shone forth with miraculous powers, and that it was the "comparison" of such miracles that evoked the regrets expressed in IGP 1. Peter says that he does not doubt that there have been good men in Italy, but until this moment he has never before heard that any of them performed miraculous signs and deeds of power (*signa atque virtutes*—lines 59-62). Thus in his handling of IGP 1 the Dialogist has already implied that it is the miraculous in the lives of holy men that Gregory holds up as a pattern with which to compare ourselves. Now, in his handling of IGP 2 the Dialogist explicitly completes his equation between *signa* and *exempla*, which will justify and usher in his whole subsequent narrative of prodigious happenings.

To do this, it appears, he has had to alter a word in his borrowed Gregorian pericope, substituting his own word *signorum*, in line 72, for the word *exemplorum* which must have been there in the original Gregorian pericope. That such a substitution has taken place can be inferred from the tenor of the argument that immediately follows. *Exempla* (line 74) clearly corresponds to the second term of the comparison that has just been made, while *praedicamenta* corresponds to the first term—i.e. expository exhortation. But to read *signorum* in line 72 is to make a crass equation between *signa* and *exempla*—an equation that the real Gregory expressly rejected. On the supposition that in line 72 Gregory had originally written *exemplorum* and not *signorum*, IGP 2 concords perfectly with his consistent teaching in those many other parallel passages in which he discusses "the examples of the fathers" as models of godly conduct. From exposition of the word of God, he says here, we learn "how virtue is to be acquired and established"; from narration of the [*examples*] of the holy fathers we see "how virtue once acquired and established, is manifested". He goes on to repeat his usual teaching about the spiritual profit of the *exempla patrum* for the hearer of a sermon: namely, to kindle in him heavenly love by emulation of the virtues of God's saints, and to humble him by the contrast between his own unworthiness and their merits. Thus to make Gregory teach, as the Dialogist does by the intrusion of the word *signorum* in IGP 2, that miraculous signs consitute the *exempla patrum* that are to have this spiritual profit for the hearer, is simply to contradict Gregory's consistent teaching throughout his works. "*Miracula in exemplum operationis non sunt trahenda.*"

Yet one can see why the Dialogist has wrested the original meaning of his first two Gregorian pericopes. He must explain why the Gregory of the *Dialogues* is going on to narrate a long series of miracles stories, and he seeks to employ those two perciopes for this purpose. Thus he must make both IGP 1 and IGP 2 seem to refer to the miraculous deeds and prodigies of his Italian fathers, and not merely to the moral and spiritual examples to be derived from the virtuous living of the just, which was the sense of both passages in their original Gregorian context. Marvellous deeds—*signa atque virtutes*—are his theme. As he makes Peter the Deacon remark, there have been plenty of good men in Italy; but what the Gregory of the *Dialogues* must do is to narrate the marvellous histories of men of thaumaturgic power. Hence the need to make the pope equate *exempla* with *signa*.

Before leaving IGP 2 I would draw attention to a significant peculiarity of the text of the Prologue which throws an interesting light on the Dialogist's methods of composition. In the concluding sentence of IGP 2 the first spiritual benefit of hearing the *exempla patrum* is stated as follows: "*ad amorem venturae vitae ex praecedentium* comparatione accenditur" (lines 76-7; emphasis mine). Now there has been a *previous* remark by Peter the Deacon which presents a direct reference to this sentence, and which supposes that the sentence had already been spoken—not by Peter but by Gregory himself. This remark is: "*Ex quorum igitur* comparatione accenderis *ignoro*" (lines 58-9; emphasis mine). This peculiarity of the text betrays a strange confusion and inversion. Peter previously makes a remark, in lines 58-9, which assumes that Gregory has himself made mention of being "set on fire by the comparison" of himself with some fathers of times past; but the very phrase which mentions being "set on fire by the comparison" that is provided by the *exempla praecedentium*—the phrase that provides the implied verbal cue for Peter's previous remark—has not yet appeared in the text! This distinctive phrase does appear *subsequently*, in line 77—and there it is attributed not to Gregory but to Peter. There is thus a double confusion: the cue phrase comes after the response it elicits, and both cue phrase and response are attributed to the same partner in the dialogue.

This textual confusion throws light on the Dialogist's scissors-and-paste method of composition. He had at hand, for use in his introductory prologue, two genuine Gregorian pericopes, IGP 1 and IGP 2, both of which had reference to recollection of the virtues of holy men. It is likely that in a first draft he placed IGP 2 immediately after IGP 1, as continuing the same general theme. He intended, therefore, to put IGP 2 into the mouth of Gregory (and indeed its language is authentically Gregorian). The phrase near the end of IGP 2, "*ex praecedentium comparatione accenditur*", would thus have conveniently provided the cue for Peter to reply (as he does in lines 58-9) that he does not know who the men were by whose example Gregory was thus "set on fire" (*ex quorum igitur comparatione accenderis*"). The stage would accordingly have been set for Gregory to begin his long recital of the names and deeds of the wonder-working Italian fathers. On closer consideration, however, the Dialogist must have seen that IGP 2 did not appositely follow on from IGP 1. Whereas in IGP 1 Gregory is sighing at the memory of holy recluses who enjoyed the contemplative peace denied to him, in IGP 2 he is giving his usual teaching about the value of preaching the *exempla patrum* in order to enkindle the love of heavenly things in the hearts of the hearers. No doubt realizing that IGP 2 had a different perspective from IGP 1, the Dialogist rearranged his draft so that IGP 2 was placed later. It was then no longer spoken by Gregory but by Peter, as a plea to his master to embark on the narration of the *exempla patrum*, which were now equated with miraculous *signa*. By retaining in his rearranged text the now misplaced cue of Peter the Deacon, "*Ex quorum igitur comparatione accenderis ignoro*", the Dialogist unwittingly left a tell-tale pointer to an earlier stage in the drafting of his prologue.

IGP 3: I.1.6-7. On the inward teaching of the Holy Spirit. From line 43, "*... lege non stringitur ...* ", to line 65, "*... veneranda sunt, non imitanda.*"

IGP 3, which occurs at the end of the first chapter of Book I, is set in a pattern that the Dialogist will repeat again and again throughout his work. First there is an account of prodigious deeds performed by a holy man; next comes a cue question from Peter the Deacon, which is somehow made to seem relevant to what has just been narrated, yet which can usually be seen to be framed expressly as a pretext for bringing in the Gregorian fragment which the Dialogist has ready for use; and then follows the inserted Gregorian passage itself, at the end of which Peter expresses his admiration for his master's teaching.

The hero of this first miracle-story in the *Dialogues* is one Honoratus, son of a serf on an estate in Samnium. As a youth he excelled in the virtue of abstinence, which led him to refuse meat at a feast provided by his family for their neighbours. Thereupon he was derided by his parents, who asked him whether he expected to have fish brought to him in those mountains. But when water was drawn from the well a fish was found in it, which provided the day's fare for Honoratus. Freed later by his lord from servitude, Honoratus grew ever more renowned for his virtues and power. He established a monastery at Fondi, where he ruled some 200 monks. The Dialogist relates one notable miracle of the holy abbot, when he saved his monastery and all the brethren from being crushed by a gigantic boulder, which had broken away from the overhanging cliff

above and was hurtling down the side of the mountain. By invocations
and the sign of the Cross, Honoratus caused the boulder to be stopped
miraculously in its course, where it could still be seen overhanging the
monastery, according to the Dialogist, at the time of writing. It is at this
point of the narrative that Peter the Deacon puts in his leading question.
Are we to suppose, he asks, that to become such a notable master of
disciples Honoratus himself had a master previously? (lines 40-1). The
reader may wonder why this question is thus brought in abruptly,
apropos of nothing that has preceded. But the reason soon appears. The
Dialogist has at hand for insertion into his text a Gregorian excerpt concerning the inward teaching of the divine master, the Holy Spirit, which
can avail even without the outward teaching of human masters. Peter's
question has been set up as a peg on which to hang this doctrinal lesson.
The Gregory of the *Dialogues* is made to answer that, to his knowledge,
Honoratus had never been any man's disciple. Then the text leads
straight on into the genuine Gregorian pericope.

In IGP 3 Gregory observes that the ordinary rule for virtuous living
is that no one should presume to exercise authority who has not first
learnt to obey. Nevertheless, he continues, there are some spiritual
masters who, even though they themselves have received no instruction
from an external master, are taught and admonished by the inward
teaching of the Holy Spirit. Such chosen souls should not be held up as
models for the weaker brethren, however, lest one or other of them
should spurn human teaching on the pretext that he is similarly filled
with the Holy Spirit, and so become a teacher of error. The veritable indwelling of the divine master is clearly attested by the presence both of
virtuous power and of humility, as in the case of John the Baptist and
of Moses. Neither was taught by a human master, but both inwardly received teaching from on high.

The passage is umistakably Gregorian, in its style and phrasing, in the
antithetical balance of its rolling periods, and in its spiritual insight. The
insistence on humility as a true sign of the Spirit's presence, and on the
need for prelates to learn to obey before they command are favourite
themes of Gregory's, paralleled by similar statements in his other works.
There is a particularly close parallel with a passage in the commentary
In 1 Regum, IV.183. Here, in IGP 3, Gregory says: "*Usus quidem rectae
conversationis est, ut praeesse non audeat qui subesse non didicerit, nec oboedientiam
subiectis imperet, quam praelatis non novit exhibere*". In the parallel passage in
his *In 1 Regum* Gregory says: "*Rectus quoque ordo electae conversationis est, ut
oboedientiam non iniungat aliis, quam ipse aliis impendere non curavit*" (*CCL*
144, p. 396).

IGP 4: I.2.7. On the humility of Elisha, which rendered him worthy to wield power like that of his master Elijah. From line 76, "*Heliseus ... magistri pallium ...*", to line 85, "*... et ipse fecit*" (Omit "*quoque*" in line 77, and "*Petre*" in line 81).

This excerpt may originally have come from the same context as IGP 3, since the subject matter—the value of the humility of a disciple who submits himself to the authority of his master—is similar to the theme of the preceding passage in our series. In his tale of the miracle of Libertinus on the road to Ravenna the Dialogist devises a somewhat strained parallelism in order to introduce IGP 4. He relates how Libertinus, out of veneration for Honoratus, carried in his clothing one of his dead master's shoes. Placing the shoe on the breast of a dead boy, he successfully prayed for a miracle of revivification. Thereupon Peter the Deacon interjects to ask whether it was the merit of Honoratus or the prayer of Libertinus that worked the miracle. The Gregory of the *Dialogues* replies that both factors contributed to the production of so wonderful a sign. Libertinus was able to perform that miracle because he trusted in the power of his saintly master, whose shoe he had placed on the corpse of the child. This provides the lead-in for IGP 4. There the real Gregory extols the excellence of humility, which was a prerequisite even for the wondrous works of the saints and prophets. He cites the episode of *2 Kings* (*4 Kings* in the Latin Bible) 2.13-14, in which Elisha, bearing the mantle of Elijah, called on the God of his master: as he struck the waters of the Jordan with the mantle they divided to give him passage. By a typically intricate turn of Gregorian exegesis, the power to obtain the miracle is linked with Elisha's humility in recalling the name of his master, after a first attempt at opening a path through the Jordan had failed (according to a detail found in the Latin, but not in the Hebrew, text of the Bible). By invoking the God of Elijah, he equivalently acknowledged his discipleship and by thus humbling himself anew he was worthy to wield miraculous powers equal to those of his master.

The Dialogist has devised the story of the miracles of Libertinus on the road to Ravenna because he sees here an opportunity to utilize IGP 4. The action of Elisha, in bearing his master's mantle and using it with pious invocation to effect the miraculous parting of the waters of the Jordan, can then be presented as a precedent and model for the action of Libertinus, in bearing his master's shoe and using it with pious confidence to effect the miraculous raising of the dead boy to life. Gregory's commentary on Elisha's humility can thus be made to apply to the conduct of Libertinus. On closer inspection, however, we find that there is discongruity in this application. The main point of IGP 4 is that after his first unsuccessful attempt to part the waters Elisha was successful at the second attempt because, by his mention of Elijah in his invocation, he duly "returned to humility under his master". This Gregorian exegesis of the Vulgate text of *2 Kings* 2.13-14 has no parallel or application in the Dialogist's story, since there Libertinus needed no second attempt to perform his miracle, but was instantly successful.

On the hypothesis that Pope Gregory wrote the *Dialogues* and was here offering a Scriptural parallel to the miraculous deed of Libertinus, the argument in this passage is a strange irrelevance. When, however, IGP 4 is seen as one more of the Dialogist's available store of Gregorian excerpts, which he employs here to embellish his story of Libertinus, the irrelevance is readily understandable. Here as in many other places he accepts inconsequentiality in his reuse of Gregorian extracts if at least one aspect of the borrowed text can be made relevant to his narrative. Thus he uses IGP 4 to set up a parallel between Libertinus using his master's miraculous shoe and Elisha using his master's miraculous mantle, even though the explanation of Elisha's success at the second attempt after initial failure is inapposite in his context. No doubt the Dialogist was aware of this inappositeness. In his parallel story he does introduce a delay before Libertinus works his miracle (lines 55-64), as if to make his account correspond with the allusion to Elisha's delayed miracle in IGP 4. However there is no apt correspondence. In the case of Libertinus the delay is due solely to his humble diffidence. Unlike the case of Elisha in IGP 4, there is no failure of supernatural efficacy when Libertinus does proceed to exercise his power, nor is there any similar need for him to "return to humility under his master" before he can succeed in working the miracle.

Another incongruity in the Dialogist's narrative may also be pointed out. In lines 74-6 the Gregory of the *Dialogues* asserts that when Libertinus placed his master's shoe on the boy's corpse "he counted on the soul of Honoratus to obtain what he prayed for". This unGregorian concept has no parallel in IGP 4 itself, where there is no suggestion that Elisha looked to the soul of Elijah to procure the miraculous effect that he desired.

IGP 5: I.4.9. On grace prevenient to works. From line 103, "*Opus ... ex dono ...*", to line 106, "*... dona succrescunt*" (Omit "*Petre*" in line 103.)

This short but unmistakably Gregorian fragment is introduced by the Dialogist somewhat inconsequentially. After he has related how the holy abbot Equitius received a divine commission to preach, he makes Peter the Deacon come in with a cue (lines 101-2) containing both the words "*opus*" and "*dona*", which provide a link with the Gregorian snippet which he has ready, concerning the human work and the divine prevenient gift of grace. But the Pauline and Augustinian principle which Gregory enunciates in IGP 5 is not aptly used in this place. The Gregory of the *Dialogues* has already related many particulars about the marvellous activity—the *"opus"*—of the holy Equitius, when Peter the Deacon now asks to know the *opus* of this Father, who had received such *dona*. While this remark provides the desired verbal link with IGP 5, the short doctrinal snippet appears out of place when compared with what precedes and follows.

IGP 6: I.4.18. On the contrast between the heavenly honour of the humble and the outward vainglory of the proud. From line 210, " ... *in quanta Dei ...*", to line 218, " ... *est ante Deum*".

Nothing could be more typically Gregorian than the lesson taught in this short excerpt, which is clearly distinguished by its style from what has preceded. The just who endure humiliation in this life have divine protection and heavenly honour, whereas the proud who seek outward vainglory are rejected by God. The contrast presented here is one of the most frequent themes in Gregory's writings, as A. de Vogüé observes (p. 55), referring to a relevant article by P. Aubin (*"Intériorité et extériorité dans les Moralia in Job de Grégoire le Grand"*, in *RSR* 62, 1974, pp. 117-66). As in so many other cases, we may suppose that this pericope was a "doublet" excised by Gregory when preparing his works for publication, when he realized that he had expressed the same sentiment in similar words elsewhere. Indeed a close parallel to IGP 6 is found in his *Homilies on the Gospels*, 28.2-3, where the same teaching is expressed in similar phraseology and is confirmed with the same Scriptural testimony from *Luke* 16.15.

As placed here by the Dialogist IGP 6 appears at first sight to be a suitable moral comment to append to his story of the meekness of Equitius when the haughty official Julian, sent by the pope of that time, arrives to conduct him to Rome to give an account of himself and of his seemingly irregular ministry. In the genuine Gregorian passage, however, the point is that, while the humiliation endured is visible and outward (*foris*), the divine vindication of the humble is invisible and inward (*intus*). It is the proud who enjoy outward honour in this life; the honour of the humble servants of God is among the citizens of the heavenly city. Yet in the story of Equitius, the Dialogist—as is usual in his narratives—wants the humble virtue of the holy man to be vindicated outwardly by prodigious signs here and now, so that the proud men who have insulted him may be discomfited before him. This happens when a supernatural terror seizes those who approach Equitius to humiliate him. First the arrogant servant, then the haughty Roman official himself, are constrained to prostrate themselves to do honour to the holy abbot. A frightening vision admonishes the pope to send a message to Julian post-haste, ordering him to leave Equitius undisturbed. The embarrassed official then takes his leave of the magnanimous abbot. Coming after this anecdote, IGP 6, though introduced by an *"igitur"* as if it were an apposite doctrinal comment upon it, does not appear so appositely placed after all.

IGP 7: I.4.19. On the proneness of the human mind to be deceived, and how a busy prelate may easily be imposed upon. From line 221, *"Quid miraris ..."*, to line 233, *" ... in multis occupatur"*. (Omit *"Petre"* in line 221.)

IGP 7 follows immediately on IGP 6. Whereas IGP 6 was brought in without a cue from Peter the Deacon, for IGP 7 the Dialogist adopts his more usual practice of presenting his borrowed excerpt as a response to a query from Peter. He has ready for use a Gregorian passage about the fallibility of the human mind and the proneness of a prelate to "subreption". Accordingly he makes Peter express surprise that the illustrious pope in the preceding story should have succumbed to "subreption" by listening to slander about so worthy a man as Equitius. It is the word *"subripitur"* in line 232 that prompts the cue word *"subripi"* put into the mouth of Peter the Deacon in line 219. The verb *subripere* has also been introduced earlier in the chapter (in line 135). There, stated beforehand in very similar terms, we find a reason given for the pope's shortcoming similar to that given in the second part of IGP 7 as an answer to Peter's query. From their style and rhythm, I judge that those two clauses in line 135-6 are a genuine Gregorian snippet and that they belong to the same original context as IGP 7.

In other Gregorian writings there are parallels to the first half of IGP 7 (lines 221-9), where Gregory cites the case of David, who though usually enjoying prophetic vision was deceived by the lying servant of Mephibosheth (*2 Samuel*, 16.1-4). David's fallibility in that episode is given in *Homilies on Ezekiel* I.1.13 as an instance of the interruption of prophetic vision. Elsewhere the same moral as that in IGP 7 is drawn by Gregory from the story of Saul's promotion of his unworthy sons to be judges of Israel, and he expresses it in similar language: *"Quid ergo mirum si falli possunt qui prophetiae gratiam non acceperunt ...?"* (*In 1 Regum* 4.3; cf. A. de Vogüé, *SC* 260, pp. 55, 436.) The Dialogist has probably changed a similar original *"mirum"* (cf. line 228) to *"miraris"* in line 221, since he requires a verb in the second person singular to concord with his inserted vocative *"Petre"*. This grammatical form contrasts with the impersonal forms that immediately follow.

In legal and canonical usage, *subreptio* means the obtaining of some favour or decision from a superior by misrepresentation; anything gained by such underhand methods ought to be of no legal avail. Gregory uses the word in this technical sense in a number of places in his letters. The case of David is in fact one of *subreptio* in the juridical sense, since by his false report the deceitful servant Ziba instigated the king to bestow upon him the estate of Mephibosheth. In the context it is an apt illustration. Gregory goes on in IGP 7 to make the further point that a prelate is often so immersed in a multitude of cares that in any one case he may through inadvertence become a prey to "subreption". (In the earlier Gregorian snippet in lines 135-6 flattery is also mentioned as a factor.) One may surmise that IGP 7 was excised by Gregory from the place originally intended for it because the first part duplicated what he had said elsewhere, and also possibly because the second part seemed to take too pessimistic a view of the proneness of prelates to be influenced by "subreption". In a letter to a bishop fearing unjust delation Gregory reassures him: "*nulla apud me subreptio locum inveniet*" (Epistola II.18; Ewald-Hartmann, I, p. 115).

IGP 8: I.5.6. The truly humble rejoice at being despised. From line 56, "*Qualis enim quisque ...*", to line 62, " *... semetipsos habuerunt*".

When the holy sacristan Constantius of Ancona found that oil was lacking for the church lamps he filled them with water and they burned brightly. The miracle thus demonstrated his great merit. Whereupon Peter asks (lines 20-3; also 28-9) to be told about the inward humility of such an excellent man. The story that follows, telling how Constantius rejoiced at being insulted by a rustic, seems to have been composed expressly to enable the Dialogist to cap it with IGP 8, which is appended as an apt comment. The language of IGP 8 is distinctively Gregorian, and contrasts with that of the preceding narrative. The teaching of the pericope is paralleled by Gregory's teaching elsewhere as A. de Vogüé notes (pp. 62-3). Similarity of subject matter suggests that, in the store of Gregorian papers in the Lateran *scrinium*, IGP 8 came from the same original context as IGP 6.

IGP 9: I.8.5-6. On the place of men's prayers in God's predestinatory decrees, illustrated from the history of Isaac and Rebecca. IGP 9a runs from line 40, " *... ea quae sancti viri ...*", to line 45, " *... disposuit donare*". IGP 9b runs from line 49, "*Certe etenim ...*", to line 63, " *... filios habere potuisset*". (In line 49 read *novimus* instead of *nosti*.)

IGP 9 is one of the most revealing in the whole series of borrowed Gregorian pericopes in the *Dialogues*. It is a profound yet limpid theological explanation of the place of men's prayers in the working out of God's predestinatory plan. Divine predestination does not mean that human prayers are otiose; but the prayers of the just have a true efficacy because they are the foreordained means by which God's immutable decree of predestination is fulfilled. (St Augustine had given a similar explanation: *De Civitate Dei* 5.10.) Gregory's measured cadences, his theological sensitivity and his skilful Scriptural illustration of the doctrine by reference to the *Genesis* history of Isaac and Rebecca, present a striking contrast between this pericope and the Dialogist's own surrounding text, which reflects his homely style and lower level of theological perception.

The anecdote leading into this passage concerns the holy abbot Anastasius, who with eight of his monastic companions was supernaturally summoned to impending death by a voice slowly calling their names from a crag above their monastery. Anastasius accordingly died within a few days and the other eight monks soon followed him, dying in the order in which their names had been called from the crag. Another monk, whose name had not been among those announced by the heavenly voice, nevertheless begged his dying abbot to obtain from God the favour that he too might depart this life within a week. The supernumerary monk did die within that time, and since his name had not been included in the heavenly roll-call, says the Gregory of the *Dialogues*, "it clearly appeared that only the intercession of the venerable Anastasius could have obtained his decease". Whereupon Peter the Deacon comes in with the comment that this event seems indubitably to imply that even things that are not predestined can be obtained by the meritorious prayer of holy men (lines 34-9). His query serves as the cue to bring in the Gregorian passage which follows. The concluding clause of his comment is a verbatim link with the opening clause of IGP 9. I note in passing that Peter expresses his interpretation of this preternatural episode with the use of the phrase, "*quid aliud datur intellegi ...?*". This is a very familiar phrase of Gregory himself, found throughout his expository works. However, when he uses it, it is always to propound a moral or mystical sense of a text of Scripture. I do not know of a single instance in which he uses it to refer to the implied meaning of a nonscriptural event, as the Dialogist does in the present case.

Before scrutinizing the way in which IGP 9 is fitted into the Dialogist's context, I must signal the fact that the same pericope is found in the compilations both of Paterius and of Tajo. (Paterius, *Liber Testimoniorum*, *Super Genesim*, Chapter LIV, *PL* 79.709-10—in the new *CCL* edition, Chapter LI; Tajo, *Libri Sententiarum*, I.35, *PL* 80.764-5). Both Paterius and Tajo commence their citation of the Gregorian passage with the words "*Ea quae sancti viri orando efficiunt ...*" In the *Dialogues*, on the other hand, these words (in line 40) follow on from a prefixed clause, "*Obtineri nequaquam possunt quae praedestinata non fuerint, sed ...*" (lines 39-40). It appears that the clause has been brought in here by the Dialogist in order to take up the words he has just put into the mouth of Peter the Deacon, and to make IGP 9 more obviously relevant to his preceding story. If we study IGP 9 more closely, leaving out of account the prefixed clause, we find that the question Gregory is elucidating there is not exactly the same as the question put by Peter the Deacon and taken up again in the prefixed clause (lines 39-40). That is, the real Gregory is not answering the question whether things that are not predestined can be obtained by the saints; he takes it for granted that everything is eternally and immutably predestined for the sake of the elect, but he is concerned to explain how human prayer can have instrumental efficacy in the working out of the divine plan.

Naturally neither Paterius nor Tajo includes the interjection by Peter the Deacon which in the *Dialogues* separates IGP 9b from IGP 9a (lines 46-7). Nor, of course, does their text include the Dialogist's mention of Peter in line 48. He has adapted the grammatical person of the verb in line 49 to concord with his intruded vocative "*Petre*", so that his text reads at the beginning of IGP 9b, "*Certe etenim nosti ...*". In contrast, neither Paterius nor Tajo has the verb in the second person singular here; both agree in the reading "*novimus*".[2] Their verb in the first person plural doubtless represents the original reading, and accords with Gregory's ordinary usage in his expository writings.

In Tajo's reproduction of the Gregorian passage IGP 9b flows on immediately from IGP 9a without any intervening words. That is, the sentence ending "*... ante saecula disposuit donare*" (line 45) is followed immediately by the words "*Certissime novimus quod ad Abraham Dominus dixit ...*" (line 49). In the text of Paterius, however, between the two sentences there is interposed the phrase, "*Quod utrum ita sit concite valet probari.*" The Dialogist alters this to make Gregory say, with unGregorian self-assertion, "*Hoc quod ego, Petre, intuli, concite valet probari*".

In the anthology of Paterius the item preceding IGP 9 is a very long allegorical exposition of the history of Isaac and Rebecca, which, as the Maurists noted,[3] is redolent of Gregory's style yet is not to be found in his known works. This juxtaposition of the long "unknown" passage about Isaac and Rebecca with IGP 9 may suggest that both were taken

---

[2] Paterius has "*Certe etenim novimus*", while Tajo has "*Certissime novimus*".

[3] *PL* 79.704. In early MSS of Paterius this long excerpt is said to be taken from "Homelia L" of Gregory's commentary on *Ezekiel*, but we look in vain for it in that work.

from a common source in the store of Gregorian remains to which Paterius had access.

After the statement of theological principle in IGP 9a the second part of the pericope (in its original form, before the Dialogist interpolated into it Peter's supplementary question) led straight on to the Scriptural illustration of that principle, drawn from the texts of *Genesis*. Using those testimonies Gregory appositely argued that the fixed divine decree, revealed in God's promise to Abraham to multiply his seed like the stars of heaven and the sands of the sea-shore, did not render otiose Isaac's prayer that his barren wife should conceive. There is ineptitude in the manner in which the Dialogist inserts this pericope into his chapter. The gem of Gregorian theology contained in IGP 9 reflects a higher plane of thought and spiritual insight than that of the Dialogist's tale of the unearthly voice from the crag naming Anastasius and his companions for imminent departure to the next life. There even seems to be the naive implication that this preternatural roll-call was an instance of predestination to heaven in the theological sense.

There is also a clumsy touch in the supplementary question by which Peter the Deacon brings in the texts relating to Isaac and to the divine promises: "I would like to have it proved to me more clearly if predestination can be helped (*iuvari*) by prayers". The word *iuvari* is not well chosen in this connection. As Gregory explains it, predestination is indefectibly predetermined in the eternal will of God. It cannot be "helped" by any created factors; but it is "fulfilled" (*impletur* is the word Gregory himself uses in IGP 9) through the instrumentality of the prayers of the just. In the theology of St Gregory, as of St Augustine and of St Paul, God's eternal decree cannot be affected by anything that man may do; but its effect is unfolded in the course of ages through divinely foreordained factors, among which are the prayers of the elect.

IGP 10: I.9.6-7. Resolution of a theological problem arising from *Matthew* 9.27-31. From line 59, " ... *redemptor noster*", to line 79, " ... *exemplum dedit*". (Lines 55-7 seem also to be authentic).

The Dialogist has just related a rather complicated miracle-story about Bishop Boniface of Ferentis, who provided a prodigious abundance of wine from a few drops of juice squeezed from spoiled grapes. Like the biographers of St Ammon and St Severinus before him (cf. Vogüé, *SC* 260, pp. 80-1), the Dialogist makes Boniface strictly forbid one who witnessed the miracle to reveal it to anyone while he himself remained in his mortal body. Thus Boniface imitated the example of Christ after his Transfiguration (*Matthew* 17.9), "who, in order to instruct us in the way of humility, himself commanded his disciples to tell what they had seen to no one until the Son of Man had risen from the dead''. These lines (55-7) have a Gregorian ring, and they seem to be a snippet from an authentic source. The same text is cited as an example of humility in Gregory's *In 1 Regum* 5.40.

The Dialogist has at hand a Gregorian passage, IGP 10, which is concerned with a similar text, *Matthew* 9.27-31. That Gospel text relates how, after Christ had restored sight to two blind men and charged them strictly to keep the miracle secret, they nevertheless went away and spread his fame through all the region. Now the commentary and purpose of IGP 10, in which Gregory resolves an apparent theological difficulty arising from the fact that He who gave the unheeded prohibition was a divine person, has no relevance to the story of Bishop Boniface. This presents a difficulty for the Dialogist. Throughout his work he usually shows astute concern to make his borrowed Gregorian passages seem relevant to the context in which he situates them. In many other places he could so write his miracle stories as to make them apposite to the Gregorian pericopes that he has ready for insertion. But here such a proceeding was impossible, since the theological problem posed in IGP 10 could apply only to the divine Son, not to any of his saints. Nevertheless, the Dialogist does not intend to forego use of this precious and otherwise unused piece of Gregorian exposition. Although the theological excursus of IGP 10 cannot be made relevant to his story of Bishop Boniface, he decides to make opportunity to bring it in anyway. In the cue he puts into the mouth of Peter the Deacon he justifies the inconsequential introduction of this theological question by saying simply that this is ''a suitable occasion'' for choosing to do so: ''*Quia occasio apta se praebuit, libet inquirere ...*'' (lines 58-9).

IGP 10 is a classic example of a Gregorian ''doublet''. There is a closely parallel passage, though differently phrased, in *Moralia* 19.36, where, as A. de Vogüé notes p. 81), ''the same theological problem is raised, in connection with the same text—*Matthew* 9.30-1—and is there given an identical solution''. In Chapter 12 I recalled that R. Étaix, when discussing the provenance of the ''unknown'' Gregorian passages contained in the *Liber Testimoniorum* of Paterius, suggested that some of them may have been drawn ''from an earlier edition of the *Moralia*''. That is an explanation which can be aptly applied to the case of IGP 10. In the long-drawn-out process of revising the text of the Moralia, Gregory would have found that IGP 10 exactly duplicated what he had written in Book 19, and thus decided to retain only the latter passage. The manuscript of the earlier redaction, or even excised fragments from it, would have been preserved in the chests of the Lateran *scrinium*, to be eventually utilized by the Dialogist.

IGP 11: I.9.9. To provoke the wrath of one in whom God dwells is a fearful thing, for it is to provoke the wrath of God. From line 106, " ... *pensandum est ...*", to line 112, " ... *invalidus non est*".

The Dialogist's possession of this short Gregorian excerpt may well account for his composition of the dramatic but disagreeable tale which precedes it. In Chapter 19, where I discuss the lack of moral and religious sensitivity which the Dialogist displays in parts of his narrative, I include among those "sub-Christian tales" the story of the strolling minstrel who, with his monkey and his clashing cymbals, unwittingly interrupted and annoyed the holy bishop Boniface as he was about to pronounce grace at table. The indignant bishop, realizing that the wretch was doomed for this unseemly interruption, declared that he was as good as dead. Sure enough, divine judgement soon avenged the annoyance that had been unintentionally caused to the sacred personage. After the minstrel had, at the bishop's behest, partaken of some refreshment, a huge block of masonry fell on the wretch and killed him. It is at this point that the Dialogist inserts his Gregorian moral.

In its original context IGP 11 was evidently a comment on one of the Scriptural texts concerning the manifestation of the wrath of God in the righteous anger of his saints. Just such a text is *I Samuel* 11.6: "And the spirit of the Lord came upon Saul when he heard these words: and his anger was exceedingly kindled". In his commentary on this text (*In 1 Regum* 5.13; *CCL* 144, p. 424) Gregory teaches the same lesson as that of IGP 11, in very similar terms: "*Quam metuenda sit ergo sanctorum ira, cernimus, si insilientem in eos Domini spiritum cogitamus ...*". Another Old Testament text on which IGP 11 would have been an apt comment is *2 Kings* 2.23-4, which tells how boys who mocked the prophet Elisha, and who were cursed by him in the name of the Lord, were torn by bears.

IGP 12: I.9.19. An axiom on divine pedagogy. Lines 215-7: "*Hoc ... ex magna conditoris nostri dispensatione agitur, ut per minima quae percipimus, sperare maiora debeamus*" (Omit "*Petre*" in line 215.)

As so often, the intruded vocative *Petre* is here the mark of an inserted Gregorian fragment. Brief though this snippet is, it repays study. The turn of phrase, as well as the teaching, is recognizably Gregory's. The same pedagogy of the divine *dispensatio*, which leads us from smaller boons to hope for greater, is explained more fully by Gregory in his *Homilies on the Gospels* 32.6. There he explains that God's *dispensatio pietatis* lay in drawing the thoughts and hopes of simpler folk to the invisible realities of eternal life, by first putting before them temporal promises for realization in this life. Thus to the Israelites in Egypt he first held out the prospect of possession of the earthly promised land; to the *rudes* among Christ's disciples he first promised that they would see the visible kingdom of God on earth as an earnest of seeing the invisible kingdom of God in heaven. The perspectives of the Dialogist are different. He goes straight on to apply the axiom of IGP 12 to a miraculous event obtained by the prayer of Boniface in childhood. The "holy and simple boy" lamented to the Lord that a fox had just snatched one of his mother's hens that he had been hoping to eat; whereupon the fox at once returned, restored its prey and then dropped dead. The point of this homely little miracle, so the Gregory of the *Dialogues* explains in answer to Peter's cue, was to show the boy how much more he could expect in greater matters. It is for this quaint usage that the Dialogist here introduces the Gregorian axiom concerning the divine *dispensatio*, which he had found unused somewhere in his store of *Gregoriana*. But his use of it here, as a comment by Gregory on the tale of the fox and the hen, reflects a mentality very different from that of the real Gregory. The difference can be appreciated by comparing this section of the *Dialogues* with Gregory's own explanation of the pedagogy of the divine *dispensatio* in the parallel passage in his thirty-second Gospel homily.

IGP 13: I.10.7. On perverse intention which vitiates actions even if they appear to be good. IGP 13a runs from line 75, "*Multa ... videntur bona ...*", to line 80, " *... rectum esse videatur*" (omitting "*Petre*" in line 75.) IGP 13b runs from line 84, "*Sunt namque nonnulli ...*", to line 87, " *... qua ceteros premunt*".

In its original setting IGP 13 was evidently one continuous paragraph, without the intrusive sentence which separates them in the *Dialogues*. IGP 13a and IGP 13b are both phrased in Gregory's usual objective style, stating general moral principles. They read on consecutively and smoothly in the same style from the words " *... quamvis rectum esse videatur.*", in line 80, straight on to "*Sunt namque nonnulli ...*" in line 84. The gloss which the Dialogist has interpolated between them, as well as the similar sentence which he adds immediately after IGP 13b, are of a different style and character, with an unGregorian emphasis on verbs in the first person singular (lines 82, 87). When we examine the use that the Dialogist makes here of IGP 13 it appears that this is another instance of his constructing a preceding miracle-story in such a way that his borrowed Gregorian pericope may be presented as an apt doctrinal reflection upon it.

IGP 13 is a typical statement of Gregory's teaching on the decisive influence of antecedent intention upon the moral quality of a subsequent act. Even though men may be mistaken in judging the worth of the outward actions of others, the eyes of the inward Judge perceive the underlying intention and cannot be deceived. There are at least three passages in Gregory's authentic works which are parallel to IGP 13, even in phraseology: namely, *Moralia* 10.41 and 28.30, and *Homilies on Ezekiel* I.7.2. In all those three passages, as in IGP 13, Gregory cites the words of Christ (*Matthew* 6.22-3) on the eye as the lamp of the body. Habitually he interprets the "eye" as the intention of the will and the "body" as the subsequent outward action.

How does the Dialogist make his narrative relevant to IGP 13? His immediately preceding miracle-story is one of a series about Bishop Fortunatus of Todi, who was gifted with "immense power" for driving out evil spirits from possessed persons. After one such exorcism the expelled demon, disguising himself as a benighted wayfarer, went about the city pleading for shelter and complaining that Bishop Fortunatus, so renowned for holiness, had turned him out of doors. A householder who heard his lament took him under his family roof. As they were chatting around the fireside the disguised demon suddenly threw the man's infant son on to the fire and killed him. At this point of the dialogue Peter the Deacon asks how it could be that the malign spirit was allowed to commit that foul deed in the house of one who had performed an act of hospitality (lines 71-4). As answer, the Dialogist puts into the mouth of Gregory the two sections of IGP 13, with which he intermingles his own explanation, applying Gregory's theology to his own story of the sinister happening at Todi.

I think the key sentence in the Gregorian passage that prompted the Dialogist's composition of his tale is the one that I have distinguished as IGP 13b. "There are some who set out to perform good actions with the aim of overshadowing the good deeds of others; they regale themselves not with the good that they do but with the praise they get for it, by which they put others down" (lines 84-7). In framing his tale about the householder who was bereaved by the devil's murderous trick, the Dialogist has ingeniously accommodated it to IGP 13. In the two glosses that he intermingles with IGP 13 (in both instances intruding verbs in the first person singular lines 80-4, 87-91), he makes Gregory explain that the householder's hospitable act, though apparently virtuous, was really performed out of ostentation. By taking the wayfarer into his dwelling, he wanted to appear more charitable than Bishop Fortunatus who had refused shelter to the stranger. Both Peter the Deacon and the Gregory of the *Dialogues* point out the conclusion to be drawn: the punishment of the man in the death of his child proved that his intention in offering hospitality had been reprehensible.

IGP 14: I.10.19. On miracles at the tomb of a saint, testifying to his better life in union with God. From line 222, " ... *post mortem melius vivere* ...", to line 228, " ... *ossa sua perseverat*"

Despite appearances to the contrary, these lines are in all probability not part of the Dialogist's own narrative, but an extract imported from a genuine Gregorian homily. Discounting the preceding clauses, IGP 14 has a fairly close resemblance to similar elogia pronounced by Pope Gregory at the tombs of Roman martyrs in his Gospel *Homilies*. For example, in his sermon to the Roman people in the basilica of Saints Processus and Martinianus in their anniversary he appealed to the miracles of healing and liberation from evil spirits, still worked at the shrine where the bones of those saints were honoured, as a testimony of the true eternal life with which they were forever living in heaven: "*Ad exstincta namque eorum corpora viventes aegri veniunt et sanantur, periuri veniunt et a daemonio vexantur, daemoniaci veniunt et liberantur. Quomodo ergo vivunt illic ubi vivunt, si in tot miraculis vivunt hic ubi mortui sunt?*" (*Homilies on the Gospels* 32.6; partially reproduced in *Dialogues* IV.6.1-2—see IGP 49 below). Carefully studied and separated from its preceding context, IGP 14 can be seen to make the same point. In the original setting Gregory was addressing a congregation in a church in which the relics of a certain saint were preserved. He argues that the miracles of liberation from evil spirits and of healing of the sick, granted at that tomb-shrine to prayerful faith, are eloquent testimonies that the saint is ever living (lines 223-6). In his mortal life he worked miracles of healing, and still he continues to do so where his dead bones lie (lines 227-8). The life that he now "lives after death is without doubt better" for this saint "who even before death sought earnestly to please Almighty God" (lines 221-3). The superiority of the life which the martyrs and the blessed live in heaven, compared to this corruptible mortal life, is a constant theme in Gregory's teaching.

It may well be that IGP 14 is a passage from a sermon preached to his flock which Gregory did not eventually include in his edited selection of forty *Homilies on the Gospels*. Among the martyrs and saints in whose basilicas he preached to the people of Rome were Saints Peter, Paul, Andrew, Felix, Agnes, Clement, Silvester, Marcellinus and Peter, Pancras, Nereus and Achilles, Menas, Lawrence, Sebastian, as well as Processus and Martinianus.[4] From his words we can deduce that some at least of those sermons were preached at the saints' tombs on their feast-days. The Pope referred at times to the presence of the martyrs' bodies and their shrines in order to raise the minds of his hearers from this transitory life

---

[4] The allocation of individual homilies to these *tituli* needs to be further researched in the MSS.

to the true eternal life. IGP 14 fits into such a pattern. Note that in this pericope Gregory appeals to the many testimonies that "*we* have" to the living power of the saint he is referring to, in the miracles that even to this day are worked at his tomb. This suggests that the tomb was that of a Roman martyr or confessor—the *teneamus* of line 225 would be less apposite in a Roman context if the tomb were at Todi, as the *Dialogues* narrative requires.

In IGP 14 there is repeated mention of the exalted "life" and "living" of a certain saint, both on earth and after death. In a manner his "life" is still powerful even on earth, in the miracles wrought at his tomb. The Dialogist has taken these references to a new and better life after death as the verbal link for his preceding story of one who returned to a better life *on earth* after dying. But since the link is merely verbal, IGP 14 does not fit well into the tissue of the Dialogist's narrative. He has just told the story (closely and strangely modelled on that of the raising to life of Lazarus by Christ—as A. de Vogüé remarks, *SC* 260, p. 107) concerning a worthy citizen of Todi named Marcellus, who was brought back to life by Bishop Fortunatus, after dying and being conducted "to a good place" (*in bonum locum*). The Dialogist proceeds in paragraph 19 to say that we must not think that Marcellus, through having to return to this life, lost the good place that had been allotted to him. As his reason for saying this, he leads straight on to his adaptation of IGP 14: " ... since there is no doubt that thanks to the prayers of his intercessor [i.e. Fortunatus] he could live better after death, seeing that even before death he sought earnestly to please the almighty Lord" (lines 220-3). It seems that the Dialogist intends to refer Gregory's phrase "*potuit post mortem melius vivere*" to Marcellus's resumed life on earth, and not to his final state of life in heaven. This appears from his statement that Marcellus was able to live better afterwards "by the prayers of his intercessor"; the prayers of an intercessor would not be needed to enable one of the blessed in heaven to live *that* better life. If IGP 14 were an integral part of the Dialogist's narrative, one would naturally expect him to say that Marcellus lived better "after his return to life", rather than "after death". This is only one of several incongruous features of the Dialogist's text. But on the recognition that IGP 14 is an already existing Gregorian pericope originally uttered in a quite different context, (akin to that of the Gospel homily 32.6), the incongruities become readily understandable. Thus the obscurity of the phrase "*post mortem melius vivere*" is at once dissipated when we realize that in its original context it *did* refer to a saint's heavenly bliss after the end of this mortal life.

Another puzzle arises from the eulogy in lines 223-8. In the Dialogist's text the verb "*vivere*" in line 222 clearly refers to Marcellus and his better life. Immediately following, in the next sentence, come the words, "But why need we say much about *his life* ...?" Grammatically and contextually it would seem that the antecedent referred to here in the words "*eius vita*" is Marcellus, about whom it has just been said that after his miraculous return to life "he remained long in this life" (line 219), and that "he was able to *live* better after death" (line 222). Likewise the subsequent description of his miracles, worked both in his mortal life and eventually from heaven, seems naturally to refer to the same person. But this straightforward conclusion is surprising, since all that we have been told about Marcellus is that he was a good-living citizen of Todi ("*quidam bonae actionis vir*"; line 188), who dwelt with his two sisters. The extraordinary elogium of his miraculous power, witnessed it seems by Gregory himself (cf. lines 224-5) is therefore unexpected. Fr Paul Antin, author of the French translation of the *Dialogues* in the *Sources Chrétiennes* edition, meets the difficulty by translating "*eius vita*" as "*la vie de Fortunat*". In my view it is probable that the Dialogist did intend the "*eius*" of line 224 to refer to Marcellus, as the context and the grammatical antecedent require. (It would be unnatural to take "*intercessoris*" as the antecedent.) Since, as I have argued, the whole of the original Gregorian pericope referred to the "life and living" of a single saint of old, it is unlikely that the Dialogist would think of making it refer to the "life and living" of two different people. He would thus have been less likely to change the subject without warning by making the *eius vita* of line 224 refer obliquely back to Bishop Fortunatus. As we have seen, he is habitually careful to make clear, by clerkish phrases of "reference back", any such change of antecedent. But in any case, whether he intended to attribute the fame of posthumous miracles to Marcellus or to Fortunatus, his main concern in this place was to find a pretext for utilizing the fragment of a genuine Gregorian homily which he had in his store. Since in its origin this fragment had a quite different bearing, it proved intractable to his attempted adaptation. As a result this section of the *Dialogues* is unusually disconnected and opaque.

IGP 15: I.12.4-5. Performance of miraculous signs is not the criterion of virtue and heavenly merit. IGP 15a runs from line 46, "*Vitae namque vera* ...", to line 49, " ... *dispares non sunt*". IGP 15b runs from line 53, "*Numquidnam ... Paulus apostolus* ...", to line 63, " ... *dispar non est in caelo*". (Omit "*nescis quoniam*" in line 53, "*Scio plane*" in line 56, and "*Quod bene ipse reminisceris*" in line 58.)

IGP 15, when the Dialogist's additions and adjustments between lines 50 and 58 have been discounted, is clearly Gregorian. Although the "water miracle motif" in IGP 15b has no exact parallel in Gregory's

authentic works, the passage has some affinity to the long comparison between St Peter and St Paul which Gregory makes in his *Homilies on Ezekiel*
II.6.9-13. In that homily he expressly limits himself to extolling the co-
excellence in virtue and merit of the two great Apostles. He there
disclaims the intention to speak of their miracles: "*Ut enim taceamus de
ostensione signorum, loquamur de virtutibus cordium*". We recognize a
resonance between these words and the opening sentence of IGP 15a:
"*Vitae namque vera aestimatio in virtute est operum, non in ostensione signorum*".

In the following sentence of IGP 15a (lines 48-9) Gregory affirms that
there are many who, though they work no miracles, are not of less worth
than those who do. In the original form of the pericope he doubtless went
straight on to illustrate his point by the Scriptural comparison between
St Peter and St Paul (IGP 15b). Peter could miraculously walk in the
water (*Matthew* 14.29), yet Paul could not—when he was shipwrecked he
had to struggle through the waves to the shore (*Acts* 27.43-4). Despite this
disparity in miraculous experience where the element of water was concerned, Paul was Peter's peer in the apostolate and in heavenly merit.
The Dialogist, using his familiar tactic, interposes after IGP 15a a query
by Peter the Deacon (lines 50-2), in order to make the Scriptural comparison in IGP 15b appear to be the demonstration which Peter asks for
in his cue question.

The opening words of IGP 15 accord uneasily with the basic assumption of the Dialogist, which underlies his whole narrative of miracle
stories—namely that the record of their miraculous deeds is the main
proof of the sanctity of the thaumaturges who have abounded in Italy in
recent times. (I would refer here to our earlier discussion of IGPs 1 and
2). Contrary to that assumption, Gregory declares in IGP 15a that "the
true reckoning of a life is in the virtue shown in good works, not in a
display of miraculous signs". Gregory's habitual teaching about the
function of miracles, and about the true criterion of holiness which is
charity and virtuous action, is plain from the following passages, which
serve to illustrate the statement in IGP 15a: *Moralia* 27.36-7; *Homilies on
Ezekiel* I.5.14-5; II.5.22; *Homilies on the Gospels* 2.1; 4.3 (which is a close
parallel to IGP 15); 10.1; 29.4. In *Homilies on Ezekiel* II.5.22 Gregory
teaches that miracles do not themselves constitute victorious virtue, "*nam
haec aliquando dantur et reprobis*". He quoted *Matthew* 7.22-3 to this effect,
and he lays down this principle: "*Unum vero signum electionis est soliditas
charitatis*". However, Gregory does allow that the miracles of the elect
are, as it were, outward images of God's inward favour to them (*ibid*).
We find the same teaching in *Homilies on the Gospels* 30.10, where Gregory
says of the servants of God: "*Quos dum mira conspicimus agere, certum nobis
fit in eorum mentibus Deum habitare*". The saints whose miracles he is there

referring to are the Apostles. What he says in these two places about miracles as a special testimony of God's favour, and of God's presence in the Apostles and martyrs, does not contradict his habitual teaching that the criterion of a good life is to be looked for not in the performance of miracles but in charity and virtuous actions.

What the Dialogist has found and reproduced in IGP 15—incongruously, in the context of his own collection of modern marvels in Italy—is a Gregorian excerpt which reflects the same reserve about miraculous signs, and the same refusal to set them up as the criterion and incentive for godly life, that is to be found in the passages I have listed above. The Dialogist is doubtless aware that this attitude of Gregory towards miracles, so trenchantly expressed in IGP 15a and elsewhere, that after the dissemination of the Gospel and the spread of the Church miracles had become in the main unnecessary and relatively[5] rare, presented a serious objection to the whole enterprise he was undertaking in the book of the *Dialogues*. That book presents a plethora of astonishing miracles worked within living memory by a host of Italian wonder-working saints. At the end of IGP 15, the Dialogist makes Peter the Deacon acknowledge that he has been convinced: *"Ecce aperte cognovi quia vita et non signa quaerenda sunt"* (lines 64-5). However, simply to accept this principle would seem to render redundant the whole conception of the *Dialogues*. It also inevitably raises the question why the author, after affirming that Gregorian principle so emphatically, should nevertheless continue to devote himself to writing a long work of hagiography which concentrates consistently and obsessively on the miraculous. The Dialogist provides some defence against the objection which would seem to arise patently from IGP 15. He makes Peter the Deacon say: *"Sed quoniam ipsa signa quae fiunt, bonae vitae testimonium ferunt, quaeso adhuc, si qua sunt, referas, ut esurientem me per exempla bonorum pascas"* (lines 66-8). This assertion is unGregorian, in its unqualified assumption (already put forward in the Prologue) that miracles are *exempla* for others. Nevertheless, it is the Dialogist's justification for continuing to narrate his stories of the miracles of the Fathers of Italy.

---

[5] There is a qualification in *Moralia* 27.36.

CHAPTER FIFTEEN

THE INSERTED GREGORIAN PASSAGES IN BOOK II OF THE *DIALOGUES*

In Book II of the *Dialogues*, devoted to the life and miracles of St Benedict, eleven genuine Gregorian passages are inserted. The first of these is of particular interest since it provides a term of comparison with a related passage in the Paterian *Liber Testimoniorum*, and offers a further indication of the independence of Paterius from the *Dialogues*.

IGP 16: II.2.3-4. Exposition of the text of *Numbers* 8.24-6, concerning the Levites, who after the age of 50 years were to be keepers of the vessels. IGP 16a runs from line 27, "*Unde et per Moysen ...*", to line 30, "*... custodes vasorum fiant*". IGP 16b runs from line 37, "*Electi ergo ...*", to line 41, "*... doctores animarum fiunt*".

From study of IGP 16 and its context it appears that the Dialogist has here made an imperfect adaptation of a passage from an alternative redaction of the *Moralia*—a passage which, in its fuller form, has been preserved independently in the anthology of Paterius.

In Chapter 2 of his second book the Dialogist relates how St Benedict overcame carnal temptation by throwing himself naked into a thicket of briars and nettles. Having by this means permanently conquered the flesh, he began to attract and instruct disciples. The Gregory of the *Dialogues* comments: "Thus freed from the vice of temptation, he worthily became a master of virtues". Then comes IGP 16a, an allusion to the text of Scripture (*Numbers*, 8.24-6) on which IGP 16b is a gloss: "Whence it was commanded by Moses that the Levites from twenty-five years and upwards ought to minister; but from their fiftieth year they should become the keepers of the vessels." Peter the Deacon interjects: "I understand something of the meaning of the text you have quoted, yet I beg you to explain it more fully". The answer that follows incorporates IGP 16b: after the fiftieth year of life the temptations of youth grow cold; the elect, their earlier fatiguing labours behind them, are now worthy to be keepers of the sacred vessels, which are taken to signify the souls of the faithful. Peter then expresses his satisfaction that Gregory has unlocked the meaning of the quoted text.

Both IGP 16 and the related extract in the collection of Paterius (*In Numeros*, cap. IV) are seen to depend on a passage in *Moralia*, 23.21. The rather intricate problems of textual interdependence here can only be studied by a synoptic comparison of the three texts. I reproduce below the relevant passage from the received text of the *Moralia* (= *RMor*), which is closely followed by Paterius in his *Liber Testimoniorum* (= *PLT*), and more remotely by *Dialogues* II.2. It will be found that while *RMor* and *PLT* have substantial identity of text, agreeing against *Dialogues*, nevertheless *PLT* and *Dialogues* agree against *RMor* in the addition of two significant sentences and also in an incidental phrase. In reproducing the following passage from *RMor* I have numbered each of its constituent elements, from (i) to (iv), for later comparison with the other two texts. To show the substantial agreement between *PLT* and *RMor* I have marked out in this text[1] of *RMor* only those words which are not identical in *PLT*:

From *MORALIA* 23.21

(i) Hinc est enim *quod,* iuxta divinae dispensationis vocem *ab anno vigesimo* et *quinto levitae* tabernaculo serviunt, sed a *quinquagesimo custodes vasorum* fiunt. (ii) *Quid* enim *per annum quintum ac vigesimum, in quo flos iuventutis oboritur, nisi ipsa contra unumquodque vitium bella signantur? Et quid per* quinquagesimum, *in quo et iubilaei requies continetur, nisi interna requies edomito bello mentis exprimitur? Quid vero per vas tabernaculi, nisi fidelium animae figurantur? Levitae ergo ab anno vigesimo et quinto tabernaculo servi*unt, *et a* quinquagesimo *custodes vasorum f*iunt, *ut videlicet qui adhuc impugnantium vitiorum certamina* per consensum delectationis *tolerant, aliorum curam suscipere non praesumant.* (iii) *Cum vero temptationum bella subegerint, quo apud se iam de intima tranquillitate securi sunt, animarum custodiam sortiantur.* (iv) *Sed quis haec temptationum praelia sibi perfecte subigat, cum Paulus dicat ... etc.*

The two principal points at which PLT and Dialogues agree against RMor are as follows: after *RMor* (ii) both include the sentence: "*Electi enim* [*Dial.* ergo] *cum adhuc in temptatione sunt, subesse eos ac servire necesse est, et obsequiis laboribusque fatigari*" (in IGP 16, lines 37-9). Immediately after this additional sentence *PLT*—but not *Dialogues*—continues with wording identical to *RMor* (iii) above. Then both *PLT* and IGP 16 conclude with the second additional sentence, not found in *RMor*: "*mentis quippe aetate tranquilla, cum calor recesserit temptationis, custodes vasorum sunt, quia doctores animarum fiunt*" (in IGP 16, lines 39-41). The incidental phrases in which *PLT* and *Dialogues* agree *partly* against *RMor* are as follows. In (i) *RMor* has, "*tabernaculo serviunt, sed a ...*"; whereas both *PLT* and IGP 16a have, "*ministrare debeant, ab anno vero ...*" Both have "*fiant*" instead of *fiunt* at the end of that sentence. However, *Dialogues* differs from both *RMor* (i)

---

[1] In Roman characters.

and Paterius by reading (in IGP 16a, line 28), "*a viginti quinque annis et supra*".

It will be seen that while *Dialogues* echoes the sense of the *RMor* passage, it has direct verbal correspondence with *RMor* only in some separated expressions—in (i), and in the linking "*Cum vero*" (IGP 16b, line 39), which, as we can see from the fuller text in *PLT*, picks out the opening words of *RMor* (iv). The opening words of IGP 16a, found only in *Dialogues*, give a familiar Gregorian turn of phrase. (The "*Unde*" is abrupt in the *Dialogist's* sequence.) Instead of *RMor* (ii) *Dialogues* has, after a cue question from Peter the Deacon (lines 31-3), a short explanation of the allegorical meaning of the *Numbers* text (lines 34-7). This seems to be a jejeune paraphrase of *RMor* (ii). In *Dialogues* the two sentences that make up IGP 16b (which are found also in *PLT* but not in *RMor*) are consecutive. They are not separated, as in *PLT*, by the three clauses (*Cum vero ... sortiantur.*) which are common to both *PLT* and *RMor* (iii). In *PLT* those three clauses harmoniously link together the two additional sentences; the only trace of them in IGP 16b is the inclusion of those two opening words, "*Cum vero ...*" Here Paterius can be seen to give a smoother and more complete reading than either *Dialogues* IGP 16b or the received text of the *Moralia* passage.

What are we to make of this synoptic comparison of the three related texts, in the *Moralia*, in Paterius and in the *Dialogues*? If you are determined at all costs to maintain that Pope Gregory had written the *Dialogues* years before Paterius made his compilation, and that where identical wording is found both in the *Dialogues* and in *PLT* (and nowhere else) it must have been copied by Paterius from the *Dialogues*, then you have to make some such reconstruction as the following. When Gregory wrote the *Dialogues* in 593-4 he briefly paraphrased, and applied to St Benedict, the exegesis of the text of *Numbers* 8.24-6 which he had earlier expounded at greater length in his *Moralia* 23.21. In doing so he repeated some phrases he had used in the work. Then he decided (so you must suppose) to add to this brief exposition two newly composed sentences, which had no counterpart in the *Moralia* (i.e. from "*Electi ergo ...*" down to "*... doctores animarum fiunt*"). After this you have to explain some rather intractable features of the corresponding text in *PLT*. You must suppose that when Paterius came to compile his Scriptural commentary out of excerpts from St Gregory's writings, he reproduced almost verbatim the exposition of the *Numbers* text as he found it in the *Moralia*. Nevertheless, you must further suppose, he also came across the similar comment on the text in *Dialogues* II.2, and decided to improve the exposition given in the *Moralia* by inserting into it the two supplementary sentences that he found only in the *Dialogues*. In doing so he realized, with astonishing editorial perceptiveness, that he could achieve a more harmonious composition by separating the two sentences, which in the *Dialogues* are consecutive, and weaving them together by deft interposition of a sentence from the *Moralia* (*RMor* iii). You must also conclude that, while he copied the wording of *Moralia* with word-for-word fidelity for most of the rest of the passage, he decided to depart from it in a couple of instances and to substitute words picked out from the *Dialogues* text. Thus when he came to *"tabernaculo serviunt"* in *RMor* (i) he chose not to copy that phrase, but instead to put in *"ministrare debeant"* from the *Dialogues*.

Instead of this far-fetched reconstruction, the commonsense conclusion from the texts we have compared is surely that Paterius is not dependent on the *Dialogues*. It is not credible that he cobbled his Gregorian extract together in such a manner, copying the *Moralia* passage faithfully while keeping an eye on a parallel paraphrase in *Dialogues* II.2 in order to insert pieces from it in an improved composite text. Rather, the text as he reproduces it reflects a harmonious Gregorian original. It would appear that Gregory's commentary on *Numbers* 8.24-6 must have existed separately in a rather longer form (with the inclusion of the two additional sentences) than that which has been transmitted in the received text of the *Moralia*. This longer form, preserved in the Gregorian papers in the Lateran *scrinium*, would have been available to Paterius when he was compiling his systematic collection of Gregory's exegetical comments. Doubtless it was still available at a later date when the Dialogist was composing his work, and it was from this that he constructed the abbreviated expository comment which he appended to his account of St Benedict's victory over temptation.

The Dialogist's use of the fragment of Gregorian exposition contained in IGP 16 is, in any case, not apposite to his context. He implies that the typology of *Numbers* 8.24-5 is to be applied to St Benedict, who, like the elderly Levites there mentioned, acquired spiritual mastery after passing beyond the temptations of the flesh. But since the Dialogist sets Benedict's victory over carnal temptation near the beginning of his monastic life, the typology is incongruous. For the Scriptural analogy to be apposite we should have to suppose that Benedict was already over the age of 50 when he overcame the temptation. Moreover the analogy is unapt also in the manner in which the victory of chastity was won. According to the Dialogist, the youthful Benedict extinguished carnal desires by a single heroic feat of ascetical violence against his flesh; according to Gregory in IGP 16, on the other hand, the elderly Levites of *Numbers* 8 typified worthy masters of souls, not because they conquered youthful passion by a like feat of asceticism, but because, after long years of fatiguing labours, "in the spiritual peace that came with age, the heat of temptation had receded" (IGP 16b, lines 39-40).

IGP 17: II.3.5-9. Explanation, with Scriptural illustrations, of what it means to "return to oneself". IGP 17a runs from line 48, "*Nam quotiens* ...", to line 59, "*... ad se rediit?*". IGP 17b runs from line 64, "*... de Petro apostolo ...*", to line 78, " *... et prius fuit*". (Omit "*Petre*" in line 69.)

IGP 17 is another typical example of the manner in which the Dialogist adapts and employs his borrowed Gregorian passages. He has available here an authentic and substantial pericope of Gregorian teaching which he seeks to make applicable to his story of St Benedict. After an introductory query from Peter the Deacon (lines 40-1), he puts into the mouth of the Gregory of the *Dialogues* some observations about Benedict (lines 42-8) which lead on to the genuine Gregorian pericope and make it seem relevant to the context. Try as he may, the Dialogist cannot adequately match the style of Gregory the Great, as can be seen by comparison of IGP 17 with the text in which it is embedded. There is also a tell-tale difference in grammatical forms between the borrowed Gregorian excerpts and the Dialogist's surrounding text—a difference that can be discerned in other similar instances. Instead of the Dialogist's use of verbal and pronominal forms relating directly to Benedict, there is in IGP 17 a change to Gregory's familiar use of his homiletic "we", enunciating general spiritual principles. The verbal forms in the first person plural mark out both IGPs 17a and 17b; they are to be found in lines 48-52 and 69-72. Note how in lines 60-1, between those two genuine Gregorian excerpts, the Gregory of the *Dialogues* reverts to the first person singular.

After reproducing Gregory's first Scriptural testimony, concerning the Prodigal Son, the Dialogist has interpolated into the middle of IGP 17 some remarks of his own composition (lines 60-3). Thereupon he leads into IGP 17b by putting Gregory's citation of *Acts* 12.11 into the mouth of Peter the Deacon, so that the subsequent exposition of the text appears as the Pope's reply to the second query of his subordinate. The remarks interposed by the Dialogist between IGPs 17a and 17b, in lines 60-3, are needed in order to return the discussion to the subject of St Benedict. The Dialogist realizes that Gregory's reflections in IGP 17a on the parable of the Prodigal Son (*Luke* 15.11-17), though they may give an authentic Gregorian flavour to his own text, are unrelated to his narrative of St Benedict's life, in which there is no analogy to the alienation and repentant return of the Prodigal Son. Indeed for the Dialogist's purpose, only IGP 17b, relating to the higher sense of "going out of oneself" as exemplified in the Apostle Peter, is relevant for application to St Benedict. He is aware that the lower kind, namely the dereliction of one's true self in the mire of sin, as exemplified by the Prodigal Son, has no application here. Nevertheless, since it is not possible to disengage the higher kind from the lower kind in his closely-knit Gregorian pericope, he has to reproduce the whole passage—IGP 17a as well as IGP 17b.

In the case of IGP 17 we can discern both the considerable degree of adroitness with which the Dialogist weaves his borrowed material into his narrative and also signs of awkwardness and inconsequence when Gregory's words, written for a different purpose, do not fit appositely into his context. It is worth tarrying for a more searching investigation of his use of IGP 17, in order to mark the peculiarities in the development and logic of his argument. The complicated mixture of ideas in paragraphs 5-9 of Chapter 3 will be seen to be the result of his injudicious attempt to use IGP 17 as a commentary on the spiritual state of Benedict in his contemplative solitude. The borrowed Gregorian pericope does not really lend itself to the Dialogist's usage here. Its subtle play of language and ideas escapes his attempt to accommodate it to his purpose, and there is thus an effect of disconnection and mystification in his text.

The key phrase which the Dialogist presents as the theme of the whole discussion is *"habitavit secum"* (line 39). When the miscreant monks tried to poison their abbot, Benedict left them and returned to his beloved solitude, where "he dwelt with himself". Thereupon Peter the Deacon puts in a cue question, saying that he does not understand what *"habitavit secum"* may mean (lines 40-1). Now in numerous instances elsewhere in the *Dialogues* a cue question by Peter the Deacon contains a word or phrase from a Gregorian passage shortly to be inserted, as a proleptic device to prepare for it. When we examine IGP 17 we do not find that the exact phrase *"habitavit secum"* occurs in that genuine Gregorian pericope. We do find there *"nobiscum non sumus"* (line 5), *"secum fuisse"* (line 52) and *"secum fuit"* (line 58). On the other hand, the phrase which Peter the Deacon has queried is twice taken up again in the comments added by the Dialogist himself: *"secum habitasse"* (line 60) and *"habitavit secum"* (line 79).

Much has been written about this phrase of the *Dialogues*, *"habitavit secum"*. It has even been asserted that "Gregory is indebted to the *Alcibiades*, with Persius as an intermediate source, for the precept "Dwell with thyself"—considered as an equivalent of the Delphic precept "Know thyself", but applied by Gregory to St Benedict's ascetic life in solitude". (P. Courcelle, *Connais-toi, toi-même, de Socrate a saint Bernard*, Tome I, Paris 1974, p. 229; quoted by A. de Vogüé, *SC* 260, p. 143.) The phrase *"habitare secum"* is not found in any of Gregory's authentic works. Why does the Dialogist include it and use it for the cue phrase in Peter the Deacon's query in lines 40-41? Why does he not fasten on a cue phrase that is readily recognizable in the borrowed Gregory passage he is about to insert? The explanation, I think, is that he used the phrase *"habitavit secum"* as a substitute for the phrase *"secum fuit"*, which does occur in IGP 17 (line 58), and for the two cognate phrases using *"secum"* with the verb to-be. (lines 50-52). It would have been a weak concluding phrase in his sentence about Benedict's retirement to prayerful seclusion (in line 39) to say simply *"fuit secum"*; so the Dialogist coined the phrase[2] *"habitavit secum"*.

He gets himself into difficulties when he uses this phrase as his cue for applying IGP 17 to St Benedict's state of solitary retirement. First he says that if the holy abbot had continued his rule over those unruly monks he might perhaps have overtaxed himself, lost his peace of mind and "turned aside the eye of his mind from the light of contemplation" (*a contemplationis lumine*; lines 45-6). Worn down by the daily struggle with his refractory subjects, he might "have been less watchful of himself" and "perhaps would have left himself" (*se forsitan relinqueret*; line 48). From these observations (and from lines 60-3) we gather that in his usual state of peaceful contemplation Benedict was "dwelling with himself": had he descended from the state he would have been no longer *secum*. Immediately after these observations, the Dialogist inserts IGP 17a. There the real Gregory states the principle that "whenever we are led out of ourselves by a movement of excess in thought, we are at the same time ourselves yet not with ourselves" (lines 48-50). Later in IGP 17 he elucidates this idea by explaining that such movements are of two kinds, and that there are two senses in which we are "led outside ourselves" (lines 69-72). The first kind of excess was that of the Prodigal Son, who was evidently not "with himself" when he was wandering afar in vice and misery before he "returned to himself" (lines 52-9). But could it be thought that when St Benedict feared he might "leave himself" (line 48) through his involvement with the unruly monks, he was in danger of the same kind of depraved alienation from self as that of the Prodigal Son? Lest such an inference could be drawn from the Dialogist's insertion of IGP 17a, he hastens to exclude it by explaining that Benedict was always watchful over himself and never allowed the eye of his mind to stray outside himself; it was in this sense that he "dwelt with himself" (lines 60-3). Now the flow of the argument is becoming complicated.

After the allusion to the case of the Prodigal Son, which has proved to be irrelevant to the case of Benedict, the discussion moves on in IGP 17b to the example of the Apostle Peter, who "returned to himself" after being rescued by an angel from the hand of Herod. This scriptural episode is interpreted by the real Gregory as meaning that the Apostle had been

---

[2] " ... *l'expression semble avoir été frappée tout exprès pour piquer la curiosité du diacre Pierre"*: J. Winandy, in *Collectanea Cisterciensium Reformatorum*, 25, 1963, pp. 343-54.

caught up in a spiritual ecstasy, and that his "return to self" was descent from "the summit of contemplation" (*a contemplationis culmine*, line 77) to his normal state of consciousness. The Dialogist's accommodation of this example to St Benedict is not altogether coherent. The venerable Benedict, he says, "dwelt *with* himself" inasmuch as he kept himself "within the cloisters of his thought"; but at times he was (like the Apostle Peter) raised *above* himself by "the heat of contemplation" (*contemplationis ardor*; line 81). Has the Dialogist forgotten that earlier he has described Benedict's habitual state as one in which the eye of his mind was held "by the light of contemplation" (*contemplationis lumine*; lines 45-6)? In that state the saint was clearly "with himself", since he feared lest by departing from that state he might "leave himself" (line 48). Now, however, the Dialogist says that whenever the heat of contemplation lifted Benedict up he was no longer with himself, but "without doubt he left himself below himself" ("*se procul dubio sub se reliquit*" lines 81-2). Perhaps, in order to defend the Dialogist from a charge of incoherence here, someone will suggest that he makes a distinction between "the *light* of contemplation", in which Benedict was "with himself", and "the *heat* of contemplation", in which he was "above himself"!

The whole sequence that follows Peter the Deacon's initial request for elucidation (lines 40-1) has a puzzling quality. The extracts of Gregorian wisdom have been set in a dialogical exchange which has an air of inconsequence, even of confusion. The reason for this is that in order to bring in IGP 17 the Dialogist has set a question which is not the same as the question the real Gregory was discussing in the original source of IGP 17. The Dialogist makes his sequence an answer to the question: What does it mean to say that Benedict "lived with himself"? But in IGP 17 the real Gregory is not answering that question: his purpose is to explain two senses of being "away from oneself". His use of the term "*secum*", and his remarks about being "with himself" or "with ourselves", are only incidental to his argument. But the Dialogist has entangled the thread of his discussion by making "*secum*" the verbal link for Peter the Deacon's cue question. The real Gregory does not consider that "being with oneself", "*secum*", requires any interpretation. He mentions it only in passing as a point of reference for his discussion of the two altered states—one below, the other above the usual state of self-awareness and self-possession. Since Scripture has the phrases, "*in se reversus*", "*ad se reversus*", the question arises: *Whither* are we taken to when "we are led out of ourselves"—"*extra nos ducimur*"? When the sinner or saint "returns to himself", *whence* does he return—"*unde ad se rediit?*" (line 59).

As his answer Gregory expounds the two ways in which we are led out of ourselves by "a movement of excess in thought". As we have seen, one, exemplified by the Prodigal Son, is to sink below oneself into sinful depravity; the other, exemplified by the Apostle Peter, is to be lifted above oneself to a state of contemplative ecstasy. Here IGP 17 clearly parallels Gregory's similar teaching in *Moralia* 22.36. There is also a short relevant passage in *Moralia* 23.41, where it is said that the Psalmist, after being "*sublevatus in ecstasi*" and being rapt in contemplation, "*ad semetipsum rediit*". It may well be that IGP 17 was excised by Gregory from an earlier draft of the *Moralia* because it duplicated what he had said elsewhere.

To recapitulate, then, the impression of inconsequence in this piece of dialogue arises from the fact that in IGP 17 Gregory's concern was not with the state of being "*secum*" but with the state of *not* being "*secum*". His intent there was to explain the two senses in which the soul can be said to be "*extra se*". Twice the Dialogist has to add glosses of his own (lines 60-4 and 78-80) in order to bring the discussion back to the question that Peter the Deacon asked in the first place—namely, what it meant to say that Benedict "dwelt with himself" when he retired to his prayerful solitude. Since the real Gregory does not address that question in the borrowed pericope, the Dialogist tries to answer it himself in those two supplementary glosses.

IGP 18: II.3.10-11. How the apostolic labourer, finding that he is labouring fruitlessly, may move to another field of greater spiritual fruit. IGP 18a runs from line 85, " ... *ibi adunati* ...", to line 90, " ... *ferre meliorem.*" IGP 18b runs from line 93, "*Et saepe agitur* ...", to line 107, " ... *campum quaesivit.*"

IGP 18 follows in quick succession to IGP 17. As usual, it is introduced by a leading question from Peter the Deacon. This harks back to the story of St Benedict's departure from the wicked monks, which had immediately preceded IGP 17. Ought Benedict to have abandoned those monks, asks Peter, once he had taken them under his charge? This cue question, unlike that which introduced IGP 17, is well chosen to lead in to the Gregorian pericope that follows. Indeed, it seems likely that the Dialogist framed his account of Benedict's departure from the dissolute monks with the prospect of an apt use for IGP 18 in his mind. The accent on the "I" in the phrase which ushers in IGP 18 ("*Ut ego, Petre, existimo* ...") is typical of the Gregory of the *Dialogues* (e.g. I.10. lines 82, 89), but not of the real Gregory.

One may question whether in the original Gregorian setting IGP 18a was immediately prefixed to IGP 18b, since there is a slight difference of perspective between the two excerpts. But in any case the main subject of both excerpts (which the Dialogist has separated by a rhetorical question of his own) is the same. A passage that very closely resembles IGP 18b (even with verbatim agreement in some phrases) is to be found in *Moralia* 31.58-9, where the same teaching is given in greater detail. There the same precedent of St Paul's escape from Damascus is cited with the same moral,[3] but the application of the lesson is explained more fully and carefully than in our pericope. In that longer passage Gregory adds warnings about the danger of grave fault if we desert one field of apostolic labour for another when the balance of spiritual advantage does not warrant it, and about the danger of self-deception in justifying withdrawal from labour and peril on the pretext of prudence. It may well be that in his revision of the *Moralia* Gregory excised IGP 18 not only because it duplicated *Moralia* 31.58 but also because, lacking the additional pastoral warnings contained in the latter passage, it could have been taken amiss by some readers. His letters show us instances of his concern about churchmen tempted to abandon vexatious responsibilities.

IGP 19: II.8.9. On the difference between the signs shown by Christ to his proud enemies and to his humble followers. IGP 19a runs from line 75, "*... spiritum ... qui per concessae ...*", to line 79, " *... omnes accepimus.*" IGP 19b runs from line 81, "*Ille autem signa ...*", to line 87, "*... gloriam potestatis.*"

The meaning and relevance of IGP 19 in this chapter of the *Dialogues* is curiously elusive. At first sight the whole of paragraph 9 (lines 74-9) seems to be a single doctrinal excursus, prompted by Peter the Deacon's cue in lines 72-3. The mention in IGP 19a of the one spirit which fills the hearts of all the elect and the quotation of the Johannine text on the plenitude of the Word who illuminates all men, provides the verbal links to which Peter the Deacon's cue is adapted. That is, when Peter the Deacon remarks of Benedict, "*spiritu iustorum omnium plenus fuit*", the word *spiritu* links with *spiritum* in line 25, *iustorum omnium* links with *electorum omnium* in line 76, and *plenus* links both with *implevit* in line 76 and with *plenitudine* in lines 78-9. But after noting these verbal links, it is difficult to see how IGP 19b, authentically Gregorian though it clearly is in content and style, fits logically into the excursus as a whole. I think the explanation of this impression of unrelatedness is to be found in recognition that IGP 19 is conflated out of two disparate Gregorian fragments.

---

[3] Both in *Moralia* 31.58 and in IGP 18 Gregory defends St Paul's escape from Damascus as the act of a brave soldier of God seeking a better field of battle; but in an earlier passage, *Moralia* 19.11, he interprets Paul's flight from that city as an act of weakness. (cf. Vogüé, *SC* 260, p. 149.)

The Dialogist prefixes to his inserted pericope a phrase purporting to be addressed by Gregory to Peter the Deacon, which will personalize and adapt his own narrative to the objective Gregorian teaching that follows: *"Vir Domini Benedictus, Petre ..."* Omitting this extraneous prefix, we ask what the original context of IGP 19a may have been. Possibly it was part of an expository comment in which Gregory reflected on the expression *"unus spiritus"* which recurs in several Pauline texts (e.g. *1 Corinthians* 6.17; 13.9; 13.13; *Ephesians* 2.18; 4.4; *Philippians* 1.27). We shall see later that the Dialogist utilizes a Gregorian excerpt (IGP 21) which comments directly on the words of *1 Corinthians* 6.17: *"Qui adhaeret Domino unus spiritus est"*. It may well be that he took both IGP 19 and IGP 21 from the same sheaf of *schedae* in the archives.

After the short Gregorian snippet of IGP 19a, the sentence in lines 79-81 (*"Nam sancti ... aliis tradere"*) is interposed by the Dialogist himself with the aim of leading on to IGP 19b and of making it seem relevant to his context. This sentence does not, however, seem to follow appositely from what has just preceded: the logical link implied by *"Nam"* is lacking. In the Johannine texts just reproduced in IGP 19a it is "every man" who is illuminated by the light of Christ, and "all we" who have received of his fulness. But the interposed sentence in lines 79-81 implicitly makes those Johannine texts refer to *"sancti Dei homines"* who have received miraculous powers from God—an unGregorian restriction. The point and purpose of this sentence only emerges when we grasp the Dialogist's drift in the whole of the passage from lines 68 to 87. He has constructed this passage in order to bring in his two Gregorian fragments, IGPs 19a and 19b, and to make them seem part of a continuous sequence. Benedict's miracles had as precedents the miracles of Moses, Elisha, Peter, Elijah and David (lines 69-72). Was Benedict then "filled with the spirit of all the just"? (lines 72-73). IGP 19a is used to provide the answer that he, like all the elect, was filled with the one Spirit of the Lord. After this the interposed sentence in lines 79-81 implicitly refers back to the five Scriptural thaumaturges of lines 69-72. Even though Benedict's miracles were modelled on theirs, the *sancti Dei homines* could not transmit to any other saint their miraculous powers: Benedict's powers, like theirs, could come only directly from the Lord. By this train of thought the Dialogist leads into the IGP 19b, the opening clause of which offers an apparent link with his preceding sentence in lines 69-71.

When we examine IGP 19b more closely, however, it appears that its original context was quite other than that of IGP 19a, and also that it is unconnected with the Dialogist's foregoing argument. It has no relevance to the Scriptural figures who provided the models for Benedict's prodigious deeds, nor to the question of the bestowal of thaumaturgic powers on the saints. Although the expression *"virtutes ... aliis tradere"* in the interposed sentence in lines 79-80 leads the reader to assume that the words *"signa virtutis dedit subditis"*, which follow in line 81, are meant to refer to Christ's bestowal of miraculous powers on his followers, IGP 19b in itself does not have such a meaning. In it the real Gregory is speaking not of the transmission by Jesus of thaumaturgic powers to others, but of the two kinds of sign that he himself gave as a testimony to his mission. The scribes and Pharisees, the "evil and adulterous generation", sought a sign; but the only sign he would give them was that of Jonah—a figure presaging his death and entombment, which would be a sign for judgement upon them (*Matthew* 12.38-41). In contrast to this sole prophetic sign which Jesus declared he would give to his proud enemies, he did vouchsafe *"signa virtutis"*, signs of *his* power, to his humble disciples, to lead them to veneration and love. This disparity in the signs that Christ gave, on the one hand to the proud, on the other to the humble, symbolically foreshadowed (*"Ex quo mysterio actum est ..."*) the disparity in their reaction to the climax of redemption. That is, the proud saw only the ignominy of Christ's death, but the humble who witnessed his resurrection apprehended his glorious power over death (lines 85-7).

This elucidated, IGP 19b is a self-coherent and noble extract of Gregorian exposition; but inserted here into the Dialogist's narrative of Benedict's miracles, it is simply adventitious.

IGP 20: II.15.3. How in the decay of the city of Rome a prophecy is mystically fulfilled. From line 25, *"Cuius prophetiae mysteria ..."*, to line 29, *" ... prosternantur videmus."*

IGP 20 is so much all-of-a-piece with the Dialogist's preceding story of St Benedict's prediction of the ruin of Rome that it must seem strange at first sight to ascribe the two parts of paragraph 3 to two different pens. Nevertheless on closer inspection IGP 20 can be discerned as an independent pericope, not originally written to refer to Benedict's prediction. There is a strikingly similar parallel in one of Gregory's homilies which provides a key for recognizing its original bearing. Short as it is, IGP 20 is authentically Gregorian in its construction and language, which further differentiate it from the Dialogist's prose.

According to *Dialogues* II.15, lines 23-5, St Benedict predicted that Rome would not be destroyed by invaders (in particular, by Totila and his Goths) but that, weakened by the forces of nature, it would sink into ruin by itself. IGP 20 is then presented as a declaration that Benedict's prophecy is being verified at the time of writing. Although the opening clause (lines 25-6) has the appearance of being a direct comment on the preceding words of Benedict's prophecy, it has a curious inappositeness in the use of the word *mysteria*. Gregory there says: "The mysterious meaning of this prophecy has now become clearer than light to us ...". He and his contemporaries see the fulfilment of prophecy in the decay of the city of Rome, which, weakened by long decrepitude, is now falling into ruins; they see its walls and buildings, broken by storm damage, crumbling to the ground (lines 26-9). Now in Gregory's terminology the phrase *prophetiae mysteria* refers to a mystic symbolism or latent typology underlying the words of an inspired prophecy. But where is the hidden significance in Benedict's prediction? There is no mystery about it; its meaning is perfectly straightforward. How can it be said that its mystic symbolism has become clarified in Gregory's own day? There is nothing arcane in the observation that the storm damage and long-continued decay of the Roman buildings (which must already have been apparent at the time of Benedict's prediction and of Totila's entry into the city, 47 years before the ostensible date of the *Dialogues*) has continued since that date to reduce Rome to a ruinous condition.

That word *mysteria* is in fact the clue that points to the native context of IGP 20, and indicates that this Gregorian fragment did not originate as a comment on Benedict's prediction. In Gregory's usage *prophetia* means Scriptural prophecy. Very frequently in his expository writings he points to a mystical, moral or allegorical significance underlying the literal sense of an Old Testament prophetic text—therein lie the *prophetiae mysteria*. I conclude that IGP 20 was in its original context a commentary on a prophetic text from the Bible referring to the coming ruin of a city, which Gregory proceeded to apply, by his mystical exegesis (*"cuius prophetiae mysteria"*), to the ruin of the once proud and magnificent city of Rome. This is no merely fanciful suggestion, for we have in Gregory's authentic writings two instances in which we find him doing precisely that. The first is in his *Homilies on Ezekiel*, II.6.22, where he cites the prophecy of *Ezekiel* 24.3-11, announcing the coming ruin of the city of Jerusalem (Samaria, in Gregory's text). He interprets that prophecy of long ago as now applicable to the present-day ruin of the city of Rome: *"Ipsa autem quae aliquando mundi domina esse videbatur qualis remanserit Roma conspicimus ...; ita ut in ea completum esse videamus quod contra urbem Samariam per hunc eumdem prophetam longe superius dicitur"*. He then proceeds to make a detailed application of his symbolic interpretation of the prophecy to the plight and decay of Rome in a passage which contains verbatim parallels to IGP 20—*"ruinis crebrescentibus, ipsa quoque destrui aedificia videmus"*. IGP 20 may well have been written to refer likewise to *Ezekiel* 24.3-11, and may have been excised in Gregory's revision of his writings because it duplicated the pericope in his *Homilies on Ezekiel*.[4] In the following section of the same homily (II.6.23) Gregory goes on to make another similar symbolic interpretation of an Old Testament prophecy as verified in the downfall of the city of Rome. This time it is the prophecy of *Nahum* (2.11) foretelling the destruction of Nineveh that is seen as also fulfilled in Rome's downfall.

IGP 20, then, which seemed *prima facie* to be aptly placed and homogeneous with its textual setting, can be seen on closer study to belong to an original Gregorian context of Scriptural exposition and to be adventitiously inserted into the *Dialogues*. The *prophetia* there referred to by the real Gregory was not the non-scriptural vaticination put into the mouth of St Benedict by the Dialogist, but was a Scriptural text such as *Ezekiel* 24.3-11 or *Nahum* 2.11. The *mysteria* of that prophecy lay in a further mystic sense latent in it, so that it presaged not only the destruction of an ancient biblical city but also the eventual ruin of the City of Rome, once the centre and mistress of the world. Yet the very aptness of IGP 20 to the use the Dialogist makes of it strongly suggests that he composed his story of the colloquy between Bishop Sabinus of Canosa and St Benedict, in which the latter uttered his circumstantial prediction of the eventual collapse of the City of Rome, precisely in order to utilize this genuine fragment of Gregorian exegesis which lay ready to his hand in the Lateran *scrinium*.

IGP 21: II.16.3-8. To what extent do the Apostles and saints know the mind of God? From line 27, "*Qui adhaeret Domino ...*", to line 79, " *... occultata non possunt*" (Omit "tibi" in line 56.)

This is one of the longest IGPs in the first three books of the *Dialogues* (52 lines in the *SC* edition). It has the unmistakable flavour of Gregory's heuristic exegesis, whereby he considers apparent contradictions arising from contrasted texts of Scripture and then makes a harmonious resolution of them to arrive at a doctrinal synthesis. IGP 21, with its many Scriptural quotations, its discursive style and its inversions and resumptions, bears the marks of a spoken colloquy taken down by scribes as Gregory spoke from pulpit or conference chair. (Note especially lines 49-50, "*Sed rursum mihi haec dicenti alia suboritur quaestio*".) Although the passage is unmistakably Gregorian, the ordering of the Scriptural quotations and commentary suggests that Gregory has not here carried out the

---

[4] We know of one particular storm that occurred at the beginning of Gregory's pontificate and that caused much damage to the buildings of Rome. He refers to it in one of his *Homilies on the Gospels* (1.5) in phrases that have echoes both in his later homily on *Ezekiel* and in IGP 20: "*Nudiustertius, fratres, agnovistis quod subito turbine annosa arbusta eruta, destructae domus, atque ecclesiae a fundamentis eversae sunt.*"

careful revision and polishing that he devoted to those of his discourses that were destined for publication. Possibly IGP 21 was extracted by the Dialogist from the *schedae* of Claudius, who took down so many of Gregory's extempore exegetical colloquies, albeit less than satisfactorily. It is possible that IGP 21 comes from an original source that also included IGP 22, which is the next passage we shall have to consider. The subject matter of these two passages is connected.

There is only a tenuous and unGregorian connection between IGP 21 and the preceding narrative to which it is appended. The Dialogist has just told the tale of a cleric who had been possessed by a demon, and who before having recourse to Benedict had sought in vain for deliverance at numerous shrines of martyrs to which his bishop had sent him. The reason for his failure to obtain relief at those shrines was that "the holy martyrs of God willed not to give him the gift of recovery so that they should show what great grace was in Benedict" (lines 3-6). After duly exorcizing the man, Benedict warned him never to presume to receive sacred orders, under pain of being at once repossessed by the evil spirit. Many years later the cleric, heedless of Benedict's warning, did obtain ordination and was straightway seized by the devil, who shook the life out of him. Thereupon Peter the Deacon provides the cue for IGP 21 by remarking that to predict this eventuality Benedict must have "penetrated even the secrets of the Deity". And why wouldn't he, retorts the Gregory of the *Dialogues*, since the saint observed the commandments of the Deity? With this remark the Dialogist leads directly into IGP 21. Beginning with the quotation of *I Corinthians* 6.17, this lengthy excursus discusses the sense in which the Apostles and prophets "knew the mind of God". It is to be noted that the Dialogist divides up this Gregorian pericope by putting a substantial section of it (lines 45-55) into the mouth of Peter the Deacon. Since this section consists of two ruminative questions which the real Gregory put to himself in the course of his original discourse, it can be made to seem part of the dialogical exchange. Those searching reflections, however, are out of character for Peter the Deacon.

In IGP 21, with its counterpoised exegesis of the various biblical texts adduced, Gregory develops his answer to the Pauline question, "Who has known the mind of the Lord?" (*Romans* 11.34). At the end of the long expository excursus Peter the Deacon remarks with satisfaction (lines 80-1) that by putting forward his "little query" (*quaestiuncula*) he has prompted the clarification of the subject. Presumably this remark refers to his initial cue in lines 23-5, since the two substantial and well posed Scriptural questions put into his mouth in lines 45-55 can hardly be called a *quaestiuncula*. But while his initial remark did provide a verbal link with the opening text cited in IGP 21, most of the long Gregorian passage, with its subtle flow and reflux of exegetical arguments, is irrelevant to his initial remark and to the tale of Benedict and the demoniac cleric. IGP 21, which was originally composed for a very different context, appears here as a long digression merely juxtaposed to the Dialogist's narrative, and having no organic unity with it.

IGP 22: II.21.3-4. God sometimes withdraws the spirit of prophecy from the minds of the prophets. From line 21, *"Prophetiae spiritus ..."*, to line 37, *" ... quid sint de semetipsis"*. (Omit *"Petre"* in line 21.)

This typically Gregorian pericope is a "doublet" of what Gregory says elsewhere. Indeed it is a "triplet", for the same theme and the same explanation is found in *Moralia* 2.89 and in *Homilies on Ezekiel* I.1.15-16. In both those passages, as in IGP 22, Gregory establishes from biblical illustrations that the prophets are not uninterruptedly illuminated by the *prophetiae spiritus*. The two biblical illustrations used in IGP 22 (namely, the nescience of the prophets Nathan and Elisha) are both included in the fuller series of examples given in the *Moralia* and in the *Ezekiel* homily. Compared with those other two passages, as A. de Vogüé observantly points out, *"Le présent passage est un raccourci mieux ordonné"* (*SC* 260, p. 199). We have already noted that there is similarity of subject matter between this pericope and the preceding one (IGP 21), which may indicate that their original provenance was from the same Gregorian discourse. The manner in which the Dialogist utilizes IGP 22 and inserts it into his narrative conforms with his pattern of composition now familiar to us. Yet despite his dexterous tailoring of it into his life of St Benedict, tell-tale indications remain to show that it is from a different weft.

The Dialogist has been relating a series of anecdotes which demonstrate Benedict's clairvoyance and his preternatural power to predict future events. These stories provide the author with an opportunity to insert a Gregorian pericope which he has at hand concerning the power of prophecy. This pericope, IGP 22, is not altogether pat to his purpose, since it discusses the *withdrawal* of the power of prophecy, whereas in the preceding series of anecdotes Benedict's powers of vaticination and preternatural insight are shown to be unfaltering. Indeed, after recounting how the holy abbot read the secret thoughts of a proud young monk, the Dialogist has commented: "Then it was patently clear to everyone that nothing could remain hidden from the venerable Benedict" (II.20.2, lines 18-19). Yet in spite of this affirmation of the infallibility of Benedict's visionary power, the Dialogist now makes Peter the Deacon introduce IGP 22 by asking whether Benedict possessed the prophetic spirit at all times or only at intervals. His reason for introducing this question is that the next Gregorian pericope which he wishes to insert is concerned with the intermittent ignorance of the prophets. Since IGP 22 gives a general conclusion by Gregory on the divine reasons for the withdrawal of prophetic powers from the Scriptural prophets, Peter the Deacon's question about Benedict receives no specific answer.

As in so many other instances, the Dialogist picks out a phrase from his borrowed Gregorian pericope to use as a cue in the introductory question posed by Peter. In this case he chooses the opening phrase of IGP 22, "*prophetiae spiritus*" and proleptically echoes it twice in Peter's leading question (lines 18 and 20). I would again observe that although here and elsewhere the Dialogist directly attributes to Benedict[5] the *prophetiae spiritus*, and in lines 21-3 he implies that Benedict is included among the prophets whose minds are irradiated by the Holy Spirit, this usage is unGregorian. I have not found any instance in Gregory's writings in which he applies the title *propheta* to a post-biblical saint, or the term *prophetia* to a non-scriptural vaticination or exercise of preternatural discernment.[6] The long discussion which he devotes in the first of his *Homilies on Ezekiel* to the nature of the prophet's mission, and expressly to the meaning of the term *prophetiae spiritus*, is wholly in the biblical context. For the real Gregory, then, a prophet is always a biblical figure, and his illustrations of prophecy are always drawn from the pages of holy writ. Even "false prophets" are mentioned only in contrast to the true prophets of God whose words and deeds are recorded in that sacred history. IGP 22 is one out of numerous examples of this consistent Gregorian usage. By making it appear that Gregory meant IGP 22 to refer to Benedict, thus applying the terms *propheta* and *prophetiae spiritus* to non-biblical prognostication, the Dialogist has once more left us with evidence of his uneasy blending of disparate elements in his literary alloy. I have already pointed out a similar significant misappropriation of the word *prophetia* in connection with IGP 20.

IGP 23: II.23.6. On the awesome authority given to men on earth to pass judgements valid even in heaven. From line 52, "*Numquidnam ... in hac adhuc ...*" to line 61, " *... est firmitas Dei.*" (Omit "*Petre*" in line 52.)

In this fragment Gregory dwells on the paradox that weak human nature (*caro*) has been raised to the high dignity of wielding spiritual

---

[5] He also attributes it to other holy men in his narrative: Cerbonius, Sabinus and Isaac.

[6] Apart from the *Dialogues*, the noun *prophetia* is used exactly 200 times in the corpus of Gregory's writings, frequently in the expression *spiritus prophetiae*, the spirit possessed by the prophets in biblical times. In *Ezekiel* I.8.32 he says "*nos per spiritum prophetiae videre non possumus*" (so we must accordingly seek "the likeness of God's glory" in sacred Scripture and divine commandments). In *Moralia* 34.7 he mentions, among the divine signs now dimmed in the Church, "*prophetia absconditur*".

authority even in the heavenly sphere. It was not only in the other-worldly regeneration (*Matthew* 19.28) that Christ promised his Apostles that they should exercise judgement on high. (It would seem likely that in the original context IGP 23 was prefaced by a direct reference to *Matthew* 19.28, in view of the implied contrast in the opening words of the pericope.) It was while still in this mortal flesh that the Apostle Peter was endowed by Christ with authority to bind and loose even in heaven (*Matthew* 16.19), and the authority bestowed on him has now passed to the rulers of the Church. This dignity given to man on earth, Gregory teaches, is made possible by the ennobling of human *caro* in the Incarnation. It was by descending even to the lowliness of human flesh (*factus pro hominibus Deus caro*; line 60) that God gave to men in their earthly flesh the awesome power to exercise judgement even over spirits (*ut iudicare caro etiam de spiritibus possit*, line 58-9). Perhaps in the original source there had also been previous mention of a text such as *1 Corinthians* 6.3: "Know you not that we shall judge angels?"

How does the Dialogist utilize this rich passage of Gregorian theology? He brings it in as an adjunct to his story of two nobly-born but bad-tempered nuns who were threatened with excommunication by Benedict if they did not curb their mordant tongues. They died without having heeded his warning, and during the liturgy they were seen to leave their tombs in the church whenever the deacon bade non-communicants to depart. When their old nurse informed Benedict of their plight he enjoined that a Mass should be offered for them, and declared that thereafter they would no longer be excommunicated. That his declaration was ratified and the ban of excommunication on the nuns was lifted was patently demonstrated by the fact that after the Mass had been offered for them they were no longer seen to leave the church when the deacon dismissed the non-communicants. It is this tale that the Dialogist uses to introduce IGP 23. Peter the Deacon expresses his wonderment that Benedict, albeit a venerable saint, could, while "still living in this corruptible flesh, liberate souls already haled before the invisible judgement seat" (lines 49-51). As usual, the Dialogist includes in Peter's query a cue phrase taken from the coming Gregorian pericope in order to provide a verbal link with it. In this case the phrase is "*in hac carne*" in line 49, which links immediately with the same phrase at the beginning of IGP 23 (line 52). As in so many other instances, one is left with the strong suspicion that the Dialogist composed his bizarre tale of Benedict's acquittal of the excommunicate nuns for the express purpose of providing an apparently apposite niche for the Gregorian fragment which he had at his disposal.

There is more than one incongruity in this chapter of the *Dialogues*. First, there is the lack of spiritual sensitivity shown by the author in joining IGP 23 to the tale of the acid-tongued nuns. It is veritable bathos to make it appear that Gregory wrote this elevated theological reflection as an answer to a query about Benedict's power to lift the ban that obliged those spectral nuns to quit their tombs whenever the liturgical dismissal of non-communicants was pronounced. What notion of eschatology, one wonders, was presupposed by the Dialogist in telling of their strange state in the other world? It was not the doctrine of Purgatory, such as Gregory himself envisaged (cf. Chapter 17 below, IGP 67). The departed souls of the excommunicate nuns were, it seems, not yet definitively judged; they are not presented in the *Dialogues* as suffering in purgatorial fire, like the souls mentioned in the stories in Book IV. Their other-worldly plight consisted in their continued severance from ecclesiastical communion. As A. de Vogüé observes, what Benedict's pardon obtained for them was simply reconciliation with the Church (*SC* 260, pp. 208-9).

Furthermore the Dialogist strikes a false note when, by his application of IGP 23 to the case of Benedict's absolution of the souls of the excommunicate nuns, he makes Gregory imply that the power of binding and loosing even in heaven, committed by Christ to the Apostle Peter and thereafter to those who are in the same apostolic succession (lines 55-7), was possessed by the wonder-working abbot likewise. The real Gregory would not have allowed that an abbot not in holy orders could exercise this apostolic power. Here I do not argue merely from the fact that the phrase *locus sancti regiminis* (line 56) and cognate phrases are habitually used by Gregory in his doctrinal treatises and letters to refer specifically to the dignity and duties of a bishop.[7] The incongruity of applying IGP 23 to Benedict does not arise from that phrase alone, but from the reference to the power of the Keys conferred on St Peter and on the successors of the Apostles (lines 53-7). Pope Gregory is clear that it is the bishops of the Church who have succeeded to the awesome power conferred by Christ on his Apostles of passing judgement on souls. In his *Homilies on the Gospels* 26.5 Gregory affirms this principle in a passage that is very relevant to our present question: "*Horum profecto nunc in Ecclesia episcopi locum tenent. Ligandi atque solvendi auctoritatem suscipiunt, qui gradum regiminis sortiuntur.*" Thus according to Gregory's teaching an unordained abbot, however highly endowed with holiness and exceptional charisms, could not possess the apostolic and episcopal authority to bind and loose

---

[7] Out of a large number of instances of Gregory's use of the term *regimen* to refer to authority in the Church, it seems that only two refer to abbatial authority (*Epistolae* X.9 and XII.6; Ewald-Hartmann II, pp. 244, 352). The rest refer to episcopal authority.

with sanctions ratified in heaven. Benedict was not a bishop, nor even a priest; it was not with him in mind that Gregory wrote the passage which, long afterwards, was to be included in the *Dialogues* as IGP 23. I shall return to this instance in Chapter 19, when discussing theological discrepancies in the *Dialogues*.

IGP 24: II.30.2-3. On two modes of miracle-working, one by prayer, the other by direct power. From line 18, "*Qui devota mente, ...*" to line 32, " *... illi reddidit orando*".

The distinction that Gregory makes in this pericope between two modes of working miracles, one *ex potestate*, the other *ex postulatione*, provides the Dialogist with the motif for three of his miracle stories. The first of these stories immediately precedes IGP 24 and provides the occasion for its insertion; the other two immediately follow it. In IGP 24 Gregory illustrates his distinction between the two modes by pointing out the differing circumstances of two miracles worked by the Apostle Peter (lines 25-32). When for their blasphemous lie St Peter consigned Ananias and Sapphira to death, he did so not by a prayer addressed to God but by a direct rebuke addressed to them. Conversely, when he raised the dead Tabitha to life he obtained that miracle by prayer. In the former instance, therefore, the miraculous sign was worked by the God-given power exercised directly by the Apostle (*ex potestate*); in the latter it was impetrated by prayer (*ex postulatione*: equivalent terms are *ex prece* and *orando*).

Gregory comments particularly on the fact that Christ's disciples and saints could work miracles by personal power. He explains that they derived that power from their divine Master, and confirms this by a reference to the Prologue of St John's Gospel (lines 21-4). The Dialogist introduces IGP 24 by telling a tale in which St Benedict produced a miraculous effect by a similar direct exercise of personal power. When the devil violently possessed one of the Cassinese monks Benedict expelled the evil spirit by a simple slap. That the Dialogist means to point out the correspondence between this act of power and that of St Peter recalled by Gregory in IGP 24 appears from his revealing use of the word *solummodo*. In IGP 24 Gregory remarks that in executing the portentous sanction on Ananias and Sapphira St Peter is not said to have prayed for that result, "*sed* solummodo ... *increpasse*" (lines 29-30). Likewise in his preceding tale the Dialogist relates that Benedict had finished his prayer (*Qua completa*—line 7) when he came upon the monk possessed by the devil. It was not by prayer but by power that he effected the miraculous exorcism: "*ei* solummodo *alapam dedit*" (line 12). We have seen that it is the customary device of the Dialogist to make a proleptic allusion to a phrase contained in the Gregorian passage he is about to insert into his text. By such verbal links he makes his borrowed pericopes seem to have an intrinsic connection with his narrative. In the present case the introductory verbal link is provided not only by Peter the Deacon's leading question (line 15-17), but also in the preceding miracle-story by echoing the *solummodo ... increpasse* of IGP 24 in his allusive phrase *solummodo alapam dedit* (line 12).

When we examine the leading question of Peter the Deacon we find that it is framed less than astutely. Although he has just heard the Gregory of the *Dialogues* recount a story which emphasizes that Benedict worked the miraculous exorcism of the possessed monk not by prayer but by direct action, Peter the Deacon now asks his master to tell him whether Benedict ''always impetrated such great miracles by the efficacy of his prayer, or did he sometimes produce them also by the sole act of his will?''. Peter the Deacon's question, then, ineptly ignores the fact that just such a miracle, worked by the sole act of Benedict's will, has just been narrated to him. Notwithstanding this incongruity the author presents the question in this form in order to provide a pretext for introducing IGP 24, in which Gregory contrasts the two modes of miracle-working.

The Dialogist appears to take a particular pride in his possession of IGP 24. The extended use he makes of this gem of Gregorian doctrine is remarkable. On closer analysis we find that the whole sequence of the three chapters, 30, 31 and 32, has been constructed around this borrowed excerpt. The story in the first part of Chapter 30 already contains anticipatory allusions to IGP 24 (lines 7, 12, 15-17). But since the story in that chapter, about the monk whom Benedict exorcized with a simple slap, corresponds to only one of the two modes in the Gregorian distinction explained in IGP 24, the Dialogist proceeds in the two following chapters to add two further stories of miracles worked by Benedict in order (as he himself expressly explains—Chapter 30, lines 33-5) to provide parallels to both of those two modes. The first story is of a miracle *ex potestate*, the second of a miracle *ex postulatione*. In telling these two stories the Dialogist repeatedly alludes to the Gregorian distinction of modes contained in IGP 24 (cf. II.31, lines 32-3, 40-1, 42-8, 48-9; II.32, lines 34-5).

IGP 25: II.33.1. Even St Paul did not obtain what he asked of God in prayer. From line 1, ''*Quisnam erit ...*'' to line 3, '' *... non valuit?*'' (Omit ''*Petre*'' in line 1.)

This snippet, short though it is, well repays examination. Disregarding the familiarly intrusive "*Petre*", we recognize the sentence as authentically Gregorian in the midst of the Dialogist's surrounding narrative. There are two other passages in Gregory's writings in which he makes a comparable comment on St Paul's *stimulus carnis*, referred to in *2 Corinthians* 12.7-9. In *Moralia* 19.11-12 Gregory says that the Apostle was left with that affliction, despite his repeated prayer to the Lord to be rid of it, as a reminder to him—and as a lesson to us—of his human infirmity even amid his sublime virtues and heavenly gifts. In his *Homilies on the Gospels* 27.6 Gregory raises and discusses the question why St Paul's prayer for release from his trial went apparently unanswered. In that homily the question is presented as a theological problem arising from the apparent contradiction between *2 Corinthians* 12.7-9 and the promise of Christ in *John* 16.23-4. A similar theological setting of the question in another Gregorian discourse was doubtless the original context of IGP 25. The Dialogist has excerpted this single sentence from his store of *Gregoriana* to make it an answer to the naive question of Peter the Deacon: "Please tell me if holy men can achieve all that they want to, and if, in answer to their prayers, they are granted everything they desire to obtain". ("*Sed quaeso te indices, si sancti viri omnia quae volunt possunt, et cuncta impetrant quae desiderant obtinere*"; II.32, lines 37-9.)

To understand the Dialogist's use of IGP 25 we have to go back to IGP 24 and to the stories that illustrated it. We have seen that by inserting IGP 24 into Chapter 30 he introduced the Gregorian distinction between miracles performed by a saint through direct power (*ex potestate*) and those obtained indirectly through prayer to God (*ex postulatione* or *orando*). Equivalent phrases used by the Dialogist himself to correspond to that Gregorian distinction are *solo voluntatis nutu* (II.30, lines 16-17) for the first mode, and *ex oratione* (line 35) for the second mode. In Chapter 31 he has gone on to give an example of the first mode of miracle-working, and in Chapter 32.1-3 an example of the second mode. Peter the Deacon's question, which follows immediately (in 32.4, lines 37-9), still reflects this preoccupation with the two modes of miraculous efficacy explained in IGP 24. That is, the phrase "*si sancti viri omnia quae volunt possunt*" refers back to efficacy *solo voluntatis nutu*; while the concluding part of the question, "*et [si] cuncta impetrant quae desiderant obtinere*", refers to obtaining desired boons by impetration or prayer to God. Notice however that in this leading question by Peter the Deacon, which serves as the cue for IGP 25, there is no longer any explicit mention of miracles, but of desired boons in general. I will comment later on the significance of this widening of the reference of the question.

Different strands of the Dialogist's thought now become entangled. He has ready for use the snippet of IGP 25, which has reference to the problem of the saints' unanswered prayer, so he frames the last part of Peter's question (in lines 38-9) directly to refer to this problem. At the same time he sees a way of using IGP 25 as a bridge to lead on to one of the most substantial and most pleasing anecdotes in the whole of his work— namely, the story of St Scholastica and how she succeeded in constraining her brother Benedict to remain in her abode against his will to spend a night in spiritual colloquy. The Dialogist sees an opportunity to make this story relevant to his present context by fastening on a phrase in IGP 25: *"quod voluit obtinere non valuit"* (line 3). He has already alluded proleptically to this phrase in Peter the Deacon's leading question; immediately after IGP 25 he repeats those very words and applies them to St Benedict: *"quod voluit ... non valuit implere"* (II.33, lines 5-6). He sees in the repetition of this Gregorian phrase a peg on which to hang his coming story of Benedict and Scholastica. "Hence it is necessary", he writes, "to relate to you, concerning the venerable father Benedict, that once there was something that he willed but was not able to fulfil." Indeed the picturesque anecdote that follows is shown clearly to be an instance in which Benedict's will was thwarted—*"contra hoc quod voluit ... miraculum invenit"* (lines 51-2).

It would seem therefore that the story of Benedict and Scholastica in Chapter 33 follows on smoothly and logically from what has preceded. On closer inspection, however, we find that it is not so. Although the Dialogist has preserved a verbal continuity from Chapter 30 to 33 by his use of similar phrases, he has lost the logical sequence. In II.30.2 he made Peter the Deacon ask whether Benedict always obtained miracles through impetration, or whether he sometimes worked them directly, *solo voluntatis nutu* (lines 15-7). The question was answered by the insertion of IGP 24 and by two illustrative tales in Chapter 31 and 32. At the end of Chapter 32 (lines 37-9) Peter the Deacon asks the further question whether saints (and, by implication, St Benedict in particular) are always successful in obtaining what they desire, whether by their direct power or by impetration. It is significant, as I remarked above, that in his phrasing of this leading question the Dialogist, although still retaining an allusion to the previous distinction between the two modes of direct power and of impetration, no longer makes explicit reference to the working of miracles, but now extends the discussion to the wider and vaguer notion of "getting what one wants". As we read on we realize that this change of reference is needed by the Dialogist since he intends Peter's question, together with the answering Gregorian snippet of IGP 25, to lead on to the Scholastica story in which Benedict worked no miracle, nor even attempted to work one, either *ex potestate* or *ex oratione*. The coming story is not about the limitations of Benedict's miraculous power, but simply demonstrates that he did not always get what he wanted and that his will could be thwarted—as it was by his sister's pious stratagem. By a kind of verbal sleight, the Dialogist has simply changed the subject.

Notice also a further incongruity in his narrative and in his use of IGP 25. In his eagerness to bring in that Gregorian snippet with its cue phrase "*quod voluit ... non valuit*", he failed to appreciate that its original doctrinal reference makes it inappropiate as an introductory text for the Scholastica story that he intends to graft on to it. IGP 25, with its Scriptural reference to Paul's three unanswered petitions to the Lord, is plainly about the failure of a saint to obtain *by prayer to God* a desired boon. (Indeed IGP 25 answers only the concluding part of Peter the Deacon's preceding question, that which refers to impetration.) But while IGP 25 refers to the problem of saints' unanswered prayer to God, the story of Benedict and Scholastica, which is expressly linked with it, does not. In that story we find that there is no mention or implication of Benedict's failing to obtain *by prayer to God* what he desired. When he refuses his sister's request for a night of spiritual colloquy it is not he but Scholastica who prays to God—and her petition is not refused but instead is answered by a miracle. When the spectacular tempest makes it physically impossible for Benedict and his brethren even to set foot outside the door he does not pray to God for the obstacle to be removed: he simply turns to reproach his sister and then accepts the inevitable. Brief and inconspicuous though IGP 25 is in comparison to the much more substantial passages of Gregorian material that the Dialogist borrows elsewhere, this discussion of its content and its placing in the *Dialogues* has helped to show both his ingenuity and his intellectual limitations. He seeks to maintain a connected sequence of thought, but it falters and fails at the very point at which he tries to use the Gregorian snippet as a connecting link.

IGP 26: II.35.6. On the mystic vision of divine light, in which the soul is taken up into the greatness of God and realizes the littleness of all else. From line 51, " ... *animae videnti creatorum* ...", to line 59, " ... *humiliata non poterat.*" (Consider also the Gregorian echoes in paragraph 2, lines 19-22 and paragraph 3, lines 24-6.)

IGP 26 is used by the Dialogist as a theological commentary on his account of the so-called "cosmic vision of St Benedict", which provides a splendid climax for his biography of the saint. The whole of Chapter 35 is conceived and composed with undeniable artistry. While it is not dif-

ficult to mark out IGP 26 as an imported passage borrowed from a genuine Gregorian source, there remain some interesting questions, and
some obscurities, about the way it has been set into the rest of the
chapter.

The teaching of IGP 26 is paralleled and clarified by a number of
passages in the *Moralia*, as A. de Vogüé observes (*SC* 260, pp. 240-1; cf.
Moralia 1.34, 4.62; 4.65; 22.35; 22.36; 23.41; 31.96.) Some phrases in
IGP 26 have verbatim resonance with those other passages: e.g. *"angusta
est omnis creatura"* (line 51), *"mentis laxatur sinus"* (line 54), *"superior existat
mundo"* (line 55), *"rapitur super se"* (line 57). The calm universality of the
vision of reality described in IGP 26 is authentically Gregorian. Unlike
the rest of the chapter, which is a narrative about a concrete individual,
St Benedict, and his personal experience, IGP 26 is characteristically
Gregorian in its objective statement of spiritual truths about the nature
of the mystic vision as such. As in so many other cases, this universality
of teaching and objectivity of style is a criterion for distinguishing a genuine Gregorian pericope from the Dialogist's narrative in which it is set.

There is a significant contrast between Gregory's own teaching about
the vision of the contemplative soul rapt in the divine light, above itself
and above all created things, and the Dialogist's preceding account (in
paragraphs 2-4) of what Benedict saw in the famous vision that came to
him as he looked out of a tower window into the darkness around his
monastery. There were three stages in his vision. First he saw the
darkness suddenly dispelled by a wondrous light from on high, brighter
than day. Secondly, "in this contemplation a very wonderful thing followed": the whole world, "as if gathered under a single ray of sunlight"
(*velut sub uno solis radio collectus*; lines 24-5), was brought before his eyes.
Thirdly, while still "intent on the splendour of this radiant light", he saw
a further marvellous apparition. It was the soul of Bishop Germanus of
Capua being borne up by angels to heaven in a fiery globe. Benedict's
immediate reaction was to wish "to provide himself with a witness of so
great a miracle" (line 30). Accordingly with an extraordinary outcry he
called his visitor Servandus, who was sleeping nearby. Servandus was
able to see a glimmer of the miraculous radiance, while the man of God
related to him all that had happened. Straight away Benedict sent to have
inquiries made in Capua; sure enough, it was found that Bishop Germanus had just died, at the very moment that Benedict had seen the
meteoric ascent of his soul to heaven.

It was natural for the Dialogist, with his constant preoccupation with
the miraculous and his practical equation of sanctity with wonder-
working, to make a prodigious apparition and a miracle of clairvoyance
the climax of St Benedict's vision. Even when he brings in IGP 26 as a

commentary on what he has related, it is Benedict's vision of the fiery globe, containing the soul of Germanus and borne aloft by angels, that is uppermost in his account. At the end of the inserted pericope in which the real Gregory speaks of the vision in which the contemplative soul is rapt above itself "in the light of God", the Dialogist immediately makes the Gregory of the *Dialogues* apply the passage to the story of that spectacular apparition: "Therefore it is beyond doubt that the man who saw the fiery globe and the angels too mounting to heaven could only do so in the light of God" (lines 59-62).

There is here a gulf between the theological elevation of Gregory's own mystical teaching and the level of the Dialogist's spiritual perception. In *Moralia* 23.42 Gregory describes how the soul truly penetrated with the sense of God and His otherness from creatures, "suppresses all corporeal imaginations which may intrude on its awareness, and fixes the gaze of the heart on the very radiance of the infinite light (*incircumscriptae lucis*)". In the soul's upreach to God, he says, "it is watchful lest imagination of some finite vision (*circumscriptae visionis*) should draw it away, and therefore it rejects all images that may come before it".[8] This teaching of the real Gregory shows how inappropriately the Dialogist has made IGP 26 a commentary on his account of Benedict's tower-experience. The apparition of the fiery globe and of the angelic escorts for the soul of Bishop Germanus is indeed an instance of those "*obviantes imagines*" and of that "*circumscripta visio*" which Gregory declares must be resolutely excluded if the soul is to be rapt above itself and above the world "*in Dei lumine*". For St Gregory the mystic, imaginative visions such as that of the Bishop of Capua's ascension in a fiery globe do not constitute the supreme contemplation of the *anima videns creatorem* of which he speaks in IGP 26 and elsewhere. For the Dialogist on the other hand, avid relator of the miraculous, it is the prodigious element that is paramount.

It is likewise instructive to compare what the real Gregory says about the *return* of the soul from the ecstasy of divine contemplation with the Dialogist's description of Benedict's reaction after his tower-experience. Gregory says of the mystic, exemplified by the Psalmist: "After that vision of inward light, which shone forth in his soul with clear radiance through the grace of contemplation, he returned to himself; and becoming aware of himself, he realized both how far he was from that supernal good and how near he was to evils here below ... Raised up he saw what here he could not see of himself; falling back on himself he sighed in lament." (*Moralia* 23.40). Compare this with what the Dialogist tells us of Benedict's comportment after his vision, with its three stages—first the

---

[8] Similarly *Moralia* 5.62: "*corporeas imagines deserit*". cf. R. Gillet, *SC* 32b, pp. 23-9.

blazing out of the wondrous light, then the world shown him in miniature, and finally the spectacular apparition of the bishop's soul in the fiery globe carried upwards by angels. Benedict's reaction to these apparitions, as related by the Dialogist, is very different from the state of the contemplative soul returning to himself after mystical rapture, as described by the real Gregory.[9] The excited abbot's first thought, even during the visionary experience, is to find a fellow witness of the miraculous phenomena he has observed, wherefore he repeatedly calls Servandus by name with a mighty shout[10] (lines 30-2). Then, after relating to his friend in due order the series of supernatural happenings, his immediate concern is to send off to Capua for corroboration of his miraculous perception of the passing of Germanus (lines 34-9). The whole story of Benedict's vision is artistic hagiography, but it is a far cry from the mystical theology of St Gregory, of which IGP 26 preserves a lost fragment.

Has the Dialogist used any other Gregorian material in the construction of his remarkable chapter on Benedict's vision from the tower? There are two other small fragments which may well have been taken from an unedited text which he found in the *scrinium*. One is the phrase, '*omnis etiam mundus, velut sub uno solis radio collectus, ante oculos eius adductus est*'' (lines 24-6). While this may echo a Gregorian phrase, it is unlikely that it was borrowed from the same original source-text as IGP 26. Although in both cases there is mention of an extraordinary light, the expression ''*velut sub uno solis radio collectus*'' is a different concept from the ''*lux creatoris*'', ''*lux visionis*'' and ''*Dei lumine*'' of IGP 26. That the Dialogist has borrowed the phrase about an apprehension of ''the whole world gathered as if under a single ray of sunlight'' from a genuine Gregorian source is suggested by the way he repeats and savours it. He introduces it no less than four times: in lines 24-5, 45-6, 62-3, and 65-6. In the first part of his leading question (lines 45-7) Peter the Deacon says that the meaning of this phrase is beyond his understanding; in the second part of his question the phrase ''*mundus omnis*'' is repeated and used as the cue to bring in IGP 26: ''How could the whole world be seen by one man?'' (lines 48-9). The Dialogist presents IGP 26 as the first part of Gregory's answer to this question. He himself composes the second

---

[9] On the desolation of the *anima reverberata*, according to the authentic teaching of St Gregory, see R. Gillet, *SC* 32b, pp. 50-4.

[10] Commenting on this feature of the story, St Thomas Aquinas argues that since St Benedict did not completely transcend the sensory, his experience of divine vision could not have been complete. (*Summa Theologica* II.II.qu.180, art. 5, ad 3; and *Quodlibetales* 1.1.)

part (lines 59-71), giving his own further elucidation of Benedict's vision, while using some of Gregory's phraseology.[11]

The other short passage in Chapter 35 that I think may well have been extracted from a genuine Gregorian source is the concluding part of the final sentence of paragraph 2 (from line 19, "... *vidit fusam lucem* ...", to line 22, "... *inter tenebras radiasset*". These clauses have the veritable ring of Gregorian language and style. Moreover, as A. de Vogüé observes (*ibid.* p. 237), there are strange resemblances between this paragraph and one of the fourteen edifying *exempla* narrated by Gregory in his *Homilies on the Gospels*. There, in Homily 34.18, Gregory recalls the story of a penitent monk of austere life who went out secretly by night to pray and afflict himself before God. The phrase Gregory uses in that homily to describe how the monk rose early before the nocturnal office of monastic prayer is quite similar to that in which the Dialogist describes Benedict's anticipation of the hour of nocturnal prayer (in line 17). Then in the story in the *Homilies* the abbot of the monastery, who has followed the penitent monk to observe him at prayer, sees a sudden brilliant radiance falling on him and lighting up the whole countryside. Some individual words in this account are the same as or cognate with words in the *Dialogues* passage (*subito, lux ... fusa, tantaque claritas, radiando*). While the phrasing of the episode in the *Homilies* is otherwise different from that of our passage in the *Dialogues*, nevertheless the overall description of the sudden effulgence of the supernatural light has a remarkable resemblance in both texts.[12]

I shall consider in Chapter 17 the questions that arise from the group of edifying *exempla* included by Gregory in his *Homilies on the Gospels*, and shall discuss the Dialogist's knowledge and use of them in his fourth book. Here I draw attention to an interesting suggestion by Pfeilschifter (*op. cit.* p. 74), based on a close study of these Gregorian anecdotes. He thinks it not unlikely that Gregory kept a written collection of edifying stories to prompt his memory when he occasionally introduced *exempla* to illustrate and enliven his sermons to the people. In the Gospel homilies which he edited for publication we find one of these stories told twice in quite different language. Accepting Pfeilschifter's hypothesis, we may see an explanation of the strange resemblance between the details in *Dialogues* II.35.2 and in *Homilies on the Gospels* 34.18. There could have been a second telling of the story of the heavenly light that fell upon the penitent monk. Thus it could have been from such a variant text, preserved in

---

[11] This section of the Dialogist's text seems to reflect Cicero's account of Scipio's dream (*De Republica* VI.8-26); cf. Th. Delforge, "*Songe de Scipion et vision de saint Benoît*", in *Rev. Bén.* 69, 1959, pp. 351-4.

[12] "*Reste que les deux scènes sont presque identiques*": A. de Vogüé, *Vie de saint Benoît*, p. 199.

Gregory's papers in the papal *scrinium*, that the Dialogist took the Gregorian clauses which he uses to describe the heavenly light that Benedict saw.

In Chapter 35 the Dialogist presents Benedict's tower-experience as the Tabor of the saint's life. In it he emphasizes that the great thaumaturge was also a great seer, who is here shown in a climax of illumination from on high. It would seem that the Dialogist has gone through his store of Gregorian remains, picking out fragments which refer to supernal light and combining them to embellish his finely-woven account of Benedict's vision from his tower window. The three kinds of light referred to in these chosen Gregorian fragments can be seen to be disparate: there is the sudden brilliance near the monastery; there is the "single ray of sunlight" under which the whole world seemed to be perceived; and there is the light of God himself, of which IGP 26 speaks. The real Gregory would not have equated the marvellous light dispelling the darkness around the monastery with the *lumen Dei* in which the ecstatic soul is rapt above all created things. The Dialogist himself realizes that these "lights" are different, and at the end of the chapter he seeks to unite them in one focus. "In that light that shone out to bodily eyes", he explains, "was the interior light in the mind that raised the seer's soul to higher things ..." (lines 68-70).

IGP 27: II.38.4. Solution of an apparent theological difficulty concerning the eternal procession of the Holy Spirit. From line 29, "*Unde ipsa quoque veritas* ...", to line 39, "*... me discitis spiritaliter amare.*"

This, the last of the inserted Gregorian passages in Book II, I have already singled out for detailed examination in Chapter 13. There I chose it as a typical and revealing example of the Dialogist's methods, illustrating how he cobbled his text together and tried to make his borrowed pericopes relevant to his own homespun narrative. For discussion of his use of IGP 27 I refer the reader to that chapter (pp. 433-8).

The Dialogist, who knows Gregory's main writings well, has in II.38 also drawn on one of the saint's *Homilies on the Gospels* in order to construct the linking argument by which he makes IGP 27 relevant to Peter the Deacon's cue question. His argument remotely and incongruously echoes a fairly long passage in one of Gregory's sermons in which the pope criticizes the ill-instructed devotion of the simpler faithful who frequent the martyrs' tombs with too much thought of the visible world, and not enough understanding of the true life and of spiritual reality. The sermon had as its text *Luke* 9.23-27, and was delivered to a congregation of Romans in the basilica of the martyrs SS Processus and Martinianus on their feast-day.[13] Gregory remarks that although the assembled congregation are present in the place where the bodies of the martyrs rest, a place where miracles are worked, it is necessary to raise the minds of the *rudes*, the simpler folk, above the quest for visible marvels, and consolations, to seek the life of the spirit and prepare for judgement and eternity. If healing is provided for the living through the dead bodies of the martyrs, how much greater is the heavenly life of the martyrs? If they gave their bodies to be put to death, is this not a greater proof of the value of the eternal life for which they accepted bodily death? Evidently, in all this there is a very different climate of thought to that of the Dialogist in his explanatory paragraph which links Peter the Deacon's question in II.38.2 with IGP 27, and which we have discussed in Chapter 13. For the real Gregory, the weakness of the *rudes* is that they are too intent on outward signs and wonders, and he seeks to raise them to a higher understanding of the visible spiritual reality. In this he is in clear contrast to the Gregory of the *Dialogues*, who presents a different antithesis between the spiritually minded and the weaker brethren. That is, the former are aware that the martyrs can hear prayers and work miracles even in places where they are not buried, whereas the latter are ignorant on this point. In order to correct this misapprehension there has to be a greater incidence of miracles in places where the saints' bodies do not rest.

Immediately following IGP 27, at the very end of Book II, there is a remark attributed to Gregory in which he says that he must cease from speaking for a while in order to restore his strength through silence (lines 41-3). As A. de Vogüé notes (*SC* 260, p. 249) the same plea is made at the end of two of Gregory's *Homilies on Ezekiel* and in his commentary *In 1 Regum*. As taken down by the papal notaries, those remarks from the pulpit reflected the physical exhaustion of the ailing pope in the delivery of his discourses. The Dialogist has either modelled the concluding sentence of Book II on those pleas for respite which he found in the Scriptural commentaries or he has borrowed it from another discourse spoken by Gregory, the written record of which he found among the *schedae* in the *Lateran* secretariate.

---

[13] *Homilies on the Gospels*, II.32; *PL* 76.1237-8.

CHAPTER SIXTEEN

THE INSERTED GREGORIAN PASSAGES IN BOOK III OF THE *DIALOGUES*

In Book III we find fifteen genuine Gregorian passages inserted into the Dialogist's narrative. They are distributed irregularly through the book, sparsely at first and somewhat bunched towards the close. The overall frequency of the inserted passages is approximately the same as in the first two books.

IGP 28: III.7.1. A disciplinary warning to those committed to celibacy. From line 5, " ... *qui corpus suum* ...", to line 8, " ... *concupitae formae famulatur.*"

This fragment has the authentic stamp of a disciplinary admonition delivered by Gregory to enforce the law of ecclesiastical celibacy. It thus differs from the other inserted Gregorian passages which we are examining, which, excerpted from expository or homiletic writings, do not have a brusquely mandatory tone as in this case. In Gregory's letters there are several admonitions parallel to that of IGP 28. One relevant disciplinary letter which Gregory sent to the rectors of the papal patrimonies in Sicily and Italy indicates the likely context in which our fragment was originally included. (Epistola IX.110; Ewald-Hartmann II, pp. 115-6.) IGP 28 may have been excised from an earlier draft of such a letter, or may have been taken from a disciplinary brief of the pope which the Dialogist found apart, not filed in the archive record of his correspondence. He has used it as a handy introduction to his long and picturesque story of the temptation of Bishop Andrew of Fondi. Its direct admonitory tone, marking it out from all the other elements in the *Dialogues*, made it somewhat difficult to insert into the text. The author solved this difficulty by directing Gregory's admonition to his "readers",[1] who—by implication—are dedicated to celibacy. It is not unlikely that the next IGP, 29, was another snippet taken from the same original context as IGP 28.

IGP 29: III.7.10. Diffidence in our weak selves and trust in God's mercy must go together. From line 88, " ... *oportet et de Dei* ...", to line 92, "... *stabilitate fiducia.*"

---

[1] Thus disregarding his chosen literary convention according to which Gregory's words are spoken to Peter the Deacon in a dialogue.

As IGP 28 provided an exordium for the chapter on Bishop Andrew's temptation, so IGP 29, unmistakably Gregorian in its style, provides a suitable hortatory conclusion to it. Indeed, from familiarity with the Dialogist's methods we may infer that one particular detail of his story about Bishop Andrew was expressly written with a view to making IGP 29 appear to be a relevant allusion to it. Fr de Vogüé admits that the story of the temptation of Bishop Andrew of Fondi is *"particulièrement troublant"*; and indeed it is troubling for those who assume the Gregorian authenticity of the *Dialogues*. Although the Gregory of the *Dialogues* claims to have the story from countless witnesses from Fondi itself (lines 8-10), the account is manifestly modelled on earlier forms of the same racy story in Cassian and in the *Vitae Patrum*. (cf. Vogüé, *SC* 251, pp. 129-30, 132-4; *SC* 260, pp. 283-5.) In Chapter 18 I discuss this as one of the many indications of counterfeiting in the Dialogist's narrative. Here my point is to draw attention to the fact that although the account in the *Dialogues* depends substantially on the earlier form of the story, it significantly differs in the very detail which offers an implicit allusion to IGP 29.

In the original form of the tale, attested both by Cassian and in the *Vitae Patrum*, the devils succeed in seducing their celibate prey into complete carnal sin; but in the Dialogist's version of the story, the most that Bishop Andrew's tempter can do is to induce him to give a playful slap to the *posteriora* of the comely nun. Repenting of this venial intimacy when rebuked by the Jew, he confesses his fault, removes the nun and all women from his household, and thereafter leads a blameless life. The incident of the unseemly slap is, in the Dialogist's narrative, made relevant to the Gregorian snippet with which he ends his story. To Bishop Andrew, giving way to the impulse to take a risky liberty with the nun but not going further into grievous carnal sin, is applied the Gregorian moral of IGP 29, with its Scriptural allusion to "the cedar of paradise, shaken but not overthrown". The sentiment expressed in IGP 29 is a favourite theme of Gregory's, found repeatedly in his genuine works (e.g. *Moralia* 2.1; *Homilies on Ezekiel* II.7.15, 20.) The somewhat elusive reference to the cedar of paradise seems to have been a comment based on the Latin text of *Ezekiel* 31.8-9. It is out of keeping with the character and gravity of the real Gregory, as we know him from his authentic works, to suppose that he would have composed these lines of elevated spiritual exhortation as a comment on the jocular tale about Bishop Andrew's *peccadillo*.

IGP 30: III.14.12-14. Those to whom God gives great gifts he leaves with certain blameworthy imperfections, in order that they should always have something to struggle against. From line 125, "... *Magna est* ... *om-nipotentis* ...", to line 158, "... *damno servetur.*" (Omit "*Petre*" in line 125.)

This fairly long pericope presents a favourite theme of Gregory's ascetical theology. Those on whom God has bestowed his great gifts are left by him to struggle unsuccessfully with their lesser faults and imperfections, in order to keep them in humility. Thus they should learn not to extol themselves for the divine gifts they have received, and they should realize how weak they are in themselves. We have seen a related lesson taught in IGP 12, which echoes the opening phrase of IGP 30. The theme of our passage is developed in *Moralia* 28.20 and 34.44. In those *Moralia* passages, as Vogüé observes *SC* 260, p. 313), there are numerous verbal parallels to the phrasing of IGP 30. The same theme is worked out at length with further Scriptural illustrations in *Moralia* 19.9-12; cf. also *Homilies on Ezekiel* I.10.35-6. As in so many other instances, we can surmise that it was because Gregory had explained this doctrine so fully in other closely parallel passages that IGP 30 came to be among the redundant pieces laid up among his literary remains.

The elevated doctrine and stately latinity of IGP 30, so different in character from the preceding narrative, provides a Gregorian climax to this chapter of the Dialogist's, in which he has been relating anecdotes about the venerable abbot Isaac. How does he make this Gregorian pericope relevant to his narrative? The answer seems to be that he has composed paragraph 10 ("*Hic itaque* ... *crederetur*") precisely in order to put in a peg on which to hang this choice quotation of Gregorian spirituality. Since in IGP 30 the real Gregory refers to minor faults which remain in the just (using *Judges* 3.1-4 as an apt Scriptural analogy) the Dialogist makes the Gregory of the *Dialogues* remark that in the midst of all his virtues the abbot Isaac had one fault—namely, that he was sometimes given to immoderate gaiety (lines 118-9). Whereupon Peter the Deacon asks whether Isaac gave himself to gaiety willingly or was drawn into it despite himself (lines 121-4). In point of fact IGP 30 gives no answer to this question, since it is a statement of general principle, in which Gregory explains why God leaves imperfections in the just. As in so many other cases, we find cue words picked out from the IGP and used to prepare for it. In this case the words "*reprehendat*" and "*reprehensibilia*" in the Gregorian pericope (lines 128 and 140) are picked out by the Dialogist and given an anticipatory cue—that is, the word "*reprehensibile*" in line 118.

IGP 30 is one of the six passage which are found both in the *Dialogues* and in the *Libri Sententiarum* of Tajo of Saragossa. There are some eight textual differences between the two forms of the passage. Of the two, the

Dialogist seems to have reproduced the original more exactly. He also includes a sentence (lines 153-6) which is lacking in the text of Tajo.

IGP 31: III.15.9-10. On the grave malice of uttering a curse. IGP 31a runs from line 75, "*... cum Paulus ...*", to line 77, "*... a regno vitae.*" IGP 31b runs from line 81, "*Si apud districtum ...*", to line 84, "*... utilitatis vacat.*" (Omit "*Petre*" in line 81.)

The story of the four envious monks who killed Florentius's pet bear, and of the dreadful fate which befell them when the holy hermit cursed them for their malicious deed (III.15.3-8) is designed to lead into the Gregorian fragment preserved in IGP 31. In the original source IGP 31b evidently led straight on from IGP 31a, without the question which is interposed in the Dialogist's text. We shall see that the second part of the pericope is a simple reinforcement of the sentiment expressed in the first, and that the Dialogist's interposed question breaks up the sense by introducing a question that is not answered in the Gregorian original.

In IGP 31a (lines 75-6) Gregory cites *I Corinthians* 6.10 to emphasize the *gravis culpa* involved in uttering a curse. For this Gregorian snippet a preparatory cue is provided by the question of Peter the Deacon, who asks whether a curse provoked by anger is *valde grave* (lines 73-4). Then, since IGP 31b goes on to refer to idle words as well as to malicious words, a supplementary question by Peter the Deacon is interposed between IGP 31a and 31b in order to make the latter appear to be a new turn in the dialogue. Peter asks in what case a man may be who chances to curse another, not out of malice, but through lack of due guard on his tongue (*ex linguae incuria*; line 79). This, we are to infer, was the case of the holy hermit Florentius, who was moved not by malice but by grief when he launched his curse against the four wicked monks who had slain his bear (cf. lines 56-71).

On examining IGP 31b, however, we find that it is not well adapted to be an answer to Peter the Deacon's supplementary question. One would expect Gregory's answer to be directed to the point of that question, namely to assess the degree of guilt attributable to a curse uttered *ex linguae incuria*. But it is not so. In IGP 31b, which is presented as the answer, the real Gregory is still emphasizing the gravity of malicious cursing; it is the heinousness of that kind of cursing that is still the point he is concerned with. He refers to "idle speaking" (*otiosus sermo*) only incidentally, to make his main point about the malice of cursing. He uses an *a fortiori* argument, with an implied reference to the fuller text of *Matthew* 12.36 and to Christ's teaching there that men must give an account in the day of judgement of every idle word they speak. If even useless words are blameworthy before the divine Judge, so Gregory argues, how much more worthy of damnation are words of cursing, which are not merely idle but wicked. Once one has realized that the question of Peter the Deacon in lines 78-80 is alien to the genuine Gregorian passage, one can easily perceive that in IGP 31b Gregory is not concerned with a possible distinction between the degree of culpability in a curse uttered out of carelessness and that in a curse uttered out of malice. The real Gregory does not envisage any such distinction between malicious cursing and non-malicious but careless cursing. For him, in the light of the Pauline condemnation, to utter a curse is (unless as the prophetic mouthpiece of divine judgement) always a grave sin, involving *malitia* which merits damnation (lines 76-7 and 82-3). His passing mention of *otiosus sermo* in his *a fortiori* argument does not refer to a supposed category of non-malicious cursing, but to idle and useless speaking in general—*"qui a bonitate utilitatis vacat"*—which is clearly contradistinguished from the category of malicious speaking to which cursing belongs.

There are parallels to IGP 31 elsewhere in Gregory's works. We find reference to *Matthew* 12.36 and the *verbum otiosum*, with a similar *a fortiori* argument, in *Moralia* 7.58, *Regula Pastoralis* 3.14 and Epistola I.33 (see Vogüé, *SC* 260, p. 321). In the opening chapters of Book IV of the *Moralia* (Praefatio and 4.1-4) there is a lengthy discussion of cursing in the light of Scriptural instances. There we find *1 Corinthians* 6.10 cited in the same abbreviated form as in IGP 31. Gregory explains that the prohibition from uttering curses was not applicable to the holy servants of God of whom we read in Scripture, in particular St Peter and Elijah, who cursed wicked men with dreadful consequences. They did so without sin because their malediction was not motivated by human vindictiveness but was a pronouncement of divine justice. But whereas the real Gregory, when citing these Scriptural instances of righteous malediction sanctioned by God, emphasizes that the saints who pronounced such divine sentence remained innocent of guilt, the Gregory of the *Dialogues* has a strangely different assessment of the lethal malediction levelled by Florentius at the four monks who had slain his bear. Although the unpleasant death of the four monks is said to be *ultio divina* (lines 61-2), nevertheless Florentius was culpable for uttering his impassioned curse against them. For the remainder of his life he wept in remorse for what he had done, accusing himself of cruelty and murder. The Gregory of the *Dialogues* then gives a curious explanation of these events. The reason why Almighty God visited so terrible a sanction on the monks whom Florentius had culpably cursed, thus leaving the hermit with life-long remorse, was to teach him the lesson that, however severely he might be tried by grief, "he should never again presume to launch the dart of malediction" (Lines 70-1). In this odd comment we are far from the spiritual perspectives and lucidity of the real Gregory.

IGP 32: III.15.13-17. From purity of heart and simplicity comes the prayer that is acceptable to God. From line 107, "*Apud omnipotentis Dei ...*", to line 143, "*... nullo modo audimus*". (Omit "*Petre*" in line 108.)

This lengthy and profound passage of Gregorian teaching about prayer is at a markedly different spiritual level from the narrative in which it is embedded. The Dialogist has just made Gregory relate a story of a miracle worked by Florentius when his cell was beset with innumerable snakes. The holy man lifted up his eyes and hands in prayer, and from a cloudless sky thunder and lightning straightway descended to kill all the reptiles. The problem of disposing of the multitude of dead snakes was solved by another appeal to heaven: an equal multitude of birds at once appeared and carried off all the remains. Peter the Deacon thereupon asks what must have been the virtue and merit of a man whose prayers were so quickly heard by God. It is as a response to this cue that the Dialogist then inserts IGP 32. In Peter's cue question the anticipatory words picked out from IGP 32 are "*ori ... proximus omnipotens Deus*" (lines 105-6), which link up with the Gregorian clause in lines 118-9 containing the same words. In the latter clause, however, Gregory laments that through our implication in wordly affairs "our mouth become the farther distant from Almighty God, the nearer it becomes to this world". The Dialogist reverses this concept in Peter the Deacon's cue question, by saying that because of the virtue and merit of Florentius, "Almighty God became near to his mouth".

Towards the end of IGP 32 *Proverbs* 28.9 is cited: "He that turns away his ear that he hear not the law, his prayer shall not be heard". In the concluding sentence of the inserted pericope Gregory comments on that text of *Proverbs* as follows: "What wonder therefore if, when we pray, God is slow to listen, when on our side we are slow to listen to God's commandments or heed them not at all?" (lines 141-3). With a swift descent to his own level, the Dialogist makes his Gregory immediately append a further comment: "and what wonder that Florentius, when he prayed, was swiftly heard, seeing that he was swift to listen to the commandments of the Lord?" (lines 143-5). This additional comment, unconsonant though it is with the preceding Gregorian pericope, is necessary for the Dialogist in order to make IGP 32 seem relevant to Peter's initial question, and to the tale of Florentius and the snakes.

There are Gregorian parallels to IGP 32 elsewhere. Both in *Moralia* 35.3 and in *Homilies on Ezekiel* 1.8.19 the same text of *Isaias* 6.5 is quoted more fully, and expounded more naturally. A. de Vogüé says of the treatment of the text in IGP 32, "*Le présent commentaire est inédit*". It may well be that realization of the inadequacy of this exegesis of the text was a reason for Gregory's excision of the pericope from its original place.

The text of *Proverbs* 28.9 cited in lines 139-40 is also quoted by Gregory four times in the *Moralia* (5.76; 10.27; 16.26; 18.15) with the same moral—namely, that those who contemn God's commandments do not deserve to have their prayers heard by him. The warning that Gregory gives in IGP 32 against the danger of being drawn away from God by becoming immersed in wordly pursuits is also paralleled in several other places: e.g. in *Regula Pastoralis* 3.14, where *multiloquium* is severely reproved. The danger of being gradually dragged down, through conversation with seculars, into taking pleasure in *otiosa* is feelingly described by Gregory in *Homilies on Ezekiel* I.11.6. It is possible that IGP 32 had a common source with IGP 31. In both excerpts we find mention of *otiosa* and *noxia verba*. A similarity between IGP 32 and IGP 1 can also be observed (cf. Vogüé, pp. 323-325).

IGP 33: III.17.7-13. It is a greater miracle to convert a sinner than to raise the dead. From line 59, "*... maius est miraculum ...*", to line 91, "*... interius vivificetur*".

This pericope takes its place with numerous other passages in which Gregory gives similar teaching, often with the same Scriptural allusions. A. de Vogüé has collected and commented on these many striking parallels (*SC* 260, pp. 341, 343, 447). It is not difficult for the Dialogist to make a niche in his narrative for this rich passage of Gregorian wisdom. In IGP 33 Gregory declares that it is a greater miracle to convert a sinner, thus restoring his soul to eternal life, than to raise the dead, which merely restores life for a time to mortal flesh (lines 59-62, 88-9). In preparation for this pericope the Dialogist tells a picturesque story of a venerable hermit from Monte Argentaro who, moved by a widow's lamentations, raised her dead husband to life. This story leads on to the cue from Peter the Deacon, who asserts his opinion that to restore the dead to life and to recall their souls to their flesh is greater than all other miracles. To this rash assertion IGP 33 is then presented as a magisterial corrective. The cue query of Peter the Deacon in lines 53-6 picks out several words which recur in the Gregorian pericope.

IGP 34: III.18.3. How the one element of fire can, by divine dispensation, produce contrary effects. From line 22, "*... tres pueri ...*", to line 29, "*... ad tormentum*".

That IGP 34 was originally set in an eschatological context is strongly suggested by comparison with a closely similar but longer passage in *Moralia* 9.102. The parallelism between the two passages, in the stages of the argument and in the language used, is very close indeed. It appears quite likely that IGP 34 represents another, more abbreviated, form of the same *Moralia* text.

The passage in *Moralia* 9.102 is an integral part of Gregory's long disquisition in that chapter on the penal fire of hell. His point in bringing in the Scriptural testimony from *Daniel* 3, relating how the fire of the Babylonian furnace burned away the bonds of the three young men while leaving them otherwise untouched, was to show that by divine ordinance the same element of fire could have *diversa virtus*, or contrary properties. Thus the fire of hell plunges the damned into lethal darkness and at the same time provides a kind of light to give them a sight of others which increases their sorrow (as is exemplified in the case of Dives—*Luke* 16.23-8). A similar eschatological context is to be supposed as the probable original setting of IGP 34. This excerpt may well come from an earlier manuscript of the *Moralia*. Alternatively, it may have belonged to an unpublished Gregorian writing on the Last Things. We shall see when we consider the inserted passages in Book IV that the Dialogist had at his disposal some considerable Gregorian fragments relating to hell. IGP 34 may have formed part of the same materials.

How does the Dialogist make IGP 34 relevant to his own non-eschatological context? First he contrives his tale of a young monk miraculously spared in a fiery furnace—a tale modelled on earlier hagiographical stories, as well as on *Daniel* 3.23-4, 91-4 (cf. Vogüé, II, pp. 345-7, 447). Since in IGP 34 Gregory stresses the circumstance that the Babylonian fire burned the bonds of the three young men but spared their persons and even their clothes, the Dialogist makes his story of the miraculous survival of the young monk amid the flames show a corresponding circumstance. When the ferocious Goths tried to burn the holy man alive in his cell, the fire consumed all the surroundings but could not burn the cell itself. Whereupon the Goths, still more enraged, threw him into a bake-furnace. Just as in the story of the three young men of Babylon, he was found on the morrow unharmed amid the flames, with not even his garments singed. Thus there is a fair correspondence between the Dialogist's story and that of *Daniel* 3. Peter the Deacon explicitly points out this correspondence between the two miracles in his cue remark (lines 19-20).

The Gregory of the *Dialogues* replies to this cue that there is some dissimilarity between the two miracles of burning, and this sentence leads immediately into IGP 34. One dissimilarity, we may conclude, lies in the circumstance noted in the opening phrase of IGP 34: that is, that the three young men of Babylon were bound hand and foot when they were thrown into the fire (lines 21-2), whereas the young monk in the Dialogist's tale was not thus bound. There is a further and more substantial dissimilarity. Observe that in IGP 34 Gregory recalls the miracle of the Babylonian fiery furnace not to extol the merit of the three young men who were miraculously spared, but to make his main point about the diverse effects which could be providentially worked by the same element of fire. If the Dialogist has realized that this is the main point of his borrowed fragment, he has not been able to work it aptly into his own narrative. In his story the fire is powerless to burn the young monk's cell, but it is not vested with the *virtus ad solacium* by which, according to Gregory in IGP 34, the Babylonian fire actively set free the three young men from their bonds. In this there is a lack of correspondence between the details of the Dialogist's tale and those of *Daniel* 3 which are stressed by the real Gregory both in IGP 34 and in *Moralia* 9.102.

The main point of the borrowed Gregorian fragment (lines 25-9) is not relevant to the Dialogist's tale which it is supposed to illuminate. Perhaps because of this he introduces a feature into his tale in the following chapter (III.19) to make the element of water—like the element of fire in the tale in IGP 34—possess two diverse miraculous properties. The water of the river Adige could not only stand up like a wall to avoid flooding a church at Verona, but it could nevertheless be drawn off to slake the thirst of those detained in the church. In this case the element of water did have a direct power for consolation, *ad adiutorium*, as did the fire in the *Daniel* story. The Dialogist points this out explicitly (lines 26-31).

IGP 35: III.19.5; 20.3. On the spiritual combat that we have always to wage against the ancient enemy. IGP 35a runs from Chapter 19, line 38, "*Sine labore certaminis ...*", to line 43, "*... accusator existat*". IGP 35b runs from Chapter 20, line 20, "*... contra inimici insidias ...*", to line 28, "*... virtute terreatur*".

The two parts of IGP 35, each introduced by a cue from Peter the Deacon, evidently belonged to an originally continuous Gregorian pericope, although the Dialogist has separated them by interposing his quaint tale of the devil who unlaced a priest's boots. Probably he has adapted the opening clauses of IGP 35b in order to fit in with the second cue which he puts into the mouth of Peter the Deacon (lines 19-21). Thus the original order of the wording at the beginning of IGP 35b (lines 20-23) would have been: "*Laboriosum non erit contra inimici insidias semper intendere et continue quasi in acie stare, si custodiam nostram ... etc.*"

The theme of IGP 35, namely our need to stand steadfast in the spiritual combat against the ancient enemy, is one to which Gregory constantly returns throughout his writings. For instance, lines 40-3 can be compared to *Moralia* 2.14, where he speaks of the enemy's attempt to find matter in our deeds, words and thoughts wherewith to accuse us before God. Similar teaching to that in IGP 35 about the *certamen* in which we must always join battle with the wicked spirits is also found in *Moralia* 31, 78-9, and 32.51, where there is the same insistence on the necessity, in our fight against the evil one, to trust not in our own strength but in God's. (cf. IGP 35b, lines 22-4). There is another parallel to IGP 35a in *Homilies on Ezekiel* II.5.22.

The two cue questions of Peter the Deacon, put in as pegs on which to hang IGPs 35a and 35b, are both unimaginative. The Dialogist has ready his Gregorian excerpt on the spiritual combat against the ancient enemy, so he simply makes Peter ask, apropos of nothing in particular: "Since I am hearing about so many men in Italy of admirable virtue, I should like to know this: did they have to suffer no cunning assaults from the ancient enemy, or did they turn such assaults to good account?" (lines 34-7). The linking phrase that the Dialogist has here picked out from IGP 35a is *antiqui hostis insidias* (lines 39-40). Note that in IGPs 35a and 35b Gregory uses the homiletic "we"; his concern in this pericope is to forewarn and encourage his hearers and readers to persevere in *"our"* struggle with the devil. (cf. IGP 35a: *nostro*, line 41. IGP 35b: *nostram, nobis, tribuimus, ipsi vigilemus*, lines 22-4). Thus the Gregorian pericope is not designed to provide an answer to Peter the Deacon's naive cue question. Perhaps the Dialogist was aware of this, and in the second sentence of IGP 35a (lines 39-40) changed original verbs in the first person plural (i.e. *"victores erimus"* and *"decertaverimus"*) into the third person plural, in order to make the pericope seem less centred on "us" and more applicable to the wonder-working Italian saints it is supposed to refer to. Alternatively the "victors" referred to in that sentence, who had won the *"palma victoriae"*, may be the same heroes of the faith to whom Gregory refers to in IGP 38, who merited to receive *"martyrii palmas"*. If so, we have an indication that both IGPs 35 and 38 come from the same original context.

When, in order to satisfy the desire expressed by Peter the Deacon, the Gregory of the *Dialogues* does provide a concrete example of diabolical *insidiae* to which the holy men of Italy were exposed, it is hardly an apt one. Although the Valerian priest Stephen is described in the usual fulsome phrase as "a man of venerable life", his manner of speaking is hardly edifying—indeed, it is his loose expletive that summons the devil to the scene. When he abusively bids his servant "Untie my boots, you devil", an invisible demon at once begins to loosen the laces. Terrified, Stephen cries out for the devil to depart, explaining that he has not meant to address *him*. From this episode the Gregory of the *Dialogues* draws the moral that if the devil is always at hand for such a physical intervention, how much more intent must he be to waylay us in our thoughts. When one compares this with what the real Gregory teaches about the *insidiae* of the evil one, one realizes how inappropriate it is to attribute to him this ludicrous anecdote about the devil untying the abusive priest's bootlaces, as if it were an illustration of his teaching (repeated in IGP 35) about the spiritual combat with the forces of evil through which we must win the palm of victory.

It is after reproducing only the first half of IGP 35 that the Dialogist makes Gregory ask Peter the Deacon whether he would like to know how the devil "is always lying in wait to deceive", and thereupon introduces his tale of the demon and the priests's bootlaces. We can see why he has interrupted his borrowed Gregorian pericope here. The cautionary tale about the priest's bootlaces can seem to be consequential after IGP 35a, which speaks of the alertness of the ancient enemy to catch us in our deeds, words and thoughts; but it would be inconsequentially placed at the end of IGP 35, since by then Gregory is speaking of the decisive discomfiture of the devil in the face of the resolute watchfulness of the just who put their trust in God's protection. This moral does not fit the tale of the Valerian priest. In order to resume the interrupted Gregorian excerpt, after the interposed tale, the Dialogist puts into the mouth of Peter the Deacon the cue word *Laboriosum* taken from IGP 35b. Gregory goes on to say in IGP 35b that it will not be irksome (*Laboriosum non erit ...*) to stand resolutely against the foe if we do so trusting in God's grace and not in ourselves. The Dialogist works IGP 35b into his text by making it an answer to a contrary assertion by Peter the Deacon—"*Laboriosum valde et terribile est ...*" (lines 19).

IGP 36: III.21.4. All things are subject to God; the malign spirit has no power except by divine permission. From line 32, "... *redemptori nostro ...*", to line 42, "... *per humilitatem*". Note also the Gregorian axiom immediately preceding IGP 36, in lines 31-2.

The subject matter of IGP 36 is connected with that of IGP 35; it may well be that both came from the same original source. The Dialogist has evidently composed his foregoing tale, modelled on the story of the Gadarene swine, in order to provide an opening for the use of IGP 36. He relates how, after a nun of Spoleto had expelled a devil from a peasant,[2] the evil spirit asked her where he should go; and how, at her bidding, the devil entered into a little pig which was feeding nearby, killed it and went off. This story is an echo of the Gospel account of the legion

---

[2] A. de Vogüé points out that the expulsion of a demon by a woman is a "*cas très rare, peut-être unique*"; *SC* 260, pp. 354-5.

of devils cast out by Jesus and permitted by him to enter into and destroy a herd of swine feeding nearby, which is referred to by Gregory at the beginning of IGP 36. (cf. *Mark* 5.1-16 and *Matthew* 8.31). The Dialogist introduces that Gregorian pericope by making Peter the Deacon, in his cue question, ask whether the nun ought to have conceded even a pig to the unclean spirit (lines 29-30; *porcum concedere* links with IGP 36, line 35). On examination of IGP 36 we shall find that it is ineptly used as an answer to this question.

The reply of the Gregory of the *Dialogues* to Peter's question is, in effect, that since Christ the Incarnate Truth did likewise, the Gospel precedent justified the nun's action. Now the axiom, "*Propositae regulae nostrae actioni sunt facta veritatis*", which immediately answers Peter's question and precedes IGP 36, has indeed a genuine Gregorian ring and is doubtless reproduced from a Gregorian source. But it would never have been placed by Pope Gregory himself as a principle to be illustrated by the passage (IGP 36) which here follows it. Gregory would never have asserted that the awesome action of Christ, in expelling the legion of devils from the demoniac who dwelt among the tombs and permitting them to destroy the Gadarene swine, was one of His deeds that "are proposed as models for *our* action" (line 31). The truly Gregorian principle discussed above in connection with IGP 2, "*Miracula in exemplum non sunt trahenda*", would apply even more forcibly when the miracle in question was one worked by Christ himself using his divine authority.

When we examine the rest of IGP 36 we realize that it presupposes a quite different context from that in which the Dialogist has placed it. Gregory's concern in this pericope, and his reason for citing the Gospel episode of the Gadarence swine, is to stress the all-mastery of God. That the evil spirit is powerless to vex men unless permitted to do so by God is proved by an *a fortiori* argument: we see that the same evil spirit was powerless even to enter the Gadarene swine until permitted by divine authority. (Gregory uses the same argument, and the same Gospel testimony, in *Moralia* 2.16 and 32.50; cf. Vogüé, *SC* 260, p. 355). The climax and moral of IGP 36 is that we must willingly subject ourselves to God, to whom all the wicked spirits are unwillingly subjected; we shall be strong against those foes in the measure in which we become united with the Lord of all things by humbling ourselves before him. This noble and typically Gregorian lesson is an irrelevance as a comment on the story of the nun of Spoleto and as an answer to Peter the Deacon's cue question.

IGP 37: III.24.3. The flesh cannot perceive what pertains to the spirit. From line 21, "*... cum Daniel propheta ...*", to line 28, "*... non valet, infirmetur*".

This extract, with its comment on *Daniel* 8.27, has been preceded in the *Dialogues* by the story of one Theodorus, a sacristan of St Peter's in Rome. Rising early to tend the light that hung by the door of the basilica, he had mounted a ladder when he suddenly beheld the Apostle Peter standing below him clad in a white stole. St Peter asked him why he had risen so early. The sacristan collapsed in great fear, his strength left him and he had to keep to his bed "for many days". This detail is brought into his narrative by the Dialogist in order to prepare for the coming insertion of IGP 37. Lines 10-12 anticipate lines 21-4: *per dies multos* in line 12 directly links with *per dies plurimos* in the Scriptural allusion in line 24.

The Gregory of the *Dialogues* explains the lesson of the alarming apparition: "The blessed Apostle wished to show those who served him that whatever they did for his honour, he always and unceasingly observed it, for the recompense of their reward". Here the Dialogist has again struck a false note. The real Gregory teaches that the saints and martyrs in heaven do know, in their knowledge of God, what passes on earth. Their intercession for those on earth is availing before the Almighty Judge, and they receive the prayers of the faithful who ask their help. This is explained, for instance in *Homilies on the Gospels*, 32.8. But nowhere does the real Gregory represent the Apostles, saints and martyrs as zealous for their own honour, and unceasingly intent on rewarding those who show veneration to them. Yet according to the Gregory of the *Dialogues* it was precisely such unceasing watchfulness on the part of St Peter to reward those who paid honour to himself that was the motive for his frightening apparition to the diligent sacristan. As usual, a query by Peter the Deacon provides the immediate cue for the coming Gregorian pericope: "I do not so much marvel that the Apostle was seen but that one who saw him, from being well, became ill". As a response to this query the Dialogist brings in IGP 37. It begins with the citation of *Daniel* 8.27, which relates how the prophet, awe-struck by his dread vision and the revelation of its meaning, "began to languish and was ill for many days". Gregory's comment is that "since the flesh cannot comprehend the things of the spirit, sometimes, it must be that the bodily vessel, which is not strong enough to bear the weight of such a burden, should become weak". This short commentary has parallels in Gregory's known works—there is the same use of *Daniel* 8.27 in *Moralia* 4.67; cf. also *Homilies on Ezekiel* I.8.19.

In those parallel passages the Danielic text is used to explain that those who contemplate in the spirit the high things of God become acutely aware of their own human and bodily frailty. A similar discourse was surely the original context of the Gregorian comment in IGP 37 which the Dialogist has borrowed. It is inspired by the Pauline text *I Corinthians*

2.14: *caro* (weak unspiritual human nature) cannot comprehend *ea quae sunt Spiritus Dei*. In IGP 37 the real Gregory is speaking of a mystical experience of the Spirit of God which leaves the human vessel conscious of its infirmity. In the story in the *Dialogues* the author has ineptly made this elevated comment refer to the apparition of the Apostle Peter beneath the ladder, which so frightened the early-rising sacristan that he had to keep to his bed for many days.

IGP 38: III.26.7-9; 28.2-4. On two kinds of martyrdom. IGP 38a runs from Chapter 26, line 52, *"Duo sunt ..."*, to line 68, *"... mortuus non est"*. IGP 38b is an incomplete fragment, running from line 70, *"... si persecutionis ..."*, to line 75, *"... martyres fuerunt"*. IGP 38c runs from Chapter 28, line 14, *"Quid ergo mirum ..."*, to line 30, *"... virtute perstiterunt"*. (Omit *"Petre"* in IGP 38a, line 52.)

This Gregorian passage is introduced inconsequentially. The Dialogist has put into the mouth of Gregory a story about a holy hermit named Menas, who demonstrated that he had supernatural insight by rejecting a concealed gift which had been sent to him by a wicked man. Then, by an abrupt transition, Peter the Deacon brings in the cue for IGP 38. His leading question, which Fr de Vogüé himself finds *"un peu inattendue"*, is worded as follows: "Many of these men, I think, would have been able to undergo martyrdom if a time of persecution had come upon them". It is through this opening that the Dialogist brings in his borrowed pericope, in which Gregory comments on *Matthew* 20.20-23 in order to explain the two kinds of martyrdom—one is actual effect, the other by inward disposition and equivalent merit.

The key words picked out of IGP 38 by the Dialogist for precursory mention are *"persecutionis tempus"* and *"subire martyrium possunt"* (IGP 38b, lines 70-71 and IGP 38c, lines 22-3). Peter the Deacon alludes to these key words in his preliminary cue (*"martyrium subire potuisse ... tempus persecutionis"*: III.26.7. lines 50-1).

In three of Gregory's *Homilies on the Gospels* (3.4; 11.3; 35.7) we find reflections on spiritual martyrdom in time of peace similar to those developed in IGP 38.[3] All three of those homilies were delivered by the pope on the feast days of martyrs in the Roman basilicas dedicated to them. It may well be that the original place of IGP 38 was in a similar sermon, which was not eventually included in Gregory's published collection of 40 Gospel homilies. The passage in Homily 35.7 is a very close

---

[3] Some other, remoter, Gregorian parallels are also noted by A. C. Rush, "Spiritual martyrdom in St Gregory the Great", in *Theological Studies*, 23, 1962, pp. 569-89.

parallel, both in wording and in reasoning, to IGP 38a. In both cases there is the same commentary, in the same sequence, on *Matthew* 20.20-23.

IGP 38c clearly comes from the same original context as IGPs 38a and 38b, although the Dialogist has separated it from them by his stories of the hundreds of rustic Christians slain by the impious Lombards. While these three sections evidently belong closely together, they do not, when rejoined, form an exactly consecutive passage. In the Gregorian original there would have been a different linking sentence between IGPs 38a and 38b to lead on to mention of the ascetic confessors of IGP 38b, who by their bloodless martyrdom in time of peace prepared themselves for the actual martyrdom they were to undergo when persecution broke out once more (IGP 38c, lines 14-17). IGP 38b is set within a long cumbersome sentence (*"De his ... pervenire?"*; lines 69-79). The Latin construction of this ungainly sentence is incoherent, while the juxtaposition of ideas in it is incongruous. Lines 75-9 are added by the Dialogist after IGP 38b in order to introduce his two subsequent stories, in Chapter 27 and Chapter 28.1, about a multitude of faithful rustics who were martyred by the cruel Lombards.

In the real Gregory's usage of the phrase *"martyres esse potuissent"*, unlike the Dialogist's, it does not refer to an unrealized hypothesis, but to something that actually occurred. In the original passage Gregory was referring to certain saintly men of austere life who had suffered physical martyrdom when, after a time of peace for the Church, persecution had broken out. It was no wonder (so Gregory's *a fortiori* argument runs in IGP 38c) that those same confessors just described in IGP 38b, who during a time of peace had followed the path of self-martyrdom through ascetical virtue, had been able to embrace a martyr's death when the persecution broke out, seeing that there were *also* some (note the *etiam* in line 18 of Chapter 28) who, although they had not followed that narrow path but the wide paths of worldly living, nevertheless had worthily received the martyr's palm when put to the test in that storm of persecution. The Dialogist's perspective is different. One must dwell on the text in order to appreciate this difference.

Gregory uses the subjunctive *potuissent* in line 15 of IGP 38c because the verb there occurs in a subordinate clause in *oratio obliqua*, following *"Quid ergo mirum ..."*. He does not mean that the heroes of the faith to whom he is referring *could* have been martyrs in deed but were not (which is what the Dialogist seeks to make him mean). But he is speaking of men who, because they had followed the path of spiritual martyrdom, were able to be, and did become, martyrs in physical fact when persecution arose. His *a fortiori* reasoning in lines 17-19 of IGP 38c depends on the premise that they were actually martyred.

Since the Dialogist seeks to make his borrowed Gregorian material seem relevant to his own context, he has to give it a different bearing to that which it had in its original context. The Italian thaumaturges to whom Peter the Deacon refers in his opening cue were not martyrs. Although the merit of spiritual martyrdom through self-mortification could be claimed for them, their situation cannot be equated with that of the saints to whom the real Gregory referred in IGP 38c, who after their hidden martyrdom of self-affliction during a previous time of peace, had been finally able to attain, in the company even of some previously worldly persons, to the palm of actual martyrdom at the hands of the persecutors. The Dialogist adapts the material in such a way as to argue that the holy Fathers of his narrative were so virtuous that they *would have been able* to be martyrs if persecution had befallen them, even though that eventuality never occurred in their case. Although in Peter's cue (26.7, lines 50-1) he has reproduced from IGP 38c the words of the key phrase, "*martyres esse potuissent*", his use of it does not bear the same meaning as in the Gregorian original from which he has drawn it. He supports his hypothetical conclusion by his own *a fortiori* argument in 26.9, lines 75-9, which is modelled on Gregory's *a fortiori* argument in IGP 38c, lines 17-9. Even in his own time, he remarks, "persons of low and worldly life, in whom there could be seen nothing that might point to expectation of heavenly glory", had attained the crown of martyrdom. These persons are the rustic Christians martyred by the impious Lombards of whom he goes on to tell in the next chapters.

Having spoken of the constancy of those who had been able to become martyrs in the time of persecution, both ascetics and seculars, the real Gregory observes that the heroic constancy of the elect souls of whom he has been speaking is not general: "When the hour of open persecution strikes, just as there are many who are able to undergo martyrdom who, during the time of the Church's peace, seem to be of no account, so on the other hand there are sometimes those who fall away in fear and weakness, who were thought to stand very constantly when the Church was at peace" (IGP 38c, lines 20-5). This observation, truly Gregorian though it is in its conception and in its antithetical rhythm, is irrelevant to the Dialogist's discussion of his Italian Fathers who were not martyrs but could have been.

In Chapter 7 I noted that IGP 38 is reflected in a short paragraph in the Isidorian *Etymologies*.[4] It may have somehow come to the knowledge

---

[4] In the Isidorian excerpt the distinction, "*unum in aperta passione, alterum in occulta animi virtute*" does not correspond verbally with the opening sentence of IGP 38. It does, however, echo the distinction found in *Dialogues* III.28.4. The last sentence (lines 28-30), should be recognized as belonging to the original Gregorian source of IGP 38.

of Isidore himself before his death in 636 or it may have been inserted by Braulio, who completed and published the *Etymologies* later in the century. Braulio could have obtained this Gregorian fragment from Tajo of Saragossa, who went to Rome seeking unknown Gregorian writings. In Chapter 9 I noted that IGP 38 is also reflected, at a later time, in a work entitled *De vana saeculi sapientia*, attributed to Valerius of Bierzo. In this opusculum the textual correspondence with IGP 38 is much closer and longer than in the Isidorian snippet.[5] The question may be raised whether the later author of *De vana saeculi sapientia* was copying from and adding to the passage as found in the *Dialogues*, or whether he had independent access to a fuller form of IGP 38. He has several additional clauses which are apposite and seem to have a Gregorian ring. In particular, he gives a longer and more harmonious form of the series of relative clauses which the Dialogist inserts somewhat incoherently in IGP 38b, lines 71-5. His concluding reflections about simple and uninstructed martyrs is different from IGP 38c, but relevant to it. Is it his own elaboration of the theme, or is it a genuine paragraph from the Gregorian original, not used by the Dialogist but preserved in Spain from Tajo's notes?

IGP 39: III.34.1-5. On two kinds of compunction, symbolized by the upper and the nether watered ground bestowed by Caleb on his daughter Achsah. From line 1, "*In multis speciebus ...*", to line 48, " *...commemorari debuisset*".

IGP 39 presents a very intriguing problem of textual comparison. This Gregorian passage is found in no less than four different early documents: namely, in the anthology of Paterius, in that of Tajo of Saragossa, in the *Dialogues*, and also in a letter sent by Pope Gregory in 597 to Princess Theoctista, sister of the Emperor Maurice, and to her consort Andrew. This letter contained an elevated discourse on the virtue of compunction, which Theoctista was meant to pass on to the Empress Constantina herself as an offering of spiritual counsel from Gregory. It is this discourse that corresponds almost verbatim with IGP 39. While in all those four different sources, as they have come down to us, the text of the passage is substantially the same, there are some interesting variations of wording between them, and also some notable differences in the order in which they present the material. Hence the question arise: What is the relationship of these four texts to one another? Can we deduce anything about the chronological order of their composition? Which of them presents the passage in the most original form? In the *Liber*

---

[5] §10; *PL* 87.428.

Testimoniorum of Paterius the passage is the first of only two expository comments on the *Book of Joshua*. In the *Libri Sententiarum* of Tajo it is the last part of Book III, Chapter 45 (*PL* 80.902). In the *Register* of Gregory's letters it is in Epistola VII.23 (Ewald-Hartmann I, pp. 466-7). We do not know to what extent the texts of Paterius and of Tajo may have been "corrected" by eighth or ninth century scribes seeking to bring them into harmony with the text of the *Dialogues*. The witness of Paterius and Tajo is chiefly significant when it clearly presents a discordant reading from that of the *Dialogues*. I offer here a summary of my own conclusions drawn from comparison of the differing forms of the passage as found in those four early documents. It is not easy to harmonize all the data in one explanation, and on some points we can have only probability, not certainty. The interpretation I offer seems to me to be the most satisfactory way of harmonizing the various elements of the problem.

It is not difficult, at least, to recognize IGP 39 as an integrally distinct pericope which as placed in the *Dialogues* is adventitious. There it is introduced so artifically that the seams of the Dialogist's cobbling are more than usually obtrusive. To prepare for the use of this long Gregorian passage on the virtue of compunction and on holy tears (*compunctio* and *lacrimae*) the Dialogist has inserted a remark at the beginning of the previous chapter, to the effect that the holy abbot Eleutherius of Spoleto was a man of great compunction, and his tears were of much avail before God (III.33.1, lines 6-9). Then at the end of Chapter 33 he supplies the immediate cue from Peter the Deacon, which will lead directly on to the passage in which Gregory discusses the virtue of compunction and explains its two main *genera*. This discourse on the theological distinction between the two categories of compunction has no relevance to what has preceded, and the cue by which it is brought in is an unusually crude device. Peter the Deacon remarks: "Because you said that this man was of great compunction, I should like to learn more fully what is the power of tears. Wherefore tell me, please, how many kinds of compunction there are". Fr de Vogüé remarks on the awkwardness of this literary device: "*Trop precise, la second demande de Pierre est bien gauche*" (*SC* 260, p. 400). The Dialogist's two preliminary cues, picking out the words *compunctio* and *lacrimae*, point forward to the frequent use of these words in IGP 39 (lines 1, 6, 7, 8, 19, 31, 40, 41-2, 46).

The first puzzle of textual comparison arises from the significantly different order in which the sections of our Gregorian passage appear in the four documents in question. Of these documents, the *Letter of Theoctista* and the *Dialogues* clearly agree together in their ordering of the material—although they present some significant differences of detail in wording. Paterius has a very different order from the *Letter* and the

Dialogues, and Tajo has an order which partly agrees with that of Paterius and partly with that of the other two documents. In Paterius, the passage begins with the text from *Joshua* and the exposition that follows it. Then it continues with the theological disquisition on the two main kinds of compunction, and ends with a demonstration of how the *Joshua* text may be applied to illustrate the theological distinction that has been establish-ed. One may conclude that the order of material given in Gregory's *Letter to Theoctista* of 597, which is also that of IGP 39, was the original order that he intended, and that Paterius, for his own reasons, rearranged the four sub-sections in his own different order. A probable reason for this rearrangement could be that Paterius desired to begin the excerpt, as was usual in his anthology, with a quotation from Scripture, and accordingly he put the text from *Joshua* at the beginning of the passage. Because Tajo, in the first part of his reproduction of the Gregorian passage, follows Paterius's order, one could also suppose that he knew of Paterius's rear-rangement and decided on a hybrid order which partly followed that of Paterius and partly that originally intended by Gregory. Tajo's order is clearly erroneous, since he introduces Gregory's commentary on the words of the *Joshua* text before that text has been mentioned.

When we compare the wording of the pericope as it stands both in the *Dialogues* and in Paterius with the wording in the *Letter to Theoctista* we recognize that the *Letter* reveals a careful editing by Gregory himself of the unrevised wording that is reproduced both by Paterius and the Dialogist. The most significant retouching occurs in the sentence in which Gregory originally wrote that, even for those who have the gift of ardent faith and magnanimous good works, "it is most necessary that, whether from fear of punishment or from love of the heavenly kingdom, they should also grieve for the evils they have committed in the past": *"oportet nimis [nimirum in Paterius] ut aut timore supplicii aut amore regni caelestis mala etiam, quae antea perpetraverunt, deplorent"*. When Gregory came to revise this passage for inclusion in his *Letter to Theoctista*, as a spiritual lesson to be communicated to the Empress Constantina, a scruple must have occurred to him when he came upon the concluding clause. The Empress, whom Gregory had known well while he was at Constantino-ple, had been praised by him as "mindful of the heavenly fatherland and of her own soul" (Epistola V.38; Ewald-Hartmann I, p. 324). Gregory had sought her help in important matters affecting the Church and churchmen. Now in the passage that he proposed to send for her edifica-tion he found that when he came to point out the necessity of compunc-tion for those magnanimously engaged in good works, he had made mention only of their need to grieve for their *past* sins. But could this not encourage a certain complacency about one's present state, as if one's sins were only in the past and there were no present sins to provide continuing matter for compunction? Accordingly Gregory changed the clause from its previous wording, so that it now read: "it is very necessary that, whether from fear of punishment or from love of the heavenly kingdom, they should daily grieve for their sins, which they cannot be without while they live": "*oportet valde, ut aut timore supplicii aut amore regni caelestis peccata, sine quibus vivere non possunt, cotidie plorent*" (*ibid.* p. 467, lines 13-14).

There are other minor retouchings of the pericope as it is found in the *Letter to Theoctista*. For instance, in the closing sentence the less felicitous expression, "*necesse fuit ut ... commemorari debuisset*" is changed to "*necesse fuit ut ... diceretur*" (IGP 39, lines 46-8; Epistola VII.23, lines 19-20). Clearly, then, the text of the passage as found in the *Letter to Theoctista* is a revised form of an earlier and slightly less carefully polished text represented by IGP 39 in the *Dialogues* and by the anthology of Paterius, which agree together at the points we have just been considering. Defenders of the authenticity of the *Dialogues* would, of course, assume that when reusing the passage for his *Letter to Theoctista*, Gregory had before him the page of his *Dialogues* from which to copy it. This assumption must be examined. It is also commonly presupposed that Paterius drew his excerpt from the *Dialogues* before rearranging it. However, there are indications in the text of Paterius, as we shall see, that in some details his wording had independent and better authority.

How are we to explain the fact that the Dialogist reproduces an earlier form of the text than that found in Gregory's *Letter* of 597? I submit the following conjectural explanation of the data. IGP 39 originated (so we may reasonably suppose) as a typical piece of Gregorian Scriptural commentary in one of the saint's expository or homiletic discourses. Its place could have been in one of the earlier and unpublished redactions of the *Moralia* or of the *Homilies on Ezekiel*. (Parallel passages to it occur elsewhere in those works—cf. Vogüé *SC* 260, pp. 401-3). Or, since it makes extensive use of the text of *Joshua* 15.18-19 (cf. *Judges* 1.14-15), otherwise unexploited in Gregory's known writings, it could have been originally delivered in one of his unpublished commentaries on the Heptateuch (cf. Epistola XII.6). When in 597 Gregory sought for a suitable lesson of spiritual edification to send through Theoctista to the Empress he selected his discourse on compunction from his reserve of unpublished writings, which comprised sermon notes, unedited commentaries and sections excised from earlier redactions of his works. Either the original or a copy of our pericope was set before the pontiff for him to approve for inclusion in his important letter to the imperial court at Constantinople. When the revised form of the pericope, with Gregory's careful theological retouching, had been copied by the notaries into the *Letter to Theoctista*, the original unrevised text remained in the Lateran *scrinium*, where it would have been available in the seventh century for use both by Paterius and Tajo, and later by the Dialogist. The Dialogist may well have thought that it was a passage otherwise unknown and so particularly pat for his purpose. Although he had access to and made use of the file copies of Gregory's correspondence in the papal archive, he would not necessarily have been familiar with the detailed contents of all those many hundreds of letters, and so may not have realized that IGP 39 had been reused and retouched by Gregory himself in that letter of 597.

I noted that in some details Paterius seems to present a reading of the text that is not only independent of but better than the reading given by the Dialogist in IGP 39. A particular instance is where Gregory, before explaining the nature of two principal *genera* of compunction, makes a preliminary reference to its countless *species*. Here, unlike the Dialogist, Paterius—with whom Tajo agrees—has a concessive subjunctive to refer to the diverse species of compunction, which are as many as the sins of the penitents: "*Et licet in multas species compunctio dividatur, quando singulae quaeque a paenitentibus culpae planguntur, unde ex voce quoque paenitentium Ieremias ait: Divisiones aquarum deduxit oculus meus; principaliter tamen compunctionum genera duo sunt ...*" (new *CCL* edition, lines 19-23). Instead of this concessive subjunctive, the Dialogist begins IGP 39 with a simple indicative. This gives independent weight to the parenthesis about *species*, illustrated by *Lamentations* 3.48, which in the Paterius-Tajo reading of the text is merely a subordinate clause to the main statement about the two principal *genera* of compunction. The articulated structure of the long sentence, following the concessive "*Licet*" accords better with Gregory's normal style. The text of the *Letter to Theoctista* cannot be used to adjudicate here between the reading of the Dialogist and that of Paterius-Tajo, since in that letter Gregory eliminated the parenthesis about the *multae species* of compunction and the supporting quotation from *Lamentations*, and composed a new sentence at the beginning of the re-used passage.

Lastly, I would point out an incongruity in the supposition, which defenders of the authenticity of the *Dialogues* must make, that when Gregory wrote his *Letter to Theoctista* in 597 he reused a section of a well-known work that he had published five or six years earlier. Remember that the teaching on compunction contained in that pericope was expressly included in the letter to the Princess Theoctista as a spiritual lesson offered by the Pope for the benefit of the Empress Constantina herself. (cf. Ewald-Hartmann I, p. 466, lines 22-8 and p. 467, lines 20-2.) Would not that great lady, and her court at Constantinople, regard it as a poor compliment, verging on disrespect, that the Bishop of Rome could find nothing better for his chosen message of spiritual edification for the Empress than to reuse a section of a hagiographical work that he had already disseminated for all and sundry to read? Would Gregory, with his sense of due respect and propriety, have sent for the spiritual instruction of the Empress a second-hand offering, already published by him as a rider to his tale of the old Italian abbot Eleutherius? On the supposition, however, that the pericope in question had *not* been previously published in the *Dialogues* (which were to be written long afterwards), but that it was selected by Gregory from his file of unedited spiritual compositions as a worthy personal offering to the Empress, its inclusion in his *Letter to Theoctista* is readily understandable.

IGP 40: III.37.18-20. On the heroic virtue of an unlettered saint who laid down his life for another. From line 166, "... *quis ille spiritus* ...", to line 188, "... *odorari nesciebat*". (Omit the reference to "*isdem venerabilis vir Sanctulus*" in line 173.)

At first sight this passage seems to be homogeneous with the Dialogist's own narrative, for it is presented as a direct eulogy on the venerable priest Sanctulus, whose miraculous deeds and heroic virtue have been the subject of the whole of the long Chapter 37 up to this point. Moreover the passage, unlike almost all the other inserted Gregorian passages in the *Dialogues*—which usually enunciate Scriptural lessons and universal theological truths—refers to concrete facts in the life of a particular individual. Thus the facts alluded to would seem obviously to be those previously narrated in the long and edifying story about the readiness of Sanctulus to die in the place of a deacon whom the Lombards were about to kill. But the passage pulls us up because of its recognizable Gregorian phraseology and style, in open contrast to the Dialogist's Latinity in the preceding narrative about the prodigious virtue of Sanctulus. We then note some details which indicate that when the passage was first composed it did not refer to the Sanctulus of the *Dialogues*, and that the mention of his name in line 173 must be an interpolation.

I conclude that IGP 40, in its original setting, was uttered as part of a homily delivered by Gregory at the tomb or on the feast day of a martyr of earlier times. No doubt it was to fit in with the details of this passage that the Dialogist carefully composed his pleasing tale of the heroic resolve of Sanctulus, who was ready to die in place of the deacon whom he had delivered from the hands of the Lombards. Much of IGP 40 can plausibly be presented as a comment on this story—but not all. Sanctulus has to survive his peril, in order to become later the friend of and frequent visitor to the Gregory of the *Dialogues*. Accordingly when the

venerable priest offered his neck to the raised sword of the executioner
the bloodthirsty Lombard was divinely stricken into powerless immobility, so that Sanctulus emerged from his peril unharmed and victorious
over the persecutors. The events leading up to this miraculous escape are
indeed made to accord neatly with the details alluded to in lines 168-72
of IGP 40 (*"Ubi enim ... non expavit?"*). In lines 178-82, however, the
Gregorian pericope does not aptly correspond to the details of the Sanctulus story. There the real Gregory cites the text of *I John* 3.16, "As he
laid down his life for us, so we too ought to lay down our lives for our
brethren". Gregory remarks that the humble and unlettered martyr
whose heroic charity he is extolling may never have read that exhortation
of the Apostle, yet he put it into practice: *"... tam sublime apostolicum
praeceptum faciendo magis quam sciendo noverat."* Now this cry of praise for
the martyr's heroic fulfilment of the apostolic precept would lose its
force—and *faciendo* would be an inappropriate word to use here—if the
saint referred to had not actually laid down his life for another, but had
only been ready to do so. Although Sanctulus was of heroic virtue, he was
not a martyr in fact. By making him escape death, the Dialogist rendered
IGP 40 less useful as a Gregorian comment with which to cap his story.

Then again, it is an awkward point that the heroic saint of IGP 40 is
so simple, humble and unlettered that Gregory doubts whether he had
ever read the New Testament text, and also says that he had a poor
knowledge even of "the very rudiments of letters" (line 174). Now Sanctulus is said in the *Dialogues* to have been a much respected priest, who
visited Gregory in Rome every year, and was loved and cherished by the
Pope. The Dialogist stresses the simplicity of Sanctulus (lines 166-7; cf.
lines 10-13), and tries to present his *docta ignorantia* as admirable despite
his lack of literacy and his unfamiliarity even with the New Testament.
Nevertheless it remains odd that a priest, and one held in such regard by
Pope Gregory (who sternly disapproved of illiteracy in priests), should
have such a degree of ignorance. Fr de Vogüé himself remarks: *"Prêtre
connaissant mal l'alphabet et la Bible: l'aveu est remarquable"* (*SC* 260, p. 425).
The strangeness of this circumstance dissolves when it is realized that
IGP 40 is not referring to the priest Sanctulus, but is a tribute by the real
Pope Gregory to an unnamed martyr of lowly estate. Because that humble martyr was not a priest there was nothing unbecoming in his hardly
knowing the rudiments of letters. Though he may never have read the
Bible or the Commandments (lines 174-5), he fulfilled God's law in the
heroic charity of his life and death. His *docta ignorantia*, says Gregory,
should humble our *indocta scientia*. It seems not improbable that the
famous phrase *"scienter nescius et sapienter indoctus"*, applied by the
Dialogist to Benedict of Nursia (*Dialogues* II, Prologue 1) was originally

uttered by Gregory in a similar context to that of IGP 40. He writes a like eulogy of a humble abbot Stephen in *Homilies on the Gospels* 25.8: *"Erat autem huius lingua rustica sed docta vita"*.

The remark by Peter the Deacon which precedes IGP 40 does not contain the usual direct link with the wording of the inserted passage. For that link we have to go back some way to an earlier remark by the Gregory of the *Dialogues*, in 37.9, lines 79-81. There he promises to throw light on the external miracles of Sanctulus by revealing what he was inwardly through divine virtue. The first part of IGP 40 is presented as an apt fulfilment of this promise, although it is separated from the cue by more than 80 lines of text, relating the long anecdote about the victory of Sanctulus over the Lombards.

IGP 41: III.37.21-22. Why good men are being taken out of this world. From line 193, *"Malitia remanentium ..."*, to line 208, *"... mentem traherent"*.

With the end of Book III in sight, the Dialogist deploys his last three Gregorian insertions in quick succession. IGP 41 follows immediately on the heels of IGP 40, but not with any relevance to the context. Fr de Vogüé, when commenting on the question by Peter the Deacon that abruptly introduced IGP 39, described it as *bien gauche*; here likewise he notes that the query of Peter the Deacon by which IGP 41 is brought in is a *"question sans lien apparent avec ce qui précède"* (*SC* 260, p. 426).

In devising the cue question the Dialogist, as is his wont, picks out words and statements from the Gregorian passage that he now intends to insert into his text. The words *"boni ... subtrahuntur ... qui ... poterant"* (lines 190-1) link proleptically with *"qui ... poterant ... subtrahantur"* in lines 194-5 of IGP 41. (cf. also *subtrahi* in line 205 and *bonorum* in line 207.) As well as these verbal cues, the two parts of Peter the Deacon's question correspond to the two parts of the Gregorian lesson. In the first and longer part of IGP 41 (lines 193-204) Gregory explains why the just are being rapidly taken out of this life as the end of the world draws near. One reason is the wickedness of those who remain: they deserve to be deprived of the presence and influence of the good. Another reason is that the just are to be spared the sight of the evils of the last days. A further reason is that it is urgent that the construction of the heavenly Jerusalem should be completed with its due number of living stones. To prepare for this Gregorian explanation, the Dialogist makes Peter the Deacon ask: "Tell me, please, why you think it is that everywhere the good are being taken away" (lines 189-190).

In the concluding sentence of IGP 41 (lines 204-8) Gregory appends a qualification to what he has just said. It must not therefore be thought, he explains, that *all* the elect are being taken away and that only the wicked remain. If there were no good men to give example, no sinners would be drawn to repentance. In the second part of the cue question with which he introduces IGP 41 the Dialogist prepares for that concluding sentence of the pericope. Why is it, Peter the Deacon asks, that "those who could live to edify the multitude either cannot now be found anywhere, or at least are becoming exceedingly rare" (lines 190-2). Thus Gregory's qualifying rider, "*Nec tamen ita electi omnes ...*", towards the end of IGP 41, can be presented as if it were an implied corrective to Peter's too absolute assumption in his question. A. de Vogüé points out (*SC* 260, p. 426-7) an inconsistency in Peter the Deacon's remarks in this place. At the beginning of the dialogue (I Prologue 7) Peter said that he had no doubt of the existence of good men in Italy, but had no knowledge of miracle-workers among them. But now, forgetful even of his earlier admission, Peter says that good men have virtually disappeared, not simply from Italy but from the world: "*ceux-ci se font à présent presque aussi rares que les thaumaturges*" (Vogüé, II, p. 427.)

IGP 42: III.38.3-4. The signs of the times point to the approaching dissolution of the world. From line 23, "*Mox enim illa ...*", to line 43, "*... ne diligatur clamat?*"

This, the last of the Gregorian passages embedded in Book III of the *Dialogues*, expresses the pontiff's poignant lament as he surveyed the misery of the devastated land in which he lived, and a vibrant exhortation to his flock to shun the doomed world and to seek what is eternal. Both in the elevation of the language and in the sentiments expressed this pericope is unmistakably the utterance of Gregory himself. It has close parallels in his other writings. We note an affinity of subject matter between IGP 41 and 42. The Dialogist has collected (perhaps from the same original source) two extracts relating to the approaching end of the world and has put them in proximity at the end of his third book.

After IGP 41 a preliminary comment by Peter the Deacon provides an early pointer to IGP 42: "Thoughtlessly do I complain that the good are taken away, when I see the wicked also perishing in their multitudes" (lines 209-10). Thereupon the Dialogist makes Gregory tell the story of what happened when Bishop Redemptus of Ferentis slept in a church next to the shrine of the martyr St Eutychius. In the middle of the night the saint arose from his tomb and appeared to the half-waking bishop to declare thrice: "*Finis venit universae carni*". Whereupon Redemptus betook himself to prayer and lamentation. It is at this point of the text that IGP 42 is inserted. The appearance of portentous signs in the sky and the descent of the fierce Lombards on Italy, described in the

Gregorian passage, are presented by the Dialogist as the sequel to the nocturnal apparition and vaticination of St Eutychius.

What was the original setting of IGP 42? Comparison between it and the several parallel passages in Gregory's works helps us to suggest an answer. All the elements in IGP 42 are found expressed, often in closely similar terms, in those other passages. The appearance of fiery portents in the skies as a prelude to the descent of the savage Lombards on the land of Italy (lines 23-8) is likewise referred to in Gregory's *Homilies on the Gospels* 1.1. There the same phrase *acies igneae* is used, and the lurid phenomena are further interpreted as presaging the human blood that was to be shed in the invasion. The destruction of cities, castles, churches and monasteries (lines 28-31) is described, with the use of identical terms, in *Homilies on the Gospels* 17.16, in *Homilies on Ezekiel* I.9.9. and II.6.22, and also in two of Gregory's letters (III.29 and V.37; Ewald-Hartmann I, pp. 187, 322). The depopulation of the countryside and the abandonment of cultivation (lines 31-4) is likewise lamented in the same texts. That the prevailing misery, destruction and desolation not merely foreshadow but give present proof of the arrival of the end of the world (lines 35-6) is also declared in the first of Gregory's Gospel homilies. (cf. also *Moralia* 21.35-6). The final paragraph of IGP 42, drawing the moral that we must cease to cling to the temporal goods of this crumbling world, and that instead we should seek the good things of eternity (lines 37-43), has several close parallels in Gregory's known writings, notably in *Homilies on the Gospels* 1.5, 4.2 and 28.3 (cf. Vogüé, *SC* 260, p. 431 and the Maurists' index, *PL* 76.1442-3).

While all those passages help to illustrate IGP 42, most light is thrown by *Homilies on the Gospels* 1.1. The correspondence between that passage and IGP 42, both in expression and in the elements of the argument, is very close. Now in that sermon, which he preached on the eschatological text of *Luke* 21.10-11, 24-32, Gregory points to the progressive fulfilment in his own day of the signs that Christ predicted as indicators of the proximate end of the world and of his Second Coming. In IGP 42 the theme is identical: "*finem suum mundus non iam nuntiat, sed ostendit*" (lines 35-6). In all probability IGP 42 was in its origin part of a similar Gregorian discourse on the imminent end of the world, perhaps omitted from the published *Homilies* or the *Moralia* because of the close parallels elsewhere in those works. IGP 42 has the stamp of homiletic urgency, especially in the impassioned exhortation of the concluding paragraph (lines 37-43).

At the beginning of IGP 42 Gregory alludes to an occurrence or sign that had happened a short time before the appearance of the fiery portents in the sky and the Lombard invasion. He says that the fiery portents "followed close after" that earlier occurrence—"*Mox ... secuta sunt''* (line 23). Close afterwards, too, came the Lombard conquest (lines 25-8). The Dialogist would have us suppose that the event alluded to by those opening words of IGP 42 was the nocturnal apparition of St Eutychius to announce to Bishop Redemptus that the end was coming upon all flesh. Putting aside, however, the assumption that IGP 42 was originally written in the context of the Eutychius story, we ask what really may have been the preceding occurrence implicitly referred to by the opening phrase of the pericope. As we have seen, it is reasonable to conclude that IGP 42 was originally composed as part of a homiletic exposition of the same eschatological texts of the New Testament that Gregory expounded in his first Gospel homily. I further infer, in answer to our present question, that the preceding occurrence, alluded to by the twofold *"mox"* of lines 23 and 25, was something that Gregory saw as belonging to the eschatological signs predicted by Christ in those Gospel texts. What were those specific signs, and how does Gregory allude to them in IGP 42?

In the Lucan account of Christ's eschatological discourse, which Gregory expounds in the parallel passage in *Homilies on the Gospel* 1.1, the following signs of the approaching end of the world are given in Chapter 21, verses 10-11: (a) the rising of nation against nation (*gens contra gentem*); (b) great earthquakes (*terraemotus magni*); (c) plagues (*pestilentiae*); (d) famine (*fames*); (e) terrifying phenomena in the skies (*terrores de coelo et signa magna*). Later, in verse 25, there is the further prediction of (f) "signs in sun and moon and stars", (g) "distress (*pressura*) of nations", and (h) "confusion of the roaring of the sea and the waves". In his homily (1.1) Gregory comments that of those signs "some we see have already come to pass, others we dread as very soon to befall us". The "many signs" he recognizes as already verified are as follows: (a) "*gentem contra gentem exsurgere*"; (g) "*earumque pressuram in terris*"; (b) "*terraemotus*"; (c) "*pestilentias sine cessatione*"; and (e) fiery portents in the skies ("*igneas in coelo acies*"). The "few signs which remain" to be verified in the near future he indicates as (f) and (h).

In the light of this exposition of Christ's eschatological predictions, in Gregory's sermon, we gain insight into the meaning of IGP 42, which is a truncated extract of what must have been a similar Gregorian discourse on the signs of the world's approaching end. We know from the Gospel homily that Gregory believed that signs (a), (b), (c), (d), (e) and (g) had already come to pass in his own age. Which of these verified signs are directly referred to in IGP 42? At the beginning of the pericope (line 23) we find express reference to (e) in the phrase "*terribilia in coelo signa*", which echoes the Gospel words, "*terrores de coelo et signa magna*". This is followed by an allusion to (a) in lines 25-8. The onslaught of the "*effera*

Langobardorum gens'' on the people and land of Italy, which followed the "terrible signs in the sky", can be seen as fulfilling the prophecy in the preceding verse of the same Lucan passage: *"Surget gens contra gentem, et regnum adversus regnum"*. (There is the very same linking of these two eschatological signs, (e) and (a), in Gregory's Gospel homily, 1.1.) The fiery portents in the skies (the *aurora borealis?*) are there likewise described, with the use of identical phrasing, as having been seen before Italy fell victim to the destructive sword of the invading Lombard nation—*"priusquam Italia gentili gladio ferienda traderetur"*.

Of the other eschatological signs which, in Gregory's view, had already been verified in his own day, there remain (b), (c), (d), and (g). In the Gospel homily it seems that he subsumes (g) under (a), or takes it as a general description of the prevailing tribulation. The presence of sign (d), famine, is doubtless implicit in what he says in IGP 42 about the desolation of the land, abandoned without cultivation (lines 31-4). In our search for the preceding occurrence that is alluded to by the word *"Mox"* at the beginning of IGP 42, namely the occurrence that preceded the coming to pass of the eschatological signs (e) and (a), we are left with the probability that it was one or other of the two remaining signs, that is, either (b), earthquakes, or (c), plagues. Both those eschatological tribulations are said by Gregory, in the parallel Gospel homily, to have been verified in the present age—*"terraemotus urbes innumeras subruat ... Pestilentias sine cessatione patimur"* (*PL* 76.1078).

From the reference in IGP 42 to the Lombard invasion which followed shortly afterwards, we conclude that the occurrence in question was something that happened not long before the year 568, when the Lombard horde under their king Alboin swept into northern Italy. Which then of those two eschatological signs is it more probable that Gregory is alluding to, as having come to pass shortly before that year—an exceptionally severe earthquake or a great visitation of the plague? We do not have historical record of an unusually severe earthquake in the period just before 568, but we do know of a calamitous outbreak of the plague at that very time. During the governorship of Narses in the middle of that decade—that is, shortly before the descent of Alboin and his horde—Italy suffered a terrible outbreak of the plague which ravaged Rome and the central provinces as well as the regions of northern Italy. The rapid subjugation of the Italians by the invaders is attributed to the devastating effects of this pestilence. "The Lombard invasions coincided with the first great plague pandemic", as J. Richards points out (*op. cit.* p. 13). It is, then, likely that it was that great plague, seen as one of the fulfilled eschatological signs, that Gregory had referred to in the section of his original discourse immediately preceding IGP 42 as we have it.

At all events, Pope Gregory's sombre and powerful peroration in this pericope breathes a different air from that of the Dialogist's narrative. The latter presents the awesome phenomena in the skies and the destructive Lombard onslaught on Italy as a sequel which is significant as fulfilling the generic prediction of St Eutychius to Redemptus in the account of the bishop's nocturnal vision by the martyr's tomb. The real Gregory, on the other hand, dwells with an anguished heart on the prophetic words of Christ himself in the Gospel, describing the apocalyptic signs of the end of the world, and sees them fulfilled in the events of his own day. With the conviction that the climax of all history and the divine judgement on the world is at hand, he expounds to his flock the meaning of the Scripture that declares the warning and sentence of the Son of God. The perspective of the real Gregory when he wrote IGP 42 was very different from that of the Dialogist when he tailored IGP 42 into his story of the spectral apparition at the tomb near Ferentis.

CHAPTER SEVENTEEN

THE INSERTED GREGORIAN PASSAGES IN BOOK IV OF THE *DIALOGUES*

Of the four books that make up the *Dialogues* Book IV is the longest of all, amounting to nearly a third of the whole work. It has several special features which distinguish it from the other three books. Indeed some commentators have conjectured that it was conceived and composed independently. "It has a kind of priority over the three preceding books", observes Fr de Vogüé, "and it may be that Gregory wrote it, at least in part, before them".[1] Professor P. Boglioni has also advanced reasons in favour of a separate origin for Book IV.[2] Patently the argument and scope of this book do not correspond with the intent announced at the beginning of the *Dialogues*, in the prologue to Book I, which was to show that saintly thaumaturges had been active and numerous in Italy. The intent of Book IV (announced in the closing paragraph of Book III) is to show "that the soul does not end with the flesh". Indeed some early manuscripts of the *Dialogues* bear a composite title which may reflect this difference between the first three books and the fourth: that is, "*De miraculis patrum italicorum et de aeternitate animarum*". At the beginning we were promised that the subject of the book would be the life and deeds of the Fathers of Italy. In Book IV those Fathers are lost sight of, for the most part. Instead we meet a motley host of departing and departed souls: among them some saints, some imperfect folk, and also—in increasing numbers—sinners, the reprobate and the damned.

Out of the 62 chapters contained in the fourth book of the *Dialogues*, no less than 25 are (as A. de Vogüé points out[3]) "pure doctrine", without narrative episodes—something that is found in only one chapter in all the other three books. The "pure doctrine" elements are contained in the 38 inserted Gregorian passages, IGPs 43-80, which will be distinguished and discussed in the present chapter. Among them we find an interesting group of "narrative IGPs", a category not to be found in Books I-III. From the viewpoint of our investigation, the most striking feature of Book IV is that it contains the greatest number of IGPs, and that these make up a far larger proportion of the text than in the rest of

---

[1] *SC* 251, p. 66.

[2] In a communication given at an international conference at Norcia in September 1980, celebrating the 15th centenary of St Benedict's birth.

[3] *SC* 251, p. 66.

the *Dialogues*. A computer word-count shows that the proportion of IGP
to non-IGP material in the first three books of the *Dialogues* is about 15%;
in Book IV this proportion rises sharply to about 40%. The wordage of
IGPs in the fourth book constitutes just over 58% of the total IGP wordage in the *Dialogues* as a whole.

For the compilation of Book IV the Dialogist assembled, from his store
of Gregorian literary remains, groups of texts related in subject matter.
There are several pericopes which relate to the theology of the Last
Things (IGPs 57, 60, 61, 63, 64, 69, 70, 71, 72), and which the Dialogist
deploys in a discernible plan. Among these, in particular, we observe
that there are passages devoted to speculative questions concerning hell.
That is a topic which can hardly be considered relevant to the declared
scope of the *Dialogues* as stated in the prologue to the whole work. It seems
that another unpublished group of Gregorian papers which the Dialogist
laid under contribution for Book IV concerned the reality of the spiritual
world of *invisibilia* (cf. IGPs 43, 44, 45, 47, 48, 49). A final group of
related IGPs (76, 77, 78, 80) concerns the oblation of the Mass and its
salvific effects.

It may well have been the Dialogist's possession of those choice and
varied fragments of Gregorian wisdom that dictated the somewhat unexpected pattern of his fourth book. The distinctive character of those
theological and expository materials led him even to depart from his
declared purpose in that book, which was to persuade doubters that the
human soul is immortal. Moreover, since the proportion of genuine
Gregorian material inserted in the final book of the *Dialogues* is far greater
than in the other three, Book IV as a whole gives a greater impression
of Gregorian verisimilitude. Several of the IGPs included there are very
lengthy. In this book the Dialogist does not diversify his text by interven-
tions of Peter the Deacon nearly as frequently as he does in Books I-III.

As well as containing a greater proportion of theological material,
Book IV is unique in being systematically arranged with a didactic plan
in view. In Book II the wonder-stories were to illustrate the life, deeds
and virtues of the holy abbot Benedict. In Books I and III they were narrated without any overall plan; they could just as well have been
presented in a different order. But in Book IV the stories, though still
numerous, are subordinated to the declared doctrinal concern with the
vicissitudes of souls after death, and are arranged in groups to illustrate
recognizable stages in the treatise. This is not to say, however, that the
Dialogist's insertion of his borrowed Gregorian passages is more skilful
in Book IV than elsewhere. His desire to bring in, come what may, the
choice Gregorian morsels he has at his disposal again leads him into the
same kind of irrelevance, literary clumsiness and defect of logical se-

quence that we have noted in the preceding books, when examining how the IGPs are set into the narrative matrix of the *Dialogues*.

A notable peculiarity of Book IV, and one very relevant to our inquiry, is the patent reuse by the author of passages which appear elsewhere in the published works of St Gregory. In our study of the IGPs in the first three books we noted that virtually all of them, although recognizably Gregorian, were otherwise unpublished and unknown. I pointed out a couple of exceptions: IGP 16, concerning the 50-year-old Levites, which is adapted from the *Moralia*, and IGP 39, a passage which is also found in a letter of Pope Gregory to the Princess Theoctista. But in Book IV we find a number of passages, some quite lengthy, which are obviously "Inserted Gregorian Passages"—beyond any possible dispute—since they are also found in Gregory's authentic works. The author of the *Dialogues* reproduces in his text nine edifying stories which had been narrated by the real Gregory in his *Homilies on the Gospels*. These nine passages form the special category of what I have called the "narrative IGPs" in the *Dialogues*. When retelling the first six of these stories (IGPs 52, 53, 54, 55, 59, 65) the Gregory of the *Dialogues* acknowledges their source, saying that he "remembers" that he has recounted them in his *Homilies*, and then repeats their text practically verbatim. But when reusing the last three of the nine stories (IGPs 66, 76, 77), he omits to mention that they are taken from the *Homilies*. We also find two long IGPs (IGP 71, on the "Origenist" objections to belief in eternal punishment, and IGP 74, on the discernment of dreams) which are reproduced with verbal identity from the *Moralia*, although the Gregory of the *Dialogues* makes no reference to this fact.

The IGPs from Books I-III were all didactic passages containing exegetical, doctrinal or moral teaching. The inclusion in Book IV of those nine edifying stories, which had also been related by the real Gregory in his Gospel *Homilies*, is a new dimension in the *Dialogues*. In preaching his sermons to the people of Rome, the pope adapted himself to their level and their needs by narrating his series of *exempla*,[4] or accounts of supernatural happenings which marked the merits of saintly persons or the demerits of the wicked. In every case he used those fourteen *exempla* to illustrate the pastoral moral that he was drawing for his flock from the Gospel text of the day. The Dialogist, however, omits the pastoral moral when borrowing the stories; he uses Gregory's *exempla* merely to add to his collection of prodigy-stories about departing souls.

---

[4] Out of the fourteen Gregorian *exempla* the Dialogist reproduces only nine. Of the four he omits, *Homilies* 23.2 and 39.10 could scarcely be presented as *animarum exempla*, though 32.7 might be. I think he has already made some allusion to 34.18 in Book II (cf. IGP 26).

Out of all Gregory's voluminous works, those fourteen anecdotes in the Gospel homilies provide practically the only "light relief" in the otherwise universal gravity of his writings. Although, as F. H. Dudden remarks, "it cannot be said that these anecdotes are particularly striking"[5] (and indeed as wonder-stories they are pale in comparison with the Dialogist's own bizarre tales), they must have been eagerly repeated by readers of St Gregory's works, many of whom would have doubtless wished there had been more such spiritual diversions. I suggest that it may well have been the presence of those anecdotal *exempla* in Gregory's *Homilies on the Gospels* that gave the Dialogist the idea of using most of them as a nucleus for composing a book of diverting stories which would satisfy the eager thirst for such literature. He would incorporate them in an ambitious work ascribed to the great Pope Gregory, which would mainly consist of a large collection of much more sensational stories composed by himself. By interweaving them, together with the many Gregorian doctrinal fragments taken from the archives, into his own narrative of wonder-stories, he could plausibly present his book as the work of St Gregory himself. In composing his fourth dialogue he may have also had in mind the discussion of Gregory of Tours with one of his priests (in his *Historia Francorum*[6]) on the Last Things, and in particular on "the life of the soul after its departure from the body".

IGP 43: IV.1.1-5. Man, exiled by the Fall, suffers blindness and doubt concerning the invisible realities; the Holy Spirit illumines hearts to heal this blindness. From line 1, "*Postquam de paradisi ...*", to line 45, "*... carceris agnovit.*"

The lengthy Gregorian extract with which Book IV opens serves as a splendid exordium for this final and longest part of the *Dialogues*. The borrowed passage directly begins the chapter, and is not introduced by the usual device of a specific cue-question from Peter the Deacon. At the close of Book III, however, there was a preliminary reference to the coming contents of Book IV. There Peter asked Gregory to provide both arguments from reason (*ex ratione*) and examples from stories about the apparition of souls (*animarum exempla*) in order to teach doubters the truth of "the life of the soul after the death of the flesh".[7] The elevated Gregorian pericope with which Book IV commences is then presented as relevant to this inquiry. IGP 43 is a jewel of Gregorian spiritual teaching, which the Dialogist has rightly prized and placed at the head of Book IV.

---

[5] *op. cit.* I, p. 254; see Chapter 19 below.
[6] 10.13; cf. A. de Vogüé, *SC* 251, p. 42, note 65.
[7] III.38.5, lines 49-52.

Although, as I shall argue, it does not harmonize with his own theme throughout that book, there is seeming plausibility in using Gregory's teaching here about the mind's knowledge of *invisibilia* as an introduction to the promised discussion of the survival of disembodied souls.

Nevertheless IGP 43 has a different perspective from that implied by Peter's request at the end of Book III. In this passage Gregory teaches that the human mind, sunk to a carnal level after the Fall and the consequent loss of the power to contemplate divine things that it originally enjoyed in Eden, is a prey to spiritual blindness. Now it is prone to doubt even the existence of those invisible realities which once it knew by experience. Among the *invisibilia* which the carnally-minded doubt are the heavenly fatherland and its citizens, the angels, to whom the souls of the just are companions.[8] Despite this reference in IGP 43 to the souls of the just, however, the real Gregory does not there assume the premise posited at the end of Book III: namely, that doubters are to be taught the truth of the soul's survival after death both by proofs *ex ratione* and by *animarum exempla*, or ghost-stories. Rather, he teaches that the reality of the *invisibilia* is now confirmed to our sense-bound race by the Incarnation of God's Son, who has sent the Holy Spirit into our hearts "that we may believe what we can no longer know experientially". It is the grace of this indwelling Spirit that provides the remedy for our mental blindness and our proneness to doubt "*de vita invisibilium*".[9] The *maiores* (the prophets, apostles and saints), who "through the Holy Spirit have direct awareness of the invisible realities" and who contemplate divine things in a higher light, can strengthen the faith of the weaker brethren, who should trust in their testimonies.

In IGP 43, §3, Gregory adapts the celebrated allegory of Plato's Cave, so often used by ancient writers. Suppose, he says, that a pregnant woman were cast into a dungeon and there gave birth to her child. She would tell the child about the sun, the moon, the stars, the mountains and fields, the flying birds and the running horses, but the child in the darkness of the dungeon would not know any of these things from personal experience. Just as such a child would have to rely on the assertions of his mother, so those weak in faith should at least give credit to the truth declared by those who are inspired by the Holy Spirit. This argument is further indication that IGP 43 was not originally written to prove the particular point of the survival of the soul after death, but to lament man's weakened awareness of the reality of the unseen world.

---

[8] Lines 6-32. cf. *Homilies on the Gospels* 32-6: "*Sola esse visibilia aestimant, invisibilia non appetunt, quia nec esse suspicantur*".

[9] Lines 33-45.

There are fairly close parallels, with frequent verbatim echoes, between IGP 43 and passages in Gregory's known works (e.g. *Moralia* 5.61-2; 8.49-50; 15.52; 16.32-3; 34.5; *Homilies on the Gospels* 2.1; *Commentary on Canticle* 1.) From these passages there emerges a coherent teaching which clearly illustrates the background of Gregory's thought in IGP 43. The perspective of this teaching is substantially different from that of the Dialogist in his fourth book. Of the parallel passages just referred to, the first two from the *Moralia* are particularly revealing. The real Gregory there describes the present opaque state of the soul, in which it can think only those things which come through imagination of corporeal objects—*per imagines corporum*. It must thrust down all such corporeal images in order even to have awareness of itself, and thus to prepare the way for contemplating the substance of eternity: "*ut semetipsam sine corporea imagine cogitet, et cogitando se, viam sibi usque ad considerandam aeternitatis substantiam paret*" (*Moralia* 5.61). The exiled and darkened human mind is restored by the Redeemer's grace so that it may at least transiently repress and transcend its bodily concerns and imaginings, and thus regain some measure of the lost contemplative experience of divine things. Only by the uncircumscribed divine light can it penetrate through the obscuring veil and again reach some contemplation of the *bona invisibilia* (*Moralia* 8.49-50). The Gregory of the fourth book of the *Dialogues*, on the other hand, describes the world beyond the grave with a wealth of corporeal images, and finds a principal assurance for the existence of that other world in his colourful ghost-stories and reports by *revenants* of their visits to the abodes of the departed. Here we are in a climate of thought distinctively different from that of the real Gregory in his teaching on how the mind may apprehend eternal life.

IGP 44: IV.2.1-2. Not even the unbeliever lives without a kind of faith. IGP 44a runs from line 1, "*Audenter dico ...*", to line 8, "*... absque dubitatione testatur*". IGP 44b runs from line 11, "*Habent etiam infideles ...*", to line 16, "*... videri non possunt?*"

In IGP 44 Gregory, echoing an argument of St Augustine (cf. A. de Vogüé, *SC* 265, pp. 22-3), points out that even unbelievers accept on faith what they have never seen—for example, their origin from their parents. It is not improbable that IGP 44 comes from the same original context as IGP 43, since there is a generic similarity of matter. In IGP 43 there is mention of *fides*, *mater* and *invisibilia*, and these words also occur in IGP 44. Even so, the two passages could not have been consecutive. IGP 44 presupposes some foregoing comment which has not been included here. From the emphatic contrast in the opening sentence, "*Audenter dico quia sine fide neque infidelis vivit*", it is probable that in the original source the immediately preceding reference had been to one of the Scripture texts such as *Habakkuk* 2.4, "*Justus autem in fide sua vivet*"; or the similar affirmations in the New Testament, *Romans* 1.17, *Galatians* 3.11 and *Hebrews* 11.6.

The cues by which the two parts of IGP 44 are brought in by Peter the Deacon are once again clumsy. Since this extract is not about the survival of the soul, which is the Dialogist's chosen theme for Book IV, he must make it seem to be so. Accordingly Peter remarks that "one who does not give credence to the existence of invisible realities is surely an unbeliever; and when this unbeliever doubts he is not seeking faith but reason" (IV.1.6). By this contrived cue the Dialogist changes the subject and leads into Gregory's commentary on the Scriptural concept of "living by faith" and on the psychological self-contradiction of the unbeliever. But Peter's cue-question is scarcely consistent with the request he made in III.38.5, in order to introduce Book IV. There he asked, since "many people within the bosom of Holy Church doubt about the life of the soul after death", that Gregory should teach such doubters the truth of the survival of the soul by arguments from reason, "*ex ratione*", and by the telling of "*animarum exempla*". The programme for Book IV announced there envisaged no appeal to Scriptural revelation and faith (though that was indeed an extraordinary methodology to attribute to St Gregory). Now, in IV.1.6, the initial esteem of *ratio* is momentarily forgotten. Peter now considers it reprehensible, and the mark of the unbeliever, to seek in these matters not the way of *fides* but the way of *ratio*. This shift of perspective was doubtless dictated by the Dialogist's desire to bring in his Gregorian excerpt on faith and unbelief.

In the middle of IGP 44 a second cue from Peter is inserted, picking out the first clause of IGP 44b. Perhaps this break in the Gregorian pericope reflects an omission in the Dialogist's citation of the original text. An indication of such a hiatus may be the change from the singular *infidelis* to the plural *infideles* which occurs just at this point. Whereas in IGP 44a the singular number is used throughout (13 grammatical uses, including verbs), in IGP 44b the number is plural throughout (11 uses).

We saw that in its original bearing IGP 43 was not specifically concerned with the question of the survival of the soul; it referred to the *invisibilia* in general, in which the sense-bound mind fails to believe. Likewise IGP 44 is at a tangent from the declared theme of Book IV. In the following chapters the Dialogist resumes his pursuit of *ratio* to demonstrate the survival of the soul. But as if to forestall a possible charge of inconsistency, after the emphasis on *fides* in IGP 44, he now hastens to add that he means "*ratio sed fidei admixta*" (lines 17-18; cf. Chapter 3, lines 21, "*rationi fidelium*".)

IGP 45: IV.3.1-3 - 4.1-8. Of the three orders of created spirits. Answer to an objection alleged from *Ecclesiastes*. IGP 45a runs from Chapter 3, line 1, "*Tres quippe vitales* ...", to lines 19-20, "... *sine fine moriantur*". IGP 45b runs from Chapter 3, line 23, "... *quid est quod Salomon ait* ...", to Chapter 4, line 81, "... *veritate definivit*".

IGP 45 is the longest of the Dialogist's Gregorian excerpts, running to 111 lines in the *SC* edition. There are clear parallels to this passage in the *Moralia* (cf. Vogüé, *SC* 265, pp. 23-5, 28-9.) For instance, §§3-6 of IGP 45b are similar to *Moralia* 4, preface, 1. Unlike IGPs 43 and 44, which were concerned with *invisibilia* in general, IGP 45 can be brought in as directly relevant to the question of the immortality and incorruptibility of the human spirit, which is the declared theme of Book IV. This pericope is a discursive exegetical answer to an objection drawn from *Ecclesiastes* 3.18-20. It does not follow on smoothly from the immediately preceding Gregorian pericope, IGP 44.

We have seen that in his initial request (III.38.5), which set out the programme for Book IV, Peter the Deacon did not ask for testimonies from Holy Scripture to witness to the doctrine of the immortality of the soul, but only for arguments drawn "from reason" and from "histories of souls". Nevertheless by inserting IGP 45 the Dialogist again ignores the premise that has limited his demonstration to *ratio* and *animarum exempla*. The passage he now inserts expounds at considerable length an answer to a possible objection that could be alleged from the pages of Scripture (*Ecclesiastes* 3.18-20) against the immortality of the soul. The objection itself (IGP 45b, lines 23-33), which in the original source was doubtless a rhetorical question posed by Gregory as arising from IGP 45a, is in the *Dialogues* put into the mouth of Peter the Deacon.

IGP 45 is typical Gregorian exposition. The obscurities of the text of *Ecclesiastes* are reverently discussed, one text being illuminated by another, until a harmonious resolution of the difficulty is reached. The words of Scripture habitually permeate the thought and writing of the real Gregory, but not of the author of the main *Dialogues* text. A passage such as IGP 45 bears the true stylistic signature of St Gregory, and, by its contrast with the characteristics of the Gregory of the *Dialogues*, implicitly discredits the pseudepigrapher.

IGP 46: IV.4.10. On "condescension" for the sake of one's weaker neighbours. From line 88, "*Cur condescendentem te* ...", to line 93, "... *praedicatoris imitaris*".

Although IGP 46 uses the second person singular and fits aptly into the dialogue, there are reasons for judging it to be a genuine Gregorian snippet brought in from another context. The lesson of "condescension" out of pastoral charity, and the application of *1 Cor.* 9.22, are paralleled in *Moralia* 6.54 and elsewhere (cf. Vogüé, *SC* 265, p. 33.) Was IGP 46 a snippet from a draft of a letter from the pope to an unknown correspondent, which the Dialogist introduced by an appropriate cue from Peter in the preceding paragraph (IV.4.9)? There are two questionable features in its use here. In the concluding paragraph Gregory praises Peter as worthy of veneration (*"in hac re amplius venerari debes"*); and in the preceding cue-request Peter reveals an ambition to do good to others by his part in the discussion. Both these points are unusual in the *Dialogues*, where Peter the Deacon is habitually presented as a naive and uninformed interlocutor who is grateful (as he says here, lines 82-3) that, as a result of questions asked in ignorance, "I have been able to learn through such subtle explanation what I did not know". Is the momentary change in his status in IV.4.9-10 due to the fact that the Dialogist had ready for use a courteous response originally addressed by Gregory to an ecclesiastical correspondent whom he honoured?

When Gregory uses the term *condescendere* in the *Moralia* and elsewhere he refers to the solicitude of a superior or preacher who, out of pastoral charity and duty, converses with inferiors, worldings or unbelievers. But the application to Peter of the phrase *"dum ex condescensione caritatis"* in the present context seems heavily overdone. Since throughout the *Dialogues* Peter shows incomprehension, naivety and lack of spiritual insight, it is accordingly odd and excessive that on this one occasion, when he proposes to put forward the kind of naive difficulties that would be voiced by the incomprehending *infirmantes*, he is highly lauded by Gregory for the charity of his *condescensio*. The oddity is explained, however, on the supposition that Gregory's words are a snippet originally written for another context.

Chapter 5 and 6 of Book IV, constituting the remaining section of the Dialogist's "rational" demonstration of the soul's immortality, are among the most confused and confusing in the whole of his work. He has available some Gregorian passages, referring primarily to the angels and to the invisible world, and he seeks to press them into service as part of that rational demonstration. The trouble is that the passages do not fit naturally into his argument; the resulting obscurity and inconsequentiality can be seen from analysis of his text.

IGP 47: IV.5.4. Invisible ministering spirits pay court to the invisible Creator. From line 22, *"... vis divina implet ..."*, to line 31-2, *"... angelos et spiritus iustorum?"*

The clumsiness with which the author inserts IGP 47 into his text is striking. In IV.5.3. Peter asks how we can know that the soul still exists after the death of the body. From the movements of a living body one can deduce the existence there of a living soul; but, he objects, there are no observable movements after death from which to make such a continuing inference. The reply given to this objection by IGP 47 is not an answer to the question asked. What the real Gregory says in this passage is as follows. The divine creative energy fills all things, giving spirit, life and existence to creatures. This transcendent God, the Creator and sustainer of all things, is invisible to us. In his service there must be ministering beings in his likeness, also invisible. Those invisible attendants are the holy angels and the spirits of the just in heaven. This discourse is clearly Gregorian—there are verbal parallels in the *Homilies on Ezekiel* and in the *Moralia* (cf. Vogüé, *SC* 265, p. 35). But it was evidently not composed as a reply to Peter's question about the soul's survival after death, and to the particular difficulty he has just raised— namely, the lack of observable movements from which to deduce the continuance of the soul once it has left the inanimate body.

IGP 47, therefore, does not belong in this place. Its original context can be seen to be the same from which IGPs 43 and 44 were taken— namely a discourse by Gregory on the existence of the invisible heavenly world, direct knowledge of which was lost when the light of the human mind was darkened by the Fall, but which is known to redeemed men through Spirit-bestowed faith. The question of the existence of the heavenly world of *invisibilia*, discussed in IGPs 43 and 44, is not the same question as that of the incorruptibility and survival of the human soul, which is the Dialogist's theme in these chapters. He tries to make IGP 47 refer specifically to the latter discussion, but its original reference was plainly to the former. In IGP 43 the world of *invisibilia*, which men can no longer know experientially, is described as that of communion with God and converse with the blessed angels and the spirits of the just in the heavenly fatherland. This—and not a "rational" proof of the survival of the human soul—is also the perspective of IGP 47. Indeed the words *invisibilia* and *dubitare* are linked in both passages, and the phrase "*sanctos angelos et spiritus iustorum*" in IGP 47 (lines 31-2) match the mention of "*angelos Dei*" and "*spiritus iustorum perfectorum*" in IGP 43 (lines 12-13).

The cue-question of Peter the Deacon in IV.5.3 asked what observable "movements and activities" could be seen after bodily death to attest the continuing life of the soul. In introducing the argument from vital movements the Dialogist is already looking ahead to IGP 48. But first he wishes to find a slot for the insertion of IGP 47. By using it as Gregory's answer to Peter's naive question about bodily movements, he is more than usually inconsequential. He himself is aware that his argument here is disconnected, for he introduces IGP 47 with an excuse for its inappositeness: *"Non quidem similiter, sed dissimiliter dico"* (lines 20-21). After the insertion of the Gregorian passage he attempts to make it seem more relevant to Peter's question by a piece of quite inept reasoning. Just as from the body's movements you conclude (*"a minimo"*) that the soul is there, so—he argues—you can conclude (*"a summo"*) that the soul can still live after its departure from the body because (as IGP 47 has shown) "it ought to be occupied in the service of the invisible Creator" (lines 35-6). The comment of Peter (ostensibly written by Gregory himself) on this limping logic is: "Well said—all of it".

IGP 48: IV.5.5-8. Invisible spirit is the moving principle of visible bodies. IGP 48a runs from line 39, *"Cum Paulus dicat ..."*, to line 42, *"... quod videri potest"*. IGP 48b runs from line 43, *"... nulla visibilia ..."*, to line 66, *"... corpora quae videntur"*. (Probably intrusive are *tui* in line 45 and *te* in line 55).

IGP 48b may well have belonged to the same original context as IGP 47, (from which it seems to take distinctive words) and also to that of IGP 43. All three excerpts are concerned with the reality of the *invisibilia*. The Dialogist introduces IGP 48 by means of a cue-comment from Peter the Deacon which proleptically picks out phrases from the Gregorian passage now to be inserted, in order to weave it into the dialogue. In this case the phrase *"quod corporeis oculis non valet videre"* (line 38) anticipates Gregory's words in IGP 48a (line 41) and in IGP 48b (lines 45-6).

Although I here consider IGP 48a and 48b together, since they are consecutive in the *Dialogues* text and there is some assonance in their wording, there is no logical continuity between the two passages. IGP 48a is concerned with faith in the theological sense (as in the text cited from *Hebrews* 11.1), and with the incompatibility between seeing and believing. IGP 48b, on the other hand, is not about faith but about the priority and control of invisible spirit over visible matter. It would seem, then, that IGP 48a was not taken from the same immediate context as IGP 48b. Although Peter's cue-comment picks out the verb *credere* to lead on to IGP 48a, he does not use the verb in the same sense as there. Whereas in IGP 48a (lines 41-2) *credi* is applied strictly to believing with theological faith, in Peter's introductory remark (line 38) the verb *credere* has merely the everyday sense of "mental acceptance".

As placed here, IGP 48b is digressive and inconsequential. In it Gregory argues that vision of corporeal objects (even the operation of the corporeal eye), and likewise the bodily movements that produce the mighty effects of human industry, depend on the governing influence of the invisible soul;[10] so too the whole visible world is under the governing influence of the invisible world of intelligent spirits, who are ultimately governed by God. As an argument for the *immortality* of the human soul all this is not pertinent. The Dialogist is finding opportunities to bring in his precious excerpts of Gregorian doctrine, but since they are often intractable to his purpose, he cannot make them consequentially relevant to the specific theme he has undertaken to demonstrate in his fourth book. A. de Vogüé duly observes the logical standstill, indeed the retrogression, of the reasoning in Chapter 5. He points out that merely to show, as the author does here, that bodily sight itself implies the existence of the invisible soul, does not directly advance the argument: "Peter has already admitted the proof of the existence of the soul based on the operations of the body (§3). With regard to the *future* life of the soul, which is the object of the debate, nothing is proved by this argument—as Peter will indicate by repeating his question in §9" (*SC* 265, p. 37). Vogüé likewise remarks that the further reflection in §7, concerning the animating power of the soul, "repeats the preceding theme under another form. There is hardly any advance in the argument". The same criticism is even more applicable to §8, concerning the sway of *invisibilia* over the visible world. This was directly relevant in its original Gregorian context, but as placed here it is an inapposite and mystifying digression.

There is a passage in the *Moralia* (15.52) which is parallel to IGP 48b and throws useful light upon its meaning. There, as in IGP 48b, Gregory uses the same example of the sightless eye in the dead body to bring home the same lesson:

> The eyes of the corpse indeed remain open, but they cannot see or feel anything. The sense of sight has perished, because the indweller has departed; and the house of flesh remains vacant, because that invisible spirit who formerly looked out through its windows has gone. Because therefore invisible things are more excellent than visible things, much more should men ponder what they can learn from their own selves, and by this ladder of consideration, so to speak, should rise up towards God.

Here, as in IGP 48b, Gregory's concern is not with the survival of the soul in the future life, but with the present certainty and superiority of the invisible reality, of which God is the summit, over the visible. The Dialogist, seizing on the incidental reference to the departure of the animating soul from the body (*discedente anima*, line 50), incongruously appropriates IGP 48b for his own different context and theme.

---

[10] There is a parallel consideration, expressed in similar language, in *Homilies on the Gospels* 2.7.

IGP 49: IV.6.1-2. The posthumous miracles of the saints testify to the reality and quality of their heavenly life. From line 2, "*Numquidnam sancti ...*", to line 15-16, "*... in tot miraculis vivunt*". Omit interpolated sentence in lines 5-7, "*Tu vero ipse inquies ... corporis agnoscis*".

The Dialogist is aware that, in his preoccupation to use his Gregorian excerpts concerning the invisible and spiritual realities, he has digressed from his chosen theme and lost the thread of his argument. Now he makes Peter the Deacon repeat the request that he made in IV.5.3. Peter acknowledges for a second time that from the movements of a living body he infers the presence of an indwelling soul, and he asks once more for proofs of the life of the soul after the death of the body, when no such vital movements are observable (IV.5.9). The answer is provided by use of IGP 49. It is the last of the "rational" proofs offered in Book IV, by which the Gregory of the *Dialogues* claims to demonstrate the survival of the soul by arguments from *ratio fidei admixta* (IV.2.3). The reasoning that eventually emerges is as follows: the apostles and martyrs continue after their death to work miracles through their bodily relics; these posthumous miracles provide the "movements" which Peter seeks as proof of their continuing vital activity; therefore their souls must survive in another life.

The key to understanding the original bearing of IGP 49 is to be found in a closely parallel passage in Gregory's *Homilies on the Gospels*, 32.6, to which I referred earlier when discussing IGP 14. There, in a sermon to the people of Rome in the church of Saints Processus and Martinianus, on the anniversary of their martyrdom, the pope raised the minds of his hearers heavenwards by the lesson of the martyrs' death and miracles. Some so-called Christians, he said, supposed that only visible things were real and so doubted the existence of the invisible realm.

> We are standing here, my brethren, beside the bodies of the holy martyrs. Would those martyrs have given up their bodies to death, unless it was most certainly clear to them that there was a life for which they ought to die? And behold those who thus believed now shine forth with miracles. (*PL* 76.1237C).

IGP 49 presents the very same argument as Homily 32.6, with verbatim correspondence of terminology and order of sentences. Comparison of the continuously parallel passages in the two writings even confirms that a sentence has been interpolated into IGP 49 by the Dialogist (lines 5-7, "*Tu vero ipse inquies ... corporis agnoscis*"). In Homily 32.6 Gregory affirms that the martyrs would not have laid down their lives if they had not been certain of a life to come. Then immediately, in the sentence, "*Et ecce ... miraculis coruscant*", he goes on to exclaim that those who thus believed in a future higher life now shine forth in observable miracles. In IGP 49 there are two similar sentences (lines 2-5 and 7-9) exactly corresponding to the same two stages in the argument as in the homily. But in IGP 49 the second sentence, *"Et ecce ... miraculis coruscant"*, is now separated from the first by the interpolated remark in lines 5-7, which refers back to the plea of Peter the Deacon in IV.5.3 and 9. From its character and its language this interjection can in any case be recognized as intrusive and non-Gregorian. The Dialogist is concerned to make IGP 49 appear to be a direct answer to Peter's request for evidence of "vital movements" to attest the continuing life of departed souls. The point of his interpolation in the text at this juncture becomes clearer in the sentence that immediately follows IGP 49 (lines 16-19). There he explicitly glosses Gregory's teaching in order to make it appear to be the answer to Peter's request.

In reproducing IGP 49 has the Dialogist simply reused and adapted the passage from Homily 32.6? At first sight it seems to be so. There are, however, sufficient differences between the two passages to indicate that he took IGP 49 from another source—possibly from a Gregorian sermon which was not included in the pope's finally approved edition of his Gospel *Homilies*, but which may have been included in the first unauthorized collection which he recalled from circulation. In IGP 49 there are additional phrases, not found in Homily 32.6, which seem to belong to a fuller Gregorian original. In particular there is the inclusion, at the end of the description of prodigies worked at the martyrs' tomb, of two further evangelical miracles: *"leprosi veniunt et mundantur, deferuntur mortui et suscitantur"* (lines 12-13). Moreover in IGP 49 the saints whose living power is manifested in their miraculous relics are described as *"apostoli et martyres Christi"*. In Homily 32.6, however, the saints at whose tomb the words were uttered were Processus and Martinianus—who were martyrs but not apostles. We know that among the Roman basilicas in which Gregory preached his sermons on the Gospel texts of the day's liturgy was that of the two apostles Saints Philip and James (cf. Homily 36). Was the original context of IGP 49 an unpublished sermon delivered at the shrine of those two "apostles and martyrs of Christ"?

IGP 49 has the same emphatic expressions as Homily 32.6 in referring to the *locus* of the martyrs' miraculous activities: *"Et ecce ... miraculis coruscant"*, and *"hic ... in tot miraculis vivunt"*. Although in the last sentence of the passage in that homily the phrase *"hic ubi mortui sunt"* seems to denote a wider locality than that of the tomb alone, and *"hic"* could there have the more general sense of "here below", it is clear nevertheless from the preceding sentences that Gregory is emphasizing that it is *here*, at this tomb-shrine containing the martyrs' bodies, at this very place where he is preaching and where his hearers are gathered,[11] that the living power of the saints is thus manifested by miracles of healing. Since identical expressions occur in IGP 49, it is a reasonable inference that these words too were originally uttered in just such a setting. Reference to the presence of the tombs and bodies of the martyrs in whose basilicas he was preaching occurs in several of Gregory's sermons on the Gospel texts. When discussing IGP 14 I argued that the original context of that passage, too, was a sermon preached at a martyr's tomb, in which he made the very same appeal to the saint's miraculous activity at the shrine, as witness to the reality of his heavenly life, that we find in Homily 32.6 and in IGP 49. The pope not infrequently repeated his favourite spiritual reflections, even with the repetition of the same phrases and exhortations.

All these considerations converge towards the conclusion that IGP 49, which in any case has the distinctive traits of St Gregory's pulpit oratory, is adventitiously introduced into the Dialogist's context. Moreover, this sole direct "proof" that he offers of the survival of the human soul after death is hardly probative even for that purpose. In IGP 49 (and in Homily 32.6) the real Gregory is not concerned to establish the general philosophical truth of the permanence of all human souls after death, whether good or wicked. In his appeal to the miraculous activity of the martyrs he is concerned to proclaim the blessed life of the saints in the heavenly realm, and to raise the minds of his hearers to aspire to that life. But the Dialogist does not wish to restrict the discussion to the heavenly realm. He has undertaken to demonstrate the immortality and survival of all souls. Indeed several of the stories of other-worldly experiences that he has ready to tell refer to the souls of the reprobate.

IGP 50: IV.11.1-2. On God's loving care for his chosen sons, even while he chastises them. IGP 50a runs from line 6, "*Hunc omnipotens ...*", to lines 9-10 "*... perfecte sanando monstravit*". IGP 50b runs from line 13, "*Sed quia nemo ...*", to line 21, "*... debeat iuste misereri.*"

We have seen that IGP 49 terminated the section of Book IV devoted to "rational" proofs of the soul's immortality. The Gregory of the *Dialogues* goes straight on to the long series of *animarum exempla* that he has promised (in III.38.5) in order to corroborate his arguments *ex ratione*. He remarks that "for the fluctuating spirit, because *ratio* does not fully convince, *exempla* are persuasive" (IV.7, lines 9-10). Accordingly he proceeds to relate a series of stories about the souls of holy men which at the moment of death were seen leaving their bodies and mounting heaven-

---

[11] "*Ad sanctorum martyrum corpora consistimus, fratres mei*".

wards. The fourth of these stories concerns a venerable abbot Spes, whose sight was restored after 40 years' blindness. The climax of the story describes how at Spes's death-bed the monks saw the soul of their abbot leaving his mouth and flying heavenwards in the form of a dove. But before coming to that climax the Dialogist inserts IGP 50, which is a theological meditation on God's severe chastisements and merciful grace. One may surmise that the author framed his narration of Spes's 40-year-long blindness in order to provide a niche for this Gregorian excerpt.

IGP 50b stands out clearly as another jewel of Gregorian spirituality set in the Dialogist's own paste of religious folklore. The series of *animarum exempla*, or tales about visions of souls departing in visible form, is interrupted by this profound Gregorian lesson on the divine pedagogy of chastisement and mercy. In order to bring the passage in, the Dialogist has to stray from his stated theme and from his discussion of the soul's survival. In contrast to the concrete and descriptive narrative in which it is set, IGP 50b enunciates universal truths of the spiritual life. Nothing is more typical of Gregory's inimitable style than this majestic passage, which consists of one sustained sentence made up of ten concatenated and balanced clauses. The concluding period may be cited as a specimen of Gregory's veritable literary signature, which the Dialogist himself is incapable of counterfeiting: "... *atque in percussione sua electis filiis nunc misericorditer iustus est, ut sint quibus postea debeat iuste misereri.*"

But what of IGP 50a? This sentence too has the ring of Gregory's style and seems to come from the same context as IGP 50b. Yet, unlike IGP 50b, it does not enunciate universal truths applicable to all mankind; rather it refers to one individual to whom God has shown the extremes both of severity and of grace. Does not this sentence, it may be objected, seem to apply naturally to Spes, who, as the Dialogist explained, was divinely consoled while afflicted with blindness, and who eventually received restoration of his sight? I submit that IGP 50a, while authentically Gregorian, was not written to refer to the blind abbot Spes, but that it was taken, like the other IGPs in the *Dialogues*, from Gregory's expository writing on Holy Scripture. That is, the individual referred to in IGP 50a was a Scriptural figure whom the merciful God spared from eternal chastisement while disciplining him on earth. To this individual God providentially reserved both his greatest severity and his greatest favour. After first afflicting him, God later demonstrated his love when he "perfectly healed him". To apply this—and also the further agonized discourse on the divine *flagella* in IGP 50b—to the blindness of the abbot Spes is overdone. But it all does apply most aptly to the heroic figure of Job, about whose affliction under God's merciful *flagella* Gregory repeatedly makes similar reflections in his great *Commentary on Job* (e.g. *Moralia* 3.3-16; 35.22).

To recapitulate, then, I judge that IGP 50 was taken by the Dialogist from the unpublished remains of Gregorian Scriptural exposition in the Roman archives—a piece either omitted by the pope in the long-drawn-out process of editing his *Moralia* or found among the unused *reportata* of his *Homilies*. I propose as a likely conjecture that the individual originally referred to in IGP 50a was none other than Job.

IGP 51: IV.12.5. On visions of saints seen by the dying. From line 40, "... *plerumque contingit iustis* ...", to lines 44-5, "... *fatigatione solvantur*".

After the story of Spes the Dialogist's series of *animarum exempla* takes a new turn. In his first four *exempla* (Chapters 8-11) he has described how departing souls were seen visibly by those who remained. With Chapter 12 he commences a series of pious anecdotes about dying persons who beheld heavenly visitants calling them to Paradise. The first of these accounts tells how an unnamed priest of Nursia was visited on his death-bed by the holy Apostles Peter and Paul, who summoned him to follow them. This story is capped by the insertion of IGP 51, which says that at the hour of their passing, in order to spare them from the terror of death, many of the just are favoured with visions of saints who have preceded them to heaven. The style of the fragment is Gregorian, and the thought here is akin to *Moralia* 24.34, where Gregory affirms that often the just, who may be purged from lesser faults by the very fear of death, receive divine consolation in the hour of dying by a kind of contemplation of their spiritual reward: "*plerumque vero contemplatione quadam retributionis internae etiam priusquam carne exspolientur hilarescunt* ...".

IGP 52: IV.15.2-5. On the heroic patience and edifying death of the poor paralytic Servulus. From line 6, "... *in ea portico* ...", to lines 42-3, "... *fragrantia non recessit*". Omit "*cuius te quoque non ambigo meminisse*" in line 8.

After two further stories of holy persons who on their death-beds had visions of saints come to summon them (Chapters 13-14), the Dialogist remarks that often heavenly sounds become audible to the souls of the elect when they are on the point of leaving their bodies. By this remark he introduces the first of the series of nine edifying histories which are taken directly from Pope Gregory's *Homilies on the Gospels*. Here, as I observed earlier, we encounter a category of "narrative IGPs" specifically different from all the other inserted Gregorian passages that we have been studying. In my introduction to the present chapter I discussed the

peculiarity and significance of this reuse in the *Dialogues* of the nine ex-
amples taken from Gregory's published homilies. The story that I list as
IGP 52 is reproduced practically verbatim from the fifteenth homily, §5.
It concerns the poor paralytic Servulus, who when dying heard heavenly
psalmody, and at whose death a sweet fragrance became perceptible to
all present. The story from Gregory's homily is exactly copied by the
Dialogist, with only very few variants. In line 4 the reference to Peter the
Deacon's personal memory of Servulus is intrusive: it replaces the words
in the homily, "*quem multi vestrum mecum noverunt*".

It is to be noted that the purpose of the relation of this story in the
Dialogues differs from Gregory's original purpose in the *Homilies*. In his
sermon to the people of Rome Gregory told the story of Servulus to teach
the lesson of patient acceptance of the penal afflictions of this life, in order
to be purified to meet the divine Judge. The concluding sentence of his
account of the life and death of Servulus—a sentence omitted by the
Dialogist in IGP 52—points to the moral of this edifying *exemplum*: "*Ecce
quo fine ex hac vita exiit qui in hac vita aequanimiter flagella toleravit.*" Gregory
then applies the example of Servulus to those present. What, he asks,
shall we, who are so torpid in good works, say in the Last Judgement
when we see Servulus, who though unable to move his limbs was not
impeded from performing good works? In his sermon, then, Gregory did
not tell the story of Servulus in order to teach the lesson of the soul's survival, a truth which he there took for granted. But the Dialogist, retelling
the story for a different purpose, omits the pope's moral lesson and
pastoral application of it. Instead, his concern is with the details of the
supernatural manifestations which attended Servulus's passing. His
reason for reproducing IGP 52 is that it provides a further *exemplum*, and
one written by the real Gregory, to include in the systematic case he is
presenting, by which he has promised to demonstrate the survival of the
disembodied soul.

IGP 53: IV.16.1-7. On the hidden virtue and wondrous death of the
holy woman Romula. From line 3, "*Eo namque tempore ...*", to line 75,
"*... elongata finiretur.*"

Immediately after the story of Servulus there follows in the *Dialogues*
the second of the nine narratives taken from Gregory's *Homilies on the
Gospels* (40.11). This story of the holy woman Romula, also poor and
paralysed, is akin to that of Servulus. Gregory praises her heroic patience
and dedication to prayer. Her end, like that of Servulus, was marked by
heavenly psalmody and the odour of sanctity, and also by spiritual radiance which filled her cell. IGP 53 is again a word-for-word copy from
the text of the *Homilies*. But, like IGP 52, it is employed for a different
purpose.

In his sermon to the people of Rome Gregory told the story of Romula in order to impress on his hearers the duty of charity and respect for the poor. He stressed that moral of the story at some length in the subsequent passage (40.12; cf. also 40.10), which the Dialogist does not quote. That humble woman, exclaimed Gregory, was poor and despised; yet she was a pearl of God lying in the midden of this world's poverty and abjection. The wondrous circumstances of her death attested her true riches; the angelic choirs honoured her true merit. From this example, Gregory urged his hearers to learn to love and honour the poor and to share their riches with them. This is not the perspective of the Dialogist in reproducing the story of Romula. He retells it in order to add to his dossier of phenomenal proofs of the other-worldly immortality of the soul. For him, the prodigious happenings at Romula's death-bed provide another item for his series of *animarum exempla*. In his pages the story of the holy recluse is shorn of the noble pastoral lesson of charity and humility which was the reason for its first telling in Gregory's sermon.

IGP 54: IV.17.1-3. On the heavenly visitors who summoned the soul of Pope Gregory's aunt Tarsilla. From line 4, "*Quae inter ...*", to line 27, "*... mortua testabatur*".

The third of the "narrative IGPs" reproduced from Gregory's *Homilies on the Gospels* follows immediately upon the first two. The Gregory of the *Dialogues* says (in line 3-4) that he recalls having told it in his homilies and will repeat it here. The manner in which he repeats it is noteworthy. We have seen that when reusing IGPs 52 and 53, which were the first two *exempla* taken from the *Homilies*, the Dialogist copied out the complete narrative while omitting the pastoral moral; but in this third instance he edits and truncates the narrative itself, because its main bearing does not suit his purpose.

In his Gospel homily (38.15) Gregory recounted the lengthy history of his three aunts Tarsilla, Aemiliana and Gordiana, in order to illustrate his homiletic commentary on the Gospel text of *Matthew* 22.1-13, especially on the concluding words, "Many are called but few are chosen". All three sisters had dedicated themselves to the life of consecrated virginity. All three "made their conversion to God's service with the same ardour, all were consecrated at one and the same time, all lived together in their own house under a strict rule." But whereas Tarsilla and Aemiliana were true to their calling, Gordiana was unworthy of it. By a life of great virtue Tarsilla "reached the height of sanctity", and when she came to die was consoled by heavenly visions—first of her ancestor Pope Felix III, then of Jesus himself—welcoming her to heaven. Soon after her death she appeared in a nocturnal vision to her sister

Aemiliana, calling her too to heaven, but also sadly lamenting the fall of their sister Gordiana. The sequel of the narrative tells how Gordiana then forswore her vows to the consecrated life, took a husband and followed a downward path of worldly improbity.

This sad contrast between the sisters is the main point and moral of the whole story as told by Gregory from the pulpit; by it he brings home to his hearers the meaning of the Gospel text which he reiterates to them: *"Multi sunt vocati, pauci vero electi"*. The Gregory of the Dialogues omits all that, and picks out from the story only the brief section which tells of the heavenly visitants at Tarsilla's death-bed, which he copies verbatim. His interest in this excerpt, as he makes plain in lines 1-2, is that it provides an instance in which a departing soul has a vision—here not merely of the saints, as in his previous *animarum exempla*, but of Jesus himself.

IGP 55: IV.20.1-4. On the virtues, edifying death and heavenly reward of the abbot Stephen of Rieti. From line 3, *"Fuit etenim vir ..."*, to line 36, *"... territi fugerunt"*. Omit *"isdem Probus et ... alii"* in line 4.

After two intervening stories (one telling of a five-year-old boy whose soul departed not to heaven, but to hell), IGP 55 presents the fourth of the series of nine "narrative IGPs" taken from Gregory's *Homilies on the Gospels* (35.8; *PL* 76.1264). In the *Dialogues*, but not in the *Homilies*, the authority for the story is named as Probus, a Roman monk. Whereas some of the other "narrative IGPs" reproduce the text of Gregory's *Homilies* as we have it, in the case of IGP 55 only one section of the excerpt—namely, the description of Stephen's holy death in lines 27-34—corresponds exactly to our received text of the *Homilies*. The introductory section (lines 3-8) agrees in sense with Gregory's praises of Stephen in his sermon, but the wording is different. The additional anecdote given in the *Dialogues*, IV.20.2-3, concerning Stephen's virtuous equanimity in the face of an enemy's spite, does not appear in the homily, but it fits well into the context and accords with it linguistically. I conclude with probability that it was originally narrated by Gregory himself, and that the Dialogist took IGP 55 as a whole from a fuller recension of the text than the one that has come down to us.

It is unlikely that lines 36-8 (from *"ut palam ..."* to *"... ferre potuisset"*), which round off IGP 55 in the *Dialogues*, are authentically Gregorian. Those concluding words are not found in the homily text which just previously has been reproduced verbatim. The Dialogist may have added that comment in order to point a contrast between the mighty force of goodness that received Stephen's soul and the black forces of evil that seized the soul of the five-year-old boy in his preceding tale (IV.39.3-4). When recounting in his homily the awe of the bystanders at Stephen's death-bed, Gregory made no mention of a mighty and mysterious force that seized his soul, but instead drew an *a fortiori* conclusion that the dread of the Last Judgement will be far greater (cf. Vogüé, *SC* 265, p. 77).

Once again in IGP 55, as in the three preceding IGPs, the Dialogist focuses on the preternatural phenomena attending a soul's departure from this world, and omits the extended pastoral moral which in his homily the pope drew from the life-story of the holy abbot Stephen. There Gregory used the narrative to teach his hearers the lesson of heroic patience and of faithfulness to that daily "bloodless martyrdom" of which Stephen was an exemplar.

IGP 56: IV.24.2-3 and 25.1. How dying may purify the elect, how divine vengeance awaits their persecutors, and a reflection on the case of the prophet slain by a lion. IGP 56a runs from Chapter 24, line 11, "*Cum scriptum sit ...*", to line 19-20, "*... crudelitatis acceperunt ...*". IGP 56b runs from Chapter 25, line 1, "*Nam vir Dei ...*", to line 12, "*... cadaver iusti*".

In IGP 56 we mark a return to the Dialogist's more usual pattern, so far infrequently observed in Book IV, by which Peter the Deacon provides a query as a convenient cue for the introduction of an IGP. Following the accounts of deathbed prodigies, the last of which was IGP 55, the author then promised (Chapter 21) to present some examples of posthumous prodigies marking the merit of departed souls. In Chapters 22-4 he narrates three stories of the slaying of holy men by cruel Lombards. At the end of the third of these stories, which tells how a Lombard who had decapitated a deacon was straight away seized by an evil spirit, comes Peter's cue-question in IV.24.2: "Why does almighty God allow such men to die in such manner, yet after their death he does not suffer their sanctity to remain hidden?" IGP 56a is brought in as the answer to this question, and IGP 56b follows as a supplementary explanation. The two Gregorian excerpts are linked ineptly by a non-Gregorian interpolation in lines 20-3.

Both IGPs 56a and 56b may well have been taken from the same original context, since both include reference to death's purifying power for the elect. In IGP 56a (lines 14-16) Gregory remarks in passing that a reason for the painful deaths of just men may be that they need to expiate some light faults thereby. IGP 56b is a commentary on the history of the erring prophet in *1 Kings* 13. Gregory concludes that the man's sin of disobedience to a divine command was purged when he was killed by a lion. Since Scripture relates that the lion then respected the body it had slain, Gregory infers that in suffering death the sinner had become just.

The two parts of IGP 56, however, do not fit neatly together. If they were taken from the same manuscript source, they could not have been consecutive there, for the transit from IGP 56a to 56b is inconsequential. After briefly mentioning (in lines 14-16) the possibility that light faults may be wiped away by death, Gregory passes on, in the last sentence of IGP 56a (lines 17-20), to emphasize that divine vengeance surely awaits the reprobate who have exercised cruel power to put the just to death. There is a parallel passage to this in *Moralia* (16.69; cf. Vogüé, *SC* 265, p. 83). Taking Gregory's reference to the divine sanction awaiting reprobate persecutors, the Dialogist makes it apply to the case of the Lombard who slew the deacon, but who "was not permitted to exult over the dead man" (IV.24, lines 21-2). To support this application he invokes the testimony of Scripture as expounded in IGP 56b, which he thereupon introduces.

He presents IGP 56b as a logical sequence to what has just preceded.[12] That is, he implies that the history in *1 Kings* 13 of the prophet slain by a lion is a Scriptural analogy to the history of the deacon slain by a Lombard. In neither case could the slayer exult over his victim's body. Thus both episodes, it would seem, illustrate the assurance, given in the last sentence of IGP 56a, that divine justice is visited on those who exercise cruel power to kill the just. But the implied analogy between the two episodes[13] is bizarre. As we have seen, Gregory's point in IGP 56b is to show that the sin of the unnamed prophet in 1 *Kings* 13, who had disobediently eaten and drunk in the way, was remitted through the ordeal of his death when he was savaged by the lion. It is the benefit which that untoward death brought to the soul of the erring prophet, not condemnation of the lion's savagery, that is Gregory's concern in this expository passage. The fact that the lion was not permitted to eat the corpse is interpreted by Gregory as a sign that the prophet in dying was justified before God, not as a sanction decreed by God against the animal. In IGP 56b there is no suggestion that the lion was considered blameworthy and an object of divine vengeance because of its lethal attack upon the prophet, or that it symbolized the reprobate who slay the just, or that its part in the episode is to be understood allegorically.

IGP 56b has its interest for the study of Gregory's own teaching. Elsewhere he refers to the disobedience of the prophet described in Chapter

---

[12] This seems to be the obvious reference of the "*Quod*" in line 22, and is taken to be so by the translator in *SC* 265, p. 83. The plea that the antecedent of "*Quod*" is the general theme enuntiated earlier by Peter in lines 8-10 seems far-fetched.

[13] That the author did intend the bizarre analogy between the Lombard who slew the deacon and the lion that slew the prophet further appears from his "... *permissus non est*" in IV.24, line 21, which parallels the coming "... *licentiam non accepit*" in IGP 56b (line 9).

13 of *1 Kings*. (cf. *Homilies on Ezekiel* I.1.15 and *Moralia* 22.54), but he does not there discuss the gravity of the man's sin. Even though there may have been an extenuating circumstance in the prophet's disregard of divine command, in that he was himself deceived by a pseudo-prophet, in IGP 56b Gregory roundly calls his act a sin of disobedience, requiring divine punishment. One may surmise that the reason IGP 56b is not to be found in any published work of St Gregory could be that he had a scruple about its theological implications. Could the prophet's sin of disobedience to a divine command really be regarded as a venial fault, as merely one of the *levia contagia* which (as Gregory taught in *Moralia* 24.34 and in IGP 56a) could be cleansed in dying? If he suppressed IGP 56b because of such a doubt, it would thus belong to that category of extracts which, as R. Étaix suggested when discussing the "unknown" Gregorian fragments preserved by Paterius, the saintly pope may have prudently excised from his writings in order "to correct certain assertions which seemed inadequate or ambiguous" (*art. cit.* p. 78).

IGP 57: IV.26.1-4. The souls of the just enter heaven immediately after death, with the exception of some who are temporarily delayed. IGP 57a runs from line 1, "*Hoc neque de omnibus ...*", to line 19, "*... aeternam in caelis*". IGP 57b runs from line 23, "*Hoc eis nimirum ...*", to line 36, "*... gloria laetabuntur*".

IGP 56 was a digression from the promised theme of Book IV— namely the proof of the survival of the human soul. IGP 57, likewise, is not concerned with any such proof. In order to introduce this passage, Peter the Deacon changes the subject abruptly and asks a new digressive question: whether the souls of the just can be received into heaven before their bodily resurrection (IV.25.2). A. de Vogüé comments: "*Cette nouvelle question de Pierre déborde sa demande initiale*" (i.e. in III.38.5.) One may well be surprised that Peter's query should be posed now, when several *exempla* have already been related by the Gregory of the *Dialogues* describing how saintly souls were welcomed into heaven by celestial visitants. But the Dialogist has at his disposal some Gregorian material relating to *novissima hominis*, so he here makes an opportunity to draw in from that source the theological teaching of IGP 57.

He has not framed Peter's cue-question aptly. It appears that in the original Gregorian context from which IGP 57a was taken the question directly under discussion was whether the souls of the just enter heaven immediately after their death. The allusion to the bodily resurrection, raised in Peter's introductory query, is not directly considered in IGP 57a. Perhaps the Dialogist mentions it here in order to prepare for the supplementary cue-question in lines 20-2, which will introduce IGP 57b.

In IGP 57a Gregory makes a distinction between "the perfect just", who immediately after death are received into their heavenly abodes,[14] and another category of the just, who in some respect fall short of perfect justice. The latter, he says, "are still delayed by some sojourning-stages from entering the heavenly realm" (*"a caelesti regno quibusdam adhuc mansionibus differuntur"*). In IGP 57b Gregory takes account of the question that would naturally arise from IGP 57a. If the disembodied souls of the just are already in heaven, what reward do they receive at the Last Judgement? His answer is that the just will then receive the additional reward of heavenly beatitude in their bodies as well as the spiritual bliss that their souls already enjoy. As A. de Vogüé notes, there are two closely parallel passages to IGP 57b in the *Moralia* (Preface, 20; 35.25), where the same texts and the same arguments are adduced in very similar language. Again, these theological speculations are foreign to the Dialogist's professed theme.

IGP 58: IV.27.14. A short snippet on the hidden judgements of God. From line 118, *"Quis occulta ..."*, to line 120, *"... discutere debemus"*.

The long 27th chapter of Book IV is devoted to stories of preternatural predictions by dying persons. IGP 58, with which the chapter closes, has the character of a genuine Gregorian aphorism. In order to bring it in, the Dialogist gives a twist to his preceding story, which describes what happened to young Armentarius while he was dying of the plague. Returning to consciousness, the boy told how he had been taken briefly to heaven, and attested the truth of his claim by demonstrations of preternatural knowledge. When, however, the definitive moment of his death was at hand, suddenly—by a hidden judgement of God (*"occulto iudicio"*) he tore his hands and arms with his teeth. Whereupon Peter the Deacon remarks that the boy's dire chastisement, after receiving such a gift of heavenly knowledge, was a terrible thing. This serves as the cue for the Gregorian snippet to be introduced as an answer. The preceding phrase *occulto iudicio* in line 110 is thus seen to be the Dialogist's pointer to *occulta Dei iudicia* in IGP 58.

IGP 59: IV.28.1-4. The death of the pious Count Theophanius. From line 5, *"Fuit namque ..."*, to line 30-1, *"... aromata ferbuissent"*.

In Chapter 28 the Dialogist resumes his series of nine borrowings of *exempla* from St Gregory's *Homilies on the Gospels*, the first four of which constitute IGPs 52-55. In IGP 59 he faithfully reproduces the wording

---

[14] He affirms the same doctrine, with the same appeal to *2 Corinthians* 5.1, in *Moralia* 4.56.

of a fifth edifying story related by Gregory in Homily 36.13, with only minor variants. It tells of the pious death of Theophanius, a count of Centumcellae. In its original setting, Gregory expressly applied this *exemplum* to teach his hearers the lesson of *1 Corinthians* 7.27: this worthy official, though involved in worldly administration, led a life of virtue and died an edifying death. There were preternatural signs to mark his heavenly worth. When the count's wife doubted whether she would be able to take his body for burial (so great was the storm outside), the dying man assured her that the weather would clear—and so it happened as soon as he was dead. After his death his ulcerated flesh was found to be whole again, and when after a few days the stone of his tomb was lifted a sweet fragrance emanated from it. The moral drawn from this *exemplum* by the real Gregory in his sermon was: "I have therefore told you these things, so that by an example from your own neighbourhood I could show you that some people, though they have a secular form of life, do not have a secular spirit". The Gregory of the *Dialogues*, however, tells the story for a different purpose.[15] As he makes clear in lines 1-3, the author uses it because it affords another instance of a soul on the point of death having a specially subtle awareness which enables him to predict the future. This instance is the count's not very extraordinary prediction that the weather would clear in time for his funeral.

The Dialogist, eager as always to stress the miraculous, adds a further laboured corroboration of the report of the marvellous fragrance emanating from the count's tomb. He makes Gregory say in the *Dialogues* that after he had narrated the event in his homilies, certain people, weak in faith, doubted the truth of the story. Whereupon, on a day when he was sitting "*in conventu nobilium*", the very workmen who had opened the tomb came in to make some plea for themselves. The Pope was able to appeal to them to verify the truth of his story, which they did with a wealth of further circumstantial detail (IV.28.5). This addition to the story, making Gregory concerned to justify the veracity of his narration against doubters, and appealing to the undertaker's workmen to provide further proof of his credibility before that august assembly, is a false note. Moreover, the Dialogist's reference to a "council of the nobles", in which Gregory sat dispensing justice, even in minor civil causes, "before the assembled clergy, nobles and people", is also suspect. Nothing in Gregory's letters, or in other contemporary records, attests the existence of such an assembly in the Rome of his day.[16]

---

[15] A. de Vogüé notes the different use of the story in the two sources: "*Ici l'homélie conclut qu'il est possible de vivre dans le monde sans en avoir l'esprit. La visée des Dialogues étant différente, Grégoire remplace cette conclusion par un confirmatur*" (*SC* 265, p. 98-9.)

[16] cf. Chapter 20 below, and J. Richards, *op. cit.*, Chapters 6 and 7.

IGP 60: IV.29.1; 30.2-3 and 5. The souls of the wicked are punished in hell before Judgement Day. IGP 60a runs from Chapter 29, lines 3-4, "*... ex retributione aeternae ...*", to line 7, "*... reprobos exurat*". IGP 60b runs from Chapter 30, line 6, "*Si incorporeus spiritus ...*", to line 24, "*... ignibus neget?*". IGP 60c runs from lines 38, "*Certe reprobis ...*", to line 43, "*... sentire tormenta?*". Omit "*Petre*" in line 6.

In all probability IGP 60 belonged to the same original source as IGP 57, a source in which Gregory discussed the *novissima hominis*. In IGP 57 he taught that the disembodied souls of the just were already in heaven, not having to await the Last Judgement; in IGP 60 he teaches the corollary, namely that the disembodied souls of the wicked are already undergoing the torments of hell before the Last Judgement.

Peter's cue-question in IV.28.6, which introduces IGP 60, is awkwardly composed. First he affirms that, by analogy with the earlier answer about the souls of the just, one must believe beyond doubt that the souls of the wicked are already in hell. Despite this affirmation, he then goes on to say that he does not know what divine truth teaches on this point, since human reason does not see how those souls can be tormented before the Last Judgement (lines 42-7). The point of his last remark, it appears, is to introduce the word *cruciari*, which is a proleptic link-word pointing to the coming use of the same verb in IGP 60—*crucientur* (line 5), *crucietur* (line 14), *crucior* (line 21), *cruciandi* (line 41). Likewise the reference to the teaching of divine *veritas* in Peter's cue-question (line 46) seems to be introduced in order to link with the references to the revelation of divine *veritas* in IGP 60b, lines 17, 23 and in IGP 60c, line 38.

Peter's supplementary question in IV.29.2 doubtless reflects a similar heuristic reflection in the Gregorian original. The subsequent exchange in IV.30.1 seems to be of the Dialogist's own devising, based on the explanation about to be given in IGP 60b. The answer put into Gregory's mouth in lines 1-3 is a duplication of the real Gregory's argument in lines 6-8. As A. de Vogüé notes (*SC* 265, pp. 100-1), Gregory's speculation in IGP 60b, about the manner in which fire can torment spiritual beings, reflects similar speculations by Augustine.

The see-saw of dialogue in IV.30.4, interposed between IGP 60b and 60c, seems to be the Dialogist's own composition. It leads on somewhat heavily to the insertion of the fragment that is IGP 60c, which I think may be out of its original order as placed here. Perhaps its original setting was immediately following IGP 60a: thus the word *reprobis* in IGP 60c, line 38, would have originally resumed and referred back to the *reprobos* of IGP 60a, line 7. By deferring the use of IGP 60c by a few lines, the

Dialogist was able to make the mention of the torments of the devils a separate item in his dialogue, introduced by the further catechetic exchange of IV.30.4.

The doctrine in IGP 60 has parallels in other writings of Gregory, notably in the *Moralia* 9.95-104 and 15.35-6. In those cases, however, Gregory does not explicitly discuss the problem of how the separated soul can be punished by corporeal hell-fire. In IGP 60b he does address himself to this problem in particular. Again, we sense the existence of a writing in which Gregory speculated on the Last Things, which he chose not to publish, and which the Dialogist may have found and dissected for insertion here and there in his own composition.

IGP 61: IV.34.1-5. In the next world both the good and the wicked have knowledge of others. From line 3, "... *cum dictum esset ...*", to line 51, "... *scientem omnia sciunt?*". Omit "*quod nequaquam ipse requisisti*" in lines 32-3.

After three cautionary tales describing how wicked men were justly consigned to penal flames immediately after their death, the Dialogist brings in IGP 61, which is a doctrinal excursus on the knowledge possessed by souls in the after-life. It may well belong to the same original Gregorian source, concerned with theological speculations about the Last Things, from which came a number of other IGPs in Book IV.

The cue-question in IV.33.5 by which Peter the Deacon introduces this excerpt is based on Gregory's statement in line 23-4 of IGP 61, which is thus made to seem to be a direct answer to the question. Not long previously (in IGP 60b), the Dialogist has reproduced another Gregorian passage in which *Luke* 16.22-4 was quoted. IGP 61 contains a fuller quotation of that Scriptural parable of Dives and Lazarus. (The Dialogist alludes to this duplication, in IV.34.1, lines 1-2.) Gregory's exegesis in IGP 61 of this Lucan passage, and the teaching about the next world which he bases upon it, is paralleled in several respects in the last of his *Homilies on the Gospels* (40.8), which is a sermon on the same text. The cue-question put by Peter the Deacon—whether in the next world the good know the good and the wicked know the wicked—is given its answer by the insertion of the first part of IGP 61 (§§1-3). The second part (§§4-5) deals with a further question, not asked by Peter—whether beyond the grave the good know the wicked and the wicked know the good.

Elsewhere in the IGPs, when he finds a new development in the course of a borrowed Gregorian pericope, the Dialogist's usual practice is to make the change appear to be a new stage in his dialogue by interposing a supplementary cue-question from Peter the Deacon. Here he does not employ that literary device. Instead he simply inserts a parenthesis before Gregory's further explanation: *"quod nequaquam ipse requisisti"*—"this is something you did not ask". The Gregorian passage continues with still further elucidations for which Peter the Deacon did not ask—that the bliss of the blessed is increased by joy at seeing their loved ones also rejoicing in bliss, and the torments of the wicked are increased at seeing their earthly associates, for whose sake they despised God's law, tortured with them in the same torments. Moreover the blessed even know and enjoy fellowship with all the other righteous ones whom they have never seen on earth. All these additional theological explanations are extraneous to the Dialogist's own theme.

IGP 61 ends with a magnificent rhetorical question, expressing a familiar sentiment of Gregory's, which is found in many variants elsewhere in his writings: *"Quid est quod ibi nesciant ubi scientem omnia sciunt?"* This concluding paragraph is used as a peg for the Dialogist's subsequent story, related in IV.35. There, immediately after the Gregorian passage about the knowledge possessed by souls in eternity, and in particular the knowledge of the blessed who know all things in God, the Dialogist has a short anecdote about a holy monk ("one of ours"), who as he lay dying testified that he could see the prophets Jonas, Ezekiel and Daniel. The author introduces it with the word *"Nam ..."*, as if the story illustrates how the blessed in heaven know all things in God; but it does not have that reference. He attempts to make it relevant by adding: "Whereby it is easy to see what kind of knowledge will be possessed in that incorruptible life, if this man still living in corruptible flesh recognized those holy prophets, whom he had never seen." There is usually a kind of logic in the Dialogist's narrative, but the lameness of his own gloss, contrasting with the harmonious and lofty exposition of Pope Gregory, betrays him.

IGP 62: IV.36.12. Increased volcanic activity is a sign of approaching doom. From lines 73, "*... prae ceteris locis*", to line 82, "*... credere recusant*".

IGP 62 may belong together with IGP 42 in a discourse by Gregory on the approaching end of the world, which is a theme he sombrely expounds in several places in his *Moralia* and *Homilies*. In the Dialogist's preceding tale the dying Eumorphius sees a vessel prepared to take him away to Sicily, together with his worldly friend Stephen, who is also suddenly summoned to his doom. Peter the Deacon asks the significance of this reference to Sicily, thus providing the cue for IGP 62. This excerpt is authentically Gregorian in its rhythmic clause-structure. In its original setting it probably did refer to Sicily and the Lipari Islands. By making IGP 62 the answer to Peter's question in lines 66-7, the Dialogist implies that Eumorphius and Stephen must go to Sicily because that is where the entrance to the nether world is located. The volcanoes of that region were in ancient folklore taken to be the mouths of hell. (cf. the Dialogist's tale of the doom of Theodoric in IV.31.2-4).

Note, however, that in its original meaning IGP 62 does not naively assert that the volcanic craters are literally the entrance gates of hell. It is not about the present location of hell, but about the portents of the approaching end of the world. In it Gregory refers to reports, doubtless from Sicily and southern Italy, of a recent increase in volcanic activity. In *Homilies on the Gospels* 1.1 he likewise refers to reports "from other parts of the world" of frequent and destructive earthquakes, indicating that the Last Days, foretold by Christ in the Gospel, are not far distant. The Dialogist uses IGP 62 to imply that the Sicilian volcanoes are physically the mouths of hell into which the souls of dying sinners are even now conveyed. Gregory's own lesson in IGP 62 is that God uses the awesome sight of those widening volcanoes as a salutary warning to the living (*ad correctionem viventium*, lines 79-80) of the eternal torments prepared for sinners as Judgement Day draws near; and that by the spectacle of those dreadful flames He presents to unbelievers a visible image of the torments of hell in which they refuse to believe (lines 80-2).

IGP 63: IV.36.13-14. The blessed in heaven all enjoy the same beatitude, but with differences of quality; likewise the damned in hell are grouped according to the different quality of their sins. From line 86, "*Ipsa [veritas] quippe propter electos*", to lines 106-7, "*... ad conburendum ligant*".

To understand the original bearing of IGP 63 we must compare it with a parallel but longer passage in *Moralia* 9.98. There, as in IGP 63, Gregory comments on *Matthew* 13.30, and also alludes to the analogous text in *John* 14.2. One sentence in the *Moralia* passage sums up the point of IGP 63: "*Sicut enim in domo Patris mansiones multae sunt pro diversitate virtutis, sic damnatos diverso supplicio gehennae ignibus subiicit disparilitas criminis.*" (*CCL* 143, p. 526.) Closer inspection of IGP 63, clarified in the light of *Moralia* 9.98, shows that the Dialogist has once again made a naive application of an elevated pericope of Gregorian theology, in order to make it refer to his picturesque tales of portents at the hour of death.

At the beginning of his 36th chapter he undertook to show that a departing soul could recognize that he would be placed together in one abode ("*in una mansione*"; IV:36.1, lines 3-4) with those who shared with him "an equality of guilt or of reward". Thereupon he makes the Gregory of the *Dialogues* relate two stories. The first tells how two holy monks, John and Ursus, were both called to heaven at the same moment.

The second story is that of Eumorphius and Stephen, who also died simultaneously and whose souls were ferried together to the same volcanic inferno in Sicily. It is then, as a confirmation of these two *exempla*, that IGP 63, with its Scriptural testimonies, is appended. This is the reverse of the habitual order in the *Dialogues*, in which illustrative stories are usually placed after the IGP on which they are based. (cf. Vogüé, *SC* 265, p. 123, note 13).

But although the Dialogist has framed his two preceding *exempla* in order to cap them with IGP 63, which he has ready to use, the cap does not fit neatly. With a view to providing an opening for his Gregorian excerpts, he fashions his two *exempla* to show that in the next world 'those who were in common case through their deeds are also delivered to common places" of retribution (lines 83-5). In the case of the two reprobate laymen, he does relate that their souls were ferried in the same boat to Sicily, presumably to be thrust down to hell through the same volcanic crater. But in the tale of the two holy monks, it is related merely that they were both called to their eternal reward at the same moment; it would be difficult to demonstrate that they were thereafter allocated to the same particular *mansio* in heaven. Nevertheless the Gregory of the *Dialogues* confidently infers from his narration that since the two monks were "peers in merit and departed from their bodies together, it was given to them to live together in one mansion" (IV.36.6).

Note also that Gregory's direct concern in IGP 63 (as in *Moralia* 9.98) is not to prove that there is a distinction of *places* in heaven—as the Dialogist makes out in lines 83-5—but to observe that there are differences of *quality*—*dispar retributionis qualitas* (lines 94-5)—within the unitary retribution which souls receive in the next world.

IGP 64: IV.38.4-5 and 39. On the obscuring stench of carnal sin. IGP 64a runs from Chapter 38, line 28, "… *eandem delectationem* …", to line 36, "… *superna patiatur.*" IGP 64b runs from Chapter 39, line 1, from "… *libro Geneseos*", to line 7, "… *delectatione tradidissent*". In IGP 64a omit *eorum habitacula* in line 32; and for "*visa sit*" in line 33-4 substitute another probable original reading such as "*dici possit*".

Although there is a considerable interval between IGP 63 and IGP 64, a part of the picturesque narrative that intervenes has been framed, as we shall see, to prepare for the introduction of the latter. A query from Peter the Deacon (IV.38.2) gives the cue for the introduction of IGP 64, which in language and thought is patently drawn from a Gregorian source. The Dialogist has slightly modified it to make it seem to refer to his own account of the experiences of a Roman soldier who briefly visited the next world, and who returned to tell of the wondrous things he had witnessed there (IV.37.7-13). In the original context of IGP 64, I conclude, the "stinking vapour" (*foetoris nebula*) mentioned there did not refer (as in the *Dialogues*) to a noxious exhalation arising from the Styxian waters of the nether world and mysteriously "touching" the dwellings of those whose moral record was ambiguous. Instead, when the real Gregory used the metaphor of *foetoris nebula* he did so to liken the delectation of the unchaste mind in carnal sin to a noisome and obscuring mist.

The original bearing of IGP 64 becomes clear from comparison with parallel passages in the *Moralia*. In *Moralia* 16.83 Gregory expounds the same text of *Job* 24.20, "*Dulcedo illius vermis ...*", that he cites in IGP 64a. In both cases he interprets the text as referring to the wretched state of the lecher, whose morbid pleasure in the putrefaction of carnal sin is accompanied by mental blindness. In *Moralia* 14.23 he explains the symbolism of his phrase *foetoris nebula*, of which the Dialogist makes such a fanciful application in his tale told by the *revenant* from the other world. In his commentary on *Job* 18.15 ("Let brimstone be sprinkled in his tent"), Gregory declares that brimstone, emitting a foul stench and serving to kindle fire, is a symbol of the foulness of carnal sin. Such sin, he explains, "filling the mind with depraved thoughts which may be likened to stenches, makes it ready for the future fire; and while it diffuses in the wicked mind the vapour of its stench (*foetoris sui nebulam*), it brings fuel, as it were, for the flames to come". (*CCL* 43a, p. 711). In that passage of the *Moralia* he goes on to give the same exegesis of *foetor* and *sulphur*, and of the punishment of the Sodomites related in *Genesis* 19.24, that he gives in IGP 64b.

Thus *Moralia* 14.23, which not only shows that the striking phrase *foetoris nebula* was one favoured by Gregory but also makes clear the metaphorical sense he gives to it, illuminates the original meaning of IGP 64. Conversely, IGP 64 makes clearer the lesson underlying the unexplained linking of *nebula* with *foetor* in *Moralia* 14.23. The same lesson is indicated by the use of the word *caecitas* in the other parallel passage, *Moralia* 16.83. That is, the *foetor* of lubricious thoughts darkens the mind like a *nebula* so that it is blinded to the true light.

What the Dialogist has done is to take an unknown Gregorian passage, in which the pope again used his metaphor of *foetoris nebula* as signifying the foul darkness in the lascivious mind, and to give it another and cruder interpretation. Thus he makes it seem to refer to his tale of the stinking vapour which arose from the infernal river and affected the habitations of those who had, in their mortal life, had good deeds, but bad thoughts (IV.38.4, lines 22-7.) The tale has been fabricated to be linked with IGP 64a. In both IGP 64a and 64b Gregory plainly expounds his allegorical sense of the Scriptural word *foetor*. Aware of this, the Dialogist makes the

Gregory of the *Dialogues* say at one point (IV.38.3) that he too is speaking allegorically; but this will not do to explain his graphic tale of what the soldier saw in the other world, which is presented as equally worthy of credence as all the other tales in the book.

The Dialogist's eschatological presuppositions in telling that tale are strange and unGregorian. The habitations thus "touched" by the *foetoris nebula* were situated, it appears, on the heavenward side of the bridge at which the departing soul's fate was decided (cf. IV.37.8-9). Only some of the habitations near the black river were affected by the stinking mist which it exhaled. The meaning of this, as the Dialogist explains later, is that "there are many people who perform plentiful good works but are still touched by carnal vices in pleasure of thought" (Chapter 38, lines 24-5). A de Vogüé points out that here it is a question of "no more than bad thoughts, which are punished by bad odours" (*SC* 265, p. 137 note 4). But what kind of doctrine of other-worldly sanctions is this? Certainly not that of the orthodox theologian and stern moralist who was Pope St Gregory. In Chapter 19 below, where I review the theological discrepancies between the statements of the Gregory of the *Dialogues* and those of the real Gregory, I shall point out a similarly unGregorian assumption in the comments made in *Dialogues* IV.37.13 on the strangely ambivalent fate of the high-born Stephen.

The Dialogist leads into IGP 64b by means of a supplementary question from Peter the Deacon. This fragment doubtless belonged to the same original source as IGP 64a, for the subject matter is similar, and the terms *foetor* and *carnis delectatio* recur. The two fragments, though related, were probably not consecutive in their original context. But as used by the Dialogist the addition of IGP 64b is inept. Peter the Deacon asks for a Scriptural proof that carnal faults are punished by "the penalty of stench" (IV.38.6). IGP 64b is given as the answer. In that pericope, however, Gregory is repeating the same argument that he uses in *Moralia* 14.23, with exposition of the same text, *Genesis* 19.24. There is verbatim correspondence between the phrasing of the *Moralia* passage and IGP 64b, which serves to show us the original sense of the latter. The Dialogist would have it that IGP 64b confirms what his preceding narration has shown—namely that there is a *foetoris poena* or minor "penalty of stench" for those who, though not burdened by evil deeds, have gone to the next world without having sufficiently expelled lustful thoughts. In *Dialogues* IV.37.8-9, as we have seen, he has described how such a minor penalty afflicts those less-than-perfect souls. Their habitations, though built in the pleasant meadows on the heavenward side of the bridge of probation, are affected by the malodorous exhalations from the dark river. But this is not what IGP 64b is about—nor the parallel passage in *Moralia* 14.23.

In both those passages Gregory is referring to the fitting retribution vented by divine justice on the perverted men of Sodom. They were destroyed by fire and brimstone, the punishment fitting the crime: *"in ipsa qualitate ultionis notavit maculam criminis"* (*Moralia* 14.23). They justly perished by fire, which consumes, and by brimstone, which suffocates in noisome vapour; thus their punishment on earth appropriately signified that they had delivered themselves to the eternal death of hell-fire through their delectation in the stench of fleshy vice (IGP 64b, lines 5-7). In the light of this Gregorian teaching, therefore, it can be seen that IGP 64b does not fit the context to which the Dialogist attempts to apply it— namely, to refer to a mild "penalty of stench" in the after-life, affecting the dwellings of souls who were sullied with impure thoughts, but whose good deeds saved them from the nether abyss.

IGP 65: IV.40.2-5. The deathbed deliverance of a dissolute young monk. From line 8, *"... in meum monasterium"*, to line 46, *"... carne soluta est"*.

IGP 65 is the sixth in the series of nine *exempla* for Gregory's *Homilies on the Gospels* found in the fourth book of the *Dialogues*. The source here is Homily 38.16. There is an interesting parallel in Homily 19.7, where Gregory tells the same story but in different words.[17] Once more the Gregory of the *Dialogues* begins by remarking that he "remembers" having told the story in his homilies to the people, and then proceeds to reproduce it with verbatim quotation from Homily 38. The story concerns a youth (in the *Dialogues* he is named Theodore) who entered the monastery of St Andrew because his brother was there, but who led a worldly and scandalous life. Dying of the plague, he cried out aghast with nightmarish dread of a dragon which he saw ready to devour him, but through the prayers of the brethren he was delivered from despair, and after purifying sufferings died worthily.

In the *Homilies* in which he narrates the story Gregory uses it to teach the lesson of humble awe before the inscrutable divine judgements and of trust in divine mercy. The Dialogist's interest in repeating the story, on the other hand, is focused on the dying monk's fearsome vision of the devouring dragon. This he points to as an example of a soul about to depart who sees "something penal from the realm of spirits", in a way that brings spiritual benefit to himself and not only to the bystanders (cf. IV.40.1). The story is thus in contrast to the subsequent story of

---

[17] There is also a somewhat similar story, told more briefly (with a black dog instead of the dragon) in a letter sent by Gregory to a pious benefactress of St Andrew's monastery in 601. Hartmann thinks it is the same story as that which concerns us here. (Ep. XI.26; Ewald-Hartmann II, p. 288.)

Chrysaurius (IGP 66), who on his death-bed had a similar terrifying vision which was of no benefit to him but only to those who heard his despairing cries. The distinction which the Gregory of the *Dialogues* makes in Chapter 40, lines 3-5, is an anticipated reference to the points made by the real Gregory in IGP 66 (IV.40.9), where he says in his homily that Chrysaurius's vision was not "for himself" but "for our benefit".

IGP 66: IV.40.6-9. The desperate end of Chrysaurius. From line 49, "*... vir in hoc mundo*", to line 79, "*... petiit non accepit?*".

The story of Chrysaurius follows at once in IGP 66. It is the seventh of the series of nine "narrative IGPs", or genuine Gregorian *exempla* taken from St Gregory's *Homilies on the Gospels*. This is the first instance in that series in which the Gregory of the *Dialogues* does not avow that he is repeating a narration already given in mostly identical words in the *Homilies*. IGP 66 is in fact a faithful reproduction of the account in Homily 12.7.

The Dialogist gives the authority for the story as Probus, doubtless intending the monk of a Roman monastery mentioned in IV.13.1, who was nephew of Bishop Probus of Rieti. In his homily the real Gregory simply says that he learned the facts from "a religious man". From his own subsequent description it would seem probable that this religious man was Chrysaurius's own son, the monk Maximus, who was an eyewitness of and participant in the deathbed drama in Valeria, and whom Gregory knew personally in his own monastery in Rome (cf. lines 58-63). The Dialogist not only asserts that Probus was Gregory's informant for this episode and that Probus was related to Chrysaurius, but in an earlier chapter (VI.13.1), he also says that the father of Bishop Probus of Rieti was named Maximus. The latter name was the same that, as St Gregory himself recorded in his homily, was borne by the son of Chrysaurius. (cf. Vogüé, *SC* 265, pp. 53, 71, 143.) Here we see the Dialogist's liking for circumstantial details and for the reuse of names taken from genuine sources.

IGP 67: IV.41.1-6. Even after death there can be purgation from light faults. From line 1, "*In evangelio ...*", to line 46-7, "*... obtineat promereatur*". Instead of "*purgatorius ignis credendus*" in lines 14, an original reading such as "*purgatio credenda*" is probable.

After narrating another story of a dying sinner's vision of a devouring dragon—a vision which, like that of Chrysaurius, did not benefit the departing soul but only those who heard of it—the Dialogist suddenly changes the subject and puts into the mouth of Peter the Deacon a cue-question that leads straight on to IGP 67: Should one believe that there is a purgatorial fire after death? The question is framed to link with Gregory's mention, in the passage now to be inserted, of a "fire of future purgation". It also prepares the way for the story, to be told in the following chapter, of the deacon Paschasius who served his purgatory tending the furnaces in the baths at Angulus. A. de Vogüé again comments on the abruptness with which Peter the Deacon's question is introduced, and its lack of connection with either the preceding or the succeeding context (*SC* 251, p. 73).

In IGP 67 Gregory discusses whether before the final Judgement there can be purgation from light faults which were not remitted in this world. First he cites Scriptural texts which shows that the vital time of decision of man's eternal lot is this life (lines 1-12). Then he cites a Gospel text which indicates that there may be remission of guilt in the next world, but he insists that this can only be for peccadilloes—"*de parvis minimisque peccatis*" (lines 12-28).One may observe that the mention of *ignis* in line 14 seems prematurely out of place. It is not improbable that the Dialogist may have interpolated it there in order to make the whole of IGP 67 seem to be about the future purgatorial fire, and thus to be a direct answer to Peter's question as to whether such a purgatorial fire after death exists. If we prescind from the mention of fire in line 14 we see easily that the original bearing of IGP 67 was not to prove the existence of purgatorial *fire*, but to establish the fact that a soul burdened with only light faults could still obtain their remission *ante iudicium*. Up to line 14, and indeed for the greater part of IGP 67 (up to line 28), Gregory is discussing the possibility of other-worldly "remission" or "relaxation" of minor faults, and is not considering the nature of the purifying agent, whether fiery or otherwise. Nothing in the Gospel text (*Matthew* 12.32) that he expressly cites in lines 14-16, to show that there can be remission of light faults both here and hereafter, requires that the purgation of such faults should be by *fire*. It is only as a final step in his discussion that Gregory proceeds (in IV.41.5) to expound the meaning of the Pauline text, *1 Corinthians* 3.11-15, which does mention a stern testing of a man's works, and the possibility of his being safe "yet as if through fire". Gregory comments first that this may be interpreted as referring to the fiery tribulations of this life, and then allows that according to another interpretation it can be taken to refer to a "fire of future purgation" (lines 36-8).

In the earlier phrase "*de quibusdam levibus culpis esse ... purgatorius ignis credendus est*", (lines 14-15), was the original reading simply "*purgatio credenda est*"? When Gregory eventually sums up his whole argument, in lines 44-45, he does use the more general phrase "*de minimis ... purgationis*". The construction, "*de culpis ... purgatio*" seems a more probable original reading than the awkward expression "*de culpis ... purgatorius ig-nis*" in lines 14-15.[18] The emphatic assertion in line 14 that the existence of a purgatorial fire after death "must be believed" is scarcely consonant with the much more guarded and concessive reference to such a belief in the later part of the passage. Did the Dialogist, then, insert the mention of fire in line 14 (anticipating the discussion in lines 30-43) in order to make the whole extract seem pertinent to his purpose and to his subsequent anecdote?

The penultimate paragraph in IGP 67 (IV.41.5) is one of the half dozen otherwise unknown Gregorian passages which are used not only by the Dialogist but also by Tajo of Saragossa. Tajo cites it in his *Libri Sententiarum* V.21. That his citation of the paragraph is independent of the *Dialogues* (and thus that he drew it, directly or indirectly, from the store of Gregorian literary remains in the Lateran *scrinium*) may be indicated by some small but not insignificant variants in the form of the text as he gives it. He has a different and shorter phrase to introduce it: "*Egregius praedicator ait ...*". Moreover after "*quamvis hoc*" (line 36 in IGP 67) he has the additional words, quoted as written by Gregory, "*quod superius protulimus*". (*PL* 80.975B-C). What did those words refer to? They would seem to be an elliptic way of saying: "Although this text can be understood as referring to what we have already discussed above, namely the fire of tribulation applied to us in this life ...". Now in the *Dialogues* there had been no such preceding discussion of purgation by the fire of tribulation in this life, so that it is not surprising that the Dialogist omits the words "*quod superius protulimus*". But such a discussion *is* found in *Moralia* 16.39: "*Quasi aurum ergo quod per ignem transit probantur animae justorum, quibus exustione tribulationis et subtrahuntur vitia et merita augentur ... (Justus) ... igne purgatur ... dum tribulationi traditus, purgari se credidit ...*" This provides a probable argument that the original context of IGP 67 was in the *Moralia*, and that it was excised by Gregory when revising that work. Tajo, and later the Dialogist, would thus have found and used the earlier recension in the *scrinium*.

Notice, too, that Tajo's text is superior to the Dialogist's in the Scriptural citation from *1 Corinthians* 3.11-15. In the *Dialogues* practically the whole of verse 13 is omitted from this citation. As A. de Vogüé suggests, the omission is probably attributable to haplography (in the Vulgate *uniuscuiusque opus* occurs twice, at the beginning and at the end of that verse). That the intervening eleven words were missing from the

---

[18] "*Purgare de* [*crimine*, etc]" is a reputable classical construction, and by extension "*de culpis purgatio*" follows naturally. But "*de culpis purgatorius ignis*" is outlandish and suggests a tampering with Gregory's phraseology.

Dialogues in its archetype can be argued from the lack of any trace of them in the manuscript tradition. Nevertheless the text we have of Tajo does not follow the telescoped form of the Scriptural citation as found in the *Dialogues*, but quotes the Pauline passage in full.

The reference in IGP 67 to a purgatorial fire after death has no close parallel in Gregory's other works. If the passage was in an earlier draft of the *Moralia* and later excised, the reason may have been that Gregory felt some misgivings about it. He may have wondered whether his exposition of *1 Corinthians* 3.13-5, allowing that the text might refer to a purgatorial fire which would remove light sins in the world to come, was somewhat novel, and not clearly based on traditional teaching in the Church. St Augustine, whose theological teaching St Gregory closely follows, does not plainly assert that sins of departed souls are remitted by a *purgatorius ignis* even before the Last Judgement. (cf. *De Civitate Dei* 21.24, and 26; *Enchiridion* 69; Vogüé, *SC* 265, pp. 148-9.) We know from Gregory's letter to Secundinus in the year 593 how scrupulously he retracted and corrected his exposition of a Gospel text which he felt he had expounded in an earlier draft *"sub quadam ambiguitate"* (Epistola IV.17a; Ewald-Hartmann, I, p. 251.)

IGP 68: IV.43.2. Twilight inklings of spiritual realities before the dawn of the world to come. From line 6, *"... quantum praesens"*, to lines 21-2, *"... ante solem videmus"*.

IGP 68 resembles IGPs 41, 42, and 62 in referring to the approaching end of the world—a favourite theme of Gregory's in his *Moralia* and homilies. In a kind of twilight before the dawn of the world to come, the darkness of this declining world is shot through with the gleam of "a certain mingling of spiritual realities" (lines 18-9), which affords an inkling of the coming light. IGP 68, with its mention of "more manifest signs" presaging the world to come, and especially the phrase *"quadam iam rerum spiritalium permixtione"*, gives the Dialogist an opportunity to introduce it into his context with a cue-question from Peter the Deacon, who asks why "in these last days so many matters concerning souls, hitherto hidden, are becoming clear, so that by these open revelations and apparitions it seems that the world to come is bearing down and showing itself to us" (IV.43.1). Thus the Dialogist makes Gregory's reference to the dawn-gleams of awareness of spiritual realities, soon to be revealed in the divine light of the world to come, seem to refer to his own collection of tales "concerning souls"—such as the extraordinary tale he has just told and commented on, about the ghost of the deacon Paschasius whom Bishop Germanus found expiating his fault by penal servitude in the hot baths, and who was liberated from his steamy purgatory by the good bishop's prayers.

Examination of what IGP 68 actually says, however, shows that it does not relate to such anecdotal knowledge "concerning souls". Gregory's point in this excerpt, as elsewhere, is that the nearer this world's darkness draws to its end, the more manifest signs are there of the approach of the next world's light. Our knowledge is still opaque: here our minds and hearts are not open to one another, but there they will be (lines 9-11). Nevertheless, as in the twilight between night and day, so there are many intimations of the spiritual realities of the world to come even in this last age of darkness. The real Gregory is not here talking about an increased incidence of reports of spectral apparitions, as the Dialogist would have us suppose.

IGP 69: IV.44.1-3. On the location of hell. From line 1, *"Hac de re ..."*, to line 26, *"... infernus credatur"*.

The cue-question with which Peter the Deacon introduces IGP 69 (in IV.43.6) refers back to the phrase *locis poenalibus* in IGP 63. IGP 64 is also relevant. IGP 69 belongs to a series of Gregorian speculative passages on hell itself, which included IGPs 60 and 61, and is now resumed, after an intermission of ten chapters devoted mainly to narrations of preternatural clairvoyance by dying persons. (A. de Vogüé remarks on this puzzling interruption of the discussion of "the question of hell": *SC* 251, p. 70). When the discussion is resumed, in Chapters 43 to 47, it is pursued in an almost unbroken succession of Gregorian passages: IGP 69, on the location of hell; IGP 70, on the diverse manners in which hell-fire torments the damned; IGP 71, on the perpetuity of the flames of hell; and IGP 72, on how the soul, although immortal, can be said to suffer lasting death and perdition in hell. The similarity in subject-matter of all these pericopes suggest that they were taken by the Dialogist from a collected sheaf of Gregorian papers which contained unused speculations on hell. (See also IGP 34, which I discussed in my previous chapter.)

Peter's cue-question is inconsequential. It is put in simply because IGP 69 is there to quote. A. de Vogüé remarks that just as the chapters on purgatory had been introduced abruptly by Peter the Deacon without apparent connection with what had preceded, so "it is in a manner just as abrupt that he passes from purgatory to the questions concerning hell" (*SC* 251, p. 73). IGP 69 may well be one of the passages which Gregory suppressed from his writings out of a desire, to quote Étaix's words again, "to correct certain assertions which seemed to be inadequate or ambiguous". He begins by saying: "In this matter I do not dare to make a rash pronouncement" (lines 1-2). The interpretation he then gives of the meaning of the Scriptural expression *infernus inferior* is (as Vogüé points out, *SC* 265, p. 157) notably different from that which he gives in

Moralia 13.49. Did he omit IGP 69 from his published works because he preferred the interpretation he had adopted in that passage of the *Moralia*?

We find that IGP 69 is another of the handful of Gregorian passages that are common to the *Dialogues* and to the *Libri Sententiarum* of Tajo of Saragossa (V.20; *PL* 80.975). Tajo's text yields a difference of word order that may provide a further pointer to his independence from the *Dialogues*. Whereas in giving the comment on the *Apocalypse* text the Dialogist places the words "*dignus inventus est*" (lines 21-2) after "*nullus subtus terra*", Tajo places them earlier, after the opening words of the sentence, "*nullus in coelo*", and he follows them with the words "*aperire librum*", missing in the *Dialogues*. Tajo's order seems to be the better reading: it reflects more closely the wording of *Apocalypse* 5.3, and it allows the explanatory clause "*quia neque animae corpore exutae*" to follow on smoothly after "*nullus subtus terra*", without being separated from its antecedent by the displaced "*dignus inventus est*" as in the Dialogist's reading.

IGP 70: IV.45.2. The same hell-fire afflicts the damned in different manners. From line 5, "*Unus quidem ...*", to line 14, "*... dissimiliter exurat*".

Once again Peter's cue-question for IGP 70, picking out the phrase "*unus est gehennae ignis*" in line 5, makes no attempt to present a logical sequence in the dialogue. The author has available a string of Gregorian excerpts about the nature of hell, so he brings them in one by one in a woodenly catechetical fashion. The argument of IGP 70 is closely paralleled in *Moralia* 9.98, which presents the same analogy between the one fire of hell which afflicts sinners differently according to their diverse demerits, and the one sun which heats different bodies differently according to their diverse constitution. IGP 70 makes one think of IGP 63, which also links with *Moralia* 9.98.

IGP 71: IV.46.1-9. On the eternity of punishment in hell. From line 4, "*... sicut finis ...*", to line 72-3, "*... subtilitate discordat*". Instead of "*Scire velim*", another linking expression must be supposed in line 18.

The next catechetical question from Peter the Deacon (Chapter 46, lines 1-2) introduces one of the most intriguing of all the IGPs. It takes us into the Dialogist's workshop, so to speak. In IGP 71 we have a sustained sequence of dialogue, with question and answer closely integrated in a unitary expression of doctrine, in which St Gregory shows his awareness of St Augustine's previous treatment of the same questions. What makes IGP 71 of peculiar interest in our investigation is the fact that this long dialogistic exchange faithfully reproduces a dialogue placed by Gregory himself in *Moralia* 34.35-8, in which he answers objections put by "Origenists" against the dogma of the eternity of hell. In IGP 71 the very same exchanges are found as in *Moralia* 34.35-68, with the same arguments, in the same order, and in many places in exactly identical words. What the Dialogist has done is to insert the name of Peter the Deacon wherever in the *Moralia* Gregory introduces the objections of the Origenists with the phrase, *"At inquiunt"*—"But they say". The Gregory of the *Dialogues* gives no hint that IGP 71 has already appeared in the *Moralia*, nor that the acute objections which are now put into the mouth of Peter the Deacon were there originally attributed to those Origenists. The verbal correspondence between *Moralia* 34.35-8 and IGP 71 is so extensive and so detailed that there can be no doubt that the two texts are variant presentations of the same sequence of dialogue. Confronted with this duplication, commentators (eg. Vogüé, *SC* 265, p. 161) conclude that when Gregory came to write the *Dialogues* he simply reproduced the exchanges that he had previously composed for the *Moralia*, in the first section abridging and modifying that text, in the second section reproducing it in virtually identical wording.

But has IGP 71 been directly culled from the text of *Moralia* 34 as we know it? It is indeed possible that the Dialogist transcribed it straight from that text, abridging it and retouching it as he did so. However, I think it more likely that IGP 71 reflects a slightly variant draft of the sequence of dialogue, which the Dialogist may have found apart in the *scrinium*. For instance, after the quotation from *Matthew* 25.46, Gregory's comment in *Moralia* 34.35 is *"si igitur hoc verum non est quod minatus est, neque illud verum est quod promisit"*; whereas in IGP 71, lines 7-8, his comment is equivalent in sense but inverted in construction: *"quia verum est quod promisit, falsum procul dubio non erit quod minatus est Deus"*. There are some other, relatively minor but interesting variants in the first part of IGP 71 which cannot easily be explained on the hypothesis that its immediate archetype was the text of *Moralia* 34.35-8 that we now possess. Another difference is that in lines 51-2, IGP 71 supplies the missing words *"ad cognoscendam veritatem"* in the quotation from *2 Timothy* 2.25—words which, as Vogüé notes (*SC* 265, p. 165) were omitted both in the *Moralia* text and in the passage in Augustine's *De Civitate Dei* which Gregory followed very closely.

The interesting sequence of dialogue in *Moralia* 34.35-8 was carefully composed by Gregory with the text of Augustine before him, from which he made fairly extensive verbatim borrowings. This dialogue may even have been first intended for another purpose. It has the character of a special *excursus* in the *Moralia*, as Gregory himself remarks. At the end of his discussion of the Origenists' objections, he says that he will now "return to the order of exposition which we put aside." The variant features that appear from comparison of IGP 71 with the *Moralia* text can be explained, I submit, by supposing that these two slightly different forms of the dialogue represent variant drafts or transcripts of this Gregorian excursus.

IGP 72: IV.47.1-2. How the damned soul, although immortal, suffers perpetual death. From line 3, "... *quomodo anima immortalis* ...", to line 17, "... *finis infinitus*".

IGP 72, the last of the group of Gregorian excerpts on theological questions concerning hell, is introduced by Peter the Deacon with an abruptness that contrasts with the skilful flow of the genuine Gregorian dialogue within IGP 71. There are resemblances between IGP 72 and statements about the unending death of the damned soul in *Moralia* 4.5 and 15.21.

IGP 73: IV.48 and 49.1. On the fear of death in the just. IGP 73a runs from Chapter 48, lines 1-2, "... *plerumque de culpis* ...", to line 3, "... *iustorum purgat,* ..."; IGP 73b runs from Chapter 49, line 1, "*Nonnumquam vero* ...", to line 3, "... *minime pertimescant*".

IGPs 73a and 73b were probably one undivided fragment, since they closely match the twofold lesson about the fear of death in the just that is contained in a similarly balanced sentence in *Moralia* 24.34. For many of the just, the experience of dread in dying purges them from light sins; others, however, do not suffer deathbed trepidation because God has fortified their souls beforehand by consoling revelations. In the parallel passage in the *Moralia* Gregory explains that the revelatory consolation accorded to those just souls, in order to fortify them for death, takes the form of "a certain contemplation of their inward reward". (cf. IGP 51.)

The Dialogist has separated IGP 73a from 73b in order to illustrate the former by the insertion of a brief tale about a holy man, said to have been well known to Gregory and Peter, who feared greatly while dying but who appeared later to his disciples to announce his honourable reception into heaven. IGP 73b is then illustrated by three subsequent stories of pious monks who were fortified for death by premonitory visions. The first of these stories (in IV.49.2-3) may be of Gregorian origin—perhaps an otherwise unpublished item from a collection of *exempla* which, as Pfeilschifter surmises, may have been kept by Gregory for use in his sermons. This narration is sober and unsensational, like those in Gregory's homilies to the people, and lacks the fantastic elements and prodigious phenomena usual in the Dialogist's own tales. Moreover it seems to reflect Gregory's own style, particularly in §2. The account of how the monk Antonius, filled with trepidation, was divinely reassured that his sins were forgiven has resemblances to the story told by the pope in his *Homilies on the Gospels* 34.18, about the monk Victorinus-Aemilianus, who, sore afraid at the thought of death and his past sin, was likewise reassured by a heavenly voice.

IGP 74: IV.50.2-6. On the discernment of dreams. From line 3, *"Sciendum ..."*, to line 45, *"... falsitate laqueare"*. Omit *"Petre"* in line 3.

IGP 74 is a notable passage of Gregory's pastoral wisdom, expounded with his typical felicity of phrase and ordered sequence of thought. As we shall see, its original setting was in the *Moralia*. The way it is introduced by a cue-question from Peter the Deacon is once more unskilful. The Dialogist has just recounted three stories in which "nocturnal visions" played a part. The same expression *"nocturna visio"* occurs in each of them (Chapter 49, lines 12, 24, 33-4, 38-9). To make IGP 74 seem consequential to this triad of stories, Peter the Deacon is immediately made to ask "whether what is shown in nocturnal visions ought to be given observance". (Chapter 50, lines 1-2; the *observari* in Peter's question picks up the *observetis* in line 15 of IGP 74). In the context it is a somewhat strange question, in view of the fact that his master has just recounted those three episodes in which nocturnal visions clearly brought true revelations from heavenly sources. Indeed he has affirmed, in the story of the monk Merulus, who saw in a vision a crown descending on his head from heaven, that it became "manifest that what he saw in a nocturnal vision was true" (IV.49.5).

IGP 74 is concerned with the more general question of discernment between different kinds of dreams, and with the various manners in which *imagines somniorum* affect the mind. This passage has special importance in our discussion of the diverse components of the *Dialogues* and of the re-editing of Gregorian materials in the early period. It sets an intriguing problem of textual inter-relationships. We find that it has almost verbatim correspondence with one part of a longer passage in the *Moralia* (8.42-3; *CCL* 143, pp. 413-5; *PL* 75.827-8), with the exception of a brief but significant pericope (lines 38-45) found in the *Dialogues* but lacking in the *Moralia*. Moreover that extra pericope is also found in the Gregorian anthology of Tajo of Saragossa (*Libri Sententiarum* IV.7; *PL* 80.919-20), which contains a fuller extract from the original *Moralia* passage than does the *Dialogues*.

In Chapter 6, when discussing the textual parallels between the *Dialogues* and the *Libri Sententiarum* of Tajo, I noted that defenders of the authenticity of the *Dialogues* have assumed that Tajo was quoting from that work. Study of IGP 74 provides a significant test of this assumption, as well as throwing further light on the Dialogist's literary artifices. To make clearer the complex pattern of textual relationships, I reproduce below a series of connected sections which together give Gregory's teaching on the discernment of dreams. Their original context is to be found in the *Moralia*, 8.42-3, which is the second half of a commentary on the text of *Job* 7.13-14: "If I say: my bed shall comfort me, and I shall be relieved speaking with myself on my couch: Thou shalt frighten me with dreams and terrify me with visions". Gregory has just given (in *Moralia* 8.41) a "moral" exegesis of this text, interpreting it as referring to the terrifying awareness of divine justice that comes to the self-searching soul. Then, in 8.42, he goes on to take account of the text *iuxta literam*, which leads him into a didactic excursus on the discernment of dream images.

I have labelled this series of sections, giving the Gregorian teaching on dreams, by the letters U, V, W, X, Y and Z. Although, as I think will be evident, they originally formed one consecutive argument, they are nowhere else—in any extant manuscript or edition—to be found in this complete sequence as I give it below. The introductory Section U is a contextual link in *Moralia*, but is abbreviated in Tajo and *Dialogues*. Sections V, W, Y and Z (but not X) appear in the *Moralia*. Sections V, W, X and Y appear in Tajo's anthology. Sections V, W, and X appear in the *Dialogues*. Thus Section X appears *only* in Tajo and the *Dialogues*, not in the transmitted text of the *Moralia*. It is the pericope which is our special concern here, and which is alleged to show the dependence of Tajo on the *Dialogues*. Section Z, which I have added for completeness, appears only in *Moralia* and neither in Tajo nor in the *Dialogues*. In the following sequence I indicate the occasional variants between the three texts, which are significant for judgement on their mutual interdependence.

On the Discernment of Dreams

Section U

(*Moralia*): *Ne quis vero haec studeat iuxta literam perscrutari, exquirendum magnopere est quot modis tangant animum imagines somniorum.*

(Tajo and *Dialogues*): *Sciendum est*[19] *quia sex modis tangunt animam imagines somniorum.*

Section V: (found in *Moralia*, Tajo and *Dialogues*)

Aliquando namque somnia ventris plenitudine, vel inanitate, aliquando vero illusione, aliquando cogitatione simul et illusione, aliquando revelatione, aliquando

---

[19] The Dialogist here interpolates "*Petre*".

autem cogitatione simul et revelatione generantur. Sed duo quae prima diximus omnes experimento cognoscimus; subiuncta autem quattuor in sacrae Scripturae paginis invenimus ... [There follow several Scriptural citations to illustrate these other four manners, taken from *Ecclesiasticus* 34.7; *Leviticus* 19.26; *Ecclesiastes* 5.2; *Genesis* 37.5-10; *Matthew* 2.13; *Daniel* 2.29, 31. In variant wording of these Scriptural citations Tajo agrees with *Moralia* against *Dialogues*, as I shall point out in detail later.]

Section W: (found in *Moralia*, Tajo and *Dialogues*)

Sed nimirum[20] cum somnia tot rerum qualitatibus alternent, tanto eis credi difficilius debet, quanto et ex quo impulsu veniant, facilius non elucet.

Section X: (found in Tajo and *Dialogues*, but lacking in all known texts of
Moralia).

Sancti[21] viri inter illusiones atque revelationes, ipsas visionum voces aut imagines quodam intimo sapore discernunt, ut sciant vel quid a bono spiritu percipiant, vel quid ab illusore[22] patiantur. Si erga somnia[23] mens cauta non fuerit, per deceptorem spiritum multis se vanitatibus immergit, qui nonnunquam solet multa vera praedicere, ut ad extremum valeat animum ex una aliqua falsitate laqueare.

Section Y: (found in Tajo and *Moralia*, not in the *Dialogues*)

Saepe namque[24] malignus spiritus his quos amore vitae praesentis vigilantes intercipit[25], prospera etiam dormientibus promittit. Et quos formidare adversa considerat, eis haec durius somnii imaginibus intentat, quatenus indiscretam mentem diversa qualitate afficiat eamque aut spe sublevans, aut deprimens timore, confundat. Saepe autem[26] etiam sanctorum corda afficere somniis nititur, ut ab intentione cogitationis solidae, ad tempus saltem momentumque deriventur, quamvis[27] ipsi protinus animum ab illusionis imaginatione discutiant. Sed hostis insidians quo eos vigilantes minime superat, eo dormientes gravius impugnat. Quem tamen haec[28] maligne agere[29] superna dispensatio benigne permittit, ne in electorum cordibus ipse saltem a passionis praemio somnus vacet.

---

[20] These two words, on which *Moralia* and *Dialogues* agree, are lacking in Tajo. In reproducing his excerpts Tajo often omits conjunctions at the beginning of sentences.

[21] *Dialogues* has "*autem*" after "*Sancti*".

[22] Vogüé's text of the *Dialogues* has "*illusione*" here. The personal "*illusore*" seems the more probable original reading in the context, since the contrast is with the activity of a "*bonus spiritus*" (IGP 74, lines 41), and Gregory goes straight on to speak of the need for wariness against the "*deceptorem spiritum*" (line 43).

[23] *Dialogues* has "*Nam*" before "*si*", and *haec* instead of *somnia*.

[24] "*namque*" is in *Moralia*, not in Tajo.

[25] A variant in many Tajo MSS is "*inspicit*".

[26] Instead of "*autem*" Tajo has here "*antiquus hostis*".

[27] Tajo has "*quamquam*".

[28] Instead of "*Quem tamen haec*" Tajo has "*Humani generis hostem*".

[29] Tajo adds here "*etiam per somnia*".

Section Z: (found only in Moralia, and neither in *Dialogues* nor in Tajo)

Bene ergo rectori omnium dicitur: "Si dixero: Consolabitur me lectulus meus et relevabor loquens mecum in stratu meo, terrebis me per somnia et per visiones horrore concuties", quia nimirum Deus mirabiliter cuncta dispensat, et ipse facit quod malignus spiritus injuste facere appetit, qui hoc fieri nonnisi juste permittit. Sed quia iustorum vita et per vigilias temptatione quatitur, et per somnium illusione fatigatur, foris corruptionis suae molestias tolerat, intus apud semetipsam graviter illicitas cogitationes portat, quid est quod faciat, ut pedem cordis a tot scandalorum laqueis evellat?

On the usual hypothesis of the Gregorian authorship of the *Dialogues*, the conclusion that would follow from comparison of the foregoing passages—it is the one that is implied by the Maurist editors of Gregory's works—is as follows. When Gregory came to write Chapter 50 of Book IV of the *Dialogues*, he copied, modified and added to the first part of a passage he had written in *Moralia* 8.42. After a new and abbreviated introductory phrase (Section U), he reproduced Sections V and W from the *Moralia*. In so doing he changed the original form of his quotation from *Ecclesiasticus* 34.7 in order to make the wording conform to the Vulgate, thus (as A. de Vogüé puts it, *SC* 265, p. 173) "re-establishing the exact form of the Scriptural text". Then—because Section X is found in the *Dialogues* and not in the *Moralia*—it is supposed that he must have decided to make a new significant addition to his text by adding those two sentences about the need for discernment between the good and evil spirits.[30] After making this addition, he omitted in the *Dialogues* all the rest of the sequence (Y and Z) as it appears in the *Moralia*. Accordingly (so it is assumed) when Tajo came to compile his *Libri Sententiarum* he reproduced Section U from the *Dialogues*, and Sections V and W either from the *Dialogues* or from the *Moralia*. Then from the *Dialogues* he copied Section X, which he would have found only there; and finally he turned back to the *Moralia* to copy Section Y, which he could only find there since it is not in the *Dialogues*. It is time to criticize this contorted and implausible reconstruction.

A closer study of Section X reveals that the argument based on it to prove that Tajo was dependent on the *Dialogues* is not probative. First it must be noted that the thought in it is integral with the preceding Sections V and W, since the words in X, *"inter illusiones atque revelationes"* refer back naturally to the previous discussion in V—e.g. *"aliquando vero illusione ... aliquando vero revelatione"*. This point alone, of course, is not

---

[30] *"Les considérations suivantes sur le discernement sont originales"*, observes A. de Vogüé *loc. cit.*

enough to rule out the possibility that Gregory added X as a harmonious afterthought when he came to compile the *Dialogues*. But when we consider the preceding sentence in W and the first in Y (sentences which are in immediate sequence in the traditional text of the *Moralia*), we realize that the insertion of X is not only in harmony with the rest of the passage but is virtually required for its logical connection. It supplies a link between W and Y, without which there is a hiatus in the reasoning—a hiatus which actually exists in the received text of the *Moralia*.

The point is worth explaining more fully. The sentence in W which immediately precedes X is to the effect that the greater the uncertainties in discerning from which impulse dreams come, the greater should be our hesitation in giving credence to them. The logical development of the discussion would lead us to expect it to follow with a reference to the discernment between those dreams which come from a trustworthy origin and those which do not. The first sentence in Y, which immediately follows W in the received text of the *Moralia*, begins, "*Saepe* namque *malignus spiritus* ...''; but the "*namque*" is not apt here. An antithesis is in fact presented, but it is not the antithesis we should expect from W, namely between the impulse of the good spirit and that of the evil, but between two diverse tactics of the evil spirit—the first promising good fortune to the sanguine and the second threatening woes to the timorous. Evidently between these two there is nothing to choose in the matter of giving them credence, or in discerning "*ex quo impulsu veniant*", since they both proceed from the same evil spirit.

But when we consider Section X, which appears both in Tajo and in the *Dialogues* but not in the *Moralia*, we see at once that it is the missing link needed to make the thought consequential. The first sentence of X, "*Sancti viri ...*", does indeed continue from Section W the theme of the discernment between the prompting of good and evil spirits, saying how holy men have a special gift for it. The second sentence, "*Si erga somnia ...*", goes on to warn, on the other hand, that if the mind is not discriminating in its attitude towards dreams it can be deluded by the evil spirit, who by mixing one falsehood with many true predictions snares the soul in the end. From this point the *Saepe namque* of the succeeding sentence of the *Moralia* (the first in Y) marks a logical progression. Gregory goes on in this sentence to observe that the deceiver often uses the present inclinations of the worldly-minded to ensnare them by one or other of alternative devices. In Section Y (which is given by Tajo as well as by *Moralia* but not by *Dialogues*) Gregory completes the argument by observing that often the evil spirit tries through temptations in dreams to trouble, at least momentarily, the minds of saintly persons.

The conclusion from all this is that Section X formed part of what Gregory originally wrote in the *Moralia*, and that it somehow dropped out of the received text transmitted to posterity. The fact that Tajo quotes it, therefore, is not proof that he was quoting from the *Dialogues*. Rather, as he goes straight on to give Section Y, which is in the *Moralia* and not in the *Dialogues*, one would naturally suppose that he was drawing from a single source, using a full original text of the *Moralia* which included the "lost" passage.

When setting out Section V above, I noted that all the three writings there add Gregory's Scriptural citations to illustrate the last four of his six categories of dreams, but for economy of space I did not reproduce those citations. Comparison of certain textual variants between the three writings, in their wording of those Scriptural references, reveals interesting points of difference. In the quotation from *Ecclesiasticus* 34.7, *Moralia* and Tajo agree in the wording, "*Multos errare fecerunt somnia, et illusiones vanae*"; while *Dialogues* has "*Multos* enim *errare fecerunt somnia, et exciderunt sperantes in illis.*" Although *Dialogues* thus conforms to the Vulgate (cf. Vogüé, *ibid.* p. 173), *Moralia* and Tajo, agreeing against *Dialogues*, evidently present the original Gregorian reading, since *illusiones* is presupposed by *illusionem* in the first part of the sentence. The "corrected" reading in the *Dialogues* suggests later origin. This discordance of Tajo from *Dialogues* and his agreement with the *Moralia* original is another indication of his non-dependence on *Dialogues*. A further such indication follows shortly afterwards. In referring to the author of *Ecclesiastes* (IGP 74, line 18), *Dialogues* has "*vir sapiens*"; whereas Tajo agrees with *Moralia* against *Dialogues* with the reading "*Salomon*". (In IGP 45b, line 1, Gregory also refers to the author of *Ecclesiastes* as Salomon.)[31]

There remains the interesting point that although Tajo agrees with *Moralia* against *Dialogues* in significant particulars, both Tajo and the Dialogist agree against *Moralia* in the variant introductory phrase in Section U, and lack the longer introductory sentence in the *Moralia* which presupposes the fuller context of Gregory's commentary on *Job* 7.13. One conjecture to explain this anomaly could be that Gregory's summary on the six kinds of dream-influence was originally composed separately from the context of *Moralia* 8.42 in which we now find it, where it has the character of a self-contained appendix. In that earlier

---

[31] The agreement of Tajo, and of the traditional text of the *Moralia* in reading *adimplendum* against the reading *et implendum* in IGP 74, line 32, and likewise the agreement of Tajo and *Dialogues* against *Moralia* editions in prefacing the *Daniel* citation with "*dicens*", are not significant. As A. de Vogüé notes, the *CCL* critical edition of the *Moralia* restores both *et implendum* and *dicens* as the best reading.

form it may well have begun with the phrase, "*Sciendum est quia sex modis tangunt ...*": The way it is introduced in the *Moralia*, with its query, "*quot modis tangant*", may reflect such an explicit numerical phrase in an original draft. Moreover the reference in Section V to *duo prima* and *subiuncta quattuor* also suggests that the existing *Moralia* text may hark back to a pristine draft which had made explicit mention of the number *sex*. Variant redactions of the passage may have remained in the *scrinium*, which would explain how Tajo, though independent of the Dialogist and presenting a more original text than his, could yet agree with him in the reading of Section U.

IGP 74, as used by the Dialogist, truncates Gregory's full argument which Tajo reproduces more completely in Section Y. In the final recapitulation of the whole discussion in the *Moralia* (Section Z) Gregory repeats the text from *Job* 7.13-4 which had been the starting-point of that discussion. He also alludes implicitly to what he has said in 8.41 and 8.42. We see a reason for the Dialogist's omission of the concluding paragraphs of the *Moralia* argument. He wished to cap the last words of his truncated excerpt, referring to the devil's final snares, (IGP 74, lines 44-5), with his own cautionary anecdote in IV.51 about "one of ours" who at his life's end was certainly ensnared by the devil. This man was promised long life in a dream, amassed ample provision for it, but died suddenly.

IGP 75: IV.52 and 55.5. On burial in church. IGP 75a runs from Chapter 52, line 5, "*Quos gravia ...*", to lines 11-12, "*... in ecclessiis ponuntur*". IGP 75b runs from Chapter 55, lines 23, "*... si in sacro*", to lines 25-6, "*... temeritatis accuset*".

Gregory's succinct explanation in IGP 75 (following the teaching of Augustine; cf. Vogüé, *SC* 265, p. 177) is intended to remove any superstitious belief about the value of being buried in a church. The sight of a tomb there encourages relatives to pray for the deceased; but if wicked persons presume to procure such burial for themselves their presumption brings more severe judgement upon them. IGP 75b, eloquently reinforcing the last sentence of IGP 75a, clearly belongs immediately after it in the same single lesson. The Dialogist, however, has divided the Gregorian excerpt into two parts, widely separated by three cautionary tales, describing dreadful sanctions which followed the burial of wicked men in church. When he eventually puts in IGP 75b to cap those three tales, he introduces it by repeating the same words "*quos peccata gravia deprimunt*" which are in the final sentence of IGP 75a, and which in the original undivided passage would have needed no repetition.

IGP 76: IV.58.1. The eucharistic devotion of Bishop Cassius. From line 3, "*Cassius, Narniensis* ...", to line 12, "*... e corpore exivit*".

From Chapter 57 onwards the concluding part of Book IV is concerned with the offering of the Mass and its salutary effects. It is presented as an extended response to a question put by Peter the Deacon in IV.57.1. After the preceding tales, showing how burial in church did no good to wicked men, Peter now asks: "What then can there be that may avail to benefit the souls of the dead?" The remaining chapters of the book, showing the efficacy of the Mass, are presented as the answer. In Chapters 57-59 a number of supernatural happenings are related to illustrate that efficacy. The first two stories (IV.57.1-16) tell of liberation of deceased souls from torrid prisons by eucharistic oblation made for them. Then follow IGPs 76 and 77, which retell in abbreviated form two edifying *exempla* taken from the 37th of Gregory's *Homilies on the Gospels*. IGP 76, the eighth of the nine "narrative IGPs", is a condensed and impoverished version of the story of Bishop Cassius of Narni related by Gregory in that homily, with some phrases reproduced verbatim.

This insertion does not fit well into the Dialogist's context. He is adducing examples to show how the Mass-oblation benefits the souls of the dead; but in the case of Cassius—as the real Gregory explains at length in his narration in *Homilies on the Gospels* 37.9—it was the bishop's piety *before* his death (shown in his devout offering of Mass, in his alms and in his tears of compunction) that merited for him a blessed death in union with Christ. The Dialogist no doubt decided to include IGP 76 in this part of Book IV because it made mention of the eucharistic oblation, and also of a vision bringing a divine message. But it is not really in place here, in his series of miracle-stories attesting how the Mass benefited *departed* souls, since—as he acknowledges in IV.58, lines 1-2—it concerns *facta viventium*, not *verba mortuorum*. He would have done better to insert it after the last paragraph in IGP 78b, with which, as we shall see, it has verbal assonance and with which it may have been originally associated.

IGP 77: IV.59.1. Temporary relief for a chained captive through the Mass-oblation. From line 1, "*... audivimus quemdam*", to line 7, "*... sacrificium recognovit, ...*".

IGP 77, the last of the nine "narrative IGPs" in the *Dialogues*, may be called a "Gregorian passage" in a looser sense, since it is a very abbreviated paraphrase of a passage found in Gregory's *Homilies on the Gospels* 37.8. There he relates a story for which he gives no more precise authority than "*fertur*"—"it is said"—and which he implies is commonly known. It is about a captive in a far land, whose wife, thinking him to

be dead, procured the offering of the eucharistic sacrifice for him on certain days. On those very days, as was later realized when he returned
home, his chains fell off. When Gregory originally recalled in his sermon
this well-known *exemplum*, he used it for an *a fortiori* argument: if the
sacred oblation could thus temporarily loosen those corporeal chains,
how much more must it avail to loosen "in us" the shackles of the heart
(*PL* 76.1279).

Although this story has no reference to the lot of souls after death, the
Dialogist reuses it in his pages because it tells of a prodigy connected with
the Mass-oblation. He omits, however, the spiritual moral that Gregory
drew from it for the hearers of his sermon. As in the case of IGP 76, we
see that IGP 77 likewise is not aptly included in a discussion intended to
show, in response to Peter's initial question, how the Mass-oblation
"benefits the souls of the dead". Both IGP 77 and the following tale in
IV.59.2-5, about the storm-tossed sailor Varaca, provide examples, not
of succour obtained through the sacred oblation for the dead, but of temporal boons obtained for the living—what in mediaeval England would
come to be called "the meeds of the Mass".[32]

IGP 78: IV.59.6, 60.1-3 and 61.1. On the efficacy and awe-inspiring
nature of the mystical sacrifice of Christ. IGP 78a runs from Chapter 59,
line 55, "... *si insolubiles culpae* ...", to Chapter 60, line 8, "... *hostias im-
molare*". IGP 78b runs from Chapter 60, line 9, "*Haec namque* ...", to
Chapter 61, line 5, "... *hostiam fecerit*".

The Dialogist himself is aware that in telling stories about temporal
boons obtained for the living through the liturgical oblation he had
strayed from his discussion of succour for the souls of the dead. He
claimed at the beginning of Chapter 58 that narration of such *facta viventium* would serve to strengthen credence in the *verba mortuorum*—namely,
those of the spectral bath-attendant of Aquae Tauri and of the monk
Justus who spoke in a posthumous vision to his brother Copiosus. The
logic of this claim is not apparent. At the end of Chapter 59 he makes
another attempt to make the *facta viventium* appear more relevant to his
discourse on the souls of the dead. This he does by means of the curious
remark in lines 53-5 which serve to introduce IGP 78a.

The phrasing of these lines is cumbrous[33] and the argument odd. The
Gregory of the *Dialogues* here asserts his belief that the reason for the

---

[32] Cf. my *Eucharistic Sacrifice and the Reformation*, pp. 60-1. The two Gregorian *exempla*
reproduced in IGPs 76 and 77 were models on which were based those later questionable
assurances about the temporal advantages of attendance at Mass. A very similar story
to that resumed in IGP 77 was related by Leontius of Neapolis (cf. Vogüé *SC* 265, p.
197, and my Chapter 6 above, pp. 109-10).

[33] The scribes were puzzled by it, as the textual variants show.

bestowal through the Mass-oblation of those miraculous boons on "living persons who were unaware of what was being done"—namely the chained captive, the sailor Varaca and those associated with them—was "to show all who were active in those events while unaware of what was being done" that the sacred rite was beneficial even to the dead, if their faults were not unforgivable. One fails to see how this specific lesson could be conveyed to those persons by the events that befell the captive and the sailor. Such a lame sequence of thought can hardly be attributed to the real Gregory. The puzzling inconsequence of the last paragraph of Chapter 59 is explicable, however, once it is recognized that, while lines 55-60 are genuinely Gregorian, lines 53-5 ("*Idcirco ... ostendatur*") are not. The Dialogist's emphatic assertion in those lines, aimed at making IGP 78a seem to be a relevant sequel to his two preceding stories in Chapter 59, is clumsy and unsuccessful.

IGP 78 marks the beginning of the extended series of theological passages about the eucharistic sacrifice which forms a splendid conclusion to the whole book of the *Dialogues*. From "*... si insolubiles*" in line 55 of Chapter 59, to the concluding word of Chapter 62 all is henceforward unmistakably the authentic writing and doctrine of St Gregory the Great. IGPs 78, 79 and 80 are all evidently related to one another, perhaps representing separate parts of an original Gregorian discourse, the order of which may have been rearranged.

IGP 78a is a self-contained passage on the propitiatory efficacy of the Mass-oblation to benefit even the deceased who are in other-worldly bondage, but whose sins are not grave. Nevertheless, Gregory insists, a safer way is not to rely on the offering of Masses by others after one's death, but so to live now that one needs no such posthumous liberation. IGP 78b is also a self-standing passage of theological doctrine, not specifically about the efficacy of the Mass-offering for the dead, but about the awe-inspiring nature of Christ's mystical sacrifice in itself and about its salvific effect for the living. Although the bearing of IGP 78b differs from that of IGP 78a, it is quite likely that in the original Gregorian source they were consecutive. A similar progression of ideas, with the use of similar expressions, is found in a homily of Gregory's now to be discussed.

IGP 78b became a classical text for the later Catholic theology of the Mass, and (together with a parallel passage in the 37th Gospel homily) it can rightly be regarded as one of the most influential theological statements in the whole of the corpus of Gregorian writings.[34] The passage is undoubtedly by Gregory himself. It has the unmistakable

---

[34] See my *Eucharistic Sacrifice and the Reformation*, pp. 405, 520, etc.

Gregorian savour, with its lofty spiritual thought, its harmonious rhythm, its use of favourite words and phrases, and its close parallelism with similar sentiments in Gregory's writings.

The tone of homiletic earnestness and personal exhortation in the concluding Gregorian passages of Book IV suggests that their original source may have been a sermon to the people which the pope omitted from his published collection of *Homilies*. A possible reason for such omission of these noble passages of pastoral theology could have been their resemblance to passages in another sermon which Gregory did publish, the 37th of his *Homilies on the Gospels*. IGP 78b is very similar—even with identical phrasing—to a section of that homily (37.7). In both cases there is the same explanation of the theology of the eucharistic sacrifice: by renewing the offering of the salvific passion of the only-begotten Son of God, who though now deathless is there mystically immolated, the sacred rite of the altar calls down divine forgiveness, and saves souls from eternal death.

It was in Homily 37 that Gregory recounted the *exemplum* of Bishop Cassius of Narni, which, as we have seen, the Dialogist has already borrowed (IGP 76). In that homily he extolled the bishop's piety in this particular respect, that when offering the sacred sacrifice Cassius also offered himself as a victim, with tears, alms and contrition of heart. Just as the theological content and forms of expression in IGP 78b closely resemble a parallel doctrinal passage in *Homily* 37, so the wording of the moral drawn in the concluding paragraph of IGP 78b (Chapter 61, lines 1-5), resembles Gregory's description in that homily of Bishop Cassius's eucharistic piety. Of Cassius Gregory says in his homily "*semetipsum cum magna cordis contritione mactabat*"; this virtue of which the bishop was a model is also the theme of Gregory's exhortation in IGP 78b, "*ut ... nosmetipsos Deo in cordis contritione mactemus*". Cassius, devoted to the oblation of the altar and imitating the mystery that he celebrated, was conformed to Christ the victim and so died a blessed death; in IGP 78b (the same lesson is repeated in IGP 80b) Gregory teaches that we must "imitate what we do", and that the divine Lord will then be a sacrificial victim to God for us when we ourselves become sacrificial victims to God.

The *exemplum* of Bishop Cassius is thus seen to be a very apt illustration for the doctrine of IGP 78b (and IGP 80), where the very words used in the Cassius passage of *Homily* 37 are picked up. It is not improbable that in its original context Gregory did illustrate the doctrine of IGP 78b by reference to the edifying example of Bishop Cassius; although the Dialogist, for the needs of his narrative, has separated the Cassius *exemplum* from its doctrinal antecedent and placed it earlier, as IGP 76. The number of sermons that Gregory preached to the people of Rome was doubtless greater than the 40 which he published in collected form. Moreover, he reused his *exempla* (e.g. in *Homilies on the Gospels* 38.16 and 19.7). As well as in Homily 37.9, did he use the edifying example of Cassius in another sermon, from the surviving text of which four of the concluding IGPs of *Dialogues* IV were taken? It is a possible hypothesis, which would explain the affinities between these concluding IGPs and *Homily* 37. The overlap between the two similar sermons would account for the suppression of one of them in Gregory's edited collection of Gospel homilies.

IGP 79: IV.61.2. On keeping the mind vigilant after times of prayer. From line 6, "*Sed studendum ...*", to line 15, "*... qoud poposcit*".

Although IGP 79 is presented as a rider to what has just been said in IGP 78 about the liturgical sacrifice, I think it much more likely that it originally came from another context. While it contains mention of compunction and tears, which could refer back to remarks in IGP 78, it has no specific reference to the eucharistic oblation, which has been the theme of IGPs 76, 77 and 78, and which will be subsequently resumed in IGP 80. Gregory's lesson in IGP 79 is the need for vigilance of mind "after times of prayer" in general, lest one should slip back into vain worldly gaiety "through carelessness of unbridled thought". The passage is paralleled by two other Gregorian texts: *Moralia* 33.43 and *Homilies on Ezekiel* I.11.27. In both these instances, as in IGP 79, there is mention of compunction and tears, and Gregory uses the same Scriptural example of Hannah's seriousness, as given in the Vulgate translation of *1 Samuel* 1.18. In neither of those other two parallel texts does the warning of the need for vigilance after prayer refer to liturgical prayer during the celebration of the Mass-oblation. In *Moralia* 33.43 the phrase "*post orationis tempora*", the very same as in IGP 79, clearly refers to times of private petitionary prayer.

It may well be that IGP 79 was a fragment excised by Gregory as a "doublet" during the process of editing the *Moralia*. Finding the unused fragment in the Lateran *scrinium*, the Dialogist may have inserted it at this point because the mention it makes of compunction and tears, and of "times of prayer", could seem to refer back to the discussion of contrition during the offering of the liturgical rite, just presented in the concluding paragraph of IGP 78b (IV.61.1). The logical order of his two final chapters could, however, have been improved. He makes IGP 79 an admonition on how to behave after the liturgy, whereas IGP 80 is an admonition on how to behave before that sacrificial celebration at the altar.

The Dialogist may also have chosen to place IGP 79 where it is because of a verbal link between the word *munere* at the end of it (line 15) and the mention of *munus* at the beginning of IGP 80 (lines 3 and 6). However, there is no intrinsic connection, since the word *munus*, although apparently taken up and repeated in the transit from one passage to the other, is used in different senses. At the end of IGP 79 it refers to the boon which Hannah asked of God; at the beginning of IGP 80 it refers to the oblation which must be offered before the altar until one is reconciled with one's brother (*Matthew* 5.23).

IGP 80: IV.62.1-3. The path to peace before the divine Judge comes. From line 1, "*Sed inter haec ...*", to line 30, "*... hostia ipsi fuerimus*".

Although IGP 80 is logically prior to IGP 79, the Dialogist's reason for placing it last may have been that the stately cadences of this urgent Gregorian exhortation provided an impressive climax with which to conclude his book. The argument drawn in IGP 80 from *Matthew* 5.23-4 is also used by Gregory in three other writings (*Regula Pastoralis* 3.23; *Homilies on Ezekiel* I.8.9, and *Epistola* VII.5; cf. Vogüé, *SC* 265, p. 205). In lines 10-15 there is reference to going out in spirit to placate, through humility and benevolence, one's neighbour who is "*longe positum*", thus making a peace-offering to God himself. This makes an implied reference to the words of Christ in *Luke* 14.32, concerning the ruler whose armed advent is feared, and who, while "*adhuc longe agente*", must be placated by the sending of a delegation of peace. Here again is an echo of the theme in Gregory's 37th Gospel homily, which was preached on that same Lucan passage. The divine Judge, Gregory there explains, is the ruler who is said to be "*longe*" distant because he delays his advent; the delegation which will plead with him for peace consists of tears of compunction, works of mercy and the pacificatory sacrifice of the altar (*PL* 76.1078D-1079A).

Further indications that IGP 80, like IGP 78, was drawn from an unpublished Gregorian discourse analogous to the 37th Gospel homily can be found not only in lines 10-15 of IGP 80 but also in lines 25-30. In that last paragraph of the *Dialogues*, the phrases "*indulgentiae temporis spatium*" and "*dum iudex sustinet*" are paralleled by similar expressions in Homily 37.7 and 10. Moreover, as in Homily 37 the *legatio pacis* sent to placate the tarrying Judge is constituted by "*oblata cum lacrimis et benignitate mentis sacri altaris hostia*", so also in a parallel sequence of ideas in IGP 80 Gregory declares that while the Judge mercifully tarries we must seek his indulgence by abasing ourselves "*in lacrimis*", by showing to our neighbour *gratia benignitatis*, and by so becoming a *hostia* to God before death, so that we shall not be in need of the *salutaris hostia* to liberate us after death. (Note how lines 28-30 of IGP 80 resume the teaching of IGP 78a.) I infer, then, that although IGP 79 was probably not drawn from the same eucharistic context to which IGP 78 belongs, IGP 80 did originate in the same discourse as IGP 78. Gregory's 37th Gospel homily makes clearer the implicit continuity between the argument in IGP 78 and IGP 80. It also clarifies the sequence of thought within IGP 80—that final jewel of Gregorian spiritual wisdom displayed in the Dialogist's paste.

CHAPTER EIGHTEEN

OLD TALES IN NEW GUISE: THE LITERARY BACKGROUND
OF THE *DIALOGUES*, AND ITS IMPLICATIONS FOR THE
THEORY OF GREGORIAN AUTHORSHIP: BORROWINGS
FROM POST-GREGORIAN SOURCES

"Deus non eget mendacio, quia veritas fulciri non quaerit auxilio falsitatis" (St Gregory, *Moralia* 12.37).

After our analysis of the textual structure of the *Dialogues* and our detailed examination of the four-score "Inserted Gregorian Passages" in their context, we must turn to consider the literary background to the main hagiographical narrative which constitutes the greater part of the book. In the present chapter I shall discuss the provenance of the stories it contains, and will show that this discussion is very pertinent to the question of the Gregorian authorship of the *Dialogues*. My submission may be summarized as follows. Although the author of the *Dialogues*, speaking in the *persona* of Gregory, claims to have heard his hagiographical accounts at first hand from numerous named informants, many of them said to be eyewitnesses of the events described, it is now established that a considerable number of those stories are old tales in new guise. We find that, with change of names, places and circumstances, they reflect and adapt old anecdotes and legends taken from pre-existing hagiographical collections. It transpires that the author of the *Dialogues* was deeply versed in the legendary literature of Late Antiquity. The discoveries made in recent years of the literary artifices and dissimulation employed in the composition of the *Dialogues* have introduced a new dimension into the study of the book, and thus raise further serious difficulties for the theory of Gregorian authorship. I shall argue that it is implausible to suppose that the unacknowledged borrowing of hagiographical motifs was made by Pope Gregory himself, or to attribute to him such familiarity with and predilection for that *genre* of legendary literature. Some commentators now attempt to explain away the devious dealings of the author of the *Dialogues* as the use of literary artifice for the sake of religious edification. They suppose, that is, that St Gregory deliberately put forward invented narratives, disguising his inventions and insistently protesting that they were well-attested and true history, as a pedagogical device to convey spiritual lessons. I shall object that this theory is contradicted by what we know of Gregory's character and life, and by the evidence of his genuine writings and teaching.

During the present century it has become more and more apparent that the *Dialogues* form part of a wider current of hagiographical literature, and that much light can be thrown on the stories told there by comparison with other writings of that *genre*. Eighty years ago Albert Dufourcq presented a pioneer study,[1] still valuable despite its many shortcomings, in which he situated the Gregorian *Dialogues* as part of "the legendary movement" of writings of the sixth and seventh centuries, relating both to the City of Rome and to the central Italian region or "duchy of Rome". He pointed out specific links between the *Dialogues* and those legends in the Roman *Gesta Martyrum*. Much of what he brought to the attention of the learned world had never been observed before. By appraising the *Dialogues* in that hagiographical context of Late Antiquity, he said, the Gregorian narrative appeared in a fresh light: "St Gregory is only the illustrious emulator of a hundred obscure writers ... By seeing him in the same literary setting as his contemporaries and his predecessors one can readily explain the origin, and more precisely appreciate the bearing, of his hagiographical work".[2]

U. Moricca, in his edition of the *Dialogues* (1924), developed this line of criticism. He—like many other independent critics—deplored the gullibility of Pope Gregory in crediting and passing on bizarre tales, which brought to the lips of the modern reader "a smile of incredulity and compassion".[3] He argued that there are not only generic analogies between the *Dialogues* and the contemporary Roman *Gesta*, but also clear affinities which can only be explained either by the dependence of one source upon the other, or by their common dependence on earlier sources. (I will return to this question of their interdependence in the second part of this chapter, and will indicate strong reasons for concluding that some *Gesta* originating in the seventh century were prior in date to the *Dialogues*). Like Dufourcq, Moricca saw the contemporary hagiographical *genre* revealed in the *Gesta* as significant for a new understanding of the *Dialogues*:

> In other places likewise, we come across analogies in the way in which the two works represent the same political, ecclesiastical and religious situations. The same preoccupations appear in both, the same anti-Arian motives, the same legendary themes, the same incidents in the struggle between Christianity and the last survivals of rural paganism. In a word, the two groups of testimonies fit into one framework and each illuminates the other. By bringing them together we can reconstruct the totality of the process of legend-formation, of which each one of them is only a part. The *Gesta* sing the praises of the martyrs, the *Dialogues* those of the confessors.[4]

---

[1] *Étude sur les Gesta Martyrum romains*, 4 vols, Paris 1900-1910.
[2] *Op. cit.* Tome 3, *Le mouvement légendaire grégorien*, Paris 1907, preface.
[3] *Op. cit.*, p. LXIV.
[4] *Op. cit.*, p. XXI.

Dufourcq and Moricca had concentrated on one particular source of literary antecedents and parallels to the narratives in the *Dialogues*—i.e. those fictitious *Gesta* of Roman martyrs. Other authors showed that the field of inquiry was far wider, and pointed out striking instances of correspondence between the motifs in the miracle-stories of the *Dialogues* and similar motifs in a whole range of other sources, both Scriptural and hagiographical. It had long been recognized that particular miracles in that book "imitate" (the word is used by the author himself[5]) miracles related in the Bible. F. H. Dudden remarked, in 1905: "It is suspicious that many of the recorded wonders exhibit striking analogies with the Bible miracles. Gregory himself noticed this (*Dialogues* II.8). The miracles of Elijah and Elisha in particular seem to have furnished suggestions to the reporters of Benedict's acts".[6] Among many authors who threw new light on the post-biblical hagiographical background of the *Dialogues*, the Bollandist Hippolyte Delehaye provided many useful pointers in his critical works published over a span of half a century.[7] In *Les légendes hagiographiques*,[8] for example, he remarked on the growing realization that many of the legends of the Middle Ages went back to earlier literary models, not only Christian but even pagan. "To give an idea of the discoveries that can be made in this field", he cited the story in the Gregorian *Dialogues*, IV.31, telling how one Stephen was erroneously summoned to death and to hell, in mistake for another man of the same name. Delehaye traced the antecedents of this story not only to St Augustine but back to Plutarch and especially to Lucian of Samosata. In the *Dialogues* we read that Gregory had the story from the lips of the very person who had returned from the other world. Delehaye put the blame for this chicanery on the pontiff's informant: "St Gregory's friend was an unscrupulous individual, boasting that he had been the hero of an adventure taken from the pages of a book".

Other Catholic commentators tended to explain the literary links between the *Dialogues* and earlier tales in a similar way—that is, by assuming that Gregory's trust had been abused by informants who told him old stories yet claimed they were new and true. The dossier of earlier hagiographical sources which were seen to have provided models for episodes narrated in the *Dialogues* has been steadily enlarged. Many such parallels to miracles in Book II were pointed out by H. Schrörs in a study

---

[5] "*Visne aliquid in operatione Nonnosi de imitatione quoque Helisei cognoscere?*" (I.7.4; cf. 1.7.3).

[6] *St Gregory the Great*, Vol II, pp. 167-8, footnote 2.

[7] Especially *Les légendes hagiographiques*, *1905; Les passions des martyrs et les genres littéraires*, *1921; Sanctus. Essai sur le culte des saints dans l'antiquité*, 1927; *Les origines du culte des martyrs*, 2nd ed. 1933; *Étude sur le Légendier romain*, 1936; all published in Brussels.

[8] Chapter 6, §5.

published in 1921.[9] Among those earlier sources J. Funk drew attention, in 1933, to the *Life of St Martin of Tours* and the *Dialogi* of Sulpicius Severus, to the *Lausiac History* of Palladius, and to the *Historia monachorum* of Rufinus.[10] Other writers who in more recent years have contributed to the study of the literary antecedents of the *Dialogues*, by comparative treatment of particular passages and themes, included O. Rousseau, B. de Gaiffier, M. Mähler, P. Courcelle, B. Steidle, K. Gross, J. Laporte and P. A. Cusack.[11] According to P. Courcelle and others, the *Dialogues* also contain direct echoes of non-Christian classical authors, including Seneca, Persius, Juvenal, Macrobius, Cicero and Virgil.

The contribution of Maximilien Mähler, in 1973, has a special interest in marking a developing trend in the literary criticism of the *Dialogues*. In a comparative study of the *Life* of St Benedict in Book II, he considerably expanded the number of biblical and hagiographical *évocations* discernible in the text.[12] He paid particular attention to the numerous themes taken from the *Books of Kings*. But whereas previous Catholic commentators had usually been reluctant to admit any literary artifice on the part of St Gregory himself, preferring to lay responsibility for instances of covert plagiarism at the door of the pope's informants, Mähler advanced the view that Gregory himself had deliberately reused earlier models in the composition and interpretation of his narrative. He had reworked his materials, "without much concerning himself with the historical value of the depositions" that were communicated to him, and so "had come to compose not so much a biography of the abbot Benedict as a spiritual portrait." Mähler explained that Gregory not merely "recognized" the similarity between Benedict's experiences and those of the prophets and saints; "he goes further" and by "a subtle transposition" gives to his recital of Benedict's experiences a "*Sitz im Leben*" borrowed from biblical and hagiographical antecedents. Even though this borrowed aureole "obscures from our eyes the historical implications", Mähler now saw it as a gain that we "possess a recital that, rather than keeping to the constraints of the original facts, has the aim of disclosing their meaning."[13]

Thus during the course of the twentieth century there has been a growing interest in the specific affinities of the Gregorian *Dialogues* to earlier

---

[9] "*Das Charakterbild des heiligen Benedikt von Nursia und seine Quellen*", in *ZkT*, 42, 1921, pp. 169-207. See especially pp. 202-4.

[10] *Op. cit.*, p. XIV.

[11] References to these comparative studies are brought together by Vogüé in *SC* 251, pp. 161-2, footnotes 73-8.

[12] "*Évocations bibliques et hagiographiques dans la vie de Saint Benoît par Saint Grégoire*", in *Rev. Bén.* 83, 1973, pp. 398-429.

[13] *Ibid.* pp. 398-9, 401, 428-9.

narratives, and a growing number of studies devoted to the interrelationships between the documents. The study of this question has now been
lifted to a new level by the searching investigations of A. de Vogüé. In
his commentary on the *Dialogues* (*SC* edition, 1978-80), he convincingly
demonstrated the debt of the author to his hagiographical predecessors,
both in his imitation of their methodology and in the detailed composition of his narrative, with its specific echoes of motifs, circumstances and
events taken from their works. Vogüé developed his demonstration in a
short work, *Vie de Saint Benoît*, published in 1982, in which he adduced
further striking evidence, drawn from Book II of the *Dialogues*, of the
author's unacknowledged use of older materials in the fabrication of his
own narrative.[14] His findings are corroborated and extensively sup-
plemented by the recent study of Dr Joan Petersen.[15]

While making full use of the findings of other scholars who had pointed
out the affinities between the stories in the *Dialogues* and earlier models,
Vogüé has added substantially to the dossier. He also made a further
decisive advance in the direction tentatively indicated by M. Mähler in
the work I have referred to above. Earlier commentators had remarked
on the similarities between miracle-stories in the *Dialogues* and older narratives, but had not ventured to assert squarely that St Gregory himself
had deliberately appropriated those pre-existing materials and tacitly
reworked them into his own hagiographical book. Such an assertion
would seem to give the lie to the great pope, who in the *Dialogues* constantly insists that the episodes he relates, most of them of recent occurrence, are verified by the testimony of trustworthy witnesses from whom
he has personally learned the facts. Those earlier commentators had
usually been content to explain the similarities as independent expressions of the common heritage of religious thought-forms in the ancient
world. Or, like Dudden and Delehaye, they supposed that in some cases
Gregory's informants had plagiarized earlier anecdotes and misled the
too-trusting pope into believing that similar events had occurred in their
own recent experience. Fr de Vogüé, while allowing that there may be
many instances in which the similarities are merely coincidental, and
while also surmising that in some instances Gregory's informants may
have garbled their reports with reminiscences of older tales, showed that
there are nevertheless several passages in which the covert reuse of earlier

---

[14] *Vie Monastique*, no 14, Bégrolles-en-Mauges 1982. Vogüé signals his new
discoveries: "*... nous avons fait, dans le présent commentaire, quantité de rapprochements nouveaux,
de sorte que cet opuscule de mince apparence marque en fait un progrès notable par rapport aux volumes
des "Sources chrétiennes"*" (p. 11).

[15] *The Dialogues of Gregory the Great in their Late Classical Background*, Pontifical Institute
of Medieval Studies, Toronto 1984.

models by the author of the *Dialogues* himself can be established beyond reasonable doubt.

Here, Vogüé remarks, "we enter on a new domain, that of the unavowed antecedents of the *Dialogues*".[16] A major concern throughout his study, he explains, "was to recognize the literary *arrière-plan* of the book, and to seek out the models that Gregory deliberately chose, or followed in a more or less conscious fashion, showing their diverse elements and entering into the details of their narrations".[17] This literary search leads to what Vogüé admits is "*un fait troublant.*" "One quickly perceives a disturbing fact: the similarities are not limited to formal resemblances, but often involve the very substance of the events narrated. In other words, more than one miracle of the *Dialogues* has a precise equivalent in such or such a prior work which Gregory knew. This disconcerting observation calls in question the historical character of the work, and obliges us to ask whether Gregory's narrations are not influenced even in their content by those literary models—whether the latter inspired the author himself or the informants whose tales he reports."[18] Elsewhere Vogüé makes still more explicit admissions that would indeed have seemed startling to the earlier generation of editors, commentators and admirers of the Gregorian *Dialogues*: "in my opinion, one cannot exclude the supposition that it was Gregory himself who thus fabricated certain anecdotes in their entirety".[19] More positively still, Vogüé wrote later that in some places "there is little doubt that the writer himself consciously arranged or even fabricated the tale altogether by copying what he had read in previous literature".[20] The same "disturbing fact", and its implications, will be the theme of this chapter.

The principal sources that the Dialogist laid under contribution for the construction of his own collection of wonder-stories may be listed as follows:[21]

    (a) the Bible, especially *1* and *2 Kings*;
    (b) the *Historia monachorum in Aegypto*, translated by Tyrannius Rufinus of Aquileia († 410);
    (c) the *Paradisus* of "Heraclid the Hermit", a Latin rendering of the *Lausiac History* of Palladius, bishop of Helenopolis;

---

[16] *SC* 251, p. 112.
[17] *Ibid.* p. 11.
[18] *Ibid.* p. 110.
[19] *Vie de S. Benoît*, p. 12.
[20] *Hallel* 11, 1983, p. 66.
[21] cf. Vogüé, *ibid.*, pp. 113-24, and the works of the other authors mentioned above, from which Vogüé has drawn many of his instances.

(d) Sulpicius Severus († c. 420): *Life of St Martin* and *Dialogi*;
(e) The *Life of St Anthony* by St Athanasius, translated into Latin by Evagrius of Antioch;
(f) the *Historia Ecclesiastica* of Rufinus, based on the Greek work of Eusebius;
(g) the collection of *Vitae Patrum*: in particular, the section called *Verba Seniorum*, which was translated into Latin from the Greek *Apophthegmata* mainly by the Roman deacon Pelagius, (probably the same Pelagius who became pope in 556);
(h) the *Collationes* of Cassian;
(i) possibly the *Historia religiosa* of Theodoret of Cyrrus;
(j) several *Lives* of individual saints and Fathers, including perhaps the *Life of Hilarion* by Jerome; the *Life of Ambrose* by Paulinus of Milan; the *Life of Severinus* by Eugippius; and the *Life of Caesarius of Arles* by Cyprian of Toulon;
(k) some edifying narratives from writings of St Augustine;
(l) legendary *Gesta* and *Passiones* of Roman and other Italian martyrs, composed in Late Antiquity.

In addition to the hagiographical sources dating from before the pontificate of Pope Gregory the Great, there are also certain late sixth and seventh-century narratives which present intriguing affinities to wonder-stories in the *Dialogues*, yet which could not have been available to Pope Gregory at the date he is alleged to have written that book. They include the *Pratum Spirituale* of John Moschus, the *Vita Burgundofarae* of Jonas of Bobbio, and in particular a number of the legendary *Passiones* of Italian saints which post-date the lifetime of Pope Gregory the Great. It is questionable whether the Roman Gregory could have had access to the collections of Gregory of Tours. This group of later writings evidently raises important questions about literary interdependence. I will return to these questions later.

In an unexpected moment of truth the Dialogist puts into the mouth of Peter the Deacon a comment on the resemblance between his miracle-stories and older exemplars: "*Habemus, ut video, de exemplis veteribus nova miracula*".[22] This comment makes momentarily explicit the implicit programme of his work. I now propose for closer scrutiny some specimens of the literary affinities and tacit borrowings which link the *Dialogues* with earlier hagiographical models, before discussing the further question whether those borrowings can reasonably be attributed to St Gregory himself. I will pass over the numerous instances in which there is similarity between texts but in which dependence is not sufficiently proved. My

---

[22] *Dialogues* I.7.4.

examples will be chosen from passages in which it is reasonably certain that the author of the *Dialogues* is covertly borrowing elements from other sources and using them to construct his own scenarios. His method is to adapt and refashion anew the stories that he has appropriated, choosing themes and episodes from those earlier models but not reproducing them in just the same pattern. Often his talented imagination makes the new form of the anecdote more entertaining and better integrated than its older exemplar. Only rarely does he borrow *verbatim* from his sources, though he does at times echo individual words or phrases. What is significant is not a strictly textual comparison of his stories with their archetypes, but his exploitation for his own purposes of their plots, incidents and dramatic situations. Though names, times and places are all changed, the disguised literary parentage of many of his tales can still be detected.

In setting out the following specimens of the Dialogist's borrowings I support my choices by reference to the invaluable commentaries of Fr de Vogüé. I follow his choice and his discussion of these examples because, despite his conviction of the Gregorian authorship of the *Dialogues*, I see his frank and clear admission of the author's unavowed borrowings as providing involuntary support for my own argument. The second book of the *Dialogues* is particularly rich in literary connections with earlier hagiographies. Indeed Vogüé's demonstration of the "second-hand" character of several of the episodes in that biography of St Benedict has proved seriously disquieting to some of his monastic brethren. The Dialogist is intent to show that St Benedict, the saintly abbot and great thaumaturge of Italy, can match the deeds and miracles of St Anthony, the patriarch of Eastern monks, and of St Martin, the wonder-working apostle of Gaul. The facts of his biography of St Benedict, the Gregory of the *Dialogues* declares at the outset, are vouched for by testimony which he has received directly from four disciples of the saint.[23]

As Vogüé painstakingly demonstrates,[24] the author of the *Dialogues* was clearly inspired in the composition of his work by the writings of Sulpicius Severus on the life of St Martin—the *Dialogi* and the *Vita Martini*. There are many close parallels between the biographies of Martin and Benedict. Each biography is divided by its author into two unequal periods, marked by a decisive change of place and activity. As Benedict moves from Subiaco to Montecassino to become founder of the abbey there, so Martin moved from Ligugé to become bishop of Tours and

---

[23] *Dialogues* II, prologue 2. Since hardly any of the miracles in Book II are attested by one specific witness, says Fr de Vogüé, "Gregory obviously enjoys more freedom to add and invent than in any other part of the *Dialogues*" (*Hallel*, 11, 1983, p. 67).

[24] *Vie de S. Benoît*, pp. 92-97.

founder of the abbey of Marmoutier nearby. There he, like Benedict later, lived a life of monastic perfection on "a mountain height". There is even a verbatim echo, in the Dialogist's description of the site of Cassino, of Sulpicius's description of the site of Marmoutier.[25] "It is at the beginning of this second period—exactly as in the life of the abbot Benedict—that is placed the struggle of the bishop Martin against superstition and paganism".[26] St Martin overthrows pagan temples, to the indignation of the false-believing rustics, and erects in their place churches and monasteries. The devil mounts many assaults to thwart the work of the holy bishop. This long-continuing apostolic activity of St Martin provides the Dialogist with a model for the period of St Benedict's life that immediately followed his arrival at Cassino. Like St Martin, he destroys the pagan temple and altar on Montecassino, where "the stupid multitude of rustics" worshipped Apollo and observed diabolical rites. He erects on the site of the pagan temple an oratory of St Martin (!) and on the site of the pagan altar an oratory of St John the Baptist. The demonic assaults on St Benedict and his disciples match those directed against St Martin. The devil hurls *convicia* against Martin and *contumeliae* against Benedict. He appears in person to both saints: to Martin as a resplendent pseudo-Christ, to Benedict, "not in disguise or in a dream, but in an open apparition", in his fearsome infernal form.[27]

In the *Lives* both of Martin and of Benedict the devil produces phantasmagorial deceptions which are dissipated by their holy presence. In the case of Martin the *phantasia* is a prodigious robe, supposedly woven in heaven, which excites the wonder of many but which vanishes when brought near to Martin. In the case of Benedict it is an illusory fire, *phantasticus ignis*, which to the alarmed monks seems to consume the kitchen building, but which vanishes when Benedict prays in his oratory.[28] In each *Life* the devil procures the death of a person associated with the saint, and visits each saint in his cell to announce his evil work in a mocking apparition. In Martin's case, the victim is at first thought to be one of the monks, but proves to be a monastery servant whom the devil has killed through the instrumentality of a goring ox. In Benedict's case, the victim is indeed one of the fledgling monks, engaged on building the Cassinese abbey, whom the devil kills by overturning a wall upon him. The youth is restored to life by his abbot's miraculous power.[29]

---

[25] "*Ex uno enim* latere *praecisa* montis excelsi *rupe ambiebatur*" (*Vita Martini* 10, 4; edition of J. Fontaine, *SC* 133, p. 274); "*in* excelsi montis latere *situm est*" (*Dialogues* II.8.10).

[26] Vogüé, *Vie de S. Benoît*, pp. 92-3.

[27] *Vita Martini* 24; *Dialogues* II.8.12.

[28] *Vita Martini* 25; *Dialogues* II.10; Vogüé, *Vie de S. Benoît*, p. 95.

[29] *Vita Martini*, 21; *Dialogues* II.11.

Mähler demonstrates the close dependence of the account of St Benedict's "oil miracles" (in *Dialogues* II.28-9) on Sulpicius's account (in his *Dialogi* III.3) of similar prodigies worked by St Martin.[30] The circumstances of these and the many other matching narratives in the *Lives* of the two saints show distinctive differences as well as similarities. This is in accordance with the Dialogist's usual practice of refashioning motifs and episodes from earlier stories to use in a new imaginative composition of his own. But it cannot seriously be doubted that in this section of his biography of St Benedict ("*dans ces pages si visiblement influencées par la Vie de Martin*", as Vogüé writes[31]), he was deliberately but tacitly using the narrative of Sulpicius Severus as a model for his own.

In his annotations Vogüé also marks the very numerous links between the biography of St Benedict in Book II of the *Dialogues* and other hagiographical sources. One example of such a link must suffice here. It is found in the story of the preternatural provision of an Easter repast for St Benedict in *Dialogues* II.1.6-7, which parallels a similar event in the life of the abbot St Frontonius, told in the *Vitae Patrum*.[32] When Frontonius and his brethren are in need, a certain rich man, with sumptuous fare prepared for him, receives stern reproaches from the Lord as he lies abed: "*Tu epularis in divitiis splendide, et servi mei in eremo fame pereunt*". The desert hermitage of Frontonius and his disciples is far off across difficult terrain, but the camels bearing the provisions sent by the rich man are directed there by an angel after a four-day journey. So too in the *Dialogues*, when St Benedict is tormented by hunger in his desert hermitage, a well-to-do priest, who has prepared an Easter feast for himself, is reproached by the Lord in a vision; "*Tu tibi delicias praeparas, et servus meus illo in loco fame cruciatur*". The priest undertakes the difficult journey across mountains, valleys and gorges to bring his provisions to Benedict's cave at Subiaco. The paschal setting of the episode in the Dialogist's version may reflect a detail from another tale, told by Rufinus, concerning the abbot Apollo, at whose cave unknown benefactors appeared at Eastertime bearing a splendid repast for his monks.[33]

Although the Dialogist uses the Sulpician biography of St Martin mainly as a model for his own biography of St Benedict, he also tacitly borrows episodes from St Martin's life as exemplars for tales he tells of

---

[30] *Op. cit.*, p. 417.

[31] *Vie de S. Benoît*, p. 96.

[32] Cap. 5-9; *PL* 73.440-2. The story is more ancient than the text reproduced by Migne; cf. Vogüé, *SC* 260, p. 438. A. Vaccari (*AB* 67, 1944, pp. 309-26) dates its first appearance in the West to about 630-640 at latest. This may be one of the Dialogist's post-Gregorian sources.

[33] *Historia Monachorum* 7, *PL* 21.416; Vogüé, *Vie de S. Benoît*, p. 38.

Libertinus, prior of a monastery at Fondi.[34] In his *Dialogi*[35] Sulpicius
Severus relates how Martin, while on a pastoral journey, encounters a
party of soldiers riding in a vehicle of the fiscal service, which is drawn
by a string of horses. The soldiers then set upon him and beat him cruel-
ly, leaving him bleeding and semiconscious. His friends lift him in this
pitiful state on to his ass. But when the soldiers attempt to set off again,
their horses refuse to budge. Though flogged with whips and cudgels, the
animals still remain rooted to the spot. Then the men begin to realize that
a supernatural power is at work. They recall how they had so brutally
maltreated Martin; they follow him and fall on their knees to implore his
pardon. When Martin, who is already aware of what has happened,
grants it to them, the now chastened soldiers can proceed on their way.
The Gregory of the *Dialogues* tells a remarkably similar story about Libertinus,[36] prefacing it with the assurance that he has received plentiful information about this holy man at first hand from a monk called
Laurentius, who knew Libertinus well and who is still alive at this very
time. According to this unimpeachable witness, while Libertinus was on
a journey for the good of his monastery of Fondi he was waylaid by a
force of Gothic soldiers, who flung him from his horse to the ground and
made off with his mount. When they reached the river Volturno their
horses refused to move a step forward. Though they flogged the animals
with their lances and bloodied their flanks with their spurs, these horses
too, like those of Martin's persecutors, remained immovable. Then one
of the men realized that the cause of this phenomenon was the injury they
had done to a servant of God. The whole band returned with haste to find
Libertinus prostrate in prayer; they called on him to rise and to accept
restitution of the stolen horse, but he declined. Whereupon they lifted
him bodily into the saddle and proceeded on their way. Thanks to their
amends to the holy man, their horses now did not hesitate an instant at
the river's brink but hastened swiftly ahead.

That the tale of the maltreatment of Libertinus is based on that of the
maltreatment of Martin further appears from the sequence in both
hagiographical texts. The very next story that Sulpicius Severus tells,
after the episode of the Gallic soldiers and their immovable horses, relates
how St Martin, turning to prayer, raised to life a dead child at his
mother's entreaty. The Dialogist likewise, after adding to his account of
the Gothic soldiers and their immovable horses another short anecdote
about barbarous soldiery, immediately tells a matching story of how

---

[34] It appears that the Dialogist also invents the history of a Campanian Martin (in
III.16) as another Italian rival to the renowned Gallic Martin.

[35] II.3.

[36] *Dialogues* I.2.1-3.

Libertinus, turning to prayer, restored a dead child at his mother's en-treaty.[37]

At the end of his series of anecdotes concerning Libertinus, the Dialogist tells a remarkable story of a happening at the monastery of Fondi—so remarkable, he says, that he cannot leave it untold.[38] His authority for the facts was Felix Curvus, whom Peter the Deacon knew well and who was recently prior of the monastery. This well-attested story concerns a monk who had charge of the kitchen garden, and set a serpent to guard it against a persistent thief of his vegetables. The serpent performed his guard duty so well that the thief was apprehended, and was then courteously invited by the monk to ask freely for vegetables when needed, rather than stealing them. This theme was a favourite one in the hagiography of Late Antiquity, and for the parentage of the Dialogist's story we look not to one antecedent alone, but to at least four. All the details of the Dialogist's story can be found in writings of Rufinus, Socrates the Scholastic, Venantius Fortunatus and Gregory of Tours, who recount very similar episodes.[39]

One of the most striking examples of the Dialogist's borrowings is the racy story of Bishop Andrew of Fondi, which I have already discussed in Chapter 16 in connection with IGPs 28 and 29.[40] It is an example given special prominence by A. de Vogüé,[41] who remarks that it is "particu-larly disturbing" to find St Gregory appealing to a large number of living witnesses in an Italian town as able to verify the facts of this tale, which nevertheless appears to be recognizably the same in substance, though with the setting and circumstances different, as an old legend found in pre-existing hagiographical sources. A briefer form of the story first ap-peared in the Greek *Apophthegmata*, translated into Latin by the deacon Pelagius about the middle of the sixth century.[42] A longer and more detailed version was recounted by Cassian in his "Second Conference of Abbot Serenus".[43] I will first summarize these two different forms of the fable before showing how the Dialogist made his own imaginative development of it. He appears to have drawn on both earlier versions.

The story in the *Apophthegmata*, reproduced in the Latin *Vitae Patrum*, goes back to the early days of monasticism in the Thebaid region of Egypt. It was told by an old monk, who in his youth had been a pagan,

---

[37] Sulpicius Severus, *Dialogi* II.4; Gregorian *Dialogues* I.2.5-6; cf. Vogüé *SC* 251, pp. 128-9.

[38] *Dialogues* I.3.1-4.

[39] Vogüé, *SC* 260, pp. 35-7, 436.

[40] *Dialogues* III.7.1-9; K. Hallinger, *Papst Gregor*, pp. 243-4.

[41] *SC* 251, pp. 129-30, 132-4.

[42] *Vitae Patrum* V.39 (*Verba Seniorum*); *PL* 73.885-6.

[43] *Collationes*, 8.16; *SC* 54, pp. 23-4.

the son of a priest who served the temple of an idol. The scene is dramatic. One day the boy follows his father into the inner shrine where sacrifice is offered to the idol. There he sees Satan seated, surrounded by his army of attendant demons. When they come in turn to adore him, he questions each closely about his success in causing ruin to mortals. Those who have been slow in bringing their evil designs to fruition he orders to be severely punished. Then the hidden boy hears how one devil, having tempted a desert monk unremittingly for forty years, has that very night at last succeeded in bringing him to commit fornication. Applauding this great victory, Satan embraces the successful tempter, places his own crown on his head and seats him at his side. The boy draws the moral: "Very great is the order of monks". Since he eventually told the story as a Christian monk, readers may infer (as the Greek original makes clearer) that his witnessing of the fearsome scene in the pagan temple led to his conversion.

In Cassian's version of the story the scene is likewise set in Egypt, but the observer is now a monk journeying through the desert, who tarries one evening in a wayside cave to recite his office. After midnight he sees the demons assemble in innumerable troops, escorting their tall and terrifying prince. As in the Thebaid apophthegm, the latter seats himself on his throne and requires a strict account from his subjects of their work as tempters. He rebukes the unsuccessful and drives them out with ignominy, but praises highly those who have been adept in their evil wiles. Then, as in the earlier story, comes the turn of a demon who had induced a monk to commit carnal sin. In Cassian's tale the victorious tempter, who is extolled with highest praise by the prince of darkness, tells his master the name of the victim he has ruined. It is that of a very well known monk, whom he has tempted for fifteen years and whom that very night he has induced to commit fornication with a consecrated virgin, and thereafter to abandon religion in order to cohabit with her. At daybreak the troubled listener makes his way to the town of Pelusium, where the monk in question lived, and finds that the demon's boast of his victim's downfall is true.

Let us see how the Dialogist adapts these materials and weaves them artistically into a new version of the story, which is undeniably a gem of dramatic composition.[44] He prefaces his narrative with an emphatic assurance by the Gregory of the *Dialogues* that its truth is guaranteed by the virtually unanimous testimony of the whole population of the city of Fondi: "The facts I am narrating are beyond doubt, for there are almost as many witnesses to them as there are inhabitants existing in that

---

[44] *Dialogues* III.7.1-9.

place''. Ironically, though the Dialogist was apparently unaware of the fact, there were no inhabitants existing in Fondi in 593, the time of the supposed composition of the *Dialogues*. We know from a letter of the real Gregory, of March 592, that the place had been completely abandoned. Writing to the exiled bishop of Fondi, he recalls that ''because of the destruction of war, it is impossible for anyone to dwell either in that city or in your church''.[45]

In the form of the story given in the *Dialogues* the observer at the devils' council is, as in the Thebaid apophthegm, a non-Christian, but in this case a Jew. The place of assembly is likewise a pagan temple—in this case a temple of Apollo near Fondi. Precise details from Cassian's story are also reproduced: the traveller is benighted, and the demons begin to congregate at midnight. The central scene is the same as in both earlier sources. The attendant devils escort their chief, who takes his seat in the centre and begins to exact from each tempter an account of how much wickedness he has achieved. Now the Dialogist's description becomes more vivid. One demon leaps out and reports with glee that through the presence of a comely nun who dwells in the household of Bishop Andrew of Fondi he has provoked carnal temptation in the bishop's soul. The presiding prince of devils listens avidly, ''counting it so much the greater gain for himself the more sacrosanct was the man whose soul was being drawn to perdition''. Whereupon the tempter adds that on the very evening that has just passed he has induced Bishop Andrew to give a risky *alapa* to the nun's person. Then the enemy of the human race exhorts his minion to complete his task, in order to capture so great a prize. The Jew, escaping from the devils (because ''although lacking the faith of the Cross, he has taken care to arm himself with the sign of the Cross''), hastens to seek out Bishop Andrew in the town. Taxed with his concupiscence for the nun and the dangerous liberty he has taken in imparting a tap to her *posteriora*, the bishop at length confesses his fault. The Jew tells him of the devils' council and design, whereupon the bishop amends his life completely and builds an oratory to St Andrew on the site of the temple of Apollo. The Jew himself, like the pagan observer in the Thebaid apophthegm, is converted to the Christian faith.

When discussing this story in connection with IGP 29, I offered an explanation of why the Dialogist chose to make a substantial change in the dramatic climax of the legend. Whereas in the two antecedents that he was following the sacrosanct person tempted by the demon was induced to fall into complete carnal sin, the Bishop of Fondi hovered on the brink

---

[45] *Ep*. III.13; Ewald-Hartmann I, pp. 172, lines 7-8. See my further discussion of this point in Chapter 20 below (p. 669).

of perdition but was saved from falling. I suggested that the Dialogist chose this variation on the dramatic theme at precisely this point because he had at his disposal a genuine Gregorian snippet on resistance to temptation, in which Gregory used the simile of "the cedar of paradise, shaken but not overthrown". By adapting his story of Bishop Andrew so that the prelate was dangerously shaken by demonic temptation but not overthrown, the Dialogist fashioned an apposite niche for his Gregorian excerpt.

Another interesting parallel between the *Dialogues* and Cassian's *Collationes* is found in the Dialogist's story of the abbot Equitius, who is mystically castrated by an angel in a vision and so freed from carnal temptation, just as is related by Cassian of the abbot Severus.[46] For a last telling example of the unacknowledged borrowing by the Dialogist from earlier legends, I cite from Book IV the case of the two characters named Stephen, one of whom, as a consequence of mistaken identity, was summoned to the nether-world instead of his namesake.[47] Once again, this is one of the examples also highlighted by A. de Vogüé. I noted above that H. Delehaye singled out this story as an example of hagiographical plagiarism, while still attributing the deceit to an unscrupulous informant who imposed on St Gregory's credulity.

The source from which the Dialogist took his story about the two Stephens is to be found in a work of St Augustine, *De cura pro mortuis gerenda*.[48] There we read the tale of an African official named Curma who, being summoned to the Beyond, finds there that he has been sent for in error. It was his namesake Curma the blacksmith who was intended. The mistake is corrected, and an order given for the blacksmith to be summoned. Sure enough, when Curma the official returns to life from his state of suspended animation, he finds that his namesake has died. In the *Dialogues* the very similar anecdote about the two Stephens—one an *illustris vir*, the other a blacksmith—is introduced by the Gregory of the *Dialogues* with an exceptional guarantee of authenticity. After recalling that Peter the Deacon himself knew the illustrious Stephen well, he then affirms that what he is going to relate was told to him by this Stephen in person. The man fell ill while in Constantinople, died, and was left unburied for a day and a night. (Vogüé remarks that the choice of distant Costantinople is apt *"pour servir de cadre à un récit fictif"*[49].) Stephen was conducted to hell, where he saw many awesome sights. But when he was

---

[46] *Dialogues* I.4.1 and Cassian, *Collationes* 7.2. A similar story is told in the *Paradisus*: cf. Vogüé, *SC* 251, p. 128; 260, p. 39, note.

[47] *Dialogues* IV.37.5-6.

[48] 12.15; cf. Vogüé, *SC* 265, pp. 125. 128-9.

[49] *SC* 265, p. 128, note.

brought before the one who presided there, that potentate dismissed him, exclaiming: "I did not send for this one, but for Stephen the black-smith". Vogüé shows that in this section of the *Dialogues* the author, although his purpose is different from Augustine's and his story has many additional circumstances, is unmistakably drawing on the latter's anecdote in *De cura pro mortuis gerenda*. Indeed in this same chapter of the *Dialogues*[50] there are verbatim echoes of that Augustinian opusculum, to which the author has already made an implicit allusion in a previous anecdote.[51] It is thus established beyond doubt that the story of the two Stephens, one a blacksmith, is an embellishment of the model provided by Augustine's story of the two men named Curma, one a blacksmith. Vogüé comments rather caustically: "*Cette fois Grégoire ne s'est pas donné beaucoup de peine pour masquer son emprunt. Visiblement, son histoire des deux Étienne n'est qu'un remploi de celle des deux Curma.*"[52]

Many other instances of the Dialogist's hagiographical plagiarisms could be cited, and may be found in Vogüé's copious annotations. Clear-ly there is still much scope for further discoveries in this field. It must now be realized that a new dimension has been introduced into the critical study of the *Dialogues* by the progressive realization in recent years that so many of the stories told there, said to be vouched for by living informants of Gregory, are based on old legends, elements of which are presented anew in disguised and diverting forms. Fr de Vogüé, who has done more than anyone else to demonstrate this second-hand nature of episodes for which the author of the *Dialogues* claims to provide original authority, repeatedly shows himself aware that his findings are discon-certing and that they raise a serious problem for the study of St Gregory's literary methods—and also for the study of the life of St Benedict, whose sole biography is Book II of the *Dialogues*. He describes the reactions aroused by the publication of his critical commentary on the text and his detection of its antecedent models:

> Here we touch a delicate point, at which my edition of the *Dialogues* has provoked mixed reactions among monks. Some have thought that the door has been opened to a radical demythologizing of the whole work, and

---

[50] IV.37.1, lines 4-6.

[51] *Dialogues* IV.32.2-4.

[52] *SC* 251, pp. 134-5. Although, as Delehaye pointed out, the original source of the tale was the *Philopseudes* of Lucian of Samosata (in which it was also a smith who was sum-moned to the tribunal of Pluto), it was not from that remoter source that the Dialogist drew it, but mediately through Augustine's version. I noted earlier that Delehaye at-tributed the deceit in the retelling of this yarn in the *Dialogues* to "an unscrupulous in-formant" who imposed on Gregory's credulity; now Fr de Vogüé squarely attributes the fabrication to Gregory himself, the author of the *Dialogues*.

especially of the life of St Benedict. With the unmasking of so many previous models lurking in the mind of St Gregory, which he consciously or unconsciously used, is one not led to consider the *Dialogues* as a work of pure fiction? Others have expressed their anxiety—and even their indignation—at seeing this venerable Life of the saint and of other similar figures made to appear "a school of error, a workshop of fraud and imposture".[53]

Vogüé attempts to provide a solution to the serious problem which he himself has brought so clearly to the forefront. To infer that Gregory himself fabricated those stories, using earlier patterns, "is not to do an injury to the great pope", he writes. The disquiet felt at the revelation of such apparently disingenuous dealing, he suggests, is due to the legacy of a naively "strict concept of veracity", which leads to a misplaced search for historicity in ancient texts which have a different *genre* of religious purpose. "When one reads the *Dialogues*, the right question is not, "Is this true?", but 'What does this mean to say?'". Thus according to Vogüé, it would be out of place to find fault with Gregory for his literary fabrications—even when he insists so earnestly that the truth of his stories is accredited by reliable witnesses in recent years:

> Instead of crying fraud and imposture, it is fitting, it seems to me, to appreciate the literary creativity and pedagogical talent of this pastor who is so concerned to edify his people. The suspicion that Gregory may have embellished or even completely invented such or such an episode in no way diminishes—let us unhesitatingly avow—the esteem and confidence he inspires. When we seemingly catch him in the act [i.e. of hagiographical fabrication] we will respectfully consider his narration as a language which demands to be understood. Happy are those who are capable of imagining such fine and striking stories in order to communicate a spiritual message![54]

Is this a satisfactory solution to the problem? We are confronted here not merely with the employment of a different literary *genre*. What we have in the case of the *Dialogues* is not just the pedagogical use of myth and imagery for pastoral ends, but something else. Much of ancient hagiography is indeed in the *genre* of pious legend, and that is no new discovery. It is the stock-in-trade of the story-tellers of those centuries: "The hagiographer spares no invented detail to heighten the interest of the story that he is telling. To accuse him of falsehood would be to use a stern word; he uses freely and without scruple the fictions which were customary according to the literary conventions of antiquity".[55] But is

---

[53] *Vie de S. Benoît*, pp. 11-12. Vogüé refers to a pained article by P. Murray, "The Miracles of St Benedict. May we doubt them?", in *Hallel*, 9, 1981, pp. 46-52. He replies to it in *Hallel* 11, 1983, pp. 64-8.

[54] *Vie de S. Benoît*, p. 13.

[55] P. de Labriolle, in *Histoire de l'Eglise*, ed. A. Fliche and V. Martin, Vol 4, Paris 1945, p. 583.

it plausible to fit St Gregory the Great into that category of pious fiction-spinners? The question to ask here is not whether St Gregory could believe and recount miracle-stories for the purpose of edification—we know that he did so in a number of instances in his *Letters* and in his *Homilies on the Gospels*.[56] The point is to ask whether he can reasonably be cast in the role of an accomplished fabricator of fictitious tales—one who constantly insists nevertheless that they are true and vouched for by an imposing array of living witnesses known personally to himself, one who is patently steeped in popular legendary literature and delights in that *genre*, one who deliberately dissimulates his borrowings from earlier legendary hagiography in order to present his rehashed tales as new and true. It can be argued, on the contrary, that all this is foreign to the real Gregory we know from his authentic works.

It is indeed now clear that the author of the *Dialogues* had an extensive and close familiarity with the hagiographical writings of Late Antiquity. He was steeped in the tradition of the *Vitae Patrum*, the *Gesta Martyrum* and the similar legendary literature that I have catalogued above. He shows himself a kindred spirit to those romancing hagiographers of the fifth, sixth and seventh centuries, whose congenial tales provided for monks and clerics "a kind of innoculation against *acedia*".[57] Whoever composed the *Dialogues* had spent much time in reading and assimilating those writings. Not only did he know them intimately, but he adopted their thought-patterns and conventions, conforming his own writing to the same tradition. Moreover, as we have seen, he made numerous borrowings of themes and incidents from that literature, disguising and adapting them for the fabrication of his own tales. Both his reading and his writing thus attest a strong predilection for that *genre* of legendary writing, the purpose of which was to edify and especially to entertain. Does all this accord with what we know of Pope St Gregory the Great? What was his knowledge of and attitude to the hagiographical sub-culture of Late Antiquity? If his mind was so exuberantly stored with the fruits of the hagiographical study to which the pages of the *Dialogues* bear latent witness, surely we should expect to find some use or signs of that knowledge elsewhere in the large corpus of his writings?

Leaving aside the *Dialogues*, there are two references in Gregory's letters, and a single reference in all his other works, to earlier hagiographical literature. The sole instance in all his pastoral and expository works is contained in a sermon preached to the people of Rome in the

---

[56] In the next chapter I will point out the distinctive difference in character between these few sober narrations of supernatural events by the real Gregory and the bizarre, trivial and sub-Christian tales so frequent in the *Dialogues*. (See pp. 634-8 below.)

[57] The phrase is that of Professor Jacques Fontaine.

basilica of St Felicity on that martyr's feast-day. He refers to an episode
in St Felicity's passion which, he says, "*in gestis eius emendatioribus
legitur*".[58] Here he is alluding to the third-century account in the *Passio
SS Perpetuae et Felicitatis*,[59] which is a classical model of sober and factual
martyrology. His phrase implies a critical awareness of Acts which were
not *emendatiora* and were thus less reputable, and suggests that he viewed
such literature with reserve. The implied comparison is doubtless with
the later fictional composition, *Passio S. Felicitatis cum vii filiis.*[60]

When, in his Gospel homilies, Gregory recounts some edifying stories
for the sake of his unsophisticated hearers, he does not take them from
the popular hagiographical literature which is the concealed background
of the *Dialogues*. When preaching those homilies to his people in the
basilica-shrines of the Roman martyrs, he occasionally refers in very
general terms to the constancy and virtues of those martyrs, but he makes
no use of the legendary *gesta* and *passiones* (which had already gained a
considerable vogue in the sixth century) to illustrate his lessons. As an
example I cite his reference to Saints Nereus and Achilles, which can be
seen not only to disregard the legendary Acts of those two martyrs, but
even to be incompatible with them. In his homily on their feast-day,
preached in the basilica in which their tomb was enclosed, he held up
their heroic contempt of the world as an example to his hearers. Among
the good things of life which they left behind by accepting martyrdom,
Gregory includes that of procreation of offspring—"*fecunditas in pro-
pagine*".[61] This was not a point he would have made if he had paid any
heed to the legendary *gesta* of Saints Nereus and Achilles, for there the
two martyrs are presented as eunuchs, chamberlains of Flavia
Domitilla.[62]

The two references in Gregory's letters do not attest any close
acquaintance with or interest in hagiographical literature. One is an incidental remark in a letter to Aetherius, Bishop of Lyons, in June 601.
The bishop had asked for a transcription of the *gesta vel scripta* of St
Irenaeus; to this Gregory replied that after long-continued search no
trace of such writings could be found in Rome. The other reference is
more noteworthy. It is contained in a letter to Eulogius, Bishop of Alex-

---

[58] *Homilies on the Gospels*, 3.3.

[59] *Acta Sanctorum*, July III, pp. 12-13; cf. *CPL* 32 and H. A. Musurillo, *The Acts of the
Christian Martyrs*, Oxford 1972, pp. 110-33.

[60] *BHL* 2853; cf. *CPL* 2187.

[61] *Homiliae in Evangelia*, 28, 3; *PL* 76.1210-13.

[62] Text in *Acta Sanctorum*, May III (1680), pp. 6-13. In the fourth-century inscription
placed on their tomb by Pope Damasus these two martyrs are simply described as
soldiers.

andria, dated July 598.[63] Eulogius had asked Gregory for a copy of a book of the *gesta* of all the martyrs, collected by Eusebius of Caesarea. Gregory replied that before receiving his friend's request, he had never even heard of the existence of that separate collection of Acts of the martyrs. Moreover a search in the archives of the Roman Church and in the libraries of the City revealed nothing of the kind, "with the exception of a volume in which a few things (*pauca quaedam*) are collected in one codex". Gregory went on:

> We do however have here the names of almost all the martyrs collected in one codex, with their different passions assigned each to its proper day, and on the respective days we celebrate the solemnities of the Mass in their honour. However, in this volume the manner in which each suffered is not indicated, but all that is recorded is his name, the place and the day of his passion. Thus many who have received the crown of martyrdom, from diverse lands and provinces, are commemorated each day, as I have said.[64] But your Beatitude has these particulars, I think. We have, then, searched for, but not found, what you requested to be sent to you. Nevertheless though we have not yet found it, we will go on searching, and if it can be found we will send it.

From the evidence of this letter of Gregory to Eulogius, written five years after the ostensible date of the *Dialogues*, it would seem that the martyrological literature with which the Pope was familiar, and which was available in the libraries of his See, was sparse. Some authors find his disclaimers in that letter perplexing. Is it really credible to suppose that the only writings on the passions of the martyrs that were available in Gregory's *curia* were (apart from the fourth-century *Ecclesiastical History of Eusebius*) one codex containing *quaedam pauca*, and a martyrological calendar without biographical information? The fruitless search for such writings in the archives and libraries of Rome, as described by Gregory in his reply to Eulogius, seems to accord ill with the implicit testimony of the *Dialogues*, which indicates that a vast hagiographical literature had been at the disposal of the author. Dufourcq's conjecture[65] that the codex containing *quaedam pauca* was a collection of the fictitious *Gesta Martyrum* of the City and duchy of Rome has been discredited. In any case Gregory's manner of referring to that solitary codex clearly indicates that he had not previously been familiar with it. Dufourcq admits that the letter to Eulogius is a difficulty. His answer is that Gregory was there not

---

[63] Ep. VIII; Ewald-Hartmann II, pp. 28-9.

[64] As I noted in Chapter 11, p. 253, L. Duchesne identified the record to which Gregory here refers as the sixth-century recension of the so-called Hieronymian Martyrology. A. Dufourcq agreed (*op. cit.*, Vol I, p. 30), but B. Krusch did not.

[65] *Op. cit.*, I (1900), pp. 78-92. B. de Gaiffier, citing also the earlier criticisms of H. Delehaye, rejects this conjecture of Dufourcq's (*AB* 72, 1954, pp. 139-40). He does, however, acknowledge the usefulness of Dufourcq's documentary data (*ibid.* p. 137).

revealing the pious "interests of his soul", but "restrained himself by a measure of prudence when an inquiry was put to him as Pope, the successor of St Peter",[66] in order to display officially the sober attitude of "his Roman predecessors and ancestors." That is, so Dufourcq implies, when Gregory received the request of the Bishop of Alexandria he dissembled his familiarity with and addiction to hagiographical literature, and pretended there was hardly any to be found in his possession or in the libraries of his Church!

Dufourcq also asserts that a letter from St Gregory to the Empress Constantina, dated June 594, demonstrates that he knew and credited the apocryphal *Acts of Saints Peter and Paul.*[67] He points to an anecdote related in that letter, which tells how some Greeks who had sought to remove the bodies of the two martyred Apostles from Rome to the East had been deterred by a violent thunderstorm.[68] Dufourcq assumes that this anecdote was taken from the apocryphal *Acts*, where a similar story is to be found.[69] Comparison of the two narrations, however, reveals significant differences between them. For example, in the *Acts* it is not a thunderstorm that deterred the Greeks but an earthquake; and several other circumstances and details of the event are different. The passage has the nature of a postscript at the end of those apocryphal *Acts*. Its date of origin cannot be determined. It is quite possible that it was added after Gregory's time, adapted from the anecdote in his letter; or both narrations may depend on a common oral tradition. The editors of Gregory's letters note that "*alias haec narratio non occurrit*", and that a garbled version of the story is inserted into the first biography of Gregory written in the early eighth century by the monk of Whitby.[70]

That lack of interest, attested in Gregory's works, in the proliferating legendary literature does indeed reflect the reserve which still prevailed in the sixth-century Church of Rome towards the effusions of the hagiographers. The Roman pontiffs remained faithful to the sober tradition of Pope Damasus, who had honoured the memory of the martyrs but had not allowed imaginative invention to supply for the lack of historical facts about them.[71] The so-called Gelasian Decree, *De libris recipiendis et non recipiendis*, dating from the first half of the sixth century, did not

---

[66] *Op. cit* I (1900), p. 383, footnote.

[67] *Ibid.* pp. 382-3.

[68] Ep. IV.30; Ewald-Hartmann, I. pp. 265-6.

[69] R. A. Lipsius, *Acta Apostolorum Apocrypha*, Hildesheim (1891), 1959 ed. Part I, pp. 175-6.

[70] *Loc. cit.*, p. 265, note 8. If Gregory took the story from the *Acts*, why should he change the earthquake into a mere thunderstorm? The former would have provided a more effective cautionary argument to the Empress.

[71] Cf. Dufourcq, *op. cit.* I, (1900), pp. 24-30.

originate as a papal decree, but it was adopted by the Roman See and it undoubtedly represented the conservative attitude of the contemporary papacy to the wave of hagiographical fantasies which continued to well up during that century.[72] The *Decretum Gelasianum* affirmed that though no Catholic had any doubts about the power of God manifested in the heroic sufferings of the martyrs, the unauthorized *gesta martyrum* were not to be approved: "according to ancient custom, and with particular caution, they are not read in the holy Roman Church, not only because the names of their authors are completely unknown, but also because misbelieving and simple folk apprize in them things that are preposterous or little conforming to reality".[73] The document goes on to show the same cautious reserve to the *vitae patrum*: as Dobschütz remarks, it makes "the same distinction between the cult of the saints and the legends of the saints" (i.e. that it has already made in the case of the martyrs). It also voices disquiet about *novellae relationes*.

The *Gelasianum*, and its reception in the Roman Church, attest the contemporary impact of the unauthorized hagiographical *gesta* which, as P. Llewellyn writes, "were beginning to gain currency as the staple Christian literature for the masses, filling out the bare lists of names in the martyrologies with all the wonders of the novellette, and which the great families and political factions were to find a convenient *genre* for propaganda in internal disputes".[74] The reaction of the new school of hagiographers against the conservatism of the Church authorities may be recognized in a curious prologue, *Omnia quae a sanctis gesta sunt*, which is found prefixed to a number of fabulous *gesta*.[75] The preface is in all probability a sequel and a direct answer to the *Decretum Gelasianum*. It defends the *gesta* of the saints which "we studiously record", and challenges the attitude, as lacking in Catholic sense, of "you who judge that they should be dismissed among the apocryphal writings." (The word *apocryphus* occurs 61 times in the *Decretum Gelasianum*.[76]) "The censorious may make prohibitions, the timid may command silence, the despisers may assail; they may rebuke those who read these works and accuse those who eagerly listen to them". But, the hagiographers retort, "We speak of, write and preach those acts of divine power", and so promote orthodoxy and edification. Since the *Decretum Gelasianum* is dated in the first half of the

---

[72] E. von Dobschütz, *Das Decretum Gelasianum*, Leipzig 1912, pp. 271, 345, 351.

[73] *Ibid.*, pp. 40-1; cf. pp. 271-3. Admittedly the *Gelasianum* does commend the three *Lives* of saints by St Jerome, which are highly legendary—presumably because of the unimpeachable renown of the author.

[74] *Op. cit.*, p. 39.

[75] See B. de Gaiffier, "*Un prologue hagiographique hostile au Décret de Gélase?*", in *AB* 82, 1964, pp. 341-53; text of the preface on pp. 343-4.

[76] *Ibid.*, p. 347.

sixth century, the anti-Gelasian preface, reflecting resentment at the continued force of the official attitude which it represents, originated some
time after that. It was copied and prefixed to diverse *gesta*, and the controversy that it reflects was doubtless topical in the lifetime and pontificate of Pope Gregory I.

The Roman Church of the sixth century did not, indeed could not,
suppress the fanciful legendary *gesta* and *vitae patrum*, which had a wide
popular appeal.[77] Rather, it showed discriminating prudence by pro-
hibiting the public reading or liturgical use of such literature. The same
prudent policy endured well after the age of Gregory the Great, until
near the end of the eighth century, when, in the time of Pope Hadrian
I, public reading of the legendary passions of the martyrs was at last
authorized.[78] The attitude implicit in the genuine writings of Pope
Gregory the Great, with his concern for *gesta emendatiora*, is still wholly in
accord with the traditional reserve of the Roman Church up to that time;
in the *Dialogues*, on the contrary, a delight in fantastic hagiography is
manifest. It is indeed because of the *Dialogues* that it has become
customary for critical historians to lay at the door of Pope Gregory I the
blame for abandoning the older prudent attitude of the Roman Church
towards the aberrations of the legendary *gesta*. A. Dufourcq, noting that
Pope Gregory stood mid-way between Pope Damasus and Pope
Hadrian, saw the *Dialogues* as marking the beginning of the decline and
the sorry departure from previous sobriety. He makes this criticism:
"The writer who takes pleasure in writing so many trivial or futile
stories, who records them without making any comment—but rather,
who presents them as worthy of faith and of praise—that man is on the
same level as the compilers of the Roman *gesta*. What wonder that he
underwent their influence?"[79] These strictures are paralleled by those of
many other critics. P. Llewellyn, for example, judges that "the *Dialogues*
and the histories they present point to the changes in Roman thinking".
He marks the contrast between the tradition represented by the *Gelasianum* and "Gregory's encouragement and adoption of these same spon-
taneous, uncritical, unintellectual literary forms which were to remain
the staple of religious reading for centuries ... Gregory's work was to be
the most perfect of the *genre*."[80] But such strictures only have point on
the assumption that St Gregory was the author of the *Dialogues*. They fail

---

[77] As I noted above (p. 586), a section of the Greek *Apophthegmata* was translated into
Latin by a deacon of the Roman Church, Pelagius, who was probably the same Pelagius
who was pope from 556 to 561.

[78] B. de Gaiffier, "*La lecture des Actes des Martyrs dans la prière liturgique en Occident*", in
AB 72, 1954: "*A partir du VIIIe siècle, l'Eglise romaine se départit de sa réserve*" (pp. 141-2).

[79] *Op. cit.*, Vol I (1900), p. 379.

[80] *Op. cit.*, pp. 98-9.

to take account of the contrast here between the *Dialogues* and the un-disputed writings in the Gregorian corpus, which show Gregory as no less conservative than his predecessors in the papal chair who, in their attitude towards unauthorized hagiography and *novellae relationes*, upheld the *antiqua consuetudo* and *singularis cautela* of the Roman Church to which the Gelasian Decree bore witness.

It must not be thought that the borrowing of elements from earlier nar-ratives by the Dialogist, in order to adapt their plots and settings for his own tales, was peculiar to him. Reuse of earlier legends in a new context was a common practice among the Latin hagiographers of those cen-turies, as H. Delehaye and B. de Gaiffier have pointed out.[81] Multiple use of the same theme by several authors was not rare. Strange as it would undoubtedly be to catch St Gregory himself in the act of literary dissimulation and legend-copying, such dealings were usual enough among the busy tribe of romancing hagiographers to whom the Dialogist so clearly belongs. What does distinguish him from most of the other plagiarists of that tribe, however, is the care he takes to dissemble his bor-rowings and the originality with which he changes and refashions them for his own purposes. His plagiarized tales are not, as in so many other cases, mere centos made up of scraps taken from earlier tales. Nor does he employ that crude form of plagiarism which Gaiffier calls *"le plagiat intégral"*—that is, the servile copying of an earlier text with change only of names and places. He does, however, have his own subtler form of *plagiat intégral*, which I have pointed out in Chapter 17—namely, his bold and mainly verbatim reproduction, in his fourth book, of nine edifying stories told by the real Gregory in his *Homilies on the Gospel*.

The Dialogist has another, quite distinctive manner of reusing hagiographical material in new shapes. It consists in the repeated use of *his own* dramatic plots and themes. Again and again episodes and miracles that he has already narrated reappear in his pages, often in a closely parallel form, to provide the basis of a different story, with per-sons and circumstances changed. A. de Vogüé has amply documented this remarkable series of what he calls "the doublets of the Gregorian narrative". In Book II, in particular, he notes frequent duplication of St Benedict's miracles.[82] Sometimes a duplicate prodigy occurs in the text only a short distance from the analogue on which it is modelled. "Even

---

[81] H. Delehaye, *Les Légendes hagiographiques*, 4th edit., Brussels 1955, pp. 87-100; B. de Gaiffier, *"Les 'doublets' en hagiographie latine"*, in *AB* 96, 1978, pp. 261-9.

[82] *SC* 251, pp. 125-8; cf. also p. 60, where Vogüé remarks on a *"curieux quatrain en-trecroisé"* of two pairs of duplicated miracle stories about St Benedict. In his commentary in *SC* 260 and 265, he notes several other "doublets".

more disquieting", Vogüé considers, "are certain cases of equivalence between a deed of Benedict and that of other thaumaturges" in the Dialogist's narrative. Benedict's miraculous provision, through prayer, of the twelve gold pieces necessary to satisfy an importunate creditor is a double of a prodigy earlier related of Bishop Boniface of Ferentis, who likewise obtained, through prayer, the twelve *solidi* needed to repay and pacify the indignant Constantius.[83] Benedict, "like Isaac of Spoleto, reveals to an unfaithful messenger that a serpent has entered a container hidden by the side of the road; like Sabinus of Canosa, his friend, he uncovers a trick of the king Totila, and also foils, by means of the sign of the cross traced over wine, an attempt at poisoning; like the abbot Spes, his compatriot, he dies in his oratory, in prayer, after communion, and his disciples see his soul mount to heaven".[84] In book IV especially there is multiplication of similar miracle motifs in illustration of a particular thesis. Vogüé singles out, as the most striking doublet of all, the two miracle-stories in that book relating the spectral apparition and eventual deliverance of two departed souls, each of whom had been condemned to expiate his sins by menial service in the baths. There is sustained and exact correspondence between the circumstances and events in both tales.[85]

I have been giving chief attention to the Dialogist's furtive use of models of miracle-stories drawn from the hagiographical writings of Late Antiquity, since those instances most strikingly illustrate his devious dealing. But also significant for our inquiry is his reuse of models from Scripture. In a number of cases he openly points out the resemblance between the recent miracles that he attributes to Italian thaumaturges and parallel events related in the Bible. The wondrous deeds of Benedict, Libertinus, Equitius, Nonnosus and other holy men in his narrative recall, he acknowledges, the deeds of Scriptural exemplars: from the Old Testament, Moses, David, and especially Elijah and Elisha; from the New, Christ himself, John the Baptist and the Apostles Peter and Paul.[86] Of this category of histories told in the *Dialogues*, A. de Vogüé writes: "If some of them—not all—probably bear the stamp of pure literary imitations of biblical models, their openly avowed character makes them less disquieting than other parallels which remain unexpressed".[87] He goes

---

[83] *Dialogues* I.9.10-13 and II.27.1-2.

[84] Vogüé, *SC* 251, p. 126. He also notes the correspondence between the heavenly ascension of the soul of Spes and that of Scholastica, and observes: "Gregory seems to have adverted to the doublets and sought to mask them" (p. 127).

[85] *Ibid.*, pp. 127-8.

[86] References in Mähler, *op. cit.*; also B. de Gaiffier, *Études Critiques*, Brussels 1967, pp. 52-6.

[87] *SC* 251, p. 137. J. Petersen makes a detailed and useful examination of the analogies

on to identify other instances, not rare and "more disturbing", in which "a story in the *Dialogues* strangely resembles an event from the Bible without any mention of it." A palmary example is the story of the raising to life of Marcellus by Bishop Fortunatus of Todi, alleged to have been reported to Gregory by an unnamed old man, which in its circumstantial details is extraordinarily similar to the Johannine account of the raising of Lazarus by Jesus.[88] "Everything suggests an imitation of the Gospel", Vogüés observes, "one that is all the more suspect because it remains unavowed. If Gregory does not breathe a word here about the Gospel model, is it not because he means to obscure it?" The same suspicion comes to mind, Vogüé remarks, when one recognizes many other unacknowledged borrowings of Scriptural types. As the biography of St Martin by Sulpicius Severus provided the Dialogist with a scheme for a whole series of parallel wonders in his life of St Benedict, so also did the life and deeds of the prophet Elisha as related in *2 Kings*.[89] "Like the hagiographical literature, the Bible seems to have furnished the author of the *Dialogues* or his informants with ready-made patterns on which a good number of their narrations were constructed".[90] We recall that the *Life of St Anthony* by Athanasius, which is one of the sources exploited by the Dialogist, also took models from the scriptural histories of Elijah and Elisha in order to apply them to Anthony.[91]

To recapitulate, then, the unmasking of the latent artifices in the composition of the *Dialogues* has set the question of Gregory's authorship in a new perspective. As we have seen, the author of the *Dialogues* was not only a spinner of fictitious hagiography, deeply versed in that *genre* of literature, but also one who went to considerable lengths to dissemble his literary wiles. He is now revealed as one of the most adroit of the romancers of that age, one who imitated and covertly refashioned for his own tales many narrations taken from Scripture and from hagiographical literature, one who even reused his own plots to fabricate further tales on the same pattern. Can this inventive legend-spinner and pious plagiarizer, who insists constantly that his narrative is veridical and authenticated by a host of living witnesses, be St Gregory the Great? Is

---

between tales in the *Dialogues* and biblical models (*op. cit.*, Chapter 2). When, however, she attempts to represent these borrowings as use of "typology" in the patristic sense, and to dignify the author's borrowings of his models as "typological interpretation" of the kind the real Gregory uses in the *Moralia*, her argument is based on a misconception.

[88] *Dialogues* I.10.17-18; *John* 11.1-44.

[89] See O. Rousseau, *"Saint Benoît et le prophète Élisée"*, in *Revue Monastique*, 144, 1956 (III), pp. 103-14.

[90] Vogüé, *SC* 251, p. 138.

[91] B. Steidle, *"Homo Dei Antonius"*, in *SA* 38, 1956, pp. 162-6.

such literary dissembling in keeping with the character of the real Gregory, whose personal writings show him as a man of transparent sincerity? Could that great pastor and mystic whose life and teaching was based, with single-minded earnestness, on the source-book of the inspired Scriptures, have been after all on a par with the writers of legendary fiction?

It remains to consider the pleas which M. Mähler, J. Petersen, and A. de Vogüé put forward to excuse the literary dissimulations of the *Dialogues* and to justify St Gregory's authorship of such fabrications. Is it a satisfactory solution to the problem to argue that Gregory was merely conforming to the common literary conventions of Late Antiquity, that the question of the veracity and historicity of his narrative does not really matter, since he was using the legendary *genre* in the service of spiritual edification, and that he is to be accounted among those happy teachers "who are capable of imagining such fine and striking stories in order to communicate a spiritual message"?

The question of the veracity and historicity of the *Dialogues* narrative cannot be dismissed as relatively unimportant, since it has important implications for a judgement of the nature of the work as a whole. A. de Vogüé, while admitting that the author "has few scruples" in embellishing his narrative with borrowings from elsewhere, suggests that his work "probably contains a mixture of history and of legend, of real and of imaginary events", and considers it likely that "a number of his wonder-stories have a foundation in reality".[92] Yet once it has been recognized—as it must be recognized from Vogüé's own critique—that *some* episodes narrated in the *Dialogues* are completely fictitious, fabricated by the author using elements from other legends yet presented as an account of real and recent happenings, then *none* of the stories contained in the book can be free from suspicion. Vogüé reassures troubled readers of St Benedict's biography with the reflection that it contains "serious topographical and chronological references", and that it must have a base—"no doubt quite large, but impossible to delimit"—of authentic facts.[93] But how can we be sure of this? Scholars have been able to detect some disguised fabrications in the *Dialogues* because their fictitious character was betrayed by the author's use of material borrowed from other sources. But what of the much greater number of stories—the majority—which have the same picturesque and entertaining quality but do not contain recognizably borrowed elements which would betray a fictitious origin? Since the author has been shown to be a skilful romancer

---

[92] *SC* 251, p. 140. Elsewhere he says that the *genre* used by Gregory in the *Dialogues* was "half way between history and fiction" (*Hallel*, 11, 1983, p. 67).

[93] *Vie de S. Benoît*, pp. 13-4; cf. *SC* 251, pp. 157-60.

who invented those circumstantial histories with recourse to elements taken from earlier sources, he could equally well have devised the other tales in his book, even without the use of earlier models, directly from the fertile source of his own imagination. We can in fact catch him in the act of forging such tales by the repetition of plots and themes which he has already used in his own pages. Thus there is no guarantee that any of his stories are true—especially since almost all the holy men whose deeds he relates are otherwise completely unknown to historical record. While he doubtless drew on knowledge of folk-traditions from the districts of central Italy to which he makes many topographical references, he could as easily have invented stories about the local worthies mentioned in those traditions as he did in the passages in which his fabrication has been detected. The most recent writer on this question, Dr. J. Petersen, goes even further than Fr de Vogüé and virtually abandons the attempt to discern historicity in the *Dialogues* narrative.[94]

But may we not view the *Dialogues* with an indulgent eye, seeing it in its age and *genre* as a Gregorian work of fanciful piety, intended for popular edification? Certainly, we must not attribute our modern concepts of history and scholarly objectivity to the mentality of that age. Certainly, fictional wonders and literary plagiarism, interspersed with protestations of historical veracity, were commonplace in the work of the popular hagiographers. Doubtless they felt that pious ends justified such means. But it is an unwarranted assumption to include in their number Pope St Gregory the Great, discriminating judge of *gesta emendatiora* and upholder of the conservative traditions of the Roman Church, whose reserve towards apocryphal hagiography reflects the attitude of the *Decretum Gelasianum*.

What of the author's statement, in the prologue to the *Dialogues*, of the purpose of his book? He there declared his intention to demonstrate to his contemporaries that saintly men had abounded in Italy in recent times, and the proof of their sanctity was to be found in their miraculous deeds which he would relate. Since many of the "facts" that he adduces in proof are shown to be fictitious, his declared aim in writing is also shown to be deceptive. To edify by means of entertaining fictions put out as true, was as we have seen, a common motive of the romancing hagiographers; but it was alien to the mind of the author of the *Moralia*, that true shepherd of souls, who taught: "Truth does not seek to be stayed up by the aid of falsehood".[95] Pious readers are assured by Fr de Vogüé that they may draw profit from the narratives in the *Dialogues*,

---

[94] *Op. cit.*, Chapters 1 and 4; cf. pp. 54-5.
[95] *Moralia* 12.37.

"without concerning oneself to disentangle fact from fiction", and that they may "forget this 'troubling' problem of historicity and be wholly intent to listen to what Gregory wishes to say to us".[96] Yet since the author of the *Dialogues* is convicted of inventing his stories and of dissembling his inventions, and since his diverting collection of prodigies has no exemplary value in the pastoral and Gregorian sense, is it plausible to present this artifice of fictional hagiography as an enterprise of spiritual edification worthy of the great pastor who was St Gregory?

Post-Gregorian sources used in the Dialogues

So far I have been discussing pre-Gregorian hagiographical sources used by the author of the *Dialogues*. We must now ask: Can any borrowings from *post*-Gregorian sources be detected in his work? Obviously, this question may be of decisive importance for our whole investigation. If it can be shown that the author uses sources which originated at a time later than the last decade of the sixth century, when the *Dialogues* were allegedly written by Pope Gregory the Great, then we have a clear disproof of the traditional ascription of the work. It is my submission that several arguments do converge towards that conclusion. I will first consider the weighty argument that can be drawn from the legendary *Gesta* of the duchy of Rome, and will then discuss other seventh-century sources which may also be seen reflected in the pages of the *Dialogues*.

At the beginning of this chapter I referred to the corpus of legendary literature known as the Roman *Gesta Martyrum* and its relevance to the study of the *Dialogues*. A. Dufourcq, who more than any other author has brought out this connection, sums it up with emphasis: "One must conclude that *there is a strict solidarity between the* Gesta *and the* Dialogues. These two series of texts complement and mutually illustrate one another. By considering them together we are able to appreciate as a whole the legendary movement of which the *Dialogues* give only a fragmentary part."[97] We must ask what can be determined about the date of origin of the various elements which make up that corpus of legendary *Gesta*. The answer, to be amplified in the following pages, is that while those apocryphal martyr-acts first developed in the Rome of the Ostrogothic period and grew in volume during the sixth century, a fair number of them—in particular, those which refer to the rural localities in central Italy and which have the closest inter-relation with the *Dialogues*—originated during the seventh century. While there is no proof that the

---

[96] *Vie de S. Benoît*, pp. 13-14.
[97] *Op. cit.* III, pp. 294-5; italics are Dufourcq's.

authors of the later *Gesta* knew the *Dialogues*, there are on the other hand positive indications that the author of the *Dialogues* knew and drew upon the fanciful inventions contained in several of those seventh-century writings.

A main motive for the origin and development of those apocryphal histories was to supply for the lack of genuine knowledge about the saintly heroes of the early persecutions. Concerning most of the martyrs of Rome and the surrounding territories, whose names had been handed down from earlier tradition, few hard facts were known. In the fourth century Pope Damasus had sought out and recorded the sparse historical details of their martyrdom, but in most cases little more was known of those heroes of the faith beyond their names, the day of the month on which they were martyred and on which they were commemorated in the Church's calendar, and topographical indications of the places at which they suffered or were venerated.[98] The authors of the new legendary *Passiones* set out to fill this biographical lacuna, and to meet a growing devotional demand, by inventing circumstantial and prodigious accounts of their heroic deeds and sufferings. A particular function of the fictional *Gesta* was to satisfy a pious yearning for information about the titular saints to whom certain Roman churches were dedicated, but about whom virtually nothing was known.

Although those legendary *Gesta* form a fairly homogeneous body of texts, which can be pieced together from a large range of manuscript sources and printed editions,[99] they do not all date from one period. They show diversity not only in time of origin but also in the contemporary preoccupations of their authors and in the manner of their composition. It appears that the corpus of those texts was produced over a span of some two hundred years, from the later fifth century to the last part of the seventh. Our main interest here is their dating in so far as it is relevant to our discussion of the dating of the *Dialogues*. It seems clear that many of the apocryphal *Gesta Martyrum* of the City of Rome were composed during the fifth and sixth centuries. This earlier phase of the development of the spurious martyrology, which Dufourcq calls "the Ostrogothic legendary movement", was the background of the so-called Gelasian Decree and the reactions it provoked. As we have seen, the official Roman Church—including Gregory the Great—continued to view that wave of fictitious hagiography with reserve. However, not all the martyr-*Gesta* relating to the City originated before Gregory's time; as Dufourcq shows, some of them must have been written in the seventh

---

[98] Cf. Dufourcq, I, pp. 17-30.

[99] Many of these texts may be found scattered through the *AA.SS.*, incorporated into individual saints' lives.

century. For example, he dates the fictitious passion of the martyr St Boniface to the first quarter of that century.[100] Its purpose was doubtless to provide a legend for the titular patron of a church dedicated to the martyr which was founded on the Aventine Hill about that time. While Dufourcq traces the origin of most of the *Gesta* of Rome and its suburbs back to the Ostrogothic period, he also admits that even some supposedly earlier *Gesta* reflect situations and preoccupations of the first part of the seventh century. He infers that the legend-spinning movement in Rome itself, after continuing "feebly" during the last part of the sixth century, was "reanimated" during the period from the pontificate of Gregory I to that of Boniface V, who died in 625.

When we turn to the apocryphal *Gesta* that relate to the rural hinterland of Rome, and in particular to the provinces of central Italy lying between Rome and Ravenna, we find that they were largely of seventh-century origin. Whereas the sixth-century *Gesta* of the City of Rome and its environs had provided legends for martyrs whose names at least were known from historical tradition, the authors of the later wave of provincial *Gesta* invented not only the life stories of their characters but even the saints themselves. The saga of the "Twelve Syrian Brothers"[101] in Tuscia and Umbria, for example, is patently pure fiction. It is those provincial *Gesta* that provide the closest links with the *Dialogues*. That later phase in the production of the legendary texts can be traced from about the beginning of the seventh century onwards, with important developments around the middle of that century, and with some further additions even in the closing decades. In contradistinction from the earlier "Ostrogothic movement", Durfourcq calls the later phase "the Gregorian legendary movement", in recognition of the striking similarities between its literature and the Gregorian *Dialogues*. He naturally supposes that the production of the *Dialogues* preceded those seventh-century *Passiones*. I shall argue that the data that he himself brought into the light provide a powerful contrary argument to that supposition. In other words, it is the *Dialogues* that reflect the provincial *Gesta* and not vice versa.

Dufourcq points out distinctive tendencies in the martyrological literature of what he misnames "the Gregorian movement".[102] "After Gregory", he writes, "the two traits that are properly *Gregorian* become accentuated: the Gothic type of legend deteriorates, and the miracles and bizarre elements multiply. The later texts, above all, are indirectly influenced by the work of Rothari and the restoration of the bishoprics" [i.e.

---

[100] *Op. cit.*, I, pp. 166-8.
[101] The *Gesta* of Abundius, Carpophorus, Anastasius and their brethren: *BHL* 1620-2.
[102] *Op. cit.*, III, pp. 283-5.

the work of consolidation of the Lombard kingdom under Rothari, 636-652]. He also shows how strongly the seventh-century *Gesta* were influenced by the ecclesiastical hellenization of Italy in that period. In contrast, the Dialogist was to react against the prevailing hagiographical fashions by asserting an Italian religious patriotism, and also by making the characters of his fanciful narrative confessors from the recent past, instead of martyrs from antiquity, as in most of the prevailing *Gesta* literature.[103]

The relevance of the seventh-century *Gesta* to the question of the authorship of the *Dialogues* has hitherto gone virtually unnoticed. Goussainville and the Maurists, and the many later apologists for the *Dialogues*, were not aware either of the dating or of the fictitious *genre* of the martyr-*Gesta*, which were not critically studied until the present century. Even after the publication of Dufourcq's volumes scholars were slow to realise the implications of the documentary data to which he drew attention in his flawed study.[104] The connection of those legendary Acts with the *Dialogues* was considered to be of minor interest. Since the commentators assumed that Gregory had written the *Dialogues* in 593-4 they considered the bizarre hagiography of the following century to have little relevance to the study of his book. Even when putting forward testimonies alleged to show knowledge of the *Dialogues* in the seventh century, they did not think of claiming the *Gesta*, and their textual parallels with the *Dialogues*, as evidence to confirm the Gregorian authorship of the latter. Fr de Vogüé, who has so painstakingly traced out the connections between other hagiographical legends and the *Dialogues*, has quite left out of account the rich and luxuriant material provided by the Roman *Gesta Martyrum*, whether of the sixth or seventh century. Only J. Petersen, most recently, has given some critical attention to possible relationships between the *Gesta* and the *Dialogues*, while accepting unquestioningly the traditional dating of the latter.[105]

In order to appreciate what Dufourcq calls "the strict solidarity" between the *Dialogues* and those *Gesta* it is necessary to dwell on the texts themselves, with the aid of the contextual and topographical commentary provided in his volumes. Between the two terms of comparison there are,

---

[103] I will return to these aspects of his work in Chapter 22, pp. 724-7, 741-2.

[104] Dufourcq's volumes had many defects, especially in methodology. Much more remains to be done to illuminate the obscure field of research in which he was a pioneer. Yet when all its defects have been recognized, his work remains substantially valuable, as the Bollandists H. Delehaye (*Étude sur le légendier romain*, p. 10) and B. Gaiffier (*AB* 72, 1954, p. 137) have acknowledged. Delehaye's severe criticism of the defects in Dufourcq's volumes was in *AB* 27, 1908, pp. 215-8. Later he was more appreciative of their merits.

[105] *Op. cit.*, Chapter 3.

of course, differences of literary convention. The authors of the *Gesta* (mainly, but not always) situate their tales in a misty age of persecution, which is spun out of fantasy, while the author of the *Dialogues* situates his in a more recent past, from the age of the Ostrogoths to that of Gregory the Great.[106] For all that, both he and they live in the same mental climate. Both imagine the same kind of conceits and envisage the same kind of readers. They share in common the same religious sensibilities, the same hagiographical motifs and the same experience of the towns and territories reached by the Roman roads radiating from the City. We have space to consider only a selection of particular instances in which there is clearly inter-relation between the *Dialogues* and the *Gesta*. In each instance I will discuss the implications of this relationship. I present here five test-cases, which together provide a strong converging argument for a seventh-century dating of the *Dialogues*.

(1) My first instance is the story of the martyrdom of Bishop Herculanus of Perugia at the hands of the Gothic king Totila. In the *Dialogues* the story is told in III.13. We find another version of the same story in the *Gesta* of Abundius and the Twelve Syrians. The latter is described by Dufourcq as "a cyclical text", that is, one in which diverse traditions are combined. Although he thinks it includes sixth-century material, he dates its composition to after the middle of the seventh century, and he sees it as the work of someone "in the pontifical administration".[107] He sets out the two texts in parallel columns, where their remarkable correspondence can be studied. There can be no doubt that the two forms of the story are closely related. The essential elements are the same. Both relate that Totila besieged Perugia for seven years (both thus stating an historical error); both recall the part of famine in the capture of the city; both say that the perfidious king thought out a way to deal with Herculanus, the bishop of Perugia; that is, as both relate, he ordered that a thong of skin should be stripped from the bishop's body "from head to heel", and that he should be beheaded on the city wall; both describe how his body was later found to be not only incorrupt in the grave but to be perfectly intact, without any trace of incision; both also relate that a child's body was placed in the same tomb.

Yet for all the striking agreement between the two accounts, there are also intriguing differences. In particular, they give quite different ac-

---

[106] J. Petersen disputes Dufourcq's assertion of a strict solidarity between the *Gesta* and the *Dialogues*, and lists several significant points of difference (*op. cit.*, pp. 88-9). The Dialogist does indeed excel all the other *Gesta* writers in his method of composition and creative talent; but he and they are none the less of the same school.

[107] *Op. cit.*, III, pp. 76-9. J. Petersen thinks it "highly likely that the bulk of the material in the *Gesta Abundii* [and allied texts] is post-Gregorian" (*op. cit.*, p. 80).

counts of what befell the child's body in the tomb. In the *Gesta* there is a further miraculous sequel, missing in the *Dialogues*. Because of those remarkable differences Dufourcq judges that "the two texts are independent one from another" and that "both derive from an oral tradition".[108] I would dissent from that view, for a number of reasons. First, there are several verbal assonances which argue even some textual connection between the two accounts. I note some of them in the following comparison:

Gesta of the Twelve Syrians[109]	Dialogues III.13
"*Perfidus Totila rex*"	"*Totilae perfidi regis*"
"*septem annis eamdem obsessit civitatem*"	"*eamdem urbem annis septem ... obsedit*"
"*quid de Herculano episcopo ... cogitabat*"	"*quid de episcopo ... iuberet*"
"*iussit ei corrigiam a capite usque ad calcaneum decoriari, caput eius super muros civitatis abscidi*"	"*praecepit ... a vertice usque ad calcaneum corrigiam tolle, et tunc caput illius amputa ... super urbis murum*"
"*corpusque ... foras proici*"	"*corpus illius extra murum proiecit*"
"*ac si nulla macula ferri abscissionis ... fuisset*"	"*ac si nequaquam fuisset abscissum ... ac si nulla hoc incisio ferri tetigisset*"
"*nullum vestigium videretur*"	"*nulla vestigia ... apparerent*"

I put this further objection to Dufourcq's supposition that the *Gesta* text originated later than and independently of the *Dialogues* account. If, as he shows, the text of the *Gesta* of *The Twelve Syrians* was composed after the middle of the seventh century, and if, as is usually assumed, the *Dialogues* of St Gregory the Great had been published over sixty years before that time and were everywhere famous, how can one explain that the author of those *Gesta* gives a version of events (especially as it concerns the child's body buried with Herculanus) that substantially differs from that given by the great Pope Gregory? Why should he rely instead on "independent oral tradition" when he had so authoritative and renowned a source from which to draw the correct facts?

Throughout the legendary *Gesta* Dufourcq marks a consistent pattern of apocryphal martyrdom-stories. He shows that the events described, and often the very persons mentioned, are fictitious. The whole *genre* is that of pious legend. In particular the Acts of Abundius and "The Twelve Syrian Brothers", in which the story of Herculanus is contained, are patently a tissue of bizarre romancing.[110] Why then does Dufourcq

---

[108] *Ibid.* p. 71. The duality of the sources gave rise later in the Middle Ages to cult of *two* saints Herculanus at Perugia. They were liturgically elided into one in 1940. cf. A. Brunacci, "Ercolano", in *BS* IV, Rome 1964, cols. 1302-8.

[109] *Gesta Abundii* etc: text in *AA. SS.*, July 1st, I, p. 13, §18; reproduced by Dufourcq, III, pp. 69-70.

[110] In the further Umbrian *Gesta* there is much more about Herculanus, and "he tends to move out of his secondary role ... and to become the principal hero": Dufourcq, III, pp. 71-2 and footnote 2.

suppose that in this particular case the seventh-century author of the *Gesta Abundii* had inherited a genuine "oral tradition", from more than a century earlier, to incorporate into his fanciful narrative? The reason for his exception in this case is that he assumes without question that the Gregorian *Dialogues* had been written at the end of the sixth century and that Gregory's recording of the story of Herculanus's martyrdom, on the testimony of a Bishop Floridus, was a proof of its historical foundation. But since the author of the *Gesta* gives the story in a strangely variant form, Dufourcq concludes that he must have had it from another tradition. If we prescind from his initial assumption, there is no reason to suppose that the story of Herculanus is any less fictional than the rest of the *Gesta* in which it is found. Dufourcq assumes that the account of Herculanus's martyrdom in the *Dialogues* is not only independent, but appears "simpler and truer than that in the *Gesta*".[111] On the contrary, I would argue that the shorter form of the story in the *Gesta*, while no truer, is more original, and that it has been picturesquely embroidered and expanded by the Dialogist according to his habitual practice when reusing earlier hagiographical models. (Compare with this his expansion and embellishment of the borrowed theme in his story of Bishop Andrew of Fondi in *Dialogues* III.7). He omits, indeed, the final miracle concerning the child's body, which the author of the *Gesta* gives; but he often departs from his models in significant details. The omission of the miracle in this case is no argument for the priority of the *Dialogues*.

(2) My second instance is that of Severus of Valeria. In the *Gesta Severii*,[112] which Dufourcq dates to about the middle of the seventh century,[113] it is related that in the time of the persecuting emperor Maximian a pious, learned and high-born Christian called Severus was ordained as priest of the church of St Mary in a valley "called in popular speech Interocrina".[114] One day a *paterfamilias* on the point of death sent for the priest, wishing to do penance before dying. Severus delayed, however, in order to finish tending his vines, and the man died before his arrival. The priest prayed with tears, and the dead man returned to life, to relate what had happened to him in the other world. Fire-breathing captors had been leading him away through dark places when a young man of resplendent appearance, with supporting companions, stood in their path

---

[111] Petersen proposes arguments for the priority of the *Dialogues* version of the tale (*op. cit.*, pp. 78-9).

[112] *BHL* 7685.

[113] *Op. cit.*, III, p. 268. Lanzoni dates the work "after the 6th century" (*op. cit.*, p. 231).

[114] *Interocrium*, now Antrodoco, in the territory of Rieti.

and commanded them: "Send him back, since Severus the priest is lamenting bitterly for him." Hearing of the prodigious event, the Emperor had Severus beheaded in the same valley. Most of the same legend is also contained in the *Dialogues* (I.12.1-3), where it forms part of a kind of appendix to Book I, relating further wonders in Valeria reported to Gregory by a venerable abbot Fortunatus.[115] There it is likewise related that a very admirable man named Severus was priest of the church of St Mary at Interorina, "which many people, in rustic language, call Interocrina". As in the *Gesta Severii*, a message came from a dying *paterfamilias*, asking Severus to come to help him to do penance for his sins. Here too, Severus delayed in order to prune his vines. Arriving too late, he bewailed his procrastination with tears of self-reproach. As in the *Gesta*, the dead man returned to life, telling how fire-breathing agents were leading him away, but were stopped by a young man of resplendent appearance, who said: "Send him back, since Severus the priest is lamenting". With the assistance of Severus, the *paterfamilias* then did penance for his sins during seven days, after which he died happily.

In this instance there can be no question but that the two accounts largely reproduce the same text. There is substantial verbal identity between them in the passage relating the experience of the *paterfamilias* in the Beyond. This can be seen by comparing *Dialogues* I.12.2, lines 27-33, with the passage from the *Gesta Severii* reproduced by Dufourcq.[116] Between the two texts, as well as a few very minor variants,[117] there is one significant textual difference, which suggests that the account in the *Dialogues* is secondary to that in the *Gesta Severii*, and is a defective reproduction of the original text attested by the latter. I cite here the sentence describing the rescue of the *paterfamilias* from his demonic captors, as given in the *Gesta Severii*. I mark (in Roman type) the words omitted by the Dialogist: "*Cumque per obscura loca* diutius *ducerent, subito pulchrae visionis iuvenis cum aliis* sodalibus suis iuvenibus *nobis euntibus obviavit qui me trahentibus dixit: Reducite illum, quia Severus presbyter* amarissime *eum plangit*". Instead of the second clause in this passage, the Dialogist has a shorter reading: "*... subito pulchrae visionis iuvenis cum aliis nobis euntibus obviam factus est*". The meaning of this, it would seem, is that the angel barred the way, "to us, as we were going along, with others". In the *Dialogues* the omission after "*aliis*" of the three words, "*sodalibus suis iuvenibus*", obscures the sense. In the rest of the narrative the pater-

[115] I.10; cf. Vogüé, *SC* 251, p. 57, note 36.

[116] III, p. 266. Fr de Vogüé has pointed out that there is a literary antecedent of the Severus story in the narrative about the catechumen of Ligugé in the *Vita Martini* of Sulpicius Severus, 7.1-6 (cf. *SC* 260 pp. 114-5).

[117] An obvious error in the transmission of the *Gesta* text is *manibus* instead of *naribus*.

familias is a lone captive. The "we" in "*nobis euntibus*" evidently means him and his demonic abductors. Who, then, are those "others" who now seem to be introduced in the *Dialogues* story as accompanying "us"?[118] This puzzle is dissipated when we look at the text of the *Gesta Severii*. The "others" are there seen to be "the other young companions" of the angelic rescuer who bids the demons to stand and deliver their captive. They were not "going along with us", but they appeared with their leader when he "stood in our path".

In the lines that follow we find further indication that the text of the *Gesta Severii*, is prior, and that of the *Dialogues* secondary. In the *Gesta* the angel's words to the demons are as follows: "*Reducite illum quia Severus presbyter amarissime eum plangit. Suis enim lacrymis et intercessionibus suis Dominus ei vitam reddidit.*" The omission of "*et intercessionibus suis*" by the Dialogist can be seen to correspond to a distinctive elaboration in his version of the story. Whereas in the *Gesta* the salutary resurrection of the defunct *paterfamilias* is due to the intercessory prayers of Severus, in the *Dialogues* the priest weeps and afflicts himself not in order to obtain the man's salvation, but to express his remorse for delaying his arrival and to bewail his own responsibility for the loss of the man's soul. (Did the Dialogist modify the story here in the light of the parallel in the *Vita* Martini?) Comparison of the two texts reveals a further significant retouching by the Dialogist, by which he corrects the Latinity of the original text. In the last sentence quoted above, the *Gesta Severii* has "*Suis enim lacrymis* ...*"; the Dialogist changes the possessive pronoun "*Suis*" to the more correct "*Eius*", since the subject of the sentence is *Dominus*.[119] Dufourcq assumes as "certain" that the narrative in the *Gesta Severii* is "a reworking of a page of St Gregory".[120] But if a plagiarist writing in the mid-seventh century were reproducing a narrative related by Pope Gregory in a book known far and wide, would he change the grammatically correct "*Eius*" to the incorrect "*Suis*"? Still more, would he change the whole setting of the history as related by the great pope? Would he give the lie to Gregory and his informant, the abbot Fortunatus, and change Severus into a martyr of the early centuries who had suffered under the emperor Maximian? But while it appears improbable that the author of the *Gesta Severii* should so deform a well known history, it is not at all improbable that the Dialogist should borrow and adapt for his own non-

---

[118] Doubtless the puzzlement of scribes on this point explains the variant reading "*cum alis*", "with wings".

[119] But in so doing he chooses the awkward phrase "*Eius enim eum* ...*" By writing "*donavit*" instead of "*vitam reddidit*" he makes "*lacrymis*" a dative case instead of the instrumental ablative in the *Gesta*.

[120] *Op. cit.*, III, p. 267. On the confusion surrounding the name of "St Severus" because of these hagiographical fictions see *BS* XI, Rome 1968, cols. 984-5 and 994-5.

martyrological narrative an obscure and recently invented story taken from the lush crop of provincial *Gesta Martyrum*. In any case, the textual comparison we have considered above undermines the too-facile assumption that the author of the *Gesta Severii* was reworking a page from the *Dialogues*.

(3) My third instance is the strange duplication of the story of the vegetable thieves and the *vangae*. It is told in the *Gesta* of Felix a priest from Nola. Dufourcq considers that these *Gesta* originated around the year 600 or at least hardly later than the end of the first quarter of the seventh century.[121] The same story is told in *Dialogues* III.14.6-7 of the prescient abbot Isaac of Spoleto (whose deeds are also strangely paralleled by those of a number of other worthies in different *Gesta*). The story of Felix and the vegetable thieves is shorter and less dramatic than the Dialogist's tale of Isaac. In both cases, however, the essential elements are the same. The thieves enter the saint's garden to steal vegetables. There they find *vangae* or rustic spades. The author of the *Gesta Felicis* uses the word *vangae* without explanation—he assumes it is known to his readers; but the author of the *Dialogues* explains that these are "iron tools, which *we* call by the colloquial name of *vangae*"—"*ferramenta, quae usitato nos nomine vangas vocamus*". (Who, we may well ask, are "we"? Is it supposed that Gregory the Great belonged to a circle in which that colloquial term for the rustic spade was current?[122]) In both cases the would-be thieves find themselves tilling the ground all night; in the morning they are still labouring; they are kindly addressed by the holy man; they confess how the Lord turned them from their dishonest intent.

Dufourcq assumes, on the authority of the *Dialogues*, that the Spoletan setting of the tale is the original, since in that book Gregory tells it of Isaac of Spoleto, testifying that he has learnt much of that holy man from "monks of our monastery", from a holy virgin Gregoria, and from a venerable abbot Eleutherius.[123] Nevertheless, Dufourcq considers, there is no need to conclude that the text of *Dialogues* III.14 influenced the author of the *Gesta Felicis* in his narrative.[124] He surmises that the latter may have drawn his model independently from an Umbrian tradition.

---

[121] *Op. cit.*, III, pp. 236-7. His reasons for this dating are fair, but not apodictic. A date later in the century is not excluded.

[122] *Vanga* is a word of Germanic origin which entered Late Latin in south-central Italy as a substitute for the Latin *bipalium*. (*Dizionario Etimologico Italiano*, ed. C. Battisti and G. Alessio, Vol. V. Florence 1957, p. 3986.)

[123] An enigmatic figure: there are *Gesta* of a martyr Eleutherius, composed, as Dufourcq argues, in the first quarter of the seventh century, when this name comes to the fore. (*op. cit.* I, pp. 319-20).

[124] Petersen likewise thinks that the two stories borrow independently from earlier models (*op. cit.*, pp. 80-2).

I would submit that an objective comparison between the two forms of the story points to the conclusion that the short and unadorned episode related in the *Gesta Felicis* represents a prior form of the story; and that the longer and more circumstantial version of it in the *Dialogues*, where the plot and the *denouement* are artistically developed with dramatic irony, is a later elaboration of that original short form.[125]

(4) A tell-tale indication that the Dialogist is copying from the authors of the *Gesta*, and not vice versa, can be seen in the grouping of stories in the *Dialogues*, especially in the third book. In topography and hagiography Book III has numerous links with the legendary *Gesta* of central Italy, relating to Tuscia, Umbria, Valeria and Sabina. In the middle chapters of that book we find a succession of anecdotes, and allusions to names and places, which are strikingly paralleled by similar anecdotes and allusions scattered in several different *Gesta*. From the standpoint of literary criticism we may ask, which is the more probable: that the several authors of those diverse legends, which we find dispersed in many different texts, separately drew their legendary models from that particular section of the *Dialogues*; or that the single author of the *Dialogues* (who, we already know, was a borrower of themes from a wide range of hagiographical literature) brought together in one section of his work stories based on models and motifs which he had garnered from the separate *Gesta*-legends of central Italy?

To appreciate these literary interconnections it is instructive to take as an example Chapter 14 of the third book of the *Dialogues*, which tells of the life and miracles of the holy abbot Isaac of Spoleto. We have already seen that the Dialogist makes Isaac the hero of the very same story (concerning the vegetable thieves and the *vangae*) that is told of Felix the priest of Nola in the *Gesta Felicis*. In the *Dialogues*, immediately before that anec-

---

[125] Dufourcq points out another suggestive inter-relation between the *Dialogues* and the provincial *Gesta*, in the details of the story of Proculus of Terni and Pope Eugenius, as given in the Acts of Anastasius-Abundius. (*op. cit.* III, pp. 73-4.) He sees in that story, "*sans crainte d'erreur*", a copy of the narrative in *Dialogues* I.4 about Equitius of Valeria and an unnamed pope. In both cases the zealous fervour of a holy man is misjudged by a pope, who sends agents to arrest him and bring him to Rome. In both cases the pontiff is terrified in the night by a severe admonition on his conduct, sent from heaven, which leads him to dispatch messengers post haste to revoke his previous unjust commands and to make amends to the holy man. In both cases the wronged saint bestows a favour on his would-be persecutors. The resemblance between those two plots is indeed striking. It may well be that the Dialogist had in mind the Proculus anecdote when writing his story of Equitius. However, as we shall see later in this chapter, there is another probable model which may have been the parent of both those similar stories: namely, the narration of John Moschus in the *SpM* concerning a bishop of "Romilla", who was in like manner misjudged by a pope (Agapitus), ill-treated and finally vindicated.

dote there is an account of Isaac's arrival in Spoleto from Syria which, as Dufourcq points out,[126] is a striking parallel to the story in the *Gesta* of John Penariensis.[127] Both John Penariensis and the Isaac of the *Dialogues* were holy strangers. Each came to Umbria from Syria in the time of the Goths; each made his way to Spoleto, where each conversed with God and resolved to make his abode there; the sanctity of each was revealed by a miracle[128] which convinced the inhabitants of Spoleto; each exorcized demoniacs; each founded a monastery at Spoleto, and each attracted there a multitude of disciples.

Thus we find that in adjacent paragraphs of the *Dialogues* Isaac of Spoleto has two doubles from the *Gesta*—Felix the priest from Nola and John Penariensis from Syria. Isaac is the only one of the Dialogist's holy "Fathers of Italy" who is not of Italian but of Eastern origin. In the *Gesta*, however, John Penariensis is one of many central Italian saints who have come from the East. In particular there is the "great legend" of the Twelve Syrians who came to Rome in the time of the Emperor Julian the Apostate, and who dispersed to Sabina, Valeria and Umbria. The legendary interconnections are still further tangled when we find that one of these Twelve Syrians, connected with Spoleto, is in fact named Isaac. Dufourcq observes[129] that he is evidently identifiable with his namesake in the *Dialogues*. So we see that the Dialogist's Isaac not only impersonates two other legendary characters from the *Gesta* (Felix and John Penariensis) but is also given the name, as well as the *persona*, of a third such character—the Isaac who was one of the twelve Syrian brethren.

Among those Twelve Syrians was Herculanus, whose legendary martyrdom as bishop of Perugia we have already discussed. The reasons given by Dufourcq for dating the saga of the Twelve Syrians to the second half of the seventh century are cogent. He also shows that there are clear literary interrelationships between the *Gesta* of the Twelve Syrians and several other seventh-century *Passiones* relating to the same regions.[130] Throughout that abundant legendary literature we find many names and situations which have intriguing echoes in the *Dialogues*. Although the Dialogist has his own creative talent, and has fashioned anew his stories about those mythical worthies of the duchy of Rome, it is surely more than a coincidence that his pages repeatedly evoke names and legends that we find scattered through the seventh-century *Passiones*.

---

[126] III, pp. 61-2.
[127] *BHL* 4420.
[128] The two miracles were quite diverse in character.
[129] III, p. 72.
[130] III, Chapters 2-7.

Thus, for instance, we find in the *Dialogues* mention of the following names borne by heroes of the *Gesta*: Anastasius, Euticius—and Euthicius—Proculus, Juvenal, Sabinus, Faustinus, Maximus, Donatus, Frigdianus, Gaudentius, Boniface, Spes, Eleutherius, as well as Herculanus, Isaac and Severus. Sometimes there is a recognizable hagiographical connection between the references to these holy persons in the *Dialogues* and those in the *Gesta*, sometimes not. Dufourcq's pages offer many suggestive indications of such allusive parallels between the texts.[131] In his own speculation about the dating and literary interdependence of the legends, however, his judgement is often swayed by his unquestioning assumption that the *Dialogues* were written at the end of the sixth century by Gregory the Great.

(5) The last argument that I draw from the evidence of the *Gesta* is perhaps the most striking of all—indeed it may prove to be one of the most significant in the whole of our discussion of the Gregorian authenticity of the *Dialogues*. In I.7.3 the author of the *Dialogues* explicitly refers to a miracle of Donatus of Arezzo, which we find narrated in the legendary *Passio Donati*.[132] After relating two miracles worked by Nonnosus, the Gregory of the *Dialogues* remarks that in working them the holy man had "imitated the power of two Fathers": namely, the moving of a gigantic rock by Gregory the Wonderworker, and the reconstitution of a broken chalice by Donatus, which Nonnosus "imitated" by miraculously repairing a shattered lamp.[133] This is the only place in the *Dialogues* in which the author overtly reveals his borrowing of models from the legendary hagiography of Late Antiquity. His source for the reference to Gregory the Wonderworker was Rufinus's *Historia Ecclesiastica*, which dated from two centuries before the time of Gregory the Great. But his reference to the miracle of Donatus of Arezzo is of the highest interest for our dating of the *Dialogues*. The apocryphal *Passio Donati*[134] forms part of the jungle of Italian legends which we have been reviewing.[135] Thus the links between the *Dialogues* and the *Gesta*, though elsewhere concealed, find here a single and singular avowal.

The key question that concerns us is the date of origin of the *Passio Donati*. Since it is the source for the prodigy referred to in the *Dialogues*

---

[131] See especially his third volume, pp. 73-5 and 293-4.

[132] *BHL* 2289-94.

[133] "... *imitatus* [*est*] ... *in reparatione vero lampadis virtutem Donati, qui fractum calicem pristinae incolumitati restituit.*"

[134] A genuine saint Donatus was commemorated in the *Martyrologium Hieronymianum* as a *confessor*. The fictitious *Passio* turns him into a martyr. (Lanzoni, *op. cit.*, pp. 358-9.)

[135] The text of the *Passio Donati* was printed in the *Sanctuarium* of B. Mombritius; Paris edition 1910, Vol 1, pp. 416-8. See also Dufourcq, III, pp. 165-8.

commentators have naturally assumed that the text must antedate the year 593. Dufourcq shares this assumption, and he suggests, for reasons that are very conjectural, that the work originated during "the last years of the Ostrogothic regime", that is, in the mid-sixth century. Plainly the *Passio Donati* is closely related to the legend of St Bibbiana, and may well be by the same author (who presents himself as a subdeacon of the Roman Church, also called Donatus).[136] However, Dufourcq's study of the relationships between the various *Gesta* shows links between these two legends (of Donatus and Bibbiana) and other *Gesta*-texts that he judges to have been written (or "reworked") in the early part of the seventh century.

Indeed he himself signals an important point which would indicate that the date of the *Passio Donati* was not earlier than the seventh century. The author of that text emphasizes that Donatus went to Rome in order to be consecrated as bishop of Arezzo by the Roman pontiff. But, as Dufourcq points out, there was no controversy about the metropolitan rights of the Roman pontiff in Tuscia-Umbria in the sixth century. That question did become a live issue, however, in the following century. The author of the contemporary *Gesta* of Juvenal of Narnia, which seems to be from the same literary workshop as the *Passio Donati*, likewise insists on the ecclesiastical subordination of Tuscia to the Roman Church. Jesus himself, he relates, confided the evangelization of the province to Saints Peter and Paul; it was therefore to Rome that Juvenal went to be consecrated as bishop of Narnia by the pope. Dufourcq also dates the origin of the *Gesta Iuvenalis* to the beginning of the seventh century.[137] As we shall see, the actual dating should probably be still later. Perplexed because that tendentious trait, which is common to the *Gesta* both of Juvenal and of Donatus, reflects a later situation, Dufourcq puts forward the surmise that the *Passio Donati* was "reworked" after the sixth century in furtherance of a pro-Roman apologetic design. He also admits that certain features of the *Passio Donati* reflect those of the *Gesta* of Victorianus-Severinus and of Agapetus, which must have been written (or, he again suggests, possibly "reworked") in the early seventh century.[138] His theory of multiple "reworkings" of the various texts is an arbitrary conjecture, brought in, it would seem, mainly because the historically indicated date for the *Passio Donati* is too late for Gregory to have had knowledge of the story when supposedly writing the *Dialogues*.

[136] Dufourcq I, pp. 89-90. He notes that these *Gesta* have literary connections with another contemporary legend, that of St Juliana. Delehaye found the model of the *Passio Donati* in the *Passio Gallicani* (*BHL* 3236-7).

[137] Dufourcq III, pp. 85-6 and 109. He notes that the author of these Narnia *Gesta* has no echo of the story about Narnia in *Dialogues* III.6.

[138] III, pp. 168-9 and footnote.

Other historians have corroborated the force of the arguments for a seventh-century date of the *Passio Donati*. Indeed there are indications in that intricate network of legendary texts that the dispute about metropolitan rights in Tuscia-Umbria may not have become relevant until about the middle of the seventh century, when the bishops of Spoleto, capital of the powerful Lombard duchy in central Italy, were vindicating for themselves rights as metropolitans over that Apennine region. There are reflections of this controversy in the *Gesta* of Felicianus of Forum Flaminii (Foligno), which Dufourcq judges to be evidently related to the *Gesta* of Juvenal.[139] Later studies have further undermined the supposition that the *Passio Donati* originated at a time before the pontificate of Gregory the Great. F. Caraffa is one of those who judge that the *Gesta* of Juvenal, which are closely related to it, and may well be by the same author, date from the seventh century.[140] G. Lucchesi considers that the only substantial objection against the arguments which point to a seventh-century date of origin for the Donatus text is the assumption that it was cited by Gregory the Great in the *Dialogues*. "It is because of this assumption", he recognizes, that authors "infer that the *Passio* must be of earlier date than St Gregory".[141] It naturally did not occur to Lucchesi that the solution to the difficulty may be found in the realization that the *Dialogues* were written after the time of Gregory the Great. Instead, the solution he proposes is to postulate that when composing the *Dialogues* Gregory did not know the text of the *Passio Donati*, which had not yet been written; but that he had the story of Donatus and the broken chalice from independent "oral tradition". Lucchesi claims that acceptance of this conjecture "removes any solid basis for dating that *Passio* to an epoch earlier than that of St Gregory the Great". Although his own recourse to a putative oral tradition preceding the publication of the legendary *Passio Donati* is an implausible hypothesis, his appreciation of the weight of evidence concerning the texts provides another corroboration of the post-Gregorian origin of that writing.[142]

The author of the *Passio Donati*, who was doubtless the inventor of the miraculous episode referred to in the *Dialogues*, belonged to the group of legend-spinners who fed the religious imagination of the people in Rome

---

[139] III, pp. 82-5.

[140] *BS* VI, Rome 1965, s.v. "Giovenale", cols. 1069-70.

[141] *BS* IV, Rome 1964, s.v. "Donato", cols. 778-9.

[142] Another may perhaps be found in an interpolation of the *Passio Pigmenii*, which is one of the *Gesta* relating to the City of Rome and can be ascribed to the sixth century. The oldest redactions contain no mention of St Donatus of Arezzo; he was, however, introduced into the story subsequently. (cf. H. Delehaye, *Étude sur le Légendier romain*, Brussels 1936, pp. 136-7.) The interpolation may well have been occasioned by the appearance of the *Passio Donati* in the seventh century.

and in the central Italian provinces during the seventh century. Although obscurity still surrounds its precise date of composition, there is good reason to conclude that this text originated well after the year 593-4 in which St Gregory is alleged to have written the *Dialogues*. The Dialogist, writing at a still later date, uncritically assumed that the *Passio Donati* was old enough to have been known to St Gregory; but in citing an anecdote from it he unwittingly betrayed the non-Gregorian origin of his own pseudepigraphal work.

Among the post-Gregorian sources probably used by the Dialogist, I include the *Spiritual Meadow* of John Moschus (written, according to Dr Philip Pattenden's findings, between 614 and 629) and the *Vita Burgundofarae* of Jonas of Bobbio (after 642). Both these works have already been considered in Chapter 6, where I indicated reasons for inferring that the Dialogist drew hagiographical models from them. His story of the monk Justus in *Dialogues* IV.57 appears to be an embellished adaptation of Moschus's story of the excommunicate monk who was granted post-humous absolution by St Gregory. There are other affinities between the *Spiritual Meadow* and the *Dialogues* that are worth studying. As well as the general similarity of *genre* there are not a few specific points of contact between the two works.[143]

Even more striking than the parallel between the two stories of excommunicate monks is the resemblance between Moschus's story of the high-handed treatment of a bishop of "Romilla" by Pope Agapitus and the Dialogist's story of the high-handed treatment of the abbot Equitius by an unnamed pope.[144] The names, places, and incidental circumstances are all quite different in the two narratives. But, as A. de Vogüé points out: "The analogies are no less impressive. In both cases a pope receives a denunciation against a holy man, sends agents to bring him to Rome, and is warned in a dream not to molest him. This common framework gives cause for thought. One has the impression of being confronted with two versions of the same story. Could not Agapitus, who has a leading role in Moschus's account, be the anonymous pope in Gregory's?"[145] Fr de Vogüé makes a persuasive argument for this identification. We observe that in this instance he does not suggest that Moschus based his

---

[143] "*Par toute sa manière*", writes A. de Vogüé, "*le* Pré Spirituel *rappelle les* Dialogues" (*SC* 251, p. 121). He notes several detailed parallels between the two texts (cf. *SC* 265, p. 304).

[144] *Pratum spirituale* 150, *PG* 87, 3013-6; *Dialogues* I.4. Agapitus was pope for one year, 535-6.

[145] "*Le pape qui persécuta saint Equitius: essai d'identification*", in *AB* 100, 1982, p. 322. See also *SC* 260, p. 436.

story on the *Dialogues*, as he does when comparing the two stories about an excommunicate monk. His reason for not doing so, presumably, is that here Moschus seems to give a correct and important historical fact which he could not have copied from the *Dialogues*—that is, the identity of the high-handed pontiff, whom he names as Agapitus.[146] But if Moschus knew this fact independently of the *Dialogues*, why should it be assumed that he must be dependent on the *Dialogues* in other instances of close similarity between the two books?

While it does indeed appear that his tale of the papal maltreatment of the bishop of "Romilla" and the Dialogist's tale of the papal maltreatment of Equitius are "two versions of the same story", comparison of the texts here suggests the priority of the *Spiritual Meadow* to the *Dialogues*, rather than the reverse. The Dialogist's dramatic elaboration of the plot accords well with his habitual practice, of which we have seen several examples, of making a new imaginative reconstruction of a hagiographical model taken from elsewhere.

It is doubtful whether the Dialogist would have been able to read Moschus's Greek text, but the anecdotes it contained could have been mediated to him through the Greek-speaking monks who became so numerous in Rome during the seventh century. We must remember that as well as the Latin legendary *Gesta* which were so popular in that age, an abundant flow of Greek legendary hagiography was also influential in Italy. The *Gesta Martyrum* of the duchy of Rome reflected that influence, and the stories from the Greek texts themselves were doubtless widely repeated among the monks and clerics of Rome. In that literature the *Spiritual Meadow* of John Moschus was outstanding. It may well be that the renown of his book among the Greek-speaking churchmen in Rome was one of the factors that prompted the Dialogist to emulate him by presenting a rival and home-grown anthology of Italian saints and miracles.

It is likely, too, that the Dialogist was indebted to the *Vita Burgundofarae* of Jonas of Bobbio for models used in the accounts of deathbed phenomena in his fourth book. The resemblances seem too strong to be explained as mere coincidence. As I pointed out in Chapter 6, Jonas's stories are jejeune compared to the boldly imaginative developments which the Dialogist makes of the same motifs. If the latter knew Jonas's collection of edifying tales about Burgundofara's convent, he could also have known his *Life* of St Columban. There are in fact a number of

---

[146] A number of passages show that Moschus had access to sources of tradition about the Roman pontiffs. Immediately after his story of the pride of Agapitus he gives a pleasing anecdote about the humility of Gregory himself.

miracle motifs in the *Vita Columbani* which may seem to be echoed by tales in the *Dialogues*. The power of Columban to exact obedience from beasts and birds is matched by the similar prowess of holy men in the *Dialogues*. Thus the crow which Columban reduced to obedience, and which was constrained to bring back a stolen glove, is resembled by the crow which brought Benedict his ration of food and was induced by the saint to carry afar off a poisoned morsel.[147] The multitude of birds which obediently provide sustenance for Columban and his starving companions are paralleled by the multitude of birds which swooped down to remove the dead snakes from around the cell of Florentius.[148] There are two stories in the *VC* which show Columban's power to exact obedience from predatory bears; they have a counterpart in the Dialogist's stories of Cerbonius before whom a savage bear became submissive, of Florentius whose pet bear tended his sheep, and of Menas who disciplined the bears that tried to eat his bees.[149] These and similar parallels suggest, but do not prove, that here too the Dialogist borrowed motifs from Jonas, and developed them into new and more artistic inventions. It remains quite possible that these resemblances between the *Dialogues* and the *Vita Columbani* are to be explained as due to independent usage of commonplace hagiographical themes.

The possible relatedness of the *Dialogues* to the writings of Gregory of Tours (especially his *In Gloria Martyrum* and *In Gloria Confessorum*) also requires consideration. The similarity of *genre* is obvious. In his commentary on the *Dialogues* A. de Vogüé signals numerous parallels with miracles and other episodes in the hagiographical works of the Gallic Gregory. "In points of detail", he writes, "the narrations in those works, like others in the *Historia Francorum*, are often so similar to those of our *Dialogues* that one cannot help asking whether Pope Gregory did not read and draw upon the writings of his namesake".[150] He calls this "a delicate question". The chronology of the various writings presents a complicated problem, and it is indeed difficult to establish that Pope Gregory himself knew, or could have known of, his namesake's writings at the time (593-4) at which the *Dialogues* were ostensibly being composed. It seems that elements of the relevant works of Gregory of Tours were still being written even between 591 and his death in 594.[151] It has

---

[147] Jonas, *Vita Columbani* I.15 (ed. Krusch, pp. 178-9); *Dialogues* II.8.3.

[148] *VC* I, 27 (Krusch, p. 215); *Dialogues* III.15.12.

[149] *VC* I, 16, 27 (Krusch, pp. 181, 216); *Dialogues* III.11.2; 15.3-6; 26.3.

[150] *SC* 260. p. 120; cf. *SC* 265, pp. 300-1; and Petersen (*op. cit.*, pp. 130-41), who makes a further detailed comparison of the miracle-stories of the two Gregories.

[151] W. Arndt and B. Krusch, (ed.), *Gregorii Turonensis Opera*, *MGH*, Hanover 1884, I, pp. 11-17.

been suggested that there are possible echoes of his story-telling in three of the *exempla* that the Roman Gregory included in his Gospel homilies;[152] but the evidence appears inconclusive.

But if it is difficult to suppose that the example of the legendary compositions of Gregory of Tours could have stimulated Pope Gregory I "to achieve for Italy what had just been done for Gaul",[153] it is altogether probable that such a stimulus was operative in the Dialogist nearly a century later. The manifold echoes in the *Dialogues* of the Gallic Gregory's narratives can thus be clearly appreciated, without being muted by the chronological problems that have made historians suppose such literary dependence to be scarcely possible.

While the *Dialogues* have a close affinity with, indeed a dependence on, the narratives of Gregory of Tours, there is one notable difference between the two collections of wonder-stories, which had puzzled commentators. A. de Vogüé observes: "It is a curious fact that our author [of the *Dialogues*] has almost nothing to say on a subject in which his contemporaries were passionately interested, namely, the miraculous cures and wonders of all sorts that happened at the tombs of the saints. Whereas the work of Gregory of Tours abounds in stories of this kind, in the *Dialogues*, in contrast, there is a dearth of them." He points out that such stories "make the writings of the bishop of Tours a veritable guide to the miraculous shrines of Christendom".[154] I see a clear reason for this contrast. Although the stories of Gregory of Tours were, like those of all the hagiographers of the age, replete with legendary wonders, he was at least writing about real places of pilgrimage, where there was historical record and present cult of the holy persons whose tombs and relics were venerated there. A practical function of his writings was to cater for the pious needs of pilgrims and clients of those saints. The *Dialogues*, on the other hand, had no such function. The Dialogist not only invented his miracle stories: he also invented most of the characters who feature in them. Although he presented the lives of his holy Fathers in the setting of central Italy, most of them belonged to a never-never land of legend; they had no anchorage in actual centres of devotion and pilgrimage. His holy men, for the most part, were unknown to historical record; they had no tomb-shrines or living cult which his wonder-stories could serve. Hence his book lacked the practical function of the works of Gregory of Tours in the previous century. The Dialogist's enterprise was purely

---

[152] A. de Vogüé, "*Grégoire le Grand, lecteur de Grégoire de Tours?*", in *AB* 94, 1976, pp. 225-33. The author recognizes "the almost insoluble problems presented by this embroiled chronology" (p. 226, footnote 1).

[153] Vogüé, *SC* 260, p. 120.

[154] *SC* 251, p. 94, and footnote 52.

literary: its function was to cater for the interests of readers (and book-buyers), not of pilgrims, devotees of the saints and seekers after miraculous cures. He had no thought of encouraging his readers to tread the roads of central Italy in search of spiritual and material help from the imaginary characters of his narrative. We shall see in Chapter 20 that devotion to and cult of the spiritual heroes of the *Dialogues* came in most cases only after the lapse of centuries—in some cases after a millennium—as a consequence of the literary success of the *Dialogues*.

There, I submit, lies the explanation for the "curious" contrast between the sixth-century Gregory of Tours and the seventh-century author of the *Dialogues*, whose works are otherwise so akin. The miracle-stories of the former refer to actual centres of cult and pilgrimage; those of the latter, for the most part, lack any such base. A similar contrast is recognizable between the sixth-century authors of the *Gesta Martyrum* of the City of Rome, who in the main provided legends for historically commemorated saints and for existing shrines, and on the other hand the authors of the seventh-century *Gesta* of the wider duchy of Rome, whose bizarre stories about provincial saints were often purely literary inventions independent of any existing cult.

Lastly, mention may be made of an etymological aside which the Dialogist may well have drawn from St Isidore of Seville. In *Dialogues* II.6.1. he gives a derivation of *falcastrum*, with assonance of wording that seems to echo Isidore's *Etymologies* 20.14.5. Direct textual dependence is probable but not certain.

CHAPTER NINETEEN

THE CHARACTER, PASTORAL STANDPOINT AND THEOLOGICAL SUPPOSITIONS OF "THE GREGORY OF THE *DIALOGUES*", CONTRASTED WITH THOSE OF THE REAL ST GREGORY

Frequently in the preceding chapters I have pointed out contrasts between the character, attitude and doctrine of the Gregory who is depicted as the author and protagonist of the *Dialogues* and what we know of the real Gregory from his expository and pastoral writings, and also from his letters. In this chapter I will resume this comparison and will point out some further significant contrasts.

Before descending to particulars, I would recall again a general methodological peculiarity of the *Dialogues*, which marks it off from all the undisputed Gregorian writings. In his article on St Gregory in the *Dictionnaire de Spiritualité*[1] Dom R. Gillet remarks that the anecdotes "constitute the fabric of the *Dialogues*, and thus reduce to a minimum the utilization of Scripture, contrary to the usual practice of Gregory." In Chapter 17 I pointed out how anomalous is this scarcity of Scriptural reference in the supposedly Gregorian *Dialogues*. The writings of the real Gregory are everywhere permeated with the words and teaching of Scripture. In the *Dialogues* the same is true only of the 80 IGPs, but not of the rest of the book. To explain this anomaly it is not enough to appeal to the narrative character of most of the *Dialogues*. Even in the personal letters[2] and popular sermons of Pope Gregory the Scriptural cast of his thought is pervasive. It is not so in the *Dialogues*. Where an occasional Scriptural phrase or reference is brought into the narrative, it is an exception and an adjunct.

Self-congratulation and defective reasoning

The dialogue form of the book, and the fact that the ostensible author makes himself the chief protagonist in that dialogue, do not of course provide an argument against Gregorian authorship. Following the example of Plato, not only classical but also ecclesiastical authors, such as Jerome,

---

[1] Vol 6 (1967), col. 879.

[2] As distinct from the many administrative letters drafted for his approval by his secretaries. See Chapter 21 below pp. 689-90.

Theodoret and Palladius, had written dialogues.[3] Sulpicius Severus, to whom the author of the Gregorian *Dialogues* is considerable indebted for models for his own tales, made himself the chief speaker in his hagiographical dialogue about St Martin of Tours. St Gregory himself adopted a dialogue form of heuristic exposition in two passages in his *Moralia*: namely 34.35-38[4] and 14.72-74. There are other shorter snatches of quasi-dialogue, apostrophizing Job, in the pages of the *Moralia*.

What is anomalous and unGregorian in our *Dialogues* is the manner in which the author and chief protagonist, ostensibly Pope St Gregory himself, conducts the exchanges with his naive interlocutor, Peter the Deacon. Particularly surprising are the self-complacent comments that he puts into Peter's mouth, on his own contributions to the debate. We find Gregory portrayed as a papal Dr Johnson, so to speak, omniscient and oracular, who constantly enlightens his docile Boswell-like disciple Peter. Again and again the latter expresses his admiration at Gregory's magisterial answers, saying how clearly the matter has been explained and how completely he has been convinced by his master's arguments. All that we know of the real Gregory's transparent humility in thought and in expression contrasts with this strange and recurrent feature of the *Dialogues*.

I give here some specimens of the self-satisfied comments which the Gregory who is supposed to be writing the dialogue puts into the mouth of his disciple. Peter's admiring interjections include the following: "What you say is very true' (I.4.19); "Because your reasoning has laid bare the secret meaning, no trace of doubt remains in my mind" (I.8.7); "All that has been said is admirable. I had no inkling of it until now" (I.12.4); "I confess that what you say is altogether satisfying" (I.12.6); "You have unlocked the hidden sense of the text cited" (II.2.5); "You relate great things, which will profit for the edification of many" (II.7.4); "The things you narrate are wonderful and most astounding!" (II.8.8; likewise II.35.5, III.5.5, III.31.8, III.32.2 etc); "Through the posing of my little query the occasion was given for your reasoning to make the matter plain" (II.16.9); "Cogent reasoning cries aloud that what you affirm is the case" (II.21.5); "Your words, I avow, are like a hand wiping away the doubts from my mind" (II.22.5); "That all is as you assert is patently certain, because you prove your premises by facts" (II.32.4); "That clear argument has solved the difficulty I had in my mind" (III.24.3); "All that you say is agreeable to the reason of the faithful" (IV.3.3); "I rejoice that I was ignorant of what I inquired about, since

---

[3] Numerous examples of this *genre* are mentioned in the article *"Dialogues spirituels"*, in *Dictionnaire de Spiritualité* III.834-50.

[4] Cf. Chapter 17, IGP 71.

through such subtle explanation I have been able to learn what I did not know" (IV.4.9); "What has been said is wholly right" (IV.5.5); "Gladly, I confess, am I constrained by your reasonings" (IV.5.9); "There is nothing, it seems to me, to counter your reasoning" (IV.6.3); "By your satisfactory response to my question, reason has made the matter plain" (IV.37.1); "There is nothing that can be replied to such an evident argument" (IV.47.1). The phrases *"placet quod dicis"*, *"multum placet"*, or *"valde placet"* recur very frequently.

Most of those expressions of self-satisfaction, ostensibly written by Gregory himself, are found immediately after the insertion of the IGPs. It is understandable that the *Dialogist*, moved by *pietas* towards the great pope under whose name he is passing off his book, should write such comments; they mark his own satisfaction at being able to reproduce those gems of Gregorian wisdom. Such a portrayal, however, does not accord with the supposition that it is St Gregory himself who is the author of these exchanges, presenting himself in this Johnsonian role. In this contradiction between the self-congratulatory smugness of the Gregory of the *Dialogues* and the profound humility and simplicity of the real St Gregory, as we know him from his authentic works, is one more tell-tale mark of the pseudepigrapher.

Banal reasoning and limping logic

Another feature of the *Dialogues* which does not accord with what we know of the real Gregory is the mediocre level of reasoning and argument in the book. Again and again in Chapters 14-17, when discussing the manner in which the author inserts the IGPs, I have pointed out the frequent inconsequentiality, naivety, clumsiness and abruptness of his arguments. In his writings the real Gregory can indeed be discursive and repetitive, but his mental acuity and power of coherent argument is unwavering. By contrast, the Dialogist's level of thought and writing is inferior. The rational links in his anecdotal composition are often weak; so too, his attempts to maintain a consequential argument are often artificial. Although some authors have attempted to present the Gregorian *Dialogues* as a skilful work of pastoral pedagogy,[5] others have recognized more realistically that the logical sequence often limps painfully.[6] In his study of the structure of the book A. Vitale Brovarone characterizes the

---

[5] E.g. C. Dagens, *Saint Grégoire le Grand: culture et expérience chrétiennes*, Paris 1977, pp. 228-33; F. Tateo, *"La struttura dei Dialoghi di Gregorio Magno"* in *Vetera Christiana* 2, 1965, pp. 101-27.

[6] F. Bruys observed: *"Les interruptions de Pierre sont souvent hors de propos et toujours fades"*: *Histoire des Papes*, La Haye 1732, p. 362-3.

development of the discussion as "*disarmonico*", and judges it outside the main literary current of reasoned dialogue.[7]

It is chiefly in Book IV, the most carefully structured of all the four parts of the work, that the Dialogist's distinctive manner of reasoning is most apparent. He there sets out to provide an apologetic demonstration of the immortality of the soul, using only *ratio* and *animarum exempla* (III.38.5). This procedure is itself unGregorian. For the real Gregory, as I have already stressed, divine revelation declared in Holy Scripture is determinative of all his thinking and writing. It would have been quite alien to his mentality and practice to set out to expound spiritual truths from mere philosophical reasoning alone, as though prescinding from the light of revelation in which he saw and discussed all reality. The theme of eternal life, of resurrection, of heavenly bliss, of the future reward which God bestows, through the grace of the Saviour Jesus Christ, on those whom He loves, is an ever-resounding theme in all his expository and pastoral writings. He frequently applies Scriptural texts to illustrate, develop and expound the reality of that true life, to which this transient earthly life is only the prelude. It would have been strange indeed for Gregory to address himself to such a subject without placing in the forefront of his discussion the New Testament texts which look forward to the heavenly kingdom and the reward of the just and which warn of the eternal punishment awaiting the wicked. None of this Scripture-based perspective on the world-to-come appears in the Dialogist's argument for the immortality of the soul in Book IV.

Another strange restriction in his treatise on the other-worldly destiny of man is that he is solely concerned with the lot of the disembodied soul. In this work of "pastoral pedagogy", in which Gregory is supposed to be reaching out to the mass of the faithful to raise their minds to the essentials of the Christian faith, there is no attempt to link consideration of the soul's after-life with that central dogma of Christian eschatology, the resurrection, with which the real Gregory was so intensely concerned in his *Moralia* and Gospel homilies.[8] Nor is there even mention of the resurrection of Jesus Christ as the proof and pledge of eventual enjoyment of eternal bliss for all the just, in both soul and body. The real Gregory's concentration on this doctrine is documented by

---

[7] "*La forma narrativa dei Dialoghi di Gregorio Magno: problemi storico-letterari*" in *Atti della Accademia delle Scienze di Torino*, 108, 1973-4, pp. 95-173. The author makes many valuable observations, but his analysis of the structure of the text is naturally conditioned by unawareness of the two disparate elements in it—one genuinely Gregorian, the other not.

[8] Cf. Vogüé, *SC* 251, p. 160. The genuine Gregorian reference to the complementary bliss of the resurrection, in IGP 57, is extraneous to the Dialogist's own perspective on the future life.

J. P. McClain,[9] who remarks: "There is probably no aspect of the
Christian revelation which Gregory laboured at greater length to bolster
by argumentation than the resurrection of the body".

If indeed St Gregory the Great had set himself to show what merely
rational argument, or even "reason intermingled with faith" (cf. IV.2.3)
could prove about the immortal nature of the human soul, can we suppose that he could produce nothing better than the painfully thin—and
even puerile—"rational proofs" contained in those first six chapters of
Book IV? (As I noted in Chapter 17, Fr de Vogüé himself observes their
lameness and irrelevance). When the irrelevant stages have been discounted, the Dialogist's main rational proof boils down to the following
argument: We know that the soul is present in the living body, even
though it cannot be directly seen, because of the body's vital movements;
similarly the continued existence of the soul after the death of the body
can be deduced from the miracles which the martyrs in heaven work
through their bodily relics on earth, thus providing "movements" to attest the continued vitality of their souls (cf. IV.5 and 6). It is surely implausible to father this odd argument on St Gregory the Great, as if it
were all that his reason could adduce to support the doctrine of the soul's
survival. The Dialogist has neglected even to use arguments which the
real Gregory does bring when he refers to the immortal nature of man—
for example, in *Moralia* 5.63, where he says: "The rational creature, for
the very reason that he is created in the image of his Maker, is fixed in
his being, so that he may not pass into nothingness; but the irrational
creature is by no means so fixed".

Differing attitudes to the miraculous

It is time to criticize more closely the pastoral and theological implications of the prodigious tales that make up the bulk of the *Dialogues*. Can
those tales with any reasonable probability be ascribed to the great pastor
and master of mystical theology who was Pope St Gregory?

From the middle of the sixteenth century, when the Gregorian authenticity of the *Dialogues* was first called into question by Huldreich Coccius,
the humanist and Protestant critics singled out two main objections to the
traditional ascription. The first was the literary style of the book, which
they judged to be different from that of the real Gregory; this will be the
subject of Chapter 21. The second was the character of the anecdotes
related in it, which they judged to be incompatible with the character of

---

[9] *The Doctrine of Heaven in the Writings of St Gregory the Great*, Washington 1956, pp.
78-103.

Gregory himself. In Chapter 3 I quoted the criticisms of Coccius, Chemnitz, Rivet, Cooke, Forbes and Cave. Robert Cooke, we recall, derided the contents of the *Dialogues* as "highly legendary and highly ridiculous", and asked: "Who indeed could suspect, without injustice to Gregory, that he was so stupidly credulous that he would himself accept such old wives' tales or that he would wish others to believe them?" In his *Vindicatio* of the *Dialogues*, published in 1668, the English Jesuit James Mumford inveighed against "modern writers" who "openly profess this book to be unworthy [of] St Gregory. Why so? Because (say they) nothing like such winter tales, as are told in that book, can be found in his most worthy and learned works ..."[10]

L. Ellies du Pin, historian of ecclesiastical literature at the Sorbonne and *Professeur Royal* in the reign of Louis XIV, saw the force of the Protestant objections. While accepting that the *Dialogues* were written by St Gregory,[11] he voiced this criticism; "It seems nevertheless that this work is not worthy of the gravity and discernment of this great pope, so full is it of extraordinary miracles and almost incredible stories. Admittedly, he relates them on the authority of others, but he ought not to have so lightly given them credence, nor to have passed them on as established facts". Not only the prejudiced Gibbon[12] and hostile critics of the Roman Church, but independent historians who esteem Pope Gregory I for his contribution to Christian civilization, have seen the tales in the *Dialogues* as a strange aberration which seriously flaws the great pope's reputation. The criticisms of F. H. Dudden, which I have already referred to in Chapter 3, may be taken as typical. After giving several examples of preposterous tales, he expressed his astonishment that Gregory, the clear-headed papal statesman, should also have been the author of the *Dialogues*, and that he should have propagated "these wild tales of demons and wizards and haunted houses, of souls made visible, of rivers obedient to written orders, of corpses that scream and walk."[13]

Defenders of the *Dialogues* and of their Gregorian authorship have varied their line of defence of the miracle-stories with the passage of time. Older apologists vindicated their credibility in the face of what they saw as rationalist prejudice against the miraculous element in Christianity. Some more recent authors excuse Gregory for narrating such tales by ex-

---

[10] *Op. cit.*, p. 3.
[11] *Nouvelle Bibliothèque des auteurs ecclésiastiques*, Tome V, Mons 1691, pp. 137-8. He refers in footnotes to the usual arguments: Gregory's supposed Letter to Maximian and the alleged witness of Paterius, Tajo and Ildephonsus.
[12] Gibbon noted: "A French critic (Petrus Gussanvillaeus) has vindicated the right of Gregory to the entire nonsense of the *Dialogues*" (*The History of the Decline and Fall of the Roman Empire*, edition of J. B. Bury, London 1898, p. 36, note 81.)
[13] *Op. cit.*, I, p. 356.

plaining that he was conforming to the thought-forms of a pre-critical age, and that he must not be judged anachronistically by our modern criteria. Some propose a ''demythologizing'' of the miraculous narrative of the *Dialogues* to discern its abiding spiritual message under the disconcerting cultural envelope.[14] Some even suggest that Pope Gregory, in telling those fanciful tales, was employing a refined pedagogy of allegory, intending to convey a ''supra-historical'' sense by his ostensibly factual narrations.[15] The plea is also advanced that ''for Gregory the teleology of an event defines its nature''; if the events narrated perform a religiously pedagogical function—to excite wonder, to warn, to console, to condemn—''why not attribute to them a divine origin and thus a miraculous character?''[16]

Despite all such attempts, however sophisticated, to rescue the miracle-stories of the *Dialogues* from disrepute, their original character, meaning and historical *genre* is too plain to be obscured. In his study of the Latin language and literature of that age E. Auerbach shared the same candid judgement that so many others had formed during the previous four centuries: ''More astonishing, in a man such as Gregory, is the extent and nature of the credence given to prodigious happenings; the *Dialogues* show forth an almost childish fairy-tale world ... Among the stories there are many of the utmost naivety ... Here the miraculous is frequently mixed with the grotesque.''[17]

But, it will be objected, to show that the tales of the *Dialogues* are legendary and often bizarre is not a cogent reason for doubting whether they were written by St Gregory. Is there not other evidence to show that Gregory was naively—even superstitiously—credulous in his acceptance and narration of reports of miraculous events? There are the fourteen *ex-*

---

[14] This is the approach of Professor Claude Dagens in his sympathetic study of the spiritual wisdom and experience of St Gregory (*op. cit.* pp. 228-33, 242). He makes a rapid and valiant effort to fit the miracle-stories of the *Dialogues* into his canvas by interpreting them as a design to guide uncultured folk by way of ''exteriority'' to ''interiority''. The ''fundamental rule'' of Gregory's ''method of hagiographical exegesis'' he expresses as follows: *''il ne faut pas s'arrêter au sens littéral des miracles, mais pénétrer leur sens spirituel, aller du visible à l'invisible ...''* (p. 233).

[15] E.g. W. F. Bolton, ''The Supra-historical Sense of the *Dialogues*'', in *Aevum* 23, 1959, pp. 206-13; other authors who have advanced similar explanations are mentioned above in Chapter 18. See also Petersen, *op. cit.*, pp. XVI-XVII, 54-5.

[16] P. Boglioni, *''Miracle et merveilleux religieux chez Grégoire le Grand''*, in *Cahiers d'études médiévales* I, Montreal—Paris 1974, p. 75. An earlier essay in ''higher criticism'' of Book II of the *Dialogues* was that of C. Lambot, *''La Vie et les Miracles de saint Benoît racontés par saint Grégoire le Grand''*, in *Revue liturgique et monastique* 19, 1933, pp. 137-65 (reprinted in *Revue monastique* 1956).

[17] *Literatursprache und Publikum in der lateinischen Spätantike und im Mittelalter*, Bern 1958, pp. 73-4. He gives several examples of the grotesquely droll character of the tales in the *Dialogues*, in which he recognizes *''eine richtige Heinzelmännchen Atmosphäre''*.

empla in his *Homilies on the Gospels*, already discussed, which show his belief in contemporary miracles and visions. There are the letters he sent to three ladies of high rank at the imperial court, which include reports of prodigious happenings. Writing to the Empress Constantina, he tells her how some who had handled the relics of martyrs temerariously came to an untimely death. In his letter to Rusticiana, who was a benefactress of St Andrew's monastery in Rome, he relates four stories, vouched for by the abbot and prior of that monastery, telling how erring monks were recalled to rectitude by preternatural happenings.[18] Moreover, continuing the custom of previous popes, Gregory sent to persons whom he wished especially to honour holy keepsakes from the Apostle's shrine in the form of "keys of St Peter", and also filings from St Peter's chains. Such hallowed objects, he declared, when "placed on the sick, are wont to show forth many miracles".[19] In his letter to the Emperor's sister Theoctista he related a dreadful punishment for irreverence that had happened in a previous pontificate. An impious Lombard, trying to extract the gold from one of those keys, transfixed his own throat with his blade and expired, to the terror of King Autarith and his men.[20] If, therefore, Pope Gregory could believe and narrate such things, could he not equally have believed and narrated the miracle-stories of the *Dialogues*? Do not those prodigy-reports in his other writings provide a counter-argument in the case against his authorship of the tales in the *Dialogues*?

I reply that there is a substantial difference between the tales in the *Dialogues* and Gregory's occasional accounts in those other writings of preternatural happenings. The real Gregory accepted, of course, that the accounts of miracles in the Bible were divinely revealed truth. He likewise accepted unquestioningly that miracles still occasionally occurred in the age of the Church, although he held that they were no longer necessary in that age, as they had been at the origins of the Church. When we examine the miracle-stories that Gregory himself credited, in the other writings referred to above, we find that they differ significantly in character from those in the *Dialogues* which so many critics have singled out for censure. The few edifying *exempla* narrated in his Gospel homilies are, in comparison with the Dialogist's tales, religiously sensitive and sober in style and content. (F. H. Dudden, we recall, found them "not particularly striking" and "uninteresting".[21]) They tell

---

[18] Ep. IV.30 and XI.26; Ewald-Hartmann I. pp. 263-6 and II, pp. 288-9. The stories repeated to Rusticiana, he says, are "*pauca de multis*".

[19] Ep. I.25: Ewald-Hartmann I, p. 39.

[20] Ep. VII.23; Ewald-Hartmann I, p. 468.

[21] *Op. cit.*, I, p. 254. They are certainly less sensational than the series of some two dozen miracle-stories appended to St Augustine's *City of God* (22.8). One Gregorian *ex-*

especially of deathbed consolations bestowed upon saintly persons, of visions welcoming them to their eternal reward, of heavenly psalmody heard at their passing, of sweet fragrance lingering about their dead bodies, of divine healing both spiritual and corporal, of appearances of Christ and of saints, of cases of preternatural knowledge and foresight. Such phenomena as these have been seriously recorded by the biographers of saints down through the centuries to modern times—for example, in the lives of St John Vianney, St Gemma Galgani, St John Bosco and many another. So too, in recognizing miraculous favours granted through relics or memorials of the saints and through offering of the Mass, Gregory was at one with a constant tradition in the Church both of West and East. Again, traditional Christian piety finds nothing objectionable in accounts of divine intervention to protect the just, to recall erring sinners and to punish the ungodly; it readily recognizes a providential meaning even in ordinary events. Gregory of course shared this religious perspective.[22]

No, it is not acceptance of the miraculous, as such, that distinguishes the Dialogist from the real Gregory, but a basic difference of *genre* in his miracle-tales and of purpose in the telling of them. As many sensitive Christians have objected, the miracles of the *Dialogues* are often sub-Christian, grotesque, absurd or trivial. Remember that we are not here comparing the book with other ancient or mediaeval works of legendary hagiography; in such a comparison the *Dialogues* do not stand out as unusual. What we are comparing is the religious character, the theological presuppositions and the "psychological climate" of the tales in the *Dialogues*, with what St Gregory himself writes in his acknowledged works. It is not a Gregorian air we breathe when we read in the *Dialogues* such stories as the following:

The tale of the half-saved nun of Sabina, who preserved her chastity but gave rein to her vicious tongue. After her burial in church, a sacristan saw in a vision her body cut in two, one half being burnt and the other remaining intact. On the morrow the vision was confirmed when the marks of burning were found on the marble flagstones before the altar. (IV.53.1-3).

---

emplum which does, however, jar on modern sensitivity is the story of the priest who was severely chastised by Christ for repeated disobedience to a divine command (*Homilies on the Gospels* 37.8).

[22] The four stories in the Letter to Rusticiana (XI.26) have been singled out as most closely approaching the mental climate of the *Dialogues*. In Chapter 12 above I pointed out features indicating that Gregory may not have personally composed that section of the letter, although he authorized it. (See p. 428n above.)

The tale of the horde of caterpillars in a vegetable garden, which were adjured by Bishop Boniface in the name of Jesus Christ to desist from eating the vegetables and to depart. The creatures obeyed, not one remaining in the garden. (I.9.15).

The tale of Bishop Sabinus of Piacenza, who, when the rising Po flooded his church's domains and a disobedient deacon would not bear a message to the invading river, summoned a notary and dictated a written injunction to bid it retreat. As soon as the document was thrown into its waters, the Po obediently retired to its bed, "and did not presume thenceforth to go up into those domains". (III.10.2-3).

The tale of the five-year-old boy whose father did not correct his habit of repeating blasphemous words that he had overheard. Because he could speak, the little one was liable to damnation. Dying of the plague, he was borne away to hell by demon blackamoors. (IV.19.1-4).

The tale of the fate of a bishop of Brescia. Charged in a vision by St Faustinus to warn the bishop that he would die 30 days later if he failed to eject from a tomb in the church the corpse of an aged rake, a frightened sacristan failed to deliver the message. Despite its non-delivery and his inculpable ignorance of the saint's warning, the bishop was still struck down by sudden death on the thirtieth day. (IV.54.1-2).

The tales of the prodigious fauna in the life of the holy hermit Florentius. His tame bear tended his sheep for him, strictly observing the due hours for its return home, according to the dictates of the monastic horarium. When four envious monks trapped and slew this pet bear, Florentius cursed them so that they were all immediately struck with leprosy. Their members putrefied and they died—to the remorse of the holy hermit. When innumerable snakes infested Florentius's cell on every side, his prayer immediately called down a thunderclap which killed them all. The sanitary problem of disposing of the multitude of dead reptiles was solved by another prayer. At once there swooped down from the sky exactly as many birds as there were carcasses to remove, and the area was cleared. (III.15.2-12).

The tale of a young novice monk who left the abbey to visit his parents' house without the permission of St Benedict, and who fell dead on the same day that he arrived home. His body, when buried, was found repeatedly cast out of the grave, until Benedict gave it rest by having the Eucharist placed upon it. The moral of the story was to emphasize that "the earth itself would throw out the body of one who had departed this world out of Benedict's favour". (II.24.1-2).

The tale of a nun who, fancying a lettuce she saw in the convent garden, ate it without first blessing it with the sign of the cross, and was thereupon possessed and tormented by a devil. When the holy abbot

Equitius came to exorcize the indigestible imp, it cried out to him from the nun's mouth, in self-excuse: "What have I done? I was sitting there upon the lettuce, and she came and bit me". (I.4.7).

The futile tale of what befell Theodore, a sacristan of St Peter's in Rome. Rising before dawn one morning, he was standing on a step-ladder to tend the lights in the basilica when St Peter suddenly appeared on the pavement below him and asked: "Comrade, why have you risen so early?". The Apostle immediately vanished, but the shock of the apparition prostrated the poor sacristan for several days. (III.24.1).

The tale of the venerable Valerian priest Stephen, who, returning home from a journey, spoke with unguarded ribaldry to his servant: "Come devil, take off my boots!" Thereupon the fastenings of the priest's boots began to loosen very quickly, "so that it should clearly be seen that he who had been called upon, the devil, obeyed the order to pull off the boots". The priest hastily explained that he had meant to address his servant, not the demon, who thereupon desisted. (III.20.1-2).

The tale of the acid-tongued nuns whom St Benedict warned he would excommunicate if they did not check their abusive speech, but who died unreformed. When during the liturgy the deacon dismissed all who were non-communicants, the spectres of the bad-tempered nuns were seen to rise from their tombs in the church and to depart hurriedly. The saint eventually lifted their other-worldly excommunication by having a Mass-oblation offered for their repose. (II.23.2-5).

The tale of the lethal indignation of Bishop Boniface of Ferentis. Sitting down to dine at a nobleman's table and about to pronounce a blessing, he was disturbed by a mendicant minstrel who appeared at the door with his pet monkey and clashing cymbals. For this interruption, the bishop realized, the wretch was as good as dead—"*mortuus est miser iste*". Nevertheless he bade them, "for charity", to give the man something to eat. Inevitably, as the doomed minstrel went out of the door a block of masonry fell on him, inflicting a mortal wound. (I.9.8-9).

These dozen tales may be taken as typical of the kind of anecdote that the Dialogist delights to tell, and they may fairly be contrasted with the small group of *exempla*, containing accounts of supernatural events and visions, which the real Gregory relates in his works. There is, I submit, a clear disparity between the two categories. In their fantastic and often ludicrous quality, and in their triviality and lack of serious moral purpose, the Dialogist's tales are not only religiously inferior but different in kind. They are alien from the gravity, reverence and pastoral wisdom of St Gregory himself, who writes at a higher level of spiritual and moral sensitivity which the Dialogist cannot match. Justly may they be called sub-Christian.

My argument is not only that the real Gregory would not have given credence or circulation to the ludicrous tales with which the *Dialogues* abound, but also that he could have had no part in the pretence and deceit with which they were consciously composed. The charge now proved against the author of the *Dialogues* is not merely that he was gullible in accepting unworthy and invented tales, but that he himself invented them and disguised his inventions. In Chapter 18 we discussed the consistent and unGregorian deviousness of that author, who is convicted of fabricating his tales with the use of earlier hagiographical models, while earnestly insisting that the events he narrates have truly occurred and are vouched for by witnesses whom he identifies in great detail. As we saw in that chapter, this dissembling cannot be explained away with the plea that in writing the *Dialogues* Pope Gregory was merely conforming to a literary *genre* common in his time. There was indeed such a *genre*, but the real Pope Gregory showed no sympathy for it. Such deliberate and sustained pretence, even as a means for edification, was incompatible with the forthright character of the saint, whose own life and teaching illustrate the axiom in his *Moralia*: "God has no use for a lie, because truth does not seek to be stayed up by the aid of falsehood". In I.7.6 the author of the *Dialogues*, after retelling a series of fictitious miracle-stories, elements of which are patently culled from earlier hagiographical writings, applies to them the text of *John* 5.7, "My Father worketh until now, and I work". Such an unseemly appeal to Holy Scripture, to attribute those spurious miracles to the present power of Christ himself, and to equate their divine authority with that of the Gospel miracles, would have seemed to the real Gregory hardly short of blasphemy.[23]

Another objection may be brought: in his *Homilies on the Gospels* St Gregory, when relating stories of preternatural happenings, does take care to cite the recent testimony of witnesses known to himself and his hearers. Is not this procedure similar to that of the author of the *Dialogues*? Against my argument in Chapter 18, then, could it not be retorted that the exaggerated *souci d'authentifier*, which Dufourcq points out as a mark of the legend-monger, can be detected in an undisputed work of St Gregory? To answer this objection one must squarely compare Gregory's manner of presenting and authenticating his small group of *exempla*, which he included in his sermons to the people of Rome, with the procedures of the author of the *Dialogues*. Gregory did indeed consider

---

[23] Compare with this his own grave and reverent use of the same Johannine text in his letter to St Augustine of Canterbury: EP. XI.36; Ewald-Hartmann II, p. 305.

that the narration of examples of virtuous living, which were near to his hearers both in time and place, was of spiritual benefit in preaching. He explained why in Homily 38.15:

> But because at times the examples of faithful lives avail more than the words of teachers to convert the minds of the hearers, I wish to tell you something from near at hand. Since it comes from your own neighbourhood, your hearts will hear it with all the more concern. For the events we are speaking of did not happen long ago; we are recalling things for which there are living witnesses, who testify that they themselves were present.

From the fact that Pope Gregory took care to name witnesses for his handful of *exempla*, it by no means follows that the vast muster of witnesses cited in the *Dialogues* to authenticate those very numerous and bizarre tales is equally real. Both the respecter of truth and the spinner of yarns may give their authorities; but that does not mean that their procedures are the same. It may be that it was St Gregory's care to cite recent witnesses for the few edifying episodes narrated in his Gospel homilies that prompted the Dialogist to provide meticulous authentication for all his miracle-stories. To appreciate what an extraordinary dossier of witnesses and informants it is, one must study it attentively.[24] However remote in place or time, almost every one of the Dialogist's tales is vouched for by some informant with whom Pope Gregory is claimed to have had personal contact. "Most often they are persons of distinction: bishops and priests, abbots and priors, noblemen and high functionaries ... If he happens to give the reports of an inferior cleric or beggar, he refrains from giving their names."[25] In some cases the Gregory of the *Dialogues* directly vouches for the story from his own experience. He claims to have personally witnessed six miracles.

"These events are pleasing, because they are marvellous; and very pleasing because they are recent", comments Peter the Deacon in III.16.11. A. de Vogüé observes that this "*marche vers l'actualité et l'environnement le plus immédiat*" accelerates in Book IV.[26] In one case the Gregory of the *Dialogues* repeats a dying prediction of a lawyer whose death occurred only two days previously, and relates events at the funeral that could only have been conducted the day before writing![27] In the

---

[24] Detailed lists are presented by Dufourcq, III, pp. 291-2 (footnote); by Moricca, pp. XXIII-XXXII; and (better) by S. Boesch Gajano, "*La proposta agiografica dei Dialogi di Gregorio Magno*", in *Studi Medievali* (3rd series), 21, 1980, pp. 642-3, footnote 114. cf. Vogüé, *SC* 251, pp. 43-4, 124-6. Petersen's discussion of the informants in the *Dialogues* (*op. cit.*, pp. 1-15) is valuable.

[25] Vogüé, *SC* 251, 43. Gajano also points out (against Moricca) that Gregory's informants are for the most part an élite, not a motley crowd of little credit. (*op. cit* p. 644).

[26] *SC* 251, pp. 46-7, 50, 63, 64.

[27] IV.27.2.

Dialogues the author's constant and obtrusive insistence on the authentification of his tales is carried to a ludicrous extreme. It is a caricature
of Pope Gregory's own careful attestation of the rare *exempla* that we find
in the *Homilies on the Gospels*.

Moreover, as I have argued in Chapter 14, the Dialogist's attitude to
the miraculous in itself, and his purpose in telling miracle-stories, differs
essentially from that of the real St Gregory. The latter's first concern is
to teach the way of Christian living. He insists that miracles as such are
not examples to be proposed for the moral instruction and edification of
the faithful: "*miracula in exemplum operationis non sunt trahenda*"[28] The
Dialogist, on the other hand, makes the miraculous his chief concern and
the touchstone of sanctity.

Although, in a number of places in his genuine works, Gregory refers
to the continuing favours of miraculous healing, and of liberation from
evil spirits, that are granted to the faithful at the tombs and through the
relics of the Apostles and martyrs, and although he recognizes that there
is still need for miraculous signs to corroborate the preaching of the faith
to pagans placed "at the ends of the earth" (as in newly evangelized
England[29]), he plainly supposes that the main incidence of and necessity
for miracles lies in the past, when they served to authenticate the origin
of the Church.[30] Then they were needed to overcome the incredulity of
unbelievers and the hostility of persecutors. Miraculous signs, says
Gregory, quoting St Paul, are for unbelievers, not for believers, and they
should be viewed with reserve.[31] Miracles do not themselves constitute
victorious virtue, since, he points out, "sometimes they are given to the
reprobate too",[32] The Apostles performed outward miracles in order to
plant the faith; the Church now daily performs inward miracles by
reforming hearts and instilling virtues. "Such miracles are the greater,
the more spiritual they are ... For those corporal miracles sometimes
show forth sanctity, yet they cannot bring it about; but these spiritual
miracles, which are performed in the mind, do not show forth virtuous
living but bring it about".[33]

The Dialogist, on the other hand, makes it his central message to proclaim the great frequency and lustre of miracles in recent times, particu-

---

[28] *Homilies on Ezekiel* I.2.4.
[29] *Moralia* 27.21; Ep. XI.36; Ewald-Hartmann II, pp. 305-6.
[30] *Moralia* 27.36-7; *Homilies on the Gospels* 4.3.
[31] *Homilies on the Gospels* 4.3 and 10.1.
[32] *Homilies on Ezekiel* II.5.22. In this sermon, and again in *Homilies on the Gospels* 30.10,
Gregory also speaks of the miracles of the saints as outward signs of God's inward favour
to them.
[33] *Homilies on the Gospels* 29.4.

larly in Italy, where they have been spectacularly performed by an innumerable host of modern thaumaturges. Moreover he claims that the age in which he is writing is one of unprecedented disclosure of super-natural "revelations and visions".[34] His principal aim in presenting his rich collection of miracle-stories is to excite in his readers the sense of the marvellous.[35] The sentiment that he both arouses and feeds is expressed in the words he puts into the mouth of Peter the Deacon: "*miracula quo plus bibo, plus sitio*"—"the more I drink in miracles, the more I thirst for them".

The Dialogist doubtless knew the teaching of St Gregory well enough to realize that a thirst for miracles for their own sake was incompatible with that teaching. Here and there he puts in remarks to admit that in-terior virtue is superior to exterior signs and wonders. Indeed such superiority is explicitly stated in genuine Gregorian passages that he in-serts in his text (e.g. IGPs 2, 14, 15, 17). But despite these occasional ad-missions, he ignores them in practice. The whole thrust of his narrative is concentrated in the external marvel. As Auerbach observes,[36] even when Peter the Deacon acknowledges (after IGP 15) that "*vita et non signa quaerenda sunt*" he goes straight on to clamour for more miracle stories. Sofia Boesch Gajano compiles a weighty dossier of instances from the *Dialogues* in which the author concentrates solely on the wonder-working of his holy men, saying nothing about their inward virtue, and simply presents those miracles as proof of sanctity and power, without using them as pedagogical incentives to virtuous living.[37] She also goes on to recall the comparatively few contrasting passages in which the author ex-alts interior virtue over external miracles, but she disagrees with C. Dagens, who supposes that in the *Dialogues* Gregory presents miracles on-ly as a pointer to interior virtues. She concludes that in the book there is "*una continua incertezza tra santità interiore e* signum *esterno della santità*".[38]

The purpose of the real Gregory, when in his sermons he occasionally narrates episodes containing preternatural happenings, is always to draw a pastoral moral which ordinary Christians can apply to themselves for their own conduct. The Dialogist, contrariwise, omits the pastoral moral, even when he reproduces Gregory's own *exempla* from the *Homilies on the Gospels*. A. de Vogüé observantly marks this change from the "original

---

[34] *Dialogues* I, Prologue, 8; IV.43.1.

[35] "Where the work has an effect, it is exercised on the imagination rather than on the spirit", observes A. Ebert (*op. cit.*, Vol. I, p. 523). He criticizes the *Dialogues* for lack of real moral purpose: therein, he says, is no sense of the spiritual value of asceticism, such as is conveyed by the hagiographical collection of Rufinus.

[36] *Op. cit.*, p. 73.

[37] "*La proposta agiografica*", pp. 637-8, footnote 98.

[38] *Ibid.* p. 640, 648.

tenor" of those narratives: "In the *Homilies* those deaths accompanied by supernatural phenomena serve only to confirm a moral lesson, which is the principal purpose of the recital ... In the *Dialogues*, on the contrary, those moral elements are not made the object of any comment ... Now it is the supernatural phenomena surrounding the death that become the proper object of the narration."[39]

Peculiarities in eschatological doctrine

Among the directly theological discrepancies between the *Dialogues* and St Gregory's main writings I draw particular attention to the peculiarities of the eschatological doctrine presupposed in Book IV. Of these "visions of the life beyond the tomb, which are at times of extravagant realism", Professor Dagens[40] justly exclaims: "What a contrast there is between these representations of paradise or of hell, these accounts of the flight of souls towards heaven, and the spiritualization of the future life that one finds in the *Moralia* ...!" He recognizes the difficulty in finding a reconciling perspective that would embrace "this diversity of literary *genres* and the undeniable contrast that exists between the moralist who seeks to stimulate the desire for eternity and the popular story-teller who seems to give credence to naive legends". To prove the "primary unity of inspiration that precedes the difference existing between the two literary *genres*", he cites a text from the *Dialogues* which has "an almost total resemblance" to a text in the *Moralia*. But we find that the *Dialogues* text which he thus adduces in proof is the genuine Gregorian excerpt that we have discussed in Chapter 19 as IGP 57b.

In Book IV of the *Dialogues* we read a number of tales about persons whose souls departed out of this world and, after adventures in the next, then returned again to earthly life to report what they had seen. Nowhere in Gregory's authentic works is there any sanction for the belief that souls can thus return from a temporary sojourn in the next world to report their experiences to those living in earth. Such notions are, however, found in the works of legendary hagiography which the Dialogist laid under contribution. From Virgil, Cicero and other classical authors such imaginative myths were well known in the ancient world, and we find their influence in some patristic writings.[41] Although the theology of St

---

[39] *SC* 251, p. 93. Vogüé claims that this concentration on the supernatural phenomena is not "a play of the imagination and catering for curiosity", but has an underlying purpose of edification (*ibid.* footnote 49, and p. 76.)

[40] *Op. cit.*, pp. 401-3.

[41] Also in apocryphal writings such as the *Visio Pauli*. Riché notes that "a great deal of Irish Christian literature is devoted to voyages to the other world and to supernatural visions. The Irish brought this literary genre to Gaul, as to England" (*op. cit.*, 1981, p. 70).

Gregory himself found no place for them, the fourth book of the *Dialogues* firmly established their popularity in Christian tradition. "In fact one may regard it as the chief Western source of those visions of heaven, hell, and purgatory which formed an important *genre* in mediaeval literature and reached its highest point in Dante's *Divina Commedia*".[42]

Sometimes, we learn from the *Dialogues*, souls are summoned to hell by mistake. In IV.37.1 Peter the Deacon inquires: "But why is it, I ask you, that some persons are, as it were, called out of their bodies by mistake, and, after returning from that exanimate state, each of them relates how he heard, down there, that he was not the one sent for?" The Dialogist makes Gregory reply: "When this happens, Peter, if you consider the matter well, it is not a mistake but a warning". Nevertheless in the remarkable case reported in IV.37.5-6 the infernal judge himself declares that his minions have made a mistake in bringing before him Stephen the magnate, instead of Stephen the blacksmith whom he had sent for.[43] Accordingly Stephen the magnate is sent back to earthly life (where he is later able to tell his adventure at first hand to Gregory himself), and Stephen the blacksmith dies forthwith to take his place in hell. Contrast this bizarre tale with Gregory's elevated teaching on divine judgement and on the awesome mystery of death and retribution.

There is more unGregorian eschatology in the Dialogist's subsequent account of an even direr predicament in which the same high-born Stephen found himself when he died, for the second and last time. Half immersed in the infernal river, he was the object of a grim tug-of-war between devils and angels. The episode was reliably reported by an eyewitness, another temporary traveller to the other world who returned to tell the tale. It is indeed a strange doctrine of the soul's judgement that is here attributed to Gregory. Stephen was partly good, having given generous alms, and partly bad, not having fully resisted carnal vices. In consequence the outcome of the eschatological tug-of-war for his person, and hence his ultimate fate, was uncertain. The real Gregory would not have imagined that the fate of the man could have hung thus unpredictably in the balance between good deeds and carnal vices. In his *Moralia* 21.19 he insists, with stern vehemence that contrasts with the Dialogist's more latitudinarian assumptions that if a man has not resisted the evil corruption of the flesh and been cleansed of carnal sin, no amount of good works, no almsdeeds or piety, can avail before the almighty Judge; he will be inevitably doomed to hell-fire.[44]

---

[42] E. Colgrave and R. A. B. Mynors (editors), *Bede's Ecclesiastical History*, Oxford 1969, pp. 128-9, footnote 1.

[43] See pp. 594-5 above, where the Augustinian antecedent for the story is noted.

[44] *Moralia* 21.19. Cf. Vogüé *SC* 265, p. 133, note 13.

In the same 37th chapter of Book IV we also read of the strange and equivocal sanction visited on those who, through substantially good life, have managed to arrive on the heavenward side of the fateful river, but who are still somewhat sullied by the delight they took in impure thoughts whilst still on earth. For this, while escaping damnation, they are subject to a minor penalty; their habitations are affected by a stinking vapour which arises from the infernal stream.[45] Can this quaint conception be fitted into the framework of St Gregory's theology? Similarly strange notions are found in the story of the half-burnt nun, referred to earlier in this chapter, which the Gregory of the *Dialogues* narrates in IV.53.1-3. There too the defunct individual had a mixture of good and bad in her record: she was praiseworthy for her continence but blameworthy for her sins of the tongue. Her fate (described in the sacristan's vision, which was corroborated by the visible marks of burning in the church pavement) was to have one half of her person burned and the other half left immune. Once again, it is hard to reconcile this preposterous conception with the eschatological doctrine of the real Gregory.

If the Dialogist's theology of the soul's judgement is not that of St Gregory and of Christian orthodoxy, it does reflect notions that were quite widespread in the ancient world. One such notion was that of the fateful bridge of souls which the good could safely cross but from which the wicked fell off into the nether abyss (IV.37.10). This notion may derive ultimately from the Zoroastrian myth of the Bridge of Ĉinvat (the Separator). Likewise the struggle between the good and evil spirits for the person of the half-sinful Stephen, the outcome of which depended on the relative weight of his good and evil deeds, reflects another popular belief. The concept of a rivalry between merits and demerits at the moment of individual judgement, weighed in a balance by rival spirits to see whether good or evil predominated, is found not only in Zoroastrian mythology but quite widely in the religious imagery of the ancient world—though not in orthodox Christian theology.

Other eschatological oddities in the *Dialogues* have been noted in preceding pages. While the real Gregory saw fiery volcanoes merely as images of hell, the Dialogist concretely identifies the location of hell in the volcanoes of Sicily and the Lipari Islands.[46] To those craters were ferried the doomed souls of the two young and dissolute laymen, Eumorphius and Stephen. Because the Arian king Theodoric the Ostrogoth had

---

[45] See Chapter 17 above, IGP 64.
[46] IV.31 (cf. Chapter 17 above, IGP 62); and IV.36.8, 10-12.

persecuted unto death Pope John I and the patrician Symmachus, he was justly damned. In *Dialogues* IV.31.2-4 we read how a hermit of great holiness saw the wicked king being thrust down into hell in the crater of Lipari, watched by his two illustrious victims. We recall Hallinger's comment:[47] "That Theodoric the Great must repine in the volcano of Stromboli until Judgement Day, is something that the theologically erudite Gregory would surely not have believed himself."

G. Cremascoli finds another doctrinal anomaly in the eschatology of the *Dialogues*. In IV.40.10-12 we read the story of the death and perdition of a monk of Iconium. Although held in high repute for his strict observance, this monk was a secret eater when he seemed to be fasting. On his death-bed, he confessed his fault to his brethren with great affliction of soul. Nevertheless his contrite confession availed him nothing, and his soul was snatched down to hell by a demonic dragon. Cremascoli remarks that this story conflicts with Christian belief.[48] To weaken Cremascoli's objection one would have to postulate that in case the author of the *Dialogues* supposes that the sinner's deathbed remorse was insufficient for salutary repentance.[49]

Purgatory and succour for souls

The doctrine of Purgatory undergoes a crass development in the Dialogist's tales. We saw in Chapter 17 (cf. IGP 67) that the real Gregory tentatively allowed that *1 Corinthians* 3.11-15 could be taken to refer to a "*purgatorius ignis*" after death, by which souls could be purged from venial sins before the Last Judgement. The already traditional practice in the Church of offering suffrages for the dead implied the possibility of other-worldly remission of sins. St Augustine had made the theological implications more explicit, and had spoken hypothetically of a "*purgatorius ignis*". Thus in putting forward the concept of posthumous purgation for light sins, and in speaking of a putative purgatorial fire, Gregory was not an innovator.[50] In my discussion of IGP 67 in Chapter 17 I argued that in IV.41.3, line 14, Gregory did not write "*de quibusdam levibus culpis esse ... purgatorius ignis credendus est*", but probably "*...*

---

[47] Already cited above, in Chapter 11, p. 199n; *SA* 42, p. 243.

[48] *Novissima hominis nei Dialoghi di Gregorio Magno*, Bologna 1979, pp. 49-50.

[49] We may compare the story of the monk damned for his secret eating with an *exemplum* related by Gregory himself in his Gospel *Homilies* (19.7 and 38.16, repeated by the Dialogist in IV.40.2-5, which is IGP 65). There too an unworthy monk saw a nightmarish apparition of a dragon come to devour his soul; but thanks to the prayers of the brethren he was restored to right dispositions.

[50] See Vogüé, *SC* 265, pp. 149-52. There is also a reference to *purgatoria poena peccati* in the Gregorian commentary *In 1 Regum* 2.107 (*CCL* 144, p. 177).

purgatio credenda est", which accords with the syntax and the context. It was probably the Dialogist who there prematurely interpolated the mention of fire and the too emphatic assertion that it "must be believed", in order to link with Peter's cue-question and to prepare the way for his stories about souls released from torrid torments. In his narrative, the conservative speculations of the real Gregory (expressed in IGP 67) about other-worldly purgation are eclipsed by those sensational tales. The latter—especially the tale of the monk Justus in IV.57—were to have great influence in shaping the popular mediaeval conception of Purgatory, and also the ecclesiastical practice that emerged from it.

In two separate but remarkably similar anecdotes the Gregory of the *Dialogues* relates how two wretched spectres were found expiating their sins by performing menial labour in the steamy heat of the public baths in two Italian towns. Both bewailed their lot to ecclesiastical clients of the baths and begged for spiritual succour to free them from their penal servitude. One of the sufferers was the deacon Paschasius, who was liberated from his torrid prison in the baths of Angulus by the prayers of Bishop Germanus of Capua.[51] The other sufferer had in his lifetime been "lord of the baths" at Tauriana, and that very same thermal establishment became the penitentiary to which his soul was consigned for the purgation of his faults. He was released from it when a sympathetic priest whose needs he had served in the baths offered a week of Masses for him.[52] The notion of later mediaeval piety, that the suffering souls in Purgatory were pleading piteously for succour from the living, drew strength from these unGregorian tales.

The tale of the nobly-born but bad-tempered nuns in *Dialogues* II.23.2-5 also raises serious questions about the theological principles presupposed. As we have seen, those two nuns, failing to heed St Benedict's warning of impending excommunication, died under that ban. Whenever, during the liturgical celebration, the deacon pronounced the dismissal of non-communicants, the spectral nuns were constrained to depart hurriedly from their tombs in the church. Eventually they were released from their singular predicament and posthumously restored to ecclesiastical communion by the intervention of St Benedict.

---

[51] IV.42. Paschasius's sin was that he had, against the judgement of the bishops of the Church, obstinately supported the anti-pope Laurence against Pope Symmachus. The Gregory of the *Dialogues* considers that this sin could be purged after death, since it was done "from the error of ignorance" (IV.42.4). Vogüé justly queries whether it would be regarded as a light matter, such as Gregory teaches can be absolved after death (cf. IGP 67; *SC* 265, p. 153, note 4). The real Gregory would hardly have considered obstinacy in schism against the legitimate pope a light fault excusable because of ignorance. (cf. *Moralia* 25.29).

[52] IV.57.3-7.

When Peter the Deacon asks how the holy abbot, while still in this life, thus had the power "to absolve souls placed in the invisible judgement", the author of the *Dialogues* replies by bringing in the Gregorian exposition of *Matthew* 16.19, a passage which I discussed in Chapter 15 as IGP 23. There I pointed out how peculiar is the Dialogist's notion of the state of those excommunicate nuns in the after-life, and also how anomalous is his supposition that an unordained abbot should have the power of binding and loosing, which in Gregory's own belief was conferred by Christ on St Peter and the Apostles and on their episcopal successors.

Another feature of the anecdote has been commented on by A. de Vogüé. He calls the affair of the excommunicate nuns "one of the strangest in the life of Benedict", and he remarks that St Benedict's action in lifting the ban of excommunication from departed souls is a great marvel, "and even greater than one would realize".[53] By applying IGP 23, and citing *Matthew* 16.19, as a justification of St Benedict's action, the Gregory of the *Dialogues* seems to depart from a principle maintained by Roman Pontiffs of the preceding century, Popes Gelasius and Vigilius. Repeatedly requested by the Eastern bishops to absolve from excommunication the patriarch Acacius of Constantinople, who had died a hundred years earlier, Gelasius firmly refused, explaining that he could not do so because in *Matthew* 16.19 Christ gave power to St Peter and his successors only to loose those who were still "on earth". Fr de Vogüé comments: "Gelasius denied that it was possible for him to absolve Acacius. Gregory affirms that Benedict did well and truly absolve those nuns"; and he contrasts the public responsibility and prudent reserve of Popes Gelasius and Vigilius, when pronouncing on matters of principle concerning the whole Church, with Pope Gregory's relation of a non-canonical act by a charismatic abbot.[54] But the alleged assertion by Gregory of Benedict's power to free those departed souls is nugatory; the author of the strange tale of the two nuns is not really Gregory I, and IGP 23 was not originally written to apply to that tale.[55]

It is not only the charismatic abbot Benedict who is related in the *Dialogues* to have arranged the release of souls from other-worldly penalties. In one of the strangest of all the stories in the book, the Gregory of the *Dialogues* narrates how he himself was confidently able to

---

[53] *Vie de S. Benoît*, p. 146.

[54] *Ibid.* p. 147.

[55] It is true that even in the genuine Gregorian pericope, IGP 23, Gregory adopts a different interpretation from that of Gelasius of the bearing of the words "*super terram*" in *Matthew* 16.19. Whereas Gelasius referred those words to the standing of the persons being judged, Gregory referred them to that of those able to judge. But Gregory, like his predecessors, assumes without question that only those in the apostolic succession of the *sanctum regimen* have the power of binding and loosing (II.23, lines 55-7).

provide effective liberation for a deceased soul who, for an unremitted sin, was being tormented by fire in the after-life. In IV.57.8-16 the *soi-disant* papal author describes the disciplinary sentence he had passed in the year 590-1 upon an erring monk of his own monastery. We read how the monk, named Justus, who had medical skills and had diligently attended Gregory himself in his many illnesses, sinned by surreptitiously concealing three gold coins for himself, in contravention of the monastic rule. His sinful secret was discovered when illness brought him to death's door. In order to correct the dying monk and to set an example to the other brethren, Gregory denied him all spiritual consolation on his deathbed, despite the wretched man's earnest pleading. He then ordered the other monks to bury him on a dunghill, where they were to stand around, casting the coins on his corpse and crying, "Thy money be with thee unto perdition". A month after the death of the excommunicate monk Gregory took thought for his plight and ordered a series of Masses to be offered for him during a sequence of thirty days. At the end of that time Justus appeared in a vision to his brother and announced that he had that day been released from torment and received into communion.

This anecdote was the starting point for a famous observance in the mediaeval and later Church, which we know as "the Gregorian Trental". If the grotesque story had a happy ending in the next world, it was only, it appears, because the prescient pope[56] who later narrated it in the *Dialogues* could be sure that the stern denial of all spiritual comfort which he inflicted on the dying monk would, without reducing the miscreant to final despair, produce contrition sufficient to save him from hell. How different is this formidably autocratic prelate, commanding that the monk should die in desolation, from the patient shepherd of souls who is revealed in Gregory's sermons and Scriptural commentaries, and from the wise spiritual guide who in his *Regula Pastoralis* wrote the celebrated axiom: "*Ars est artium regimen animarum*". Far from the real Gregory would it have been to arrogate to himself the preternatural insight and confident knowledge of divine judgement that the Gregory of the *Dialogues* claims in this story. The claim implies not only that he was unerringly sure that his diagnosis of the dying monk's interior dispositions was accurate, and that the bitter experience of his lonely death would render him pardonable, but also that Gregory subsequently knew that by prescribing the trental of Masses he could secure the other-

---

[56] Many commentators have supposed that Gregory was acting as abbot of his monastery in this episode. In Chapter 20 I note how some modern authors dissent from this view, and place the episode during his pontificate. See the comments of J. Richards (*op. cit.*, pp. 32-3), who discredits the view (first advanced by John the Deacon) that Gregory became abbot of St Andrew's.

worldly absolution of the sinner and his liberation from Purgatory. If in the course of centuries all this seemed unobjectionable to mediaeval Christians, it would have seemed objectionable to Pope St Gregory himself.

It is mainly because of those tales in Book IV that St Gregory has been called "the father of the doctrine of Purgatory". In his controversial book, *La Naissance du Purgatoire*,[57] J. Le Goff, while admitting that Gregory remains very Augustinian in his reference to Purgatory in the doctrinal passage in IV.41 (i.e. IGP 67), concludes that in the *Dialogues* "the novelty comes above all from illustration and anecdote". He adds: "Gregory's stories are all the more important because they became the model for the anecdotes by the aid of which the Church of the thirteenth century expanded the belief in Purgatory, which by then was fully existing and defined.[58] Le Goff realizes, however, that despite those pregnant narratives in the *Dialogues*, on the strength of which he calls Gregory "the last founder of Purgatory", that pope himself made strangely little of the doctrine which was to become so important in mediaeval Christendom: "For all that, Gregory accords to this belief only a very secondary interest. For him the essential is still that at the Day of Judgement there will no longer be more than two categories—the elect and the reprobate".[59]

Many other critics agree that the Gregorian *Dialogues* marked a decisive departure from the earlier Christian attitude to departed souls. "With Gregory I there comes a complete change ... For Gregory and all subsequent tradition, prayers—and Masses in particular—now have the effect of bringing about the release of souls from Purgatory and of procuring their beatitude. This change in eschatology supposes a change in religious sensibility which is still insufficiently explained."[60] An important part of the explanation, I suggest, is that the religious sensibility of the author of the *Dialogues*, although it was not that of St Gregory himself, strongly influenced mediaeval piety and practice because the book was universally assumed to have the teaching authority of that great pope and Doctor of the Church.

The demonology of the Dialogues

Instructive, too, is comparison between the demonology of the Dialogist and the teaching of Gregory the Great about the powers of

---

[57] Gallimard 1981, p. 125.
[58] *Ibid.* p. 128.
[59] *Ibid.* p. 129.
[60] C. Vogel, in an (unpublished) abstract of a paper intended for the Chantilly conference on St Gregory the Great in 1982.

darkness. That teaching runs as a sombre strand throughout Gregory's writings. The evil spirits are fallen angels, still potent to conduct spiritual warfare against all that is good. In God's mysterious providence they are permitted to tempt mankind, for the proving of the just and the punishment of the wicked.[61] Satan, the apostate archangel and prince of darkness, is the *antiquus hostis*, the universal agent of evil, who with the terrible subtlety of his still angelic intelligence[62] conducts an unceasing campaign to bring spiritual ruin upon men. When the real Gregory speaks of the menace of this demonic power he does so in words of dread and anxious warning, never with light derision or trivial imagery. The elect must know that, in humble reliance on God's grace and almighty power, they need fear no lasting harm from the ancient enemy.[63] Although at the end of time Satan will, embodied as Antichrist, mount his final assault with enormous force against God's kingdom, he and his counter-kingdom of evil will eventually be vanquished for ever.[64] But when we turn from this sombre vision in Gregory's theological works, of cosmic menace presented by the powers of darkness, to the pages of the *Dialogues*, we find there a significantly different conception of the place and activity of the demons in the world. It was observed by F. H. Dudden eighty years ago. His account of it is still worth quoting, though he did not appreciate that the demonology of the *Dialogues* was not novel, but had plentiful antecedents in the past:

> It should be noticed that Gregory's *Dialogues* have a peculiar interest in this connexion, because in them we meet, for the first time, with the fully developed conception of the mediaeval devil. Here Satan is represented, no longer as the portentous power of darkness, but as a spirit of petty malice, more irritating than awful, playing all manner of mischievous pranks and doing at time serious damage, but easily routed by a sprinkling of holy water or the sign of the cross ... He is represented at one time as making his appearance all on fire with flaming mouth and flashing eyes, yet condescending to make a pun on the name of a saint; at another time, disguised as a physician, carrying horn and mortar, and riding on a mule; again under the form of a little black boy, or a bird with flapping wings. He haunts a house in Corinth, rendering it uninhabitable through his imitations of "the roaring of lions, the bleating of sheep, the braying of asses, the hissing of serpents, the grunting of hogs, and the squeaking of rats" (III.4). He begins to strip off the stockings of a priest ... He holds his court in a ruined temple of Apollo on the Appian Way ... He lives for three years, under the form of a serpent, in the cave of a holy hermit of Campania. In such representations as these the devil has lost much of his terror, and has

---

[61] E.g. *Moralia* 2.38; 14.46; 16.47.
[62] Cf. *Moralia* 2.4.
[63] *Moralia* 32.51.
[64] *Moralia* 32.27; 33.37.

become comparatively innocuous. He is already the cunning imposter, full of tricks and devices, with whom the Middle Ages were familiar. And his attendant demons have undergone a similar transformation.[65]

The crafty imps of the *Dialogues* were akin to the malicious hobgoblins of pre-Christian religion, and the same notions were doubtless still common in the folklore and superstitious fears of the Italian countryfolk whose world the Dialogist reflects. They are already found in the hagiography of the fifth and sixth centuries and in earlier sources. But this is not the thought-world of St Gregory himself. In his discussion of Gregory's teaching about "Demons and the Devil", Dudden documents the distinctive difference between Gregory's teaching in the *Moralia* and the peculiar demonology of the *Dialogues*. He concludes: "On the whole, Gregory's most important contribution to the science of demonology is the collection of stories in the *Dialogues*."[66] Since Dudden assumes the Gregorian authenticity of the *Dialogues*, he has to explain its peculiar demonology as one more instance of the paradoxes in Gregory's character which the *Dialogues* supposedly reveal. I submit, on the contrary, that the unGregorian demonology of the *Dialogues* is one more indication of the spuriousness of that book.

Differences in ecclesial and social perspective

The lack in the *Dialogues* of the *ecclesial* dimension, so prominent in St Gregory's pastoral and didactic writings, is significant. His letters, his commentaries and his *Regula Pastoralis* show him constantly aware of his grave responsibility as bishop to bring succour to his flock in their needs, using the means and administrative structure of the Church.[67] The bishop must instruct, correct, guide, protect and assist all those committed to his care—priests and laity, monks and nuns, officials and servants of the ecclesiastical domains. He must build up, and where necessary reform, the institutions of the Church—the diocesan administration, the organization of local churches and communities, the monasteries and nunneries—and must supervise the charitable provision for the relief of the poor and afflicted. Even though the Lombard invasions had wrought havoc in Church life in mainland Italy, Pope Gregory still resolutely attempted to apply the Church's resources to alleviate the resulting distress and disorder in Christian life.[68]

---

[65] *Op. cit.*, II, p. 367-8.

[66] *Ibid.* II, p. 369.

[67] See especially his long and trenchant letter of July 592 to the sub-deacon Peter, rector of the Sicilian patrimony, which is vibrant with zeal for social justice: Ep. II.38; Ewald-Hartmann I, pp. 133-9.

[68] See O. Bertolini, *Roma di fronte a Bisanzio e ai Longobardi*, Bologna 1941, pp. 270-3.

This social perspective on the Church's responsibility, which made Gregory I a model for effective pastoral action, is missing from the viewpoint of the author of the *Dialogues* and from his picturesque portrayal of church life in Italy. The Gregory portrayed there shows no pastoral concern similar to that shown by the wise ecclesiastical statesman of the *Registrum*. [69] Nor do the wonder-working bishops, who are fairly numerous in the *Dialogues* (especially in Book III), show the kind of pastoral care and institutional commitment that Gregory himself practised and held up as the norm of episcopal duty. Sofia Boesch Gajano had drawn attention to the strange "absence of any urban dimension" in almost all the stories about holy bishops in the *Dialogues*. The bishop's office, in the age and in the conception of Pope Gregory, is intimately bound to his city and its citizens; in the *Dialogues*, however, "the holy bishops do not operate in a typically urban ambience ... There is a kind of absorption of the city into the countryside, or perhaps rather a lessening of any precise delimitation between the two ... The city is never truly presented as a spatial, social or institutional entity".[70] In the *Dialogues*, in fact, the holy bishop has usually the same kind of charismatic freedom from institutional constraints as the holy abbot or hermit.

Indeed the abbots, monks and hermits who throng the Dialogist's pages are strangely independent of the ecclesial structure and of episcopal oversight, such as Pope Gregory in his day still tried tirelessly to maintain. When in those pages succour occasionally comes to the afflicted Christians of Italy, it is not provided by the activity or charity of the institutional Church but by the prodigious intervention of a thaumaturge. The holy fathers who are the heroes of the book do not seem to have a mission to work through the organs of the Church, in the ecclesiastical setting that we know from Gregory's letters.[71] Their excellence lies in their miraculous powers. The Dialogist's perspective is individualistic, not social. His main concern, unlike Gregory's, is not to move his

---

[69] This contrast between Gregory's own earnest concern for and activity on behalf of the poor *rustici* and the lack of such perspectives in the *Dialogues* emerges from the paper of Professor Marcella Forlin Patrucco, "*La vie quotidienne dans la correspondance de Grégoire le Grand*", read at the International Colloquium on St Gregory the Great held at Chantilly in September 1982, to be published in the *Acts* of that gathering.

[70] "*La proposta agiografica*", pp. 632-3.

[71] G. Cracco sees in this charismatic freedom of the wonder-working saints of the *Dialogues* the author's assertion of the central dimension of Christian sanctity, in its pure form uncluttered by "clericalization": "*Uomini di Dio e Uomini della Chiesa nell'Alto Medioevo: per una reinterpretazione dei 'Dialogi' di Gregorio Magno*", in *Ricerche di Storia Sociale e Religiosa*, N.S. XII, 1977, pp. 163-202. J. Petersen finds a significant difference between the *Dialogues* and the contemporary *Gesta* in their differing presentation of the function of a bishop. In the *Gesta* (as indeed in Gregory's own works) the stress is on his ecclesiastical function; in the *Dialogues* it is on his personal charismata (*op. cit.*, p. 63).

readers to reform of life and to social charity, but to arouse their wonder. For consolation he offers them the reflection that holy men are channels for supernatural forces which can triumph over all the ills and adversities of ordinary life.

Another aberrant trait in the Gregory of the *Dialogues* may be described as his socio-religious snobbery. He conveys a sense of the superiority of a higher clerical caste; he has scant spiritual esteem for the laity, even those of higher station; and he has a contempt for the *rustici*. S. Boesch Gajano has aptly described and documented the sacral élitism of the author,[72] which is also remarked upon by A. de Vogüé. The latter writes: "Usually the *Dialogues* do not show much esteem for and interest in the *rustici*; if some of them appear, it is to bring out their lumpishness, their "stupidity", their incongruous judgements and attitudes towards sanctity and the sacred ... As for the townsfolk, Gregory seems to be no more interested in them particularly ... In the main, the consecrated persons go to paradise, and the layfolk to hell ... Gregory tends to present monasticism and the ecclesiastical ministry as the normal paths to salvation ... Indeed, the Christian people receive from the book only scanty encouragement to bring to fruition the spiritual values proper to their state and the riches of grace latent in everyday life."[73]

Signora Boesch Gajano likewise shows that although the peasant world is the background to many of the episodes, it is largely extraneous to the world of ecclesiastical sanctity which the author describes. The peasants and lower orders are just *there*, passive, subordinate, despised.[74] The episode of the strolling minstrel and Bishop Boniface of Ferentis in I.9.8-9, which we have already discussed, typifies the socio-religious gulf in the *Dialogues* between those "*due mentalità, due mondi contrapposti*". The wretched fellow, seeking by his tricks and tunes to gain a bite to eat, appears with his cymbals and his monkey at the door of the hall in which the holy bishop is about to dine as the guest of the charitable nobleman Fortunatus. His clanging disturbs the ritual prayer and affronts the dignity of the holy bishop; his death from falling masonry is the inevitable sequel and sanction of his temerity. The bishop expressly marks the contrast between his own sacredness and the vulgarity of the minstrel, a sacredness that "has a superior and untouchable role, socially opposed to other roles and ways of life."[75] The cautionary tale told in I.10.6-7 is

---

[72] "*Dislivelli culturali e mediazioni ecclesiastiche nei Dialogi di Gregorio Magno*", in *Quaderni Storici* (Ancona), 41, 1979, pp. 398-415.

[73] *SC* 251, pp. 36-9.

[74] "*Dislivelli*", pp. 402-4.

[75] *Ibid.* p. 402.

similar. There a dweller in Todi is punished by the violent death of his infant son for an apparently hospitable act, which is nevertheless implicit irreverence to a holy bishop.

All this tells us much about the mentality and prejudices of the author of the *Dialogues*. But it does not square with what we know of the pastoral attitudes of St Gregory himself, who in his genuine writings shows no such "sacral snobbery". In his letters he is concerned to safeguard the rights and human dignity of the peasants and the poor, and in his pastoral works he seeks earnestly to promote the spiritual welfare and eventual salvation of all classes and conditions of men—poor as well as rich, layfolk as well as clerics and monks, *coniugati* as well as *continentes* and *praedicatores*.[76]

The strongly monastic colouring of the *Dialogues* has often been remarked. But it is an exaggerated colouring, which does not accord with Gregory's own pastoral perspective. Leaving aside the intrusive "monastic passages" in the commentary *In 1 Regum* (which, as I argued in Chapter 11, were interpolated by a later hand), we find that his genuine works do not put forward a specifically monastic spirituality, nor do they hold up abbots and monks as models and heroes of Christian life. The real Gregory did indeed esteem the monastic life. He recalled with nostalgia the period in which he himself had been *"in monasterio constitutus"*, giving himself to contemplative seclusion in the monastery of St Andrew which he had established in his paternal home on the Coelian Hill. When he was reluctantly raised to the episcopate and to the *culmen regiminis* he still held the monastic vocation in high regard, and took very seriously his responsibility as bishop and patriarch to provide for the due ordering of monastic life. Nevertheless, his understanding of the place of monks in the Church and of the nature of contemplative perfection differs from that of the Dialogist.

For Pope Gregory the monk was part of an institution which existed in the Church for the service of God and of souls. Although he also esteemed the eremitical vocation,[77] for him the norm of monastic observance was that of the common life in obedience to community discipline. In the *Dialogues*, on the other hand, we find monks habitually held up for admiration who lead an eremitical rather than a coenobitical life, as Dom R. Gillet points out.[78] The individual abbots and monks whose marvellous deeds enliven those pages are put forward primarily as wonder-workers to be admired, not as teachers of godly living or masters

---

[76] See his exhortation to his Roman flock in *Homilies on the Gospels* 36.11-13.
[77] Cf. his letter to the hermit Secundinus, IX.147 (Ewald-Hartmann II, pp. 142-8).
[78] *Op. cit.*, *"Spiritualité et place du moine selon saint Grégoire"*, p. 334.

of the contemplative life. They fascinate by their aura of miraculous power and clairvoyance, not by their wisdom as spiritual guides. In the perspective of the real Gregory there is no such concentration on the personality and prowess of holy recluses, nor is spiritual perfection considered to be the special preserve of monks. Rather, the height of perfection is found in the mixed life of apostolic devotion.[79] In what seems to be an autobiographical reflection in his *Homilies on Ezekiel*,[80] he describes the progress of contemplative souls who become truly enlightened only when they "reluctantly accept the ministry of souls and are assigned to the government of the faithful". Only then, in the grievous trials of the active ecclesiastical ministry, do they arrive at humble realization of their own weakness and find the path to true interior progress. Both the spiritual humility and the pastoral earnestness of St Gregory the Great are missing from the *Dialogues*-narrative.

As well as holy hermits, there are also some coenobitical communities in the book. Features of their observance do not accord with Gregory's own standards, though they pass muster with the Dialogist. For example, we find the author of the *Dialogues* praising Galla, a nun of a convent near St Peter's, and also Merulus, a monk of his "own monastery", for exercising the virtue of generous almsgiving.[81] As A. de Vogüé remarks,[82] it is surprising to find resources for almsgiving possessed by religious who should have renounced proprietorship; it is still more surprising to find such almsgiving praised as a personal virtue by Pope Gregory, who regarded any possession of money by monks as a pestilential evil and as the bane of peace and charity in a monastic community.[83]

Other doctrinal contrasts and anomalies

In Chapters 14-17, when pointing out incongruities in the Dialogist's deployment of the 80 Inserted Gregorian Passages, I noted many other doctrinal anomalies in his narrative. Of these I here recall the following instances, which still further indicate the disparity between the doctrinal presuppositions of the Gregory of the *Dialogues* and those of the real Gregory. In each case I cite the relevant IGP, in order to refer to my discussion in Chapters 14-17.

---

[79] Cf. Gillet, *ibid.* p. 350, and *DS* VI, pp. 886-7.

[80] II.7.12.

[81] IV.14.3 and 49.4.

[82] *SC* 265, p. 170.

[83] See Ep. XXII.6; Ewald-Hartmann II, pp. 352. The Dialogist himself later depicts Gregory as sternly enforcing the rule of poverty in his own monastery (IV.57.10-13.)

In *Dialogues* I.8.5-6 the author's remarks about the doctrine of predestination are inept, and do not fit the borrowed Gregorian text. (cf. IGP 9).

In II.3.5-9 the Dialogist is confused about what Gregory means when he refers to the spiritual state of "being with oneself" and "returning to oneself". (cf. IGP 17).

In II.15.5, and again in II.21.3-4, the Dialogist applies the term *prophetia* to the predictions of St Benedict. This contrasts with the usage of Gregory himself, who restricts the term to Scriptural prophecy, and does not apply it, as the Dialogist does here, to non-biblical vaticination. (cf. IGPs 20 and 22).

In II.35.2-4 and 7 there is a gulf between the level of the Dialogist's description of the spectacular phenomena in St Benedict's cosmic vision and the elevation of Gregory's own teaching about the mystical vision, in which the soul must suppress all such imaginations in order to fix its gaze on the infinite divine light. (cf. IGP 26).

In III.24.2, after telling the story of a frightening apparition of St Peter to a sacristan, the Dialogist explains that the Apostle's purpose in thus appearing was to show how unceasingly watchful he is to reward those who show honour to him. Such a notion finds no warrant in Gregory's own teaching about the saints in heaven. (cf. IGP 37).

In III.37.19-20 the Gregory of the *Dialogues* highly praises the wonder-working but illiterate priest Sanctulus, with whom he had for many years been on intimate terms. He states, without any hint of regret but rather with complacence, that this priest, who used to confer with him in Rome each year, may never have read in the New Testament St John's words about Christ's sacrifice, that he did not know the Commandments, indeed that he was unfamiliar with the very rudiments of letters. For the real Gregory such a state of affairs would have been scandalous, and he would have given it no countenance. He held that ability to read the sacred books was essential for priestly life, and that it was a grave abuse for priests to be illiterate. In his disciplinary letters enforcing the Church's discipline he sternly opposed the ordination or promotion of such men.[84] (cf. IGP 40).

I offer one last item for discussion in our comparison between the pastoral and theological presuppositions of the author of the *Dialogues* and those of Pope Gregory himself. It is the account of the apparition of the Virgin Mary to the little girl Musa. In *Dialogues* IV.18.1-3 we read how the Blessed Virgin, accompanied by white-clad handmaidens of the same age as Musa, asks the child whether she would like to join them and

---

[84] Cf. Ep. II.37, IV.26, V.51, X.15; Ewald-Hartmann I, pp. 133, 261, 351; II.247.

become one of her heavenly attendants. Musa accepts the invitation, re-
nounces all childish levity as her celestial visitor enjoined, and, falling ill,
is duly called to heaven when, thirty days later, the Mother of God reappears escorted by her handmaids.

Fr Marc Doucet has pointed out that the Mariology of St Gregory is,
in comparison with developments elsewhere, both in East and West, very
reserved—he even calls it "*incontestablement pauvre*".[85] St Gregory does indeed write of the Mother of God with high reverence—but always in the
context of the economy of salvation. Whenever he speaks of her it is to
refer to her role in the coming about of the Incarnation: that is, to affirm
that she was *Dei genetrix*, whose motherhood was the guarantee of the
truth of the Incarnation, and also that she virginally conceived and bore
her divine Son.[86] From those basic data of Mariology, theological
speculation in East and West, before and during Gregory's lifetime,
developed further doctrines about the personal prerogatives, heavenly
glorification and special intercessory power of the Blessed Virgin Mary.
But on such developments, as Fr Doucet observes, St Gregory is completely silent. Although from his sojourn in Constantinople he could not
have been ignorant of the luxuriant Mariological developments in the
contemporary East, there is no echo of them in his writings. The extension to the whole empire of the eastern feast of Mary's Assumption on
August 15 was decreed by the Emperor Maurice during Gregory's pontificate; but he nowhere made reference to that belief, nor was the feast
introduced in Rome in his age.[87]

Leaving out of account the story of Musa in the *Dialogues*, there is no
Gregorian text which attributes to Mary any role as intercessor, or any
salutary activity apart from her all-important co-operation in the Incarnation. In contrast to this silence and theological reserve of Pope
Gregory, the touching story in *Dialogues* IV.18, in which Mary appears
as a heavenly personality acting in her own right, surrounded by her
virginal retinue and issuing invitation, instructions and the promise of
heaven[88] to little Musa, can be seen as one more unusual and problematic feature of the book.

---

[85] "*La Vierge Mère de Dieu dans la théologie de saint Grégoire le Grand*", in *Bulletin de Littérature ecclésiastique*, 84, 1983 pp. 163-77.

[86] *Ibid* p. 165.

[87] *Ibid* pp. 174-6.

[88] It is especially this feature of the story that appears to depart from Gregory's
habitual reserve about the prerogatives of the Blessed Virgin. I do not, of course, argue
that he would have any difficulty in relating an apparition of a heavenly visitant to
prepare someone for death. He relates more than one such apparition in his Gospel
homilies.

CHAPTER TWENTY

HISTORICAL DISCREPANCIES

The book of the *Dialogues* is presented as a recital of historical facts, which is supported by circumstantial references to people and places. The events related are linked with Gregory's own experience and with that of other persons well known to him. There are chronological indications of when they occurred or were reported to him. All this gives to the book an appearance of almost judicial documentation, which commentators have taken as proof of its authenticity, as well as of its value as a historical source. When, however, one attempts to test the *Dialogues* against an objective framework of fact known from the history of Gregory's age, one encounters a tangle of contradictions and inconsistencies. In this chapter I can indicate only some of the main historical discrepancies which tell against Gregorian authorship of the *Dialogues*, with discussion of particular examples.

In the course of the preceding chapters I have already pointed out numerous instances in which the theory of Gregory's authorship of the *Dialogues* appears incompatible with what is established from other sources as historical fact. In Chapter 11, for example, I showed that the whole pattern of the early history of Benedictine monasticism provides a systematic argument against the supposition that Book II of the *Dialogues* originated in the age of St Gregory and was known throughout the seventh century. The Dialogist does indeed strive, with considerable ingenuity, to maintain an overall historical consistency in his narrative. To a large extent he safeguards himself from discernible mistakes by peopling his pages with characters who are completely unknown to historical record and by narrating events that are beyond the range of any historical verification. Yet from time to time he does venture a historical reference which can be tested against other sources. Moreover he has to make his narrative concord with Pope Gregory's own position and experience at the ostensible time of the book's origin, namely in the autumn of 593.[1] Thus he exposes a weak flank to historical criticism.

I do not argue that the real Pope Gregory would have been incapable of making mistakes in historical reference, or that if he had been minded to write a work of fanciful hagiography he would necessarily have main-

---

[1] In Chapter 5, pp. 81-93 I pointed out how historically improbable it is that Gregory could have had time or inclination to write the *Dialogues* in those months.

tained internal consistency in his narrative. My submission is that there are historical discrepancies and inconsistencies in the *Dialogues* that cannot plausibly be attributed to the real Gregory, in the light of what we know from other sources of his attitudes and experience. To show what I mean I will begin by citing three examples of historical blunders, which may be taken as test-cases.

Three test-cases

The first occurs in *Dialogues* III.32.1, where we read the story of some confessor-bishops whose tongues were cut out by order of the persecuting Arian king of the Vandals in North Africa. The wonder was that, although thus mutilated, the heroic confessors were still able to speak. They took refuge in Constantinople, where their miraculous speech continued and was witnessed by many. The Gregory of the *Dialogues* affirms that while papal representative at the imperial court he himself had spoken with an old prelate who had personally known those refugee bishops and heard their prodigious utterance. The episode referred to here is known to us from other sources, both Greek and Latin. The cruelty of the Vandal persecutors and the subsequent prodigy (which some think could have had a natural explanation) were related by no less than six earlier authors who wrote before the age of Gregory the Great: namely, Victor Vitensis, Marcellinus, Procopius of Caesarea, Victor Tunnunensis, Justinian, and Aeneas of Gaza.[2]

It must have been a well-known story in Constantinople, and during the six years he passed there as papal *apocrisarius* Gregory would surely have heard it, at least sufficiently to locate the event in the right century. In the *Dialogues* he is represented as saying that it had occurred during the reign of the Emperor Justinian, that is, about half a century previous to the putative date of the book. But, as Dudden pointed out, to place the event (and the outbreak of the Vandal persecution in Africa) in the reign of Justinian was "an extraordinary mistake".[3] In fact, as the contemporary historians make clear, the episode occurred during the Arian persecution in Africa under the Vandal king Huneric (447-484). Moreover that date was so remote that the claim by the Gregory of the *Dialogues* to have heard the facts from a man who had known the bishops personally strains the bounds of credibility. According to Victor Tunnunensis, the confessors were mutilated in the year 479; according to Marcellinus, five years later. In either case, it would have been a good

---

[2] Cf. Dudden *op. cit.* I, p. 341, note 2; A. de Vogüé, *SC* 260, pp. 390-1.
[3] *Op. cit.* I, p. 342.

hundred years afterwards that the Gregory of the *Dialogues* allegedly received the testimony of one who had heard them speaking. As we shall see, this is only one out of many instances in which the pope's informants in the *Dialogues* were of extraordinary longevity and length of memory—in an age when average life-spans were short.

A second test-case in which the Dialogist makes one of his rare incursions into the wider arena of history beyond the shores of Italy is likewise instructive. Here again we find the Gregory of the *Dialogues* giving a version of events which the real Gregory would hardly have given. In III.31 a graphic account is given of the circumstances of the death of the Visigothic prince Hermenigild, and of the conversion of the Spanish kingdom to the Catholic faith. It describes how the wicked king Leovigild attempted to force his Catholic son Hermenigild to apostatize to the Arian heresy. The heroic prince, who had been converted to the true faith by Bishop Leander of Seville, rebuffed his father's attempt to make him receive sacrilegious Easter communion from an Arian bishop, and was consequently put to death. Miraculous phenomena around the martyr's body then attested his heavenly reward, and he was rightly venerated by all the faithful. Leovigild was struck by remorse. On his death-bed he commended his other son and successor Reccared to Leander, whom previously he had sorely afflicted, begging the bishop to achieve in the still unconverted Reccared what by his exhortations he had achieved in Hermenigild. After ascending the throne, Reccared embraced the Catholic faith, through the noble example and merits of his martyred brother, and thereby the whole Visigothic kingdom was converted. The author of the *Dialogues* gives the principal credit for this glorious triumph of the faith to Hermenigild the martyr, whom he calls "God's confessor" and "a man dedicated to God".

The Dialogist's account is at variance with that given by the contemporary historians of Spanish affairs—Isidore of Seville (brother of Leander), John of Biclaro and Gregory of Tours—who were in a position to know the facts at first hand. Moreover it does not square with what we know of Gregory's own knowledge of the events, and of his attitude to the principal characters involved in those events. Hermenigild is mentioned by those contemporary Catholic historians of Visigothic Spain not as a martyr, but as the leader of a faction in a civil war, and as a usurper. St Isidore, greatest light of Visigothic Catholicism, merely records: "*Hermenigildum deinde filium imperiis suis tyrannizantem obsessum* [*Leovigildus*] *superavit*".[4] He does not present Hermenigild as a Catholic martyr, nor

---

[4] *Historia Gothorum* 49; likewise *Historia Suevorum* 91; *MGH, Auct. Antiqu.* XI, 1893, pp. 287, 303.

even mention his death. John of Biclaro, himself a sufferer from the same Arian persecution of Leovigild, likewise describes Hermenigild as a rebel, who was eventually captured and sent to Tarragona by his father, where he was slain by his father-in-law Sibert.[5] Gregory of Tours, although not as near to the events as the Spaniards Isidore and John of Biclaro, adds some further details. He does mention the religious factor of Hermenigild's conversion to Catholicism (through the influence, it would seem, of his young Frankish wife) at his viceregal residence in Seville, where he was confirmed by Bishop Leander. Like Isidore and John of Biclaro, Gregory of Tours shows no approval of Hermenigild's resistance to his father, but describes him as a rebel against the king, as a fomenter of domestic strife, and as a wretch who was "unmindful of divine justice". Like them, he does not present Hermenigild as a martyr; he simply records that Leovigild had him put to death. He does however refer to reports that Leovigild was converted to the Catholic faith on his death-bed.[6]

All three chroniclers record Reccared's adherence to the Catholic faith in 587, which was followed by the famous Third Council of Toledo in the spring of 589, establishing Catholic orthodoxy as the national religion. For this they give the credit to Reccared. They give no hint that Hermenigild was regarded even after that event as the one who by his example and merits promoted the conversion of Spain from Arianism to the true faith. Even though they were apologists for the Catholic cause and were writing after the triumph of that cause in Visigothic Spain, they give no countenance to any suggestion that he was a Catholic champion who died for the faith. Nor do they make any mention of a deathbed commission given by Leovigild to Leander for the conversion of Reccared. Isidore, in particular, was writing well after the time when, it is supposed, Pope Gregory's *Dialogues* had become generally known. If that supposition were correct, it would follow that Isidore equivalently gave the lie to the saintly pope whom he so highly esteemed.

According to the Dialogist, Bishop Leander of Seville had a central role in those dramatic events. It was to his exhortations that the dying king Leovigild attributed the conversion to Catholicism of the heroic Hermenigild, and it was also to Leander that he committed the task of converting Reccared to the true faith. Now Leander, brother of Isidore, brother-in-law of Leovigild and uncle of both Hermenigild and Reccared, was certainly in a position to know the facts of those cardinal events in the history of his nation and of the royal family to which he be-

---

[5] *Chronicle*, anno 585; *MGH, Auct. Antiqu.* XI, 1893, p. 217.

[6] *Historia Francorum*, V.38; VI.18, 40, 43; VIII.28, 46. *MGH, Script. rer. merov* I, pp. 229-31, 260, 278-9, 282-3, 341.

longed. One would suppose that he and his brother Isidore, leaders of the Catholic party in Spain, would surely have extolled their nephew's glorious martyrdom for the faith if they had known that version of the events. Leander's great address at the Third Council of Toledo, when the Spanish kingdom collectively embraced the Catholic faith, survives;[7] it contains no reference to any part played by Hermenigild in the triumph of that faith.

Leander, it must also be remembered, was a most intimate friend of Pope Gregory. The two men had been constant companions during the years when both were living in the imperial court in Constantinople. To Leander Gregory dedicated his great work, the *Moralia*, and in his correspondence he addressed him as the one he best loved. Those stirring events in Spain—Hermenigild's insurrection against his father about the year 579, his exile in 584, followed by his violent death in 585, and Leovigild's own death in 586—were happening in the very years in which Gregory and Leander were together in the Byzantine capital. From his close contact with his friend during those years, Gregory would have been able to avoid the many historical discrepancies contained in the *Dialogues* account.

Another odd feature of that account is that while attributing Hermenigild's conversion from Arianism to the preaching of "the most reverent bishop of Seville, Leander, with whom I have long been joined in familiar friendship", the Gregory of the *Dialogues* nevertheless gives, as his authority for his narrative of the facts, not Leander himself but "many people who have come hither from Spanish parts".[8] This ignoring of any testimony from Leander is all the more surprising since we know from a letter of Gregory to his friend, dated April 591, that Leander had written to him some time previously relating Reccared's conversion and merits.[9] In his reply to Leander the pope expresses his great joy at the news of the king's conversion and good dispositions. By sending this information, he tells Leander, "You make me love even one whom I do not know". Nevertheless, Gregory makes no reference in his letter to the dramatic events leading to Reccared's conversion, nor to the crucial part played in them by the royal martyr Hermenigild and by Leander himself, which he supposedly narrated with such fervent emphasis in the *Dialogues* only two years later.

There is also a letter from Gregory to Reccared himself, dated August 599,[10] in which he warmly praises the great work that Reccared has

---

[7] *Concilios Visigóticos e Hispano-Romanos*, ed. J. Vives, Barcelona-Madrid 1963, pp. 33-8.
[8] III. 31.1.
[9] Ep. I.41; Ewald-Hartmann I, p. 57.
[10] Ep. IX.228; Ewald-Hartmann II, pp. 221-5.

brought about: "through Your Excellency the whole nation of the Goths has been brought from the error of the Arian heresy into the firmness of the right faith". According to the *Dialogues*, as we have seen, Gregory considered Reccared's role and merit in the conversion of Visigothic Spain as consequent upon the example and merits of Hermenigild. It is supposed that in that book, published five years previously, he had referred to those very recent events, which he saw as still influencing Reccared's conduct: "And it is no wonder that this king became a preacher of the true faith, seeing that he is the brother of a martyr, whose merits help him in his task of leading so many souls back to the bosom of Almighty God. Wherein we have to consider that all this could never have come to pass had not Hermenigild the king laid down his life for the truth ... For in the Visigothic nation one died that many might live; one grain was sown in faith that a mighty crop of faithful souls might spring up therefrom."[11] Nevertheless in his long personal letter to Reccared, which includes a reference to Leander, there is no word about the king's martyred brother or any of the circumstances which in the *Dialogues* are presented as so important in the conversion of the Visigoths to Catholicism.

Many historians have severely criticized Gregory for a major historical blunder in his relation of Hermenigild's death and its sequel. Dudden, for example, comments: "the account which Gregory gives of 'the martyrdom' of Hermenigild cannot be credited for a moment in view of the silence of the Spanish historians, and the glaring inaccuracies in the narrative itself. It is pure fiction."[12] Others,[13] however, have rallied to Gregory's defence, especially Catholic authors who take account of the eventual proclamation of Hermenigild as a saint and martyr by the Roman Catholic Church. Some historians have in recent times sought to emphasize the religious factor in Hermenigild's rebellion, to which Gregory of Tours seems to allude, and to present the rebel prince as a Catholic crusader. To explain why Isidore and John of Biclaro refer so unfavourably to Hermenigild, and why there was a general silence in the Spanish Church about his alleged merits, J. N. Hillgarth[14] even proposes the theory that those Catholic bishops and churchmen had been implicated in his rising against the royal authority, and hence that they prudently wished to distance themselves from their recent embarrassing

---

[11] *Dialogues* III.31.8.
[12] *Op. cit.* I, p. 342; cf. pp. 403-11. So also R. Altamira, *CMH* XI (1913) p. 170.
[13] E.g. Garcia Villada and J. F. Alonso.
[14] "*La conversión de los Visigodos*", in *Analecta Sacra Tarraconensia*, 34, 1961, pp. 3-11, 15-26; see also E. A. Thompson, "The Conversion of the Visigoths to Catholicism", in *Nottingham Medieval Studies*, 4, 1960, pp. 4-35. cf. B. de Gaiffier, *AB* 80, 1982, pp. 390-5.

situation. B. Cignitti, while accepting—on the evidence of the *Dialogues*—Hermenigild's claim to martyrdom and saintdom, discounts those conjectures.[15]

Whatever may have been Hermenigild's personal motivation, it remains highly improbable that Pope Gregory could have written the singular narration in *Dialogues* III.31. As Dudden and Richards remark, he showed prudent caution in his attitude to the Spanish kingdom.[16] The imperial province in southeastern Spain, reconquered by Justinian, was resented by the Visigothic rulers. Both the Byzantine and the Visigothic courts regarded the City and Church of Rome as an integral part of the Empire and associated with its cause. The imperial government had supported the rebellions against the Visigothic crown by both Athanagild and Hermenigild.[17] Gregory took care to antagonize neither of the two courts. It would have been at variance with his habitual diplomatic prudence to publish a book which asserted unquestioningly a partisan account of a Spanish prince's opposition to the Visigothic king, the father and predecessor of the reigning monarch Reccared: an account, moreover, that conflicted with the view of events taken by the Spanish court and bishops, which, from his intimacy with Leander, Gregory was in a position to know at first hand.

The attitude of disapprobation shown towards Hermenigild by the contemporary Spanish chroniclers lasted for centuries in the Church of his native land. Although it is asserted in the *Dialogues* that "all the faithful" were led to venerate the prince as a martyr by the testimony of wondrous happenings around his body, there is not a trace of any such cult, either in the records of the Visigothic period or in the Mozarabic liturgy, which testifies to the ardent devotion of the Spanish Christians under Muslim rule to their earlier saints and martyrs.[18] Even the author of the *Vitas Patrum Emeritensium*, which, as I have argued in Chapter 8, is of later date, continued that tradition of Visigothic history. While he copied verbatim from the *Dialogues*, he refused to reproduce the phrases that represented the rebel Hermenigild as a martyr for the Catholic faith, and substituted a corrective phrase of his own.

We may ask how the Dialogist came to insert into his work this version of a chapter in Spanish history so much at variance with that of the

---

[15] "Ermenigildo" in *BS* V, cols, 38, 44. In a study on *"La rivolta di Ermenigildo"* B. Saitta concludes that Hermenigild "certainly did not favour or hasten the passage of the Visigothic world to Catholicism": *Quaderni catanesi di studi classici e medievali*, I, 1979, pp. 81-134.

[16] Dudden, I, p. 411; Richards, pp. 210-1.

[17] Cf. W. Goffart, "Byzantine Policy in the West under Tiberius II and Maurice", in *Traditio*, 13, 1957, pp. 73-118.

[18] cf. Garcia Villada, *op. cit.*, Vol. II, pp. 54-5.

Visigothic authorities. Perhaps he was following a fanciful and tendentious tradition of those events that had been developed by a Spanish faction during the seventh century. The visitors to Rome who had "come hither from Spanish parts" may have been descendants of followers of Hermenigild himself, who presented the execution of the prince as a martyrdom for the Catholic faith, adorned with a legend of miracles. Their viewpoint may also be reflected in the short treatise, *De vana seaculi sapientia*, which, as we saw in Chapter 9, was formerly attributed to Valerius of Bierzo. There we find a passing reference to Hermenigild as a royal martyr—the only exception in any Spanish document of those centuries to the prevailing censure on the rebel prince's memory.

It was Bede in far away Northumbria who, reading the *Dialogues* in the eighth century, first celebrated the glory of the martyred Spanish prince. But it was not until many generations later that the authority of the *Dialogues* in resurgent Spanish Christendom rehabilitated Hermenigild's reputation in his own homeland. Eventually, a thousand years after his death, through the age-long influence of the *Dialogues*, his cult in Spain was solemnly approved by Pope Sixtus V in 1586, at the request of king Philip II. It was extended to the whole Catholic Church by Pope Urban VIII in 1636.

There is another rare case in which the author of the *Dialogues* ventures into the wider sphere of verifiable Church history. It provides our third example of a historical blunder which cannot reasonably be laid at the door of the real Gregory. In III.1 there is a long and attractive story about the great St Paulinus of Nola. This story (which parallels similar themes in other hagiographical collections[19]) tells of an act of heroic charity by the saintly bishop. When the Vandals devastated Campania, it is narrated, they carried off into slavery the son of a poor woman. To redeem him Paulinus took his place in Africa as slave to the son-in-law of the Vandal king. When his identity was revealed preternaturally, he was honourably sent back to Italy with all his fellow-captives from Nola. The author of the *Dialogues* knows and refers to the account of St Paulinus's death by Uranius—a rare instance in which he explicitly makes mention of a written source for his narrative.[20] But he is strangely ignorant of the chronology of the century in which the renowned St Paulinus lived. The Vandal invasions of Italy did not in fact begin until a quarter of a century after that saint's death at an advanced age in 431.

---

[19] Cf. Vogüé *SC* 260, p. 259.

[20] *"apud eius ecclesiam scriptum est"*; III.1.9. cf. Vogüé, *SC* 251, p. 111. Uranius's *Epistula de obitu Paulini* (*BHL* 6558) is in *PL* 53.859-66.

Would not the real Pope Gregory I have known that the active life of St Paulinus, friend and correspondent of St Ambrose, St Augustine, Pope Anastasius and many another famous contemporary, antedated by many decades the first shock of the Vandal onslaughts on Italy, marked by their capture of Rome in 455? Dudden comments: "it is certain that Gregory made a serious mistake, which, by a little care, he might easily have avoided".[21] A. de Vogüé likewise makes a critical comment on this anachronism, which he sees as indication of the legendary character of the narrative.[22]

Local "history"

When we turn from that wider sphere of documented history to the Italian provincial scene in which most of the episodes of the *Dialogues* are set, we find that they are virtually beyond the range of historical verifiability. In the preface to his edition of the *Dialogues*, Moricca remarks that the narrative abounds in "indications of a historical character", but adds that it is so lacking in chronological precision that we find ourselves "sailing in the midst of dense darkness", and unable to give firm dates for the events described.[23] Nevertheless the *Dialogues* are commonly taken to be a valuable historical source. In the view of A. de Vogüé, "it is above all in the area of regional and local history that the *Dialogues* are precious". Not only does the book present "a very lively picture of Italian society in the sixth century", but, he says, "there is also in it an abundant documentation of prosopography and topography. Moreover many persons, monuments and sites of Italy in that epoch are known to us solely, or for the first time, in the *Dialogues*".[24] It cannot be said, however, that the historical credit of the book is restored by those circumstantial details which Fr de Vogüé finds so precious.[25] The author does indeed give us a lively picture of Italian society. He has set his florilegium of miracles in a homely setting which he knows from personal observation. Yet nothing authenticates that setting as belonging to the

---

[21] *Op. cit.*, I, p. 341. Ellies du Pin had pointed out the mistake over two centuries previously.

[22] *SC* 260, p. 257. J. Petersen considers it otiose to attempt to defend the historicity of those three narratives: "Gregory was not writing history but following the conventions of hagiographical writing in his own day" (*op. cit.*, p. 20).

[23] *Op. cit.* p. XLV. Moricca draws up a putative chronological table in which he tries to arrange the various events and miracles (pp. LIII-LIV).

[24] *SC* 251, p. 155.

[25] Dr Petersen points out pertinently: "Once it is acknowledged that Gregory's raw material for the *Dialogues* consisted of a corpus of traditional stories common to both East and West, the claim that they are an important source for Italian social and economic history needs to be reconsidered" (*op. cit*, p. XX).

sixth century; it could equally, or rather more probably, belong to the
seventh century.

V. Recchia set out to write a study of what can be learned about the
rural society of Gregory's age, from the data contained both in the
Registrum and in the *Dialogues*. He found himself confronted by the puzzling contrast between those two sets of data: "But it must be said at once
that the picture of agricultural society which is drawn from the *Dialogues*
is very diverse from that which is presented in the administrative
letters."[26]

Fr de Vogüé considers that the information furnished by the *Dialogues*
is particularly important for the history of the dioceses and monasteries
of Italy in that dark age. "Without those indications", he remarks, "we
should know nothing of Honoratus and of Fondi, of Equitius and his
Valerian foundations, of Anastasius and of Suppentoma, nor of so many
other cenobitical institutions ..."[27] One might comment, on the other
hand, that it is surprising that such notable saints and such extraordinary
happenings should be so completely unknown, and unmentioned, in any
other documentary record from the sixth and seventh centuries. In
Chapter 11 I pointed out how singular it is that there is elsewhere no
trace, in any record before the close of the seventh century, of biographical knowledge of St Benedict, who should surely have been the most remarkable Italian saint of that age—if we are to credit Book II of the
Dialogues. Similar critical doubts must be raised about much of the
regional "history" in the *Dialogues*, and about other miracle-working
saints in that book, whose cult and existence was for long unknown in
the localities in which they are alleged to have been active. The artificial
renown they acquired when, in a later age, the *Dialogues* became known
could not easily supply for the lack of any cult or knowledge of them in
their supposed homelands. Only after many centuries was their cult introduced as a long-delayed legacy from the *Dialogues*.[28]

A particularly striking example of the strange historical *incognito* of the
saints of the *Dialogues* appears from the narration in III.27 and 28.1.
There we read how about the year 578 (the date is indicated in the text)
440 Italian countryfolk died steadfast and glorious martyrs at the hands
of the Lombards. First 40 captive peasants were slain because they
refused to eat food immolated to idols; then no less than 400 others were

---

[26] *Gregorio Magno e la Società Agricola*, Rome 1978, p. 6.

[27] *SC* 251, p. 155.

[28] Cf. B. de Gaiffier, "*Les héros des Dialogues de Grégoire inscrits au nombre des saints*", in
AB 83, 1965, pp. 53-73, The tardy introduction of such "new saints" into the Roman
martyrology, says the Bollandist author, was unjustified, "since there is not the least
trace of any cult rendered to them" (pp. 72-3).

martyred for refusing to adore a goat's head that the impious Lombards had sacrificed to the devil.[29] Now if such an exceptional demonstration of the highest Christian fortitude by so many hundreds of the faithful, who deliberately chose martyrdom rather than deny their faith, had really occurred at that time, how is it that—outside the pages of the *Dialogues*—there is no trace of knowledge of it either in the lifetime of Pope Gregory or for a century and more later? No place can be assigned to it, no local church claimed the honour of it or treasured the martyrs' graves. Surely Pope Gregory himself, if he were so well informed about this recent martyrdom, would have ensured that the hallowed locality was known and venerated? Some commentators are prepared to recognize that this story should be classified in the *genre* of legendary hagiography; but can we suppose that St Gregory would impose on the piety of the faithful by putting out such a false report of a recent mass martyrdom? At all events, if in 593-4 he had recorded the event in the *Dialogues*, surely the great pope's announcement of the glorious constancy of that multitude of martyrs would have made some discernible impression in the Christian Church in an age when the cult of martyrs was at its height?

There are instances in which we are able to compare the assertions of the author of the *Dialogues* about regional and local matters with statements made in the writings of Gregory himself, and to observe that the two do not tally. I have already referred in Chapter 18 to a notable example of such discrepancy. In III.7.1 the Gregory of the *Dialogues* prefaces to his vivid and apocryphal story about Bishop Andrew of Fondi the assurance that the facts as he will narrate them are indubitably true, because "there are as many witnesses to them as there are inhabitants existing in that place". We have seen that the real Gregory, writing in the year previous to that in which the *Dialogues* were ostensibly written, makes it clear that there were no inhabitants existing in Fondi at that time. In his letter to Bishop Agnellus of Fondi in 592, he laments that "because of the destruction of war it is impossible for anyone to dwell either in that city or in your church." While leaving Agnellus nominal bishop of the abandoned city of Fondi, Gregory put him in charge of the church at Terracina,[30] where many of his first flock probably gathered round him.

---

[29] The Dialogist may have drawn this detail of his story from a letter of Gregory, dated 597, in which he urged the Frankish queen Brunhild to restrain her subjects from "sacrilegious sacrifices with the heads of animals" and "from the cult of devils" (VIII.4; Ewald-Hartmann, II, p. 7).

[30] *Ep.* III.13 and 14; see Chapter 18 above, p. 591; also Chapter 16, p. 497.

A suspect pattern of personal names

Despite the rich profusion in the *Dialogues* of personal names and topographical references, it proves impossible to obtain from them any independent historical confirmation of the book's authenticity or date of origin. Many names of individuals who are mentioned in the *Registrum* of Pope Gregory are also found in the *Dialogues*, either as witnesses to miracles, or as relatives or associates of other characters, or sometimes as participants in the episodes narrated. Yet although the Dialogist supplies some further particulars about those individuals, which give his narrative an appearance of verisimilitude, nothing in his book adds convincingly to the knowledge which we have of them from the papal correspondence.

Studying those instances of repetition of personal names, we may distinguish three categories. First, there are several instances in which it is clear that the author of the *Dialogues* intends to identify a character in his narrative with a person named in the papal letters. Secondly, there are other instances in which the names are the same, and identity of the persons may be implied, but there are other circumstances which make such identification doubtful. And thirdly, in numerous other instances, while there is identity of names it is clear that the characters so mentioned in the *Dialogues* could not be the same as their namesakes in Gregory's *Registrum*. This pattern of nomenclature raises some intriguing questions and doubts. Did the author of the *Dialogues*, having access to the file copies of Pope Gregory's letters, use them as a source for naming the actors in his drama of miracles? While we can see that in some cases he borrowed real characters from the Gregorian letters to bring them into his fictitious episodes, did he in other cases choose names at random from the letters to give to his own fictitious characters?

In the first category, there are several instances in which we can be reasonably certain that characters named in the *Dialogues* are intended by the author to be identified with individuals of the same name whose existence is known from the Gregorian letters. Even though in the Dialogist's lifetime those letters were not published, and were available only to those who could consult them in the papal *scrinium* in Rome, it doubtless appealed to his ingenious mind to introduce into his narrative historical characters mentioned by Gregory himself. As a first and problematic example I propose for discussion the story of Exhilaratus in *Dialogues* II.18. This individual, mentioned more than once in Gregory's letters, was an important notary and member of the papal secretariate— indeed, his name and importance may well have been still known to clerks in the secretariate a century later.

According to the story in *Dialogues* II.18 Exhilaratus was in his youth a servant, and was sent by his master to take a gift of two wine kegs to St Benedict. Dishonestly, he delivered only one, having hidden the other by the wayside for his own use. The prescient abbot warned the deceitful servant not to drink from the keg he had hidden, but to tilt it cautiously to see what was inside. When Exhilaratus, covered with confusion, did so, a serpent emerged from the keg. In telling this tale the Gregory of the *Dialogues* identifies the servant as "our Exhilaratus"—"*Exhilaratus noster*"—and he reminds Peter the Deacon, "You yourself knew him after his conversion". The possessive epithet "*noster*" is applied by Pope Gregory to members of the papal household. The Dialogist seems plainly to be referring here to the Exhilaratus who was *secundicerius*, or second-in-rank in the guild of notaries of the Roman Church, who is known to us from Gregory's *Registrum*. In Epistola V.6, written in the autumn of 594, mentioning his earlier intention of sending Exhilaratus on a mission to Constantinople, the pope refers to him by the very same familiar phrase—"*Exhilaratus noster*"[31]—that we find the author of the *Dialogues* using in II.18 to describe the reformed rogue of the wine-keg story. In June 597 Exhilaratus, now described as *secundicerius*, is still occupied on papal business, and returning from a journey to the East.[32] It is possible that this high-ranking clerical official was later raised to the episcopate, and is the same as the "*coepiscopus noster Exhilaratus*" whose misconduct in Sicily Gregory laments in a letter of September 603.[33] (Did this apparent turpitude of Exhilaratus in his later life prompt the Dialogist to attribute to him dishonesty in his earlier days?)

Now St Benedict's abbotship at Cassino is placed in the time of the Gothic kingdom in Italy, in the first half of the sixth century. Yet we find that *Exhilaratus noster*, who had been already active as a wine-stealing servant at that remote date, is still active at the end of the century as a curial official. This is another of the not infrequent instances of surprising longevity attributed to the characters in the Dialogist's narrative, upon which I have already remarked. We may also note in passing that the story of Exhilaratus and St Benedict is in itself very suspect. It is a "doublet" of a tale told of Isaac of Spoleto and a deceitful servant in *Dialogues* III.14.9, where all the circumstances are practically identical. A. de Vogüé points out this suspicious duplication of the miraculous episode, which suggests legendary creation.[34] He thinks, however, that

---

[31] Ewald-Hartmann I, p. 287.

[32] *Ep.* VII.29; Ewald-Hartmann I. p. 477.

[33] XIV.4; Ewald-Hartmann II, p. 423.

[34] A. Haggerty-Krappe traces the origins of this story to the East, where it is found in many forms. The serpent itself, he argues, was obviously Indian at the outset: Indian

it is the story of Isaac that should be judged fictitious rather than that of Benedict—his reason being that the witness cited for the latter story is the historical character Exhilaratus, who was still alive in 593.[35] As further support for this conclusion he remarks that "Exhilaratus plays there a role which is little to his credit, which Gregory could hardly have attributed gratuitously to a person of his court." With this remark concerning Gregory himself, I fully agree.

Another Roman ecclesiastic well known in Gregory's pontificate is mentioned in the *Dialogues* in connection with a further story of St Benedict's preternatural knowledge. He was the subdeacon Florentius, referred to in Epistola III.15 and in *Dialogues* II.8. The Gregory of the *Dialogues* narrates the story of a wicked priest of Subiaco who first attempted to poison Benedict (but was frustrated by the saint's clairvoyance), who then tried to seduce the minds of his disciples by sending seven naked maidens to dance in the monastery garden, and whom divine justice finally crushed to death by a prodigious fall of masonry. This wicked priest is said by the author to have been also named Florentius, and to have been the grandfather "of this subdeacon Florentius of ours"—"*huius nostri subdiaconi Florentii*". Commentators agree that this is meant to be a reference to the same Florentius, "*subdiaconus noster*", whose pusillanimity Pope Gregory deplores in his letter of December 592, relating how the man fled in order to avoid being consecrated as bishop of Naples.[36]

Here once again we find a Roman official, who is referred to (with disfavour) in one of Gregory's letters, also mentioned in connection with a story of wickedness detected by St Benedict's clairvoyance. Here too A. de Vogüé considers that the attribution of discreditable ancestry to the Roman subdeacon Florentius, whose existence is documented in Gregory's letters, provides a guarantee of the historical existence of the wicked priest Florentius of Subiaco, and consequently of the historicity of St Benedict himself whom Florentius persecuted. He comments: "Even if the pope had reason to be indignant with this faint-hearted subdeacon, can one imagine that he would have calumniously attributed to him so dishonourable a grandfather?"[37] With this comment, too, as

---

cobras like to slip into man-made receptacles, but Western snakes shun men and are thus less dangerous! ("*Sur un récit des Dialogues du Pope Grégoire le Grand*", in *Le Moyen Age* 50, 1937, pp. 272-5.)

[35] *SC* 251, p. 159, note 68; cf. *SC* 260, p. 310, note 9.

[36] III.15; Ewald-Hartmann, I, p. 174. cf. Vogüé *SC* 251, p. 159, note 68. Was the faint-hearted subdeacon the same as "our beloved son the deacon Florentius" mentioned by Gregory six years later in a letter of September 598? (Ep. IX.8, Ewald-Hartmann, II, p. 46).

[37] *SC* 251, p. 159, footnote 68.

with the Benedictine scholar's similar comment in the case of Ex-hilaratus, I concur! The historicity of the dramatic episodes of *Dialogues* II.8 is as dubious as that of any of the tales in the book, the legendary character of which Fr de Vogüé himself has done so much to demon-strate. The story of the jealous spite of the wicked priest Florentius who afflicted St Benedict at Subiaco contains echoes of phraseology in the earlier *Life of St Martin* by Sulpicius Severus.[38] As Fr de Vogüé rightly remarks, fictitious aspersions on the good name of living contemporaries cannot reasonably be laid at the door of Pope Gregory. Fiction there was in those tales of Exhilaratus and Florentius, but it must be attributed to someone else.

Several other Roman ecclesiastics and members of the papal curia who are named in Gregory's letters appear in the *Dialogues* as connected with miraculous happenings. These cross-references, brought in to support legendary tales, give an impression of historical verisimilitude. They show ingenuity on the author's part, and suggest his close familiarity with the archival records in the Lateran. One instance out of many may be cited. It is the mention in *Dialogues* III.20.1 of Boniface, "this our deacon and paymaster of the church"—"*huius nostri Bonifatii diaconi atque dispensatoris ecclesiae*"—who is introduced as a near relative of Stephen, the priest of the province of Valeria whose bootlaces were loosed by an invisible devil. The reference intended, it appears, is to the Roman deacon Boniface, an important ecclesiastical administrator who is repeatedly mentioned in Gregory's letters. His function in the treasury is indicated by a reference in a letter of 598 to his receipt of a deposit of ten gold pounds.[39] He was probably the future pope Boniface IV (608-615). The Dialogist was doubtless familiar with the *Liber Pontificalis*, which records that Boniface IV was a native of the province of Valeria.[40] In Chapter 22, and elsewhere I give other instances of the Dialogist's many allusions to, and even verbatim echoes of, details and phrases which he would have found in the file copies of Gregory's letters in the Roman archives.

A lengthy study would be necessary to discuss all the instances of com-mon nomenclature between the *Dialogues* and Gregory's letters. Where is appears that characters of the *Dialogues* are clearly, or probably, intend-ed to be identified with persons known from Gregory's correspondence, we have at least some historical data with which to compare the author's

---

[38] 27.3; Vogüé points out the parallel in *SC* 260, p. 161, note 1.

[39] Ep. IX.72; Ewald-Hartmann II, p. 91. The actual title *dispensator* could have been known to the Dialogist from official letters which have not survived, or from other records in the archives.

[40] See Vogüé, *SC* 260, pp. 350-1, note 1.

references. But there are also other instances in which names of the Dialogist's *dramatis personae* correspond to names found in Gregory's *Registrum*, but in which identity of the persons is evidently excluded by the circumstances of the tale. From mere coincidence of names we cannot, of course, infer that the Dialogist used Gregory's letters as a quarry from which to draw names for his own characters. Many personal names were of general currency. But the frequency and nature of the coincidence of names, and the curious echoes in the *Dialogues* of incidental details in the pope's letters, are, to say the least, surprising. Sometimes the coincidence is quite remarkable. I will cite one such example.

In the account of the inception of St Benedict's monastic life at Subiaco in *Dialogues* II.1.5 we read how he was befriended by one Romanus, who dwelt in a nearby monastery under the rule of an abbot named Adeodatus. That would have been in the early years of the sixth century. Now there is a letter written by Pope Gregory in the year 600 to an abbot named Adeodatus, whose monastery, in Naples, was established in the house that had belonged to a person named Romanus.[41] Fr de Vogüé remarks that the same two names linked in the chapter of the *Dialogues* are also linked, "*curieusement*", in the Gregorian letter.[42] Yes, the correspondence of those two pairs of names, both cited in a monastic context, is curious. We have two texts in which mention of a Romanus is closely linked with mention of an abbot Adeodatus, yet the pairs concerned are separated in time by a century. It could be mere coincidence. But we note it as one out of several coincidences of nomenclature. Our question remains: Did the author of the *Dialogues*, intent on giving a Gregorian flavour to his work, page through the codex of file-copies of the great pope's letters and pick out names to use in his own colourful book of legends? The instances I have cited, and other similar indications, do not prove that conclusion; but they point towards it. I have already remarked, in Chapter 18, on the echoing in the *Dialogues* of several names which are found independently in the legendary *Gesta* of the sixth and seventh centuries.

A web of unhistorical authentification

Many commentators on the *Dialogues* have drawn reassurance from the author's careful attestation of his sources, giving a specific witness or informant for practically every episode he relates. This they see as an index of his concern for accuracy, even though they concede that he may have been misled by some of his informants. On the contrary, the exaggerated and mendacious appeal in the *Dialogues* to an unending stream of

---

[41] Epistola X.18; Ewald-Hartmann II, p. 253.
[42] *SC* 260, p. 133, note 5.

eyewitness informants provides a telling counter-argument against both the historicity and the Gregorian authorship of the book. We have seen that it is no longer possible to exculpate the Gregory of the *Dialogues* by assuming that he passed on, in good faith, the untrustworthy reports of others; it has been proved that the author himself is implicated in the invention of at least some of his tales and thus in their spurious authentification. Hence the piling up of first-hand testimonies to the truth of the tales, far from enhancing the narrator's credit, undermines it.

I have remarked that, in his desire to make Gregory claim to have learnt his facts from the narration of eyewitnesses whom he had known personally, the Dialogist shows a marked tendency to make his characters live for improbably long periods. Another notable example of this is to be found in the case of the witnesses to the marvellous life of the holy abbot Equitius, which is related in *Dialogues* I.4. Moricca wrestles with the difficulties encountered in attempting to date the life of Equitius, and of reconciling the assertions made in the *Dialogues* with other data. He confesses frankly: "Concerning the time in which Equitius lived, and in which the miracles here narrated by Gregory can be located, there exists discord and confusion in the sources".[43] Confusion there is indeed in the *Dialogues*, the sole source of information about Equitius. It arises mainly from the extraordinary length of time alleged by the author both for the holy abbot's active life and for the lifespan of those who witnessed his miracles. On the one hand, the Dialogist presents him as already a renowned and experienced abbot when he unmasks a magician, Basilius. The process against this magician and his associate Praetextatus, who were accused of practising magic arts, is recorded by Cassiodorus, and can be dated accurately to the years 510-511.[44] The wonder-working ministry of Equitius continued for many more years after that date. In *Dialogues* I.4.11-17 we read how he was summoned to Rome to appear before a pope, whom A. Dufourcq thought was John III (561-574), but who A. de Vogüé suggests was Agapitus (535-6).[45] Since he was already a venerable abbot, renowned for his virtue and authority, at the time of his encounter with the magician Basilius before 510, it is reasonable to suppose that he would have been past middle age at that time; his active ministry could have lasted as long as a quarter of a century after that date. Yet the Gregory of the *Dialogues* asserts that at the time he is writing "many are still alive" who knew and can testify to the wondrous deeds of Equitius (I.4.9). Could there really have been many alive in 593 who

---

[43] *Op. cit.*, p. 27, note 2.

[44] *Variae* 4.22-3; cf. A. de Vogüé, *SC* 260, pp. 39-41, note 3.

[45] Dufourcq, *op. cit.* Tome III, p. 73; A. de Vogüé, *SC* 260, p. 436, and "*Le pape qui persécuta S. Equitius*", in *AB*, 100, 1982, pp. 319-25.

could witness to events, such as the downfall of Basilius, that had happened over 80 years before—or even later events in the life of the miracle-working abbot, which had happened perhaps 70 or 60 years previously? The author of the *Dialogues*, writing in a later age and possibly echoing folklore tradition, has got himself into a chronological tangle.

A contemporary of Equitius in the time of the Goths was Boniface of Ferentis, who was already a venerable bishop some time before 540.[46] A priest Gaudentius, who was brought up in Boniface's service and took part in the episodes described, is still alive at the time that the Gregory of the *Dialogues* writes, and is his source of information about the bishop's miracles. This memory-span is conceivable. But what are we to think of another informant, an old cleric who has recently arrived, and who is so long-lived that he can even witness to Boniface's prodigious acts when a child (I.9.16)? This implies that his memories must reach back a hundred years or more.

The references by the Gregory of the *Dialogues* to the abbots of "my monastery" (that is, St Andrew's *ad clivum Scauri*), when taken in conjunction with firm facts known from the Gregorian letters, lead to a conflicting pattern of names and dates which it is difficult to rationalize. The first abbot of the newly founded monastery that we hear of is Valentio, from Valeria; in *Dialogues* IV.22 it is related that he ruled the community while Gregory was a monk there. (John the Deacon says that Gregory wore the monastic habit under two abbots, Hilarion and Maximian.[47]) In *Dialogues* III.36.1 it is stated that Maximian was abbot of St Andrew's while Gregory was papal representative at Constantinople—that is, from about 579 to 586. A letter sent in 584 by Pope Pelagius II to Gregory in the imperial capital,[48] which seems to refer to Maximian (described there as *presbyter*), demands his return to Rome because he is needed "in our monastery" and also by Pelagius himself for some specific task. We have seen, however, that the Dialogist presents Gregory in IV.57 as acting with governing authority at St Andrew's after his return from Constantinople. If, as more recent authors suppose, Gregory was not acting there as abbot but as pope and patron of the monastery, one would have to conclude that the office of abbot was vacant, since Gregory issued his instructions through the prior, named as Pretiosus (IV.57.11-14). On the other hand, in a letter of Gregory's dating from the end of 590, Maximus

---

[46] Cf. I.9.14 and Vogüé, *SC* 260, p. 88, footnote. Moricca dates his activity somewhat earlier.

[47] *Vita Gregorii* I.6. By Hilarion is Valentio intended?

[48] Ewald-Hartmann II, pp. 440-1.

(Maximianus) is recorded as being abbot of St Andrew's at that time.[49] By October 591 Maximian had left Rome to become Bishop of Syracuse and papal vicar in Sicily (Epistola II.8). Then in *Dialogues* IV.49.5 we are told that an abbot named Peter was governing the monastery at the time of writing (i.e. 593); he had been abbot long enough to have prepared a tomb for himself at some time previously. Finally we know from the *Registrum* that in 598 the abbot was Candidus (Epistola VIII.12).

If one accepted all those statements as accurate, one would have to conclude that six superiors governed the monastery of St Andrew's in that span of some score of years (taking into the reckoning either the prior Pretiosus[50] or Gregory himself), and probably that Maximian had two spells of abbotship separated by an intermission. But if we discount the historicity of the *Dialogues*, and look only to the evidence of the papal letters, we need postulate only two abbots in that period—Maximian and Candidus. In his references to the abbots of St Andrew's it does not seem that the Dialogist has been successful in making his details concord aptly with those in Gregory's letters.

It is remarkable how many of the episodes in the *Dialogues*, especially in Books I and III, are connected with the region of central Italy in which the provinces of Valeria, Sabina, Tuscia and Umbria came together. In Book II the setting is in the hill-country east of Rome and in the district traversed by the Via Latina towards Campania. In Chapter 22, when discussing the biographical background of the Dialogist himself, I will say more about the significance of his topographical references. It appears that he had a special interest in and local knowledge of those rural regions. I will argue later that whoever wrote the *Dialogues* may well have had a function in the administration of the Roman Church which gave him the opportunity to become familiar with the papal patrimonies or agricultural estates, which still survived in central Italy and Campania even after the Lombard conquests. He shows no similar familiarity with the important papal patrimonies in Sicily. Many of Pope Gregory's letters were concerned with Sicily, where there were also estates of his own family, and where he himself founded six monasteries.[51] Nevertheless we find in the *Dialogues* only occasional mention of that island, and no stories about abbots, monasteries, ecclesiastical functionaries and local

---

[49] Ep. I.14a; Ewald-Hartmann I, p. 14. The authenticity of this letter could be questioned.

[50] Only one Pretiosus is mentioned in Gregory's letters—a "*servus Dei*" whom for some fault he had dismissed from Rome, but in July 592 wished to recall. (Ep. II.38; Ewald-Hartmann I, pp. 136-7.) Did the Dialogist pick a name for the prior from this letter?

[51] Cf. F. Gregorovius, *History of the City of Rome in the Middle Ages*, English trans., Vol. II, London 1894, p. 31.

churches, such as are abundantly related of the regions of central Italy.

When we turn to Rome we find two strange features in the list of testimonies concerning miracles and visions in the City. First, it is extraordinary how many of the community of Gregory's own monastery of St Andrew were witnesses of or participants in such prodigious happenings. Hallinger lists no fewer than 27 instances in connection with which monks of St Andrew's are named.[52] We note that a curiously high proportion of those informants in the Roman monastery were knowledgeable about events in the remoter provinces, especially Valeria and the country in the neighbourhood of Spoleto and Nursia, spanning southern Umbria and the northern part of the old Sabine country. Secondly, there is a curious progressive pattern in the localization of the episodes. In the first three books of the *Dialogues*, the persons mentioned live mainly in provincial and remote localities. In Book II Rome is mentioned as the place from which the youthful St Benedict fled, but the theatre of his activities is elsewhere. Only in the second part of Book III does Rome begin to be a place of supernatural occurrences. Then in Book IV the Roman episodes multiply. A score of stories tell of marvellous events—mainly visions—in the City, six of them relating to the monastery of St Andrew. There is, however, a dearth of thaumaturges in Rome. Although prodigious happenings occur, hardly any miracles are actually performed there. The healing of a paralytic girl by Acontius, sacristan of St Peter's, is a rare exception (III.35). If we accept the view that Book IV has the nature of a free-standing opuscule, perhaps first conceived independently, the non-Roman perspective of the first three books stands out even more clearly. The centre of gravity of the miraculous narratives in the *Dialogues* is outside Rome and in the Italian countryside. This would be a surprising bias if the author of the book were Gregory the Great, Roman of the Romans. It may point rather to an author who, although familiar with Rome and the administration of the papal curia, was even more familiar (and perhaps connected by origin) with the countryside, small towns and monasteries of provincial Italy. These implications we must explore further in Chapter 22.

The puzzle of Peter the interlocutor

The manner in which the figure of Peter the Deacon, Gregory's interlocutor, is presented in the *Dialogues* is not free from inconsistency. Was he intended to be the same as the individual of that name who is known to us from Gregory's correspondence as an important dignitary of the Roman Church and one of the pope's most trusted aides and ad-

---

[52] *Papst Gregor*, pp. 252-4.

ministrators? Although K. Hallinger considers this identification to be a "mere opinion", and leaves the question open,[53] most commentators, following the Maurists, conclude that it is well founded. A. de Vogüé agrees that it is "altogether probable" and marshals the arguments in its favour.[54] From all the mutually corroborative indications given in the text, it seems patent that the author of the *Dialogues* does intend this identification. At the very beginning of the dialogue he introduces Gregory's interlocutor as "*dilectissimus filius meus Petrus diaconus*"—the very phrase used by the pope in a letter of 595 (V.28) to refer to the former rector of the Sicilian patrimony, who had been appointed to that post in 590. In IV.59.6 he makes Peter refer to the time he was "*in Sicilia positus*".

Indeed the Dialogist seems to have chosen the *persona* of Gregory's interlocutor with shrewd attention to the dates in the file of the papal correspondence. In a letter of Gregory dated June 593 (III.39), we find Peter, then still a subdeacon, addressed as rector of the papal patrimony in Campania in that month. Another letter (III.54), sent only a month later, makes mention of a deacon Peter, who in a previous pontificate had been sent on a mission to Ravenna, and who is—it would seem—now available in Rome for consultation by the pope. Many authors conclude that this deacon Peter was the same as the erstwhile subdeacon who had been successively rector of the papal patrimonies in Sicily and Campania. Another letter of March 595 confirms that the former rector of the Sicilian patrimony had by that time been promoted deacon.[55] But was the deacon and sometime *defensor* who is repeatedly mentioned as having been sent on a papal mission to Ravenna,[56] the same man as the deacon Peter who had been patrimonial rector in Sicily and Campania? A. de Vogüé has no doubt that he was.[57] L. Hartmann observes that Wisbaum had "not ineptly conjectured" that the envoy to Ravenna and the rector in Sicily were the same Peter.[58] I confess that I find this indeed merely conjectural, and not proven. If one follows up the many references in the index of the Ewald-Hartmann edition of Gregory's *Registrum*, where there is mention of "Peter" as subdeacon, deacon and *defensor*, one becomes aware of the complexity of the question.[59] From the Gregorian

---

53 *Ibid.* p. 258.
54 *SC* 251, pp. 44-5; cf. *SC* 260, pp. 11 and 435.
55 Ep. V.28; Ewald-Hartmann I, p. 308.
56 See also Ep. VI.24; Ewald-Hartmann I, p. 402.
57 *SC* 251, p. 44 and notes 79 and 81.
58 Ewald-Hartmann I, p. 308, note 2.
59 If the deacon Peter mentioned in the letter to Ravenna of July 593 was the same as the Peter who was still a subdeacon in June 593, one might expect Gregory, writing to the bishop of Ravenna (who could not have known of a promotion that had happened only two or three weeks previously) to put in a phrase to explain the otherwise puzzling title given to the former papal envoy to Ravenna. In other letters (e.g. V.28) Gregory takes care to mention such a change of status.

letters alone it cannot be demonstrated with certainty that there was only one deacon named Peter active in the papal service at that time. Those who conclude that there is certainty on the point are basing their conclusion on the *Dialogues* in conjunction with the *Registrum*. Nevertheless it is apparent that the author of the *Dialogues* did assume that there was only one deacon Peter. As a trusted and well-loved member of Gregory's immediate circle, promoted to the diaconate in June-July 593 and seemingly settled in Rome from the middle of that year, he would be a suitable character to portray as the pope's partner in the dialogue, ostensibly set in the autumn of that year. The Dialogist presents him as an old and familiar friend of Gregory's.

Yet does the *persona* of the Peter of the *Dialogues* really fit that of the administrator of the papal patrimonies? There is a contrast between, on the one hand, the experienced and shrewd official known to us from Gregory's letters, from whom the pope expects responsibility, prudence and initiative, and on the other hand the rather obtuse interlocutor in the *Dialogues* whose contributions to the discussion are so often banal, naive and inconsequential. There is a difference between the tone and terms of Gregory's letters to Peter and the way he is made to address him in the *Dialogues*. To these objections it may be answered that in the *Dialogues* the character of Peter the Deacon is portrayed with literary licence, and need not correspond strictly to reality. Even so, the discrepancies remain, one more knot in the web of incongruities.

Peter the administrator had most recently been rector of the patrimony in Campania; yet the Peter of the *Dialogues*, in discussion a few months later, has never heard of the great saint and wonder-working abbot Benedict of Cassino.[60] He has never even heard that there have existed any holy thaumaturges in Italy. This is surprising ignorance to attribute to such a close associate of Gregory, who, we are told, had been linked with him in friendship and study since his youth. It is even more surprising since we also learn from the *Dialogues* that in the papal household and all around the City there was a multitude of witnesses attesting the marvellous deeds and extraordinary lives of numerous saints and wonder-workers of Italy.

"tam peritus fallendi artifex"?

Although the *Dialogues* do in several places reflect correct information of particular historical circumstances and localities, this information could have been drawn fairly easily by the author from the writings of

---

[60] As Hallinger observes: *Papst Gregor*, p. 258.

chroniclers or from the file of Gregory's letters. An example may be cited from II.14, where the author narrates Totila's trick to try the prophetic spirit of St Benedict. Although this story is manifestly fictitious, modelled on similar stories in earlier writings,[61] the Dialogist does give in recognizable form the correct names of Totila's three "counts", Vult, Ruderic and Bledin. These Teutonic names, variously spelt, are found in other contemporary records,[62] and could have been familiar in Italian folk tradition. To take another instance, an allusion in *Dialogues* IV.55.1 seems to reflect awareness that many dignitaries and members of the church of Milan were living in exile in Genoa in the later sixth century, refugees from the Lombard invaders. The Dialogist could have been aware of this fact from a letter of Gregory, dated April 593.[63] Similar explanations may be applied to other instances in which the author of the *Dialogues* is right in his references to historical and regional circumstances.

The same astuteness that I attribute to the pseudepigraphal author of the *Dialogues*, in the care that he takes to make the origin of his narrative seem to date from Gregory's lifetime, was attributed to him three centuries ago by the humanist and Protestant critics who then strenuously disputed the authenticity of the book. The Maurist editors and defenders of the *Dialogues* were aware of their opponents' explanation, which they stated as follows: "But, you will say, the author of the *Dialogues*, who chose to disguise himself as if in the person of Gregory, had steeped himself in the history of the holy Father by assiduous reading of his works, and so took pains to depict and adorn himself in those colours".[64] Their answer was that such a degree of astuteness in deception was hardly credible: "*Quasi vero tam peritus fallendi artifex esse potuisset ...*". However, as we saw in Chapter 18, it has now been established that the author of the *Dialogues* did boldly fabricate stories which he yet protested had been told to him by named and unimpeachable witnesses, and that he was adroit in concealing his artifices. An author who could be so astute in adapting and disguising his hagiographical borrowings could also be astute in giving to his fabricated narrative an appearance of historical congruity to the age of Pope Gregory I. We know of other examples of such craftiness in that age. The contemporary authors of the legendary *Gesta Martyrum* which I discussed in Chapter 18 often showed historical

---

[61] Cf. P. A. Cusack, "Some literary antecedents of the Totila encounter in the Second Dialogue of Pope Gregory I", in *Studia Patristica* XII, Berlin 1975, pp. 87-90.

[62] Cf. Vogüé, *SC* 260, p. 180-1, note 1.

[63] *Ep.* III.30; Ewald-Hartmann I, p. 188.

[64] "*Verum, inquies, qui sub Gregorii persona latere voluit Dialogorum scriptor, cum sancti Patris historiam ad unguem ex assidua operum eius lectione didicisset, iis se coloribus pingere ac ornare studuit.*" (*PL*.77.139).

knowledge as well as cunning in maintaining the fiction that they were chronicling events from the early centuries of persecution. The Dialogist was one of their company, albeit the cleverest.

For all his astuteness, however, he was often unsuccessful in his attempts at historical verisimilitude—as we have seen throughout the preceding chapters of Part Three of this book. The manner in which he represents the Gregory of the *Dialogues* is historically inept. He cannot match the spiritual depth, theological insight and pastoral wisdom of the real St Gregory; in several places he puts into Gregory's mouth statements that conflict with the saint's own teaching and attitudes; and he gives to the Gregory of the *Dialogues* a false tone of oracular self-complacency. In addition to those many discrepancies which I have already discussed, I note here some further points at which the representation of Pope Gregory in the *Dialogues* can be seen to be anomalous or historically improbable:

— The Gregory of the *Dialogues* is a religious chauvinist, extolling the thaumaturgic power of the holy men of Italy, who, he insists, have abounded in the peninsula in recent times. By implication, he wishes to establish Italy's claim to wonder-working sanctity, to match the lives of holy monks and thaumaturges from the Greek-speaking East and other lands. The writings of Gregory of Tours had been a powerful assertion of the corporate national sanctity of Gaul; the *Dialogues* ascribed to Gregory of Rome would match them with a saga of corporate Italian sanctity. The spiritual vision of the real Gregory, on the other hand, was universal; he wrote as a citizen of the one City of God. Though he did indeed firmly maintain the rights and interests of his Church in the face of Byzantine dominance and intrusions, he showed no such spiritual chauvinism as motivates the *Dialogues*.

— In *Dialogues* IV.37.3 Iberia, or Hiberia, evidently means Spain. When Pope Gregory wrote a letter to the Catholic bishops of Hiberia (Iberia)[65] he meant the Caucasian country of Georgia.

— The social and economic background of contemporary Italy, in so far as it is reflected in the *Dialogues*, does not correspond to the more organized social and political system which still survived during Gregory's pontificate, and which is well documented in his letters. In the everyday world of the *Dialogues* there is now no sign of administrative control either by the Exarch of Ravenna or by his subordinates. Imperial taxes,

---

[65] Ep. XI.52 (Ewald-Hartmann II, pp. 324-5. cf. D. Norberg, *CCL* 140A. p. 952: "*provincia Pontica, ut videtur*"). Hiberia is also given by Ewald-Hartmann (I, p. 150) in the title of Ep.II.49. Accordingly Vogüé at first considered that there too it designated Georgia (*SC* 265, p. 127). In his new edition of the *Registrum*, however, D. Norberg rejects the mention of Hiberia in the title of that letter (*CCL* 140, p. 131; Ep. II.43).

soldiery and harsh administrators, still a grievous burden for the countryfolk in Gregory's day, as his letters show, do not feature in the *Dialogues*. In so far as there is administrative authority in the districts where Roman ways survived, it is exercised not by civil but by ecclesiastical officials. As Professor R. Markus has remarked, "The *Dialogues* are set in a world in which the 'secular' is absent."[66]

—In *Dialogues* IV.28.5 the author refers to a "council of nobles", *conventus nobilium*, presided over by Gregory "in the presence of clergy, nobles and people", in which judgement was given in civil causes. In Chapter 17, when discussing IGP 59, I pointed out the oddity of that reference. No such institution is known to us from the records of Gregory's day. He ruled the Roman Church and its temporal affairs with hieratic authority; there is no trace of an aristocratic assembly over which he presided to administer civic justice.[67]

Still in Gregory's day, "besides the City Prefect and the Magister Militum or Dux, there were in Rome other Imperial officials; ... occasionally an Imperial messenger appeared, whose despotism occasioned no slight dismay ... Although the records of the government of the city at this time are very scanty, so much at least is certain, that the military, civil and political power in the city was in the hands of the Emperor's officials, while a certain supervision belonged to the Pope to whom recourse was made in case of appeal."[68] But in the Rome reflected in the Dialogist's pages, that imperial presence has faded. We glimpse a later stage in the evolution of the ecclesiastical city-state towards independent authority. C. Diehl well documented the reality and officiousness of imperial control in Rome and the Exarchate during Gregory's pontificate,[69] and also its erosion and disintegration during the turbulent seventh century.[70] By the end of that period (the time, that is, when the *Dialogues* first appeared into the light), he wrote, "for those Byzantines of the seventh century the influence of the Roman Church on the civil administration had become an evident and undeniable fact".[71]

---

[66] In a paper read at the Ninth Oxford Patristic Conference in 1983. In *Dialogues* III.10.1 there is a passing reference (perhaps reflecting Ep.X.8) to a "*Johannes in hac modo Romana civitate locum praefectorum servans*".

[67] "*Ubi enim senatus? ... senatus deest*", Gregory lamented: *Homilies on Ezekiel* II.6. Not once in his letters is there mention of any survival of the Senate, or of any civic assembly.

[68] Gregorovius, *op. cit.* II, pp. 51-3. cf. P. Llewellyn, *op. cit.* pp. 93-4. Gregory even intervened in military matters when necessary, sending officers to garrisons and organizing the defence of Rome against the Lombards.

[69] *Études sur l'administration byzantine dans l'Exarchat de Ravenne (568-751)*, Paris, 1888, pp. 133-90.

[70] *Ibid.*, pp. 331-7.

[71] *Ibid*, p. 333.

CHAPTER TWENTY ONE

COMPARATIVE STUDY OF THE LITERARY STYLE, VOCAB-
ULARY AND CONSTRUCTION OF THE *DIALOGUES*

Of all the reasons for doubting the Gregorian authorship of the *Dialogues*, the argument from language and style is not only one of the most important but was the earliest to be put forward. When in the middle of the sixteenth century the Swiss scholar Huldreich Coccius initiated the long debate about the book's authenticity, he pointed out how vastly it differed from all Gregory's other works in its form of expression. As we saw in Chapter 3, later critics proceeded to develop this stylistic argument. Robert Cooke found in the unGregorian language and style of the book a principal proof of its spuriousness. He noted in the text "many barbarisms in language, phrasing and expression", and judged that the style was very dissimilar to Gregory's own. From this linguistic argument, even by itself, he concluded that "we must dismiss these *Dialogues*: in no way can they be by Gregory the Great". Likewise William Cave emphasized "the immense discrepancy in style" and observed that in the book "many expressions are used which are those of a man with only a mediocre competence in the Latin language".[1]

Even the Catholic apologists who vehemently defended the Gregorian authorship of the *Dialogues* against the critics were constrained to admit the marked difference in style and wording from Gregory's other writings. They sought to explain this disparity by appealing to the difference of *genre*. Moreover they could point to the doctrinal pericopes (i.e. those that I have distinguished as the "Inserted Gregorian Passages"), which have the unmistakable ring of Gregory's Latin. "Regarding the style", wrote Peter Goussainville, "I acknowledge that there is some diversity, but it is not complete. Who does not know that ... style varies according to the nature of the treatise and of the subject matter? ... Nevertheless it is clear to the reader that in these *Dialogues* there are many things which do exhibit the style, power and elegance of Gregory's other works, indeed the loftiness of his wisdom as well".[2] Even the barbarisms objected by the critics (*"phrases et dictiones barbarae"*) were dismissed by Goussainville as quite usual among the Fathers, "who sought truth and

---

[1] Cooke gave several examples of barbarisms and uncouth Latinity in the *Dialogues*; a much larger collection could be made. Here is a random specimen: *"hoc ei currentes per circuitum et carmine nefando dedicantes"* (III.28.1).

[2] *Vindiciae Dialogorum, PL* 77.133-4.

simplicity rather than linguistic elegance''. Did not Gregory himself, in his letter to Leander, express his unconcern for such elegance?

Later apologists for the *Dialogues* have in the main continued this line of defence, admitting the linguistic contrast between the *Dialogues* and Gregory's other works, but explaining it as due to the different scope and level of the book, which, unlike his main didactic works, was intended for popular edification. Moricca was a spokesman for this view.[3] G. Pucci likewise explained that ''it was from direct contact between the soul of the great pope and that of the people that are derived the very language and style, which reflect popular influence much more than do Gregory's other writings. For this reason, too, the *Dialogues* have a distinctive character contrasting with theirs.[4] ''In this charming work'', remarks Dom R. Gillet, ''Gregory has voluntarily sacrificed the *genre*, the language and the rhythmic *cursus* of all his other works''.[5] ''By the singularity of the style and of the structure'', writes G. Cremascoli,[6] this work appears decidedly distant from the other writings of St Gregory''. Another critic of the Latinity of the *Dialogues* refers to ''*son style barbare et ennuyeux*''.[7] Numerous similar judgements could be cited. Nevertheless A. de Vogüé, almost alone among the commentators, does not recognize any significant difference in style between the *Dialogues* and the other works edited by Gregory himself. He speaks of the ''relationship which unites the musicality of Gregory's style with his spirituality''; but we find that all the six ''*belles pages*'' that he cites from the *Dialogues* to illustrate this Gregorian character of the writing are IGPs.[8]

In the controversies about the style of the *Dialogues* the critics—with the sole exception of William Cave—assumed that the whole text was from the same hand. Thus it was always possible for defenders of the Gregorian authorship to point to the doctrinal passages which have the stamp of the master—as did Goussainville in the passage quoted above. But once the IGPs, distinctively Gregorian, have been separated from the main narrative matrix in which they are incongruously set, a new and surer perspective becomes available for study of the language and style of the *Dialogues*. The disparity between the Dialogist's own Latinity and that of St Gregory stands out unmistakably when the genuine Gregorian

---

[3] *Op. cit.*, p. XIII.

[4] *Enciclopedia Italiana*, Vol. XVII, p. 931.

[5] *Op. cit.*, DS 6, col. 859.

[6] *Novissima hominis nei Dialogi di Gregorio Magno*, Bologna 1979, p. 10.

[7] A. Haggerty-Krappe, in *Le Moyen Age*, 50, 1937, p. 272.

[8] *SC* 251, pp. 83-4. Vogüé observes in a footnote that ''to these choice morsels'' there ought to be added examples of narrative passages, since ''Gregory is a master of the art of story-telling''. But if he did adduce such additions, he would hardly be able to demonstrate that the narrative text of the *Dialogues* is written in a similarly harmonious Gregorian style.

insertions in the text have been discounted. Several specialist studies have been devoted to the language of the book, but all of them are distorted to some extent by lack of awareness of the two disparate elements in its structure. Even when the difference of *genre* between narrative and spiritual theology is duly taken into account, the author of the *Dialogues*-narrative can be seen to have a fundamentally diverse use of language from that of Pope Gregory himself in his undisputed writings. This diversity can also be observed within the book of the *Dialogues* itself, where the same contrast appears between the main text and the IGPs.

Gregory's "literary signature"

There is hardly need for a lengthy demonstration to establish that the style of the main narrative text of the *Dialogues is* recognizably different from that of Gregory's undisputed writings, since this fact is commonly admitted by almost all commentators. In the course of this chapter I will offer a sufficient body of evidence to support such a demonstration. Meanwhile we must consider more closely the plea that the difference in style can be explained as due merely to the disparity of subject matter and purpose. There is undoubtedly a difference between the elevation and eloquence of Gregory's Scriptural commentaries and the more everyday forms of expression in his sermons to the people and in his letters. At a deeper level, however, his earnest and idiosyncratic style still permeates all that he personally wrote or dictated. Literary *genre* does indeed occasion changes in an author's style; but like every prolific author, Gregory has his own "literary signature" which remains recognizable through changes of *genre*, time and circumstances. Among the Fathers of the Church, none has a more distinctive style than his. Sixtus of Siena observed, in his *De falsa librorum inscriptione*, that "nothing is more difficult than to imitate the style of another"; and he said of Gregory's writings in particular that "in them there is such a consistency of diction, always such a similarity of style and such an aptly sustained order of expression, that it is impossible to discern in his writing anything which could seem to be imitated from elsewhere or supplied by another author".[9]

In the phrase of Professor Jacques Fontaine, Gregory is "a lyrical poet in prose". Even though there are variations of style within the *Moralia* itself, his inimitable "literary signature" is immediately apparent throughout his writings—including his "popular" homilies. I would emphasize again that this lyrical and idiosyncratic style is not absent from

---

[9] *Bibliotheca sancta ex praecipuis catholicae ecclesiae autoribus collecta*, Venice 1566, lib. IV, pp. 510, 374. There is a curious ambiguity in Sixtus's own reference to the *Dialogues*.

the pages of the *Dialogues*; but it is found there only in the IGPs. There indeed we meet the *cursus rhythmicus* that is the acknowledged hallmark of his style, the *homoeoteleuton* or rhyming clauses that so many later mediaeval writers were to imitate, and the other identifying marks well known to specialist students of his Latinity. There, especially in the longer IGPs,[10] we find the familiar language-structure that corresponds to the patterns of his theological and pastoral thinking. There we can recognize the three "stylistic types" distinguished by Dom Verbraken:[11] first, the "balance" of two adjacent syntactical elements which normally would be linked by co-ordinating conjunctions; secondly, the "cascade" type of sentence in which supple developments of the author's thought, introduced by subordinating conjunctions or by relative pronouns, flow on one from another; thirdly, another type of balance or "parallelism" between a subordinate proposition and its principal, often emphasized by the use of correlatives or alliterations. In the IGPs, likewise, we find exemplified the features of Gregory's style highlighted by Professor Fontaine:[12] the "psalmlike" enunciation of synonymous parallelisms; the density and intricacy of metaphors; the poetic rhythm of the stately periods and harmonized clauses; the exceptional fidelity to the Latin classical order of words.

From most of the *Dialogues* those features are strikingly absent. The architectonic structure of Gregory's Latin is there replaced by a basically different style in which the meaning is expressed by grammatical steps and clauses which are "not subordinated but juxtaposed", as Dom R. Gillet has observed. If the defenders of the authenticity of the *Dialogues* argue that the style is different from that of Gregory's other works because the *genre* is different, how can they satisfactorily explain that the familiar Gregorian style *is* eloquently present in some passages in the book (i.e. in those which I distinguish as the IGPs) but is lacking in all the rest? It is hardly plausible to reply that Gregory radically altered his style from paragraph to paragraph in the same book, because of the alteration of subject-matter between hagiographical narrative and pastoral reflection.[13] The *genre* and style of the book is supposed to have been deliberately chosen by St Gregory in order to reach a broad readership and to give it a wide influence; but if so, is it not disconcerting to find

---

[10] E.g. IGPs 1, 3, 9, 17, 21, 30, 32, 33, 38, 39, 43, 45, 48, 53, 57, 61, 63, 67, 68, 69, 71, 74, 78, 80.

[11] *Op. cit.*, *Rev. Bén.* 1956, pp. 179-81.

[12] In an address at the 1982 Chantilly conference on St Gregory the Great.

[13] F. Tateo attempts to rationalize this strange alternation of style and structure within the *Dialogues* by representing it as an unusual technique which St Gregory chose in order to obtain a special dialectic effect. "*La struttura dei Dialoghi di Gregorio Magno*", in *Vetera Christianorum*, 2, 1965, pp. 102-27; see especially p. 107.

such a master of pastoral pedagogy intermittently abandoning his chosen *genre* and deliberately unpolished style, with abrupt reversions to his usual elevated manner of writing?

If the style of the main narrative of the *Dialogues* contrasts sharply with that of the *Moralia, Regula Pastoralis, Homilies on Ezekiel* and the commentary *In 1 Regum* (and also with that of the IGPs within the *Dialogues*), how does it compare with Gregory's other, less theological, writings? Stylistic comparison with the Gregorian letters is of limited usefulness, for reasons which I will discuss later; but there too the difference is unmistakable. However, the Gregorian work to which we must give special attention for the purposes of our comparison, since it approaches most nearly to the so-called "popular" level of the *Dialogues*, is the *Homilies on the Gospels*. We find that the main part of those sermons—expository and hortatory like the exegetical commentaries but simpler in expression—is still markedly diverse in style from the *Dialogues*. Even in the group of 14 narrative *exempla* in the Gospel homilies the special flavour of Gregory's personal style can be tasted, whereas it is missing from the Dialogist's own narrative.

The argument from formal clausulae

In the study of the structure of Gregory's writings special attention has been directed to his use of final clausulae in sentence-endings, and to his observance, or otherwise, of the formal rules of stylistic *cursus*. A pioneer investigation in this field was the monograph of Sister Kathleen Brazzell, *The Clausulae in the Works of Saint Gregory the Great*,[14] in which she attempted a statistical comparison of the incidence in his individual works (but mainly the *Registrum*) of both metrical and accentual clausulae which terminate sentences and syntactical equivalents. The subject has been further explored, as far as it relates to the *Registrum*, by Professor Dag Norberg, particularly in his article "*Qui a composé les lettres de saint Grégoire?*"[15]

K. Brazzell's scrutiny of the *Registrum* revealed that Gregory's letters had been composed with studied attention to the disposition of final clausulae (especially accentual), according to the formal rules of the *cursus*. Such punctilious concern was not reflected to the same extent by a similar analysis of Gregory's other main writings. In the latter, although the incidence of the accentual clausulae was less than in the *Registrum*,

---

[14] Washington DC 1939.

[15] *Studi Medievali*, Series 3, 21, 1980, pp. 1-18; cf. also, the preface to his critical edition of the *Registrum* in *CCL* 140-140A, p.V. Norberg's later discoveries were already foreshadowed in his study, *In Registrum Gregorii Magni studia critica*, Uppsala 1937; e.g. pp. 5, 30.

their unstudied use still presented a consistent statistical pattern. It is not surprising to find such an unconscious consistency in rhythm in an author who habitually spoke and wrote in the same elevated and semi-poetical style.[16] In her table of percentages setting out the incidence of the clausulae, Brazzell showed the *Dialogues* as conforming to the same consistent pattern as that of the other main Gregorian writings. In that overall pattern there are only relatively minor mathematical variants. Fr de Vogüé points out that her table presents the incidence of the clausulae in the *Dialogues* as slightly less than in the *Moralia* and in the first book of Gospel homilies, and slightly more than in the second book of the latter and in the *Homilies on Ezekiel*. He comments: "Our text, then, in no way deviates in this respect from the Gregorian writings as a whole".[17] Do Brazzell's findings, therefore, contradict my argument in this chapter, and the opinion of so many other commentators who have found in the *Dialogues* a marked difference of style from that of Gregory's other works? The use of final clausulae is, of course, only one stylistic feature out of many to be considered. But in any case it transpires that Brazzell's findings cannot be cited as a valid argument in support of the Gregorian authorship of the *Dialogues*. The conclusions that have been drawn from her work are open to serious question.

Professor Norberg has shown that Brazzell's work on the *Registrum* contained an implicit "error of method". In her survey she failed to distinguish between, on the one hand, a relatively small class of Gregorian letters that from internal evidence can be seen to have been dictated personally by Pope Gregory, and, on the other hand, the remaining administrative letters, different in character, which make up the major content of the *Registrum*.[18] Among the latter, Norberg distinguishes two further categories. First, there are the routine administrative letters; these reproduce in places the stereotyped formularies of the chancery, which were used also by Gregory's predecessors and successors, and models of which can be found in the *Liber Diurnus*.[19] Secondly, there is

---

[16] "St Gregory shows no conscious striving for accentual clausulae but rather a general tendency and a fine feeling for them" (Brazzell, p. 65).

[17] *SC* 251, p. 34.

[18] Norberg resumed his long years of study of this question in a paper given at the Chantilly conference on St Gregory the Great in 1982 "*Style personnel et style administratif dans le* Registrum epistularum *de saint Grégoire le Grand.*" He wrote: "*Le* Registrum *de saint Grégoire contient, selon les mots du pape, deux genres de lettres: celles qu'il a dictées personnellement en tant que père spirituel* de animarum salute, *et celles qui ont été composées* de rebus terrenis *par un de ses secrétaires. Il y a des différences stylistiques entre les deux genres. Grégoire par exemple ne se soucie pas de la manière dont il termine les phrases, tandis que ses secrétaires s'empressent d'orner leur style par des clausules métriques et en même temps accentuelles ... D'un autre côté, il a lui-même dicté certaines lettres* de rebus terrenis, *quand une question lui tenait à cœur.*"

[19] The frequent repetition in the *Registrum* of standardized formulas had already been documented by M. B. Dunn, *The Style of the Letters of St Gregory the Great*, Washington 1931.

another category of administrative letters which were written for special needs arising in Gregory's pontificate, yet which do not bear the stamp of his own personal dictation. When these two latter categories of administrative correspondence are scrutinized separately from the relatively small group of letters which were evidently dictated personally by Gregory, they are found to exhibit a significantly high percentage of the formalized accentual clausulae—especially the three forms of *cursus planus*, *cursus tardus* and *cursus velox*. But when the group of letters personally composed by Gregory is analysed separately their percentage of usages of such clausulae is found to be at the same statistical levels, and even lower, than those registered for the other main Gregorian writings.[20] In other words, the conscious and meticulous observance of the formal rules for terminal clausulae in the main body of the *Registrum* must be attributed not to Gregory personally but to the officials of the chancery to whom he committed the task of composing his administrative and disciplinary letters, and who were trained to observe the conventions of formal literary style.[21]

Norberg's findings have wider implications for our present inquiry. In the first place, they show that the Gregorian letters can be used only to a very limited extent as a term of comparison when discussing whether or not the style of the *Dialogues* is Gregory's own. In Chapter 12, when considering the obtrusive *"style de notaire"* which A. de Vogüé accurately discerns as a trait of the author of the *Dialogues*, I pointed out that those clerkish mannerisms are absent from Gregory's own expository and pastoral writings. If, to counter my argument, the plea is put forward that similar clerkish features and *phrases de renvoi* can be discerned in Gregory's administrative letters,[22] that plea is rebutted by Norberg's demonstration that the administrative letters were substantially composed by notaries. In the group of Gregory's personalized letters such traits are not similarly discernible.

As far as the present question of the clausulae is concerned, I would point out that a similar criticism to that brought by Norberg against Brazzell's statistical survey of the *Registrum*—namely, that she fell into an "error of method" by failing to distinguish the diverse origin of the disparate elements in that collection—can be brought against her treatment of the clausulae in the *Dialogues*. Here, too, I would object that there

---

[20] Norberg, *art. cit.*, *Studi Medievali* 1980, pp. 3-13.

[21] In a very personal letter containing an ironic rebuke to Bishop Marinianus of Ravenna, Gregory refers to the employment of a *consiliarius* for the composition of his merely routine letters. (*Ep.* VI.63; Ewald-Hartmann I, p. 440.)

[22] Even there, however, they do not rival the excessive reduplications of phrase that are so obtrusive in the *Dialogues*.

is an unwitting defect of method, in that she was not able to distinguish in her survey between the main narrative text of the *Dialogues* and the doctrinal *excursus* which are the IGPs. She did not give a list of the clausulae that she analysed, nor did she state any principle of selection. But is seems from the accentual models that she cites that she chose her terminal clausulae from those passages in the *Dialogues* that had an articulated and euphonious literary structure—and those naturally are the IGPs. Hence, it is not surprising that the statistical pattern of the incidence of metrical and accentual clausulae in those passages is found to correspond closely to the unstudied but regular pattern found in Gregory's main theological works. An indication that Brazzell's selection of sentence-endings from the *Dialogues* was restricted can be gained by comparing the number of instances which she took from the *Dialogues* with the number she took from the *Registrum*. The word-content of the *Registrum* is 3.9 times larger than that of the *Dialogues*; accordingly, for her analysis one would expect her to draw clausulae in approximately the same proportion from the two works. Yet in taking sentence-endings for examination she took eleven times more from the *Registrum* (4,521 instances) than from the *Dialogues* (407 instances).[23] In view of this imbalance in her selection, and the circumstance that she doubtless took her specimen sentence-endings in the *Dialogues* from the IGPs, to the neglect of those in the main narrative text, the appeal to her findings, in order to argue that the *Dialogues* text "in no way deviates in this respect from the Gregorian writings as a whole", is not probative. Indeed her whole study is vitiated by the fragility of her statistical base. While she classified fully the clausulae from some books of Gregory's letters, she chose her examples from the other Gregorian works arbitrarily and in quite insufficient quantity. Thus while she analysed 3,261 clausulae from 5 out of the 14 books of the *Registrum*, she picked out only a random 605 from the vast *Moralia*, on which to base an ostensibly meticulous comparison of the incidence of the various classical forms.

Distinctive grammatical "phenomena"

There is much scope for further detailed study of the linguistic peculiarities of the *Dialogues*. The Low Latin forms found in the text can be paralleled in some cases by similar usages in the Gregorian letters, and indeed in other sixth-century texts. But, as we have seen, comparison with usages in the *Registrum* are inconclusive, since to a large extent the Gregorian letters were composed by secretaries. Judgement on the

---

[23] Brazzell, *op. cit.*, p. 63.

linguistic forms in the *Dialogues* should be based on direct comparison with the writings that Gregory composed personally.

One of the many valuable features of Fr de Vogüé's edition of the *Dialogues* is his grammatical index, in which he records "some phenomena" in the author's usage, with selected examples.[24] Almost all the forms and linguistic habits that he lists could profitably be made the basis for a detailed study and comparison with the usage in Gregory's undisputed works. For example, the luxuriant use of verbal periphrases was a common trait in Late Latin,[25] and can be found not infrequently in Gregory's own writing; but the author of the *Dialogues* has a predilection for such usages that is obtrusive and disproportionate. He is especially fond of periphrases using the verbs *posse, valere, videri, debere* (almost always in the subjunctive), *coepisse, consuevisse*. He has a further dozen or so favourite verbs which he uses to make similar constructions.[26]

There are many less noticeable usages in the *Dialogues* which prove to have a distinctive pattern. To take a random example, Fr de Vogüé lists sixteen occurrences of the word *citius*, in which this comparative form of the adverb is used in place of the positive, *cito*.[27] *Citius* is a favourite word of the Dialogist's. He uses it a score of times, but it does not occur at all in the IGPs. It is a word that is employed, with a frequency that is proportionately much less, in the rest of the Gregorian corpus.[28] Its usage there (unlike that in the *Dialogues*) does not show a ruling preference for the comparative in place of the positive.

Among the many grammatical "phenomena" in the *Dialogues* that Fr de Vogüé lists, special mention may be made of the following: the genitive case used after an indefinite pronoun (e.g. *"aliquid caritatis"*— IV.57.14); the genitive replaced by a preposition (e.g. *"de domo ... utilitas"*—IV.4.4); *valde* used as an equivalent for a superlative; the very frequent use of the present tense instead of the future; the use of the pluperfect subjunctive instead of the imperfect, especially in periphrastic constructions involving *debere* and *posse*; frequent use of the indicative mood rather than the subjunctive in indirect questions; frequent and special use of *"cum"* as a linking relative word, meaning "and then ...".[29]; a consequential use of *quatenus* following *ut; sicut* in an explanatory

---

[24] *SC* 265, pp. 267-81.

[25] The Maurists are not correct when they single out the otiose use of *debere* as "almost peculiar to Gregory" (*PL* 79.11).

[26] See Vogüé, *SC* 251, p. 83, note 167, and *SC* 265, pp. 275-6.

[27] Gregory does himself use the comparative form of some adverbs rather than the positive: cf. Verbraken, *op. cit.* p. 177, note 3.

[28] There is also a striking difference here to usage in the *Registrum*. Proportionately, *citius* is used 24 times more frequently in the *Dialogues* than in the letters.

[29] Vogüé notes that many times later copyists and editors of the *Dialogues* hesitated when confronted with this peculiarity of usage (*SC* 265, p. 277, note 1.)

sense, equivalent to "seeing that ..."; clumsy interrogatives (e.g. *"quid est quod"*, *"quid ergo quod"*, *"quidnam hoc esset quod"* etc.); pleonasms; inelegant repetition of words; and, not rarely, the grammatical sequence flounders in awkward anacoluthon.

I observe that the grammatical and stylistic peculiarities that Fr de Vogüé lists in his index are, with only a few exceptions, all taken from the narrative text of the *Dialogues* and not from the IGPs. This in itself is a pointer to the distinctiveness of the Dialogist's own linguistic usage. I do not dispute that instances can be found in St Gregory's genuine writings of Late Latin usages which parallel some of the interesting "phenomena" that Fr de Vogüé notes in the *Dialogues*. I do, however, submit that an overall comparison shows a distinctive frequency and pattern of their use by the author of the *Dialogues* which marks off his linguistic habits as different from those of St Gregory himself.

Cybernetics and stylometry

In questions of disputed authorship, study of the "involuntary markers" discernible in an author's vocabulary may be even more significant, when tracing his literary signature, than study of his deliberate style and of his favourite turns of expression. Involuntary markers are provided by such textual features as frequency of individual words, recurring grammatical forms, word order and word clusters, preferences in the usage of synonyms and alternative word-forms, incidental use of enclitics and adverbs, and similarly unstudied usages. In this field, evidently, the computer is today an indispensable tool. For my investigation I have separated the text of the eighty Inserted Gregorian Passages (the IGPs) from the main narrative text of the *Dialogues*, and have subjected each element to a separate computer scrutiny, in order to compare the linguistic patterns of each of those elements with the patterns in the other writings of the Gregorian corpus.

For this statistical survey I am indebted to the technical resources provided by the Open University Academic Computing Service (OUACS), with collaboration from the Oxford University Computing Service in registering the data; and also to the *Centre de Traitement Électronique des Documents* (CETEDOC) of the University of Louvain-la-neuve in Belgium. CETEDOC, under the direction of Professor P. Tombeur, has prepared an invaluable instrument of study in this field, the *Thesaurus Gregorii Magni*, which charts the frequency and distribution in the individual writings of every one of the 1,172,830 words and 60,830 different grammatical forms in the eight works that are commonly accepted as constituting the Gregorian corpus.[30] These are: the *Moralia* (483,569 words), the *Regula Pastoralis* (40,638 words), the *Homilies on Ezekiel* (112,035 words), the *Homilies on the Gospels* (81,847 words), the fragmentary commentary *In Cantica Canticorum* (7,483 words), the still problematic commentary *In 1 Regum* (180,165 words), the *Registrum Epistularum* (211,341 words), and the *Dialogues* (over 54,000 words). OUACS recorded a total wordage for the *Dialogues* of 54,056, with the main narrative text containing 41,171 words and the IGPs 12,944 (i.e. the two constituents are respectively 76% and 24% of the total). CETEDOC, on the other hand, recorded the wording of the *Dialogues* as 55,755. The difference of 1,699 between the two computations is almost entirely accounted for by the fact that CETEDOC included in their survey the wording of the tables of the 146 chapter-titles for the four books. Here and there I noted elision or duplication of words in one or other of the two computer surveys. I must also state that occasionally I found other minor discrepancies between the statistics recorded by OUACS and those by CETEDOC. These odd variations, which naturally arise when large numbers of words are being registered, do not make any significant difference to the statistical patterns which I present below.

The craft of "stylometry", or the use of numerical methods to investigate literary style, especially to probe "problems of authorship, of integrity and of chronology",[31] has developed vigorously with the advent and ever-increasing sophistication of computer science. I would say at the outset that I am one of many who do not think that any cybernetic methods yet devised can alone lead to apodictically certain conclusions about literary authorship. Writing on "Stylistic Analysis and Authorship Studies", Susan Hockey gives warning of the limitations of such quantitative methods. "Frequently they may only provide negative evidence", she observes; and we must surely agree with her when she remarks, "Good historical evidence may carry more weight than stylistic analysis".[32] My submission here is that, despite the difference of *genre*, computer-aided scrutiny of the main narrative text of the *Dialogues* provides an argument, of high probability, that it was not composed by Gregory the Great, and thus even by itself undermines the current presumption in favour of the Gregorian authorship of that text. The

---

[30] By the kindness of Professor Tombeur, I was able to consult the Gregorian *Thesaurus* at Louvain-la-neuve before its publication. The statistical data I use from it in this chapter are taken from the pre-publication proofs of that survey.

[31] S. Michaelson and A. Q. Morton, "Positional stylometry", in *The Computer and Literary Studies*, edited by A. J. Aitken, R. W. Bailey and N. Hamilton-Smith, Edinburgh 1973, p. 69.

[32] *A Guide to Computer Applications in the Humanities*, London 1980, pp. 129-30.

statistical arguments, then, reinforce those based on non-numerical study of the text.

Of the methods used by stylometrists to investigate questions of disputed authorship, some are not apposite to our present inquiry. When measuring the *Dialogues* against the main works of St Gregory, we cannot rely on such methods, for example, as comparison of sentence length, or of word position and word mobility. Use of the dialogue form naturally means that there is a high proportion of short sentences, in comparison with the long explanatory periods found in Gregory's Scriptural expositions. So too a narrative style is of its nature simpler in its syntax and word order than a reflective and didactic style. Again, we should expect to find more concrete terms in a hagiographical narrative than in a theological work of abstract thought. When all these reservations have been made, however, study of the Dialogist's vocabulary usages, and especially of the "involuntary markers" in his use of words, does offer significant results. Our possession of a "control text" of well over a million words in the other seven main works contained in the accepted Gregorian *corpus* gives us a very serviceable base from which to examine distinctive patterns of word frequency and usage in the *Dialogues*. Direct statistical comparison between the two strands within the *Dialogues* is less reliable, since the IGPs offer a relatively exiguous body of material for scrutiny, totalling just under 13,000 words. Analysts regard such a total as too small for reliable statistical conclusions. Nevertheless, with due allowance made for that more restricted word base, separate statistical analysis of the IGPs does provide some suggestive results.

Two possible distortions in the use of those seven main works of the Gregorian corpus as a composite control text should be mentioned here. The vocabulary of the *Registrum* does indeed have generic similarities to that of the *Dialogues*, inasmuch as it mainly deals not with abstract concepts but with concrete situations and objects. Nevertheless, as has become clear from the work of Professor Norberg and others, the greater number of the letters in the *Registrum* were not composed by Gregory personally, but by secretaries who would present their drafts for his approval. Thus the vocabulary of the *Registrum* cannot simply be taken as Gregory's own, and its inclusion in our overall statistics introduces an irregular element into the resulting calculations. There are instances in which there is similarity of word-frequency between the *Registrum* and the *Dialogues*, but not between those two works and the other six writings in the Gregorian *corpus*. Discounting concrete terms from everyday life, I will note later some instances in which this agreement between the *Registrum* and the *Dialogues*, in contrast with the other writings, relates to terms which can be classified as "notarial" or clerkish. A second possible distortion arises from the commentary *In 1 Regum*. As I have argued in Chapter 11, there is a not inconsiderable strand of non-Gregorian material in that work, which has not yet been satisfactorily delimited. Thus the inclusion of *In 1 Regum* when charting the overall pattern of word-frequencies may also introduce a degree of inaccuracy into the statistics on which we are basing our survey. Neither of those two distorting factors produces a bias in favour of the conclusions I am proposing. Rather, they produce some contrary bias, inasmuch as they dilute the proportion of specifically Gregorian vocabulary in the control text material, taken as a whole.

I present below specimen tables of word-frequencies based on the computer data described earlier. It would be possible to extend the cybernetic study of the *Dialogues* far beyond the limits of space to which I have had to restrict myself here. I doubt whether a vastly extended survey would produce more positive results than those which I offer here as fairly representative. From Tables 1-3, I submit, arguments of reasonable probability emerge. I present Tables 4 and 5 as the foundation of a strong argument for the non-authenticity of the *Dialogues*.

When presenting Tables 1 and 3 I again stress the reservations made above. Taken singly, the word-frequencies listed there do not provide sure arguments against the Gregorian authorship of the *Dialogues*. Vagaries of word-frequency in different texts by the same author are not unusual. Although my tables reveal significant disproportion between word-frequencies in the *Dialogues* compared with those in the seven Gregorian works, I must also record that I have found occasional instances in which a disproportion can be found between occurrences of words in one or other of the seven works, when compared with its occurrence in the remaining six taken together. Thus in Tables 1 and 3 I do not argue from single, or from merely a few, items of vocabulary, but from the cumulative evidence, which indicates with probability that the overall disparity in word-frequency reflects the different usages of two different authors.

In Table 1, I list some word-forms that occur in the Dialogist's narrative (i.e. the non-IGP text), which have a pro-rata frequency notably less than that found in the other seven main works of the Gregorian corpus. The word-form that is listed in the first column (a) should be taken to refer also to occurrences of all case-declensions or conjugated forms of the same word. In the second column (b) I give the number of occurrences of the word in the other seven main works of the Gregorian corpus. In the third column (c), showing the statistical "Probability for Dialogues-narrative", I show the estimated number of times that the word would be expected to occur in the *Dialogues* according to purely numerical regularity. In that column I have rounded the values up or down to the nearest whole number. The fourth column (d) gives the total number of the word's actual occurrences in the *Dialogues*-narrative. The "statistical probability" is arrived at by using as a norm the proportion of 27.13 to 1, which corresponds to the number of times by which the total wordage of the other seven Gregorian works (i.e. 1,117,075 words) is greater than the total wordage of the main non-IGP narratives in the *Dialogues* (i.e. 41,171 words). By comparing the values in (d) with those in (c) one can gain an overall impression of the under-use in the *Dialogues* of usual Gregorian vocabulary.

TABLE 1

Words frequent in Gregorian corpus and rarer in Dialogues-narrative

(a) Word-form	(b) In other 7 Gregorian works	(c) Probability for *Dialogues-* narrative	(d) Actual total in *Dialogues-* narrative
aliter	519	19	1
amare, amor	1,165	43	11
ambulare	213	8	nil
anhelare	110	4	1
animadversio, animadvertere	112	4	nil
animal	294	11	nil
annuntiare (adn-)	102	4	nil
appellatio (adp-)	117	4	nil
apprehendere (adp-)	133	5	nil
arrogantia, arrogans	267	10	1
concupiscere	471	17	1
condere	235	9	1[33]
confessio	189	7	1
coniungere	222	8	2
conscientia	193	7	1
consideratio	240	9	1
contemnere	342	13	1
contemplatio, contemplari	971	36	1
contradicere, contradictio	174	6	1
conversio	191	7	nil
cor	2,210	81	13
delictum	109	4	nil
delinquere	265	10	1
describere, descriptio	370	14	2
desiderare	420	15	4
desiderium	1,056	39	9
designare, designatio	747	28	5
diligere	686	25	8

[33] In special sense of "to embalm".

(a) Word-form	(b) In other 7 Gregorian works	(c) Probability for *Dialogues-* narrative	(d) Actual total in *Dialogues-* narrative
dilectio	404	15	3[34]
dissipare	119	4	nil
districtus	627	23	nil
doctor(es)	572	21	nil
enim	5,702	210	32
ergo	5,224	193	16
excusare	202	7	nil
exercere	302	11	2
exprimere, expressio	452	17	nil
hinc	1,408	52	5
innocens	286	11	1
interpretari, interpres	160	7	nil
mysterium	278	10	3
profecto	699	26	3
psalmista	431	16	nil
recte	1,134	42	1
rectus	668	25	2
rectitudo	334	12	1
resurrectio	267	10	1[35]
roborare, robor	358	13	nil
sapientia	654	24	nil
subditur	690	25	nil
tamquam	156	6	1
torpescere, torpere, torpor	273	10	nil
ungere, unctio, unguere	259	10	nil
unitas	182	7	nil

From Table 1 we see that several favourite words of Gregory are rarely used by the Dialogist. We must allow for the abstract nature of some of those words, which would in any case make them less frequent in a concrete narrative of events. But the table includes words which are, as it were, connatural for Gregory to use: words such as *amare* in all its forms, with *amor*; *contemplari* and *contemplatio*; *cor*, *diligere* and *dilectio*; *desiderare* and *desiderium*; *recte*, *rectus* and *rectitudo*; and *resurrectio*. Table 1 shows the high frequency of those words in the other seven works of the Gregorian corpus and their proportional rarity in the Dialogist's pages. *Recte*, for instance, is a significant Gregorian "marker-word". It occurs 1,137 times in the rest of the Gregorian corpus (and three times in the small IGP text) but only once in the *Dialogues*-narrative. Usual Gregorian words which are found to be completely absent from the Dialogist's vocabulary in-

---

[34] No occurrences with the meaning of "love"; all three occurrences are of the title "*tua dilectio*" applied to Peter (which is also a usage in the *Registrum*).
[35] Meaning Easter Sunday.

clude *districtus* (which occurs 627 times in the other seven works), *sapientia* (654 occurrences elsewhere), *exprimere-expressio* (452 elsewhere), *roborare-robor* (358 elsewhere), *doctor(es)* (572 elsewhere), and *animal* (294 elsewhere). The word *conversio* is also completely absent from the Dialogist's vocabulary. It is a word found fairly often in the seven Gregorian works (191 times), and is found twice in the IGPs of the *Dialogues*—which conforms to the "statistical probability" of its appearance there, since the wordage of the IGPs is 1/80th of that of the seven works. Although the Dialogist does not use it, he does employ the alternative *conversatio* (especially to express the embracing of the monastic life) 21 times.

Since the claim is made that the linguistic level of the *Dialogues* approximates to that of Gregory's *Homilies on the Gospels*, it is particularly relevant to note several common words which appear relatively frequently in those *Homilies* and rarely or not at all in the *Dialogues*-narrative. Since the wordage of the latter is almost exactly half of that of the *Homilies*, one would expect the respective occurrences to be roughly in the ratio of 1:2, if both works were of similar origin. I set out a sample contrast of seven such words in Table 2. In column (c), after recording the number of actual occurrences of each of the specimen words in the *Homilies*, I add in brackets the statistical probability of its occurrence there, based on the statistic that the *Homilies* constitute 13.65% of the total wordage of the seven works. It will be seen that there is a remarkably consistent correspondence between the mathematical expectation and the actual occurrences in the *Homilies*. While the *Homilies* thus conform to a predictable regular pattern of Gregorian usage, the utter disconformity of occurrences in the *Dialogues*-narrative from the predicted ratio of 1:2, in comparison with those in the *Homilies*, is striking.

TABLE 2

(a) Word-form	(b) no. of occurrences in 7 works	(c) occurrences in Gospel *Homilies*	(d) occurrences in *Dialogues*-narrative
consideratio	240	21 (18)	1
contemnere	342	27 (25)	1
delinquere	265	14 (19)	1
excusare	202	27 (15)	nil
exprimere, expressio	452	36 (33)	nil
interpretari, interpres	160	14 (12)	nil
rectus	668	36 (49)	2

While Table 1 offered a survey of the Dialogist's significant under-use of Gregorian vocabulary, Table 3 will offer a survey of his use of word-forms that occur with significantly rarer frequency in the other seven works taken as a whole. These words are not specific to the hagiographical *genre*. The arrangement of the columns is similar to that in Table 1. Column (b) shows the special frequency of the word-form in the Dialogist's text; the "statistical probability" shown in column (c) indicates the number of times the word would be expected to occur in the corpus if the frequency from the *Dialogues* were extrapolated there; and column (d) shows the significantly lower frequency of its actual occurrence in the rest of the corpus. Once again the word-form listed includes declined or conjugated forms of the same word.

Although those seven works are together 27 times greater in volume than the *Dialogues*-narrative, there are several words found in the latter text which never occur in them. Examples of such words are: *aestuatio, agnatio, albatus, accitus, armamenta, biduum, conlibertus, crepido, crepitus, crepusculum, crocitare, devexus, dilaceratus, exfugare, maturescere*. Strange as it may seem, even *pons*, used 8 times by the Dialogist, is never used by Gregory in the more than million words of his seven works. I have not included in Table 3 any of the non-Gregorian words which occur only once in the Dialogist's narrative. It will be seen that many other fairly ordinary words are used by the Dialogist in striking disproportion to their much rarer occurrence in the seven Gregorian works: for example, *famulus*, of which the frequency in the seven works is, *pro rata*, 20 times less than in the *Dialogues*-narrative; *defunctus* (14 times less frequent); *alveus* (37 times less); *sepulchrum* and *sepelire* (14 times less); *quaeso* (26 times less); *familiariter* (10 times less), *urbs* (11 times less). The adjective *devexus*, which is never used by Gregory, nor even by the drafters of his letters, is used by Dialogist 5 times, always in a set phrase which must have been a personal favourite of his: *devexum montis latus*.[36] *Obitus*, which he uses 8 times, occurs only thrice in all the six works personally composed by Gregory, and in the *Registrum* 28 times. The Dialogist uses *specus* 16 times to refer to caves. All 6 uses of the word by the real Gregory are from one sequence in the *Moralia* (30.26 seq.), where he echoes the phrase in *Job* 38.40: "... *et in specubus insidiantur*". Apart from this Scriptural reference, Gregory never uses the word *specus* himself—but instead *spelunca, caverna* or *antrum*.

My selection of words for Tables 1 and 3, showing anomalies in word-frequency, is relatively small, but it may be taken as representative. I

---

[36] Another phrase favoured by the Dialogist is "*neque hoc sileam*"; he uses it 6 times in his narrative. This, however, has some Gregorian assonance.

TABLE 3

Words frequent in Dialogues-narrative and rarer in Gregorian corpus

(a) Word-form	(b) Total in *Dialogues*- narrative	(c) Probability for other 7 works	(d) Actual total in other 7 works
accitus	3	81	nil
albatus	3	81	nil
alveus	11	298	8
biduum	6	163	nil
certatim	3	81	1
defunctus	63	1,709	119[37]
devexus	5	136	nil
diutius	10	271	57
exfugare	2	54	nil
familiariter	6	163	16
famulus	46	1,248	61
fatigare	16	434	144
fere	9	244	20
fuisset	c.50	1,356	130
idem	438	11,883	2,437
indicavit	19	515	64
lampas	19	515	62
monachus	66	1,791	149
mox	74	2,007	431
narravit	18	488	30
obitus	8	217	31[38]
parum	10	271	52
pons	8	217	nil
pontifex	10	271	68[39]
praedictus	51	1,384	360[40]
presbiter	49	1,329	233[41]
presbitera	2	54	1[42]
protinus	70	1,899	488
quadam	61	1,817	121
quadragesimus	11	298	8
quadriennium	3	81	1
quaeso	34	922	35
-que suffixed words	c.545	14,786	3,431
relatione	17	461	45[43]
repente	33	895	190
retransmisit	2	54	nil
sepulchrum, sepelire	c.75	2,034	147

[37] Including 43 in *Registrum* alone.

[38] 28 of these in *Registrum*.

[39] Almost all in *Registrum*; the word is very rarely used by Gregory personally: only 3 times in *Moralia*, not at all in *Homilies on the Gospels*.

[40] Including 333 in *Registrum*.

[41] 227 of these occurrences are in *Registrum*.

[42] In *Registrum*; the sense of the word is different in *Dialogues*.

[43] Including 39 in *Registrum*.

(a) Word-form	(b) Total in *Dialogues*- narrative	(c) Probability for other 7 works	(d) Actual total in other 7 works
sese	28	760	199
specus	16	434	6
statim	36	977	153
stupendum (-a)	9	244	2
valde	79	2,143	698
vehementer	40	1,085	206
vervex, verveces	7	190	1
ulterius	16	434	67
urbs	c.80	2,170	189[44]
ursus	16	434	6
vir (nominative)	255	6,918	896

have sought to include in Table 1 only words which were in general literary usage in Late Antiquity and the Early Middle Ages, and which could reasonably be expected to occur both in hagiographical writings and in doctrinal and pastoral literature. I have also tried to exclude from Table 3 terms from the *Dialogues* which, while absent from the rest of the Gregorian corpus, would in any case be unlikely to occur there. Such are words like *capisterium, matta, vanga, falcastrum* and similar words which reflect the rustic setting in which so many of the *Dialogues* stories are set. I must repeat the warning that arguments based on comparative word-frequencies need to be critically weighed. In the frequency of individual words, anomalies can be found even within the genuine Gregorian corpus. The significance of individual items in Tables 1 and 3 may be disputed; I point rather to a general pattern that emerges from them.

Two critical test-cases

Still more significant than analysis of the frequency of nouns, verbs and adjectives is the study of larger statistical patterns in a writer's use of simple and ubiquitous parts of speech, such as common adverbs and conjunctions. These provide the most useful of all the "involuntary markers" of his literary signature. Their use reflects unstudied and in-grained linguistic habits. The number of occurrences of such words provides the safest statistical base for a study of word-frequency, since they are largely independent of variation in *genre* and they occur so often that they provide a much more satisfactory volume of statistics for comparison. In Table 1 I noted some examples of such Gregorian "markers"

---

[44] Including 109 in *Registrum*.

that are significantly scarce in the Dialogist's writing: *aliter*, which is used 519 times in the seven Gregorian works but only once by the Dialogist, thus deviating by a factor of 19 from the statistical probability; *hinc*, which occurs 1,408 times in the seven works[45] but only five times in the *Dialogues*-narrative—a deviation from the statistical norm by a factor of 10; *profecto*, of which there are 699 Gregorian uses contrasted with the Dialogist's 3, a variation factor of 9; and *tamquam*, variant by a factor of 6. Table 3, on the other hand, showed examples of disproportionate use by the Dialogist of other everyday marker words, such as: *mox* (exceeding Gregory's use by a factor of 5); *parum* and *repente* (both over-frequent by a factor of 5); *sese* (factor of 4); *statim* (factor of 6); *valde* (factor of 3); *vehementer* (factor of 5); and *ulterius* (factor of 6). Some of these words, of course, would be expected to occur more frequently in narrative writing.

As two test-cases in this field I propose for detailed scrutiny the usage of two of the most ordinary and "neutral" words in the Latin language: namely, the conjunction *enim* ("for", "indeed") and the conjunction or adverb *ergo* ("therefore", "and so"). In Latin several possible alternatives to each of these two words are available for use instead. The scrutiny provides a striking indication of a distinctive difference between the unstudied linguistic choices of Pope Gregory and those of the author of the *Dialogues*.

In Tables 1 and 3 I used as control material all words from the other seven works of the Gregorian corpus, including the *Registrum* as well as Gregory's expository, pastoral and homiletic writings. As we have seen, the inclusion of statistics from the *Registrum* had some distorting effect on the totals; since, as Norberg's findings remind us, the language of the letters is to a considerable extent not the personal choice of Gregory himself, but is most often the language of the secretaries and administrators who drafted them for his approval. Thus one would expect it to have greater affinity with the language of the Dialogist, which, as we have seen, has curiously clerkish traits. Hence the inclusion of the *Registrum* text in the control material used as the basis for Tables 1 and 3 somewhat diluted those statistics. Its omission there would still further have highlighted the divergence between the vocabulary of the Dialogist and that of Gregory himself. For greater accuracy in discussing our two critical test-cases of *enim* and *ergo* I have in Tables 4 and 5 separated the data relating to the *Registrum* from the rest, and have used as a control text not the seven works hitherto taken together but the six works which (with certain reservations in the case of *in 1 Regum*) can be taken as reflecting the personal linguistic signature of Gregory himself.

[45] One factor explaining its high frequency there is its use as a link word after Scriptural quotations.

It will be seen from Table 4 that the mean frequency of *enim* in those six Gregorian works taken collectively is one occurrence per 174 words of text. The standard deviation from this mean among the six works, expressed as a percentage, is 17%. Column (d) shows the pattern of *enim*-frequency in the individual works. In the *Moralia* for instance, *enim* occurs once per 161 words of text, a frequency slightly greater than the mean by about 7%. Similar remarkably close approximations to the mean are found in the *Homilies on Ezekiel*, *Homilies on the Gospels*, *Regula Pastoralis* and *In 1 Regum*, all of which have substantial wordage to provide a firm base for statistical analysis. Thus those five main works which Gregory composed personally show striking consistency in his use of *enim*, within a relatively narrow band of variation. In them its frequency varies merely between one occurrence per 155 words and one per 227 words. More erratic fluctuations from the mean are to be expected where the material available for analysis is exiguous, as in the commentary *In Cantica Canticorum*. This fragmentary text, containing only some 7,500 words, shows a deviation from the frequency mean of +40%. Likewise in the exiguous IGP text of the *Dialogues*, which contains under 13,000 words, the frequency of *enim* is one occurrence per 294 words of text—a deviation of —69% from the mean. The frequency of *enim* in the papal letters, which to a considerable extent were drafted by secretaries and not by Gregory personally, is one occurrence per 453 words, which gives a still wider deviation from the mean of the six "personal" works, in the order of —111%. But when we come to the main (non-IGP) narrative of the *Dialogues*, which has a word-count of just over 41,000 (almost exactly equal to that of the *Regula Pastoralis*) we find that *enim* has a frequency of *only one occurrence per 1287 words*. Compared with the average for the six Gregorian works this rarity of usage represents a deviation from the mean of -740%.

Our first test-case, based on the little word *enim*, thus demonstrates an extraordinary discordance in linguistic usage between the *Dialogues*-narrative and the pattern of all the other works of the Gregorian *corpus*. Its frequency in that narrative differs most dramatically from the six doctrinal and pastoral works, which together show a remarkable consistency of usage. It also differs sharply from the IGP sections of the *Dialogues*. It differs significantly even from that of the *Registrum*, which has its own diversity from the rest. Whereas *enim* is used, *pro rata*, 2.6 times more frequently in the six Gregorian works, taken as a whole, than in the *Registrum*, it is used over seven times more frequently in those works than in the Dialogist's narrative.

When we turn to the second of our two test-cases, that of the frequency of *ergo*, the same discordance is demonstrable, but its extent is even more

TABLE 4

Occurrences of *enim* in the Gregorian corpus

(a) Title of work	(b) Total wordage	(c) Number of occurrences of *enim*.	(d) (b) ÷ (c) to show frequency of *enim* (i.e. number of words per occurrence of *enim*.)	(e) Percentage variation of (d) from mean frequency[46] of *enim* in the 6 works.
Moralia	483,569	2985	161	+ 7%
Homilies on Ezekiel	112,035	722	155	+ 11%
Homilies on the Gospels	81,847	408	201	— 16%
Regula Pastoralis	40,638	211	193	— 11%
In 1 Regum	180,165	795	227	— 30%
In Cantica Canticorum	7,483	71	105	+ 40%
Totals for the above 6 works together	905,737	5192	(mean frequency) 174	(standard deviation 17%[47])
Registrum	211,341	466	453	— 111%
Dialogues-IGPs	12,944	44	294	— 69%
Dialogues-main text	41,171	32	1287	— 740%

[46] The positive and negative values in this column show greater or less frequency of occurrences, relative to the mean.
[47] The standard deviation is 30, here expressed as a percentage (17%) of the mean frequency (174).

striking. We find a remarkable parallel between the general patterns of
occurrence of *ergo* and *enim*, as can be observed by comparing Table 5
with Table 4. Like *enim*, *ergo* is used by Gregory in the six works with a
degree of frequency which fluctuates within a normal distribution band.
The *Homilies on Ezekiel*, with an *ergo*-frequency of once per 208 words,
conforms almost exactly to the average of the six works. Occurrences in
the *Regula Pastoralis*, once per 341 words, are less frequent than the mean
by 68%. The small IGP wordage in the *Dialogues* has a notably lower frequency, deviating by 398% from the mean. This relatively greater rarity
of *ergo* in the IGPs calls for some comment. As I have already remarked,
much more erratic statistical patterns are to be expected when only an
exiguous body of material is being analysed, since the chance variation
of only a very few occurrences of a word can cause a major shift in its
proportional frequency. Moreover many of the IGPs are short excerpts,
divorced from their fuller original context; hence the consequential word
ergo would be less likely to occur—or to survive—in them.

In the main narrative text of the *Dialogues*, however, which has a
substantial wordage almost exactly matching that of the *Regula Pastoralis*,
we find an abnormal rarity of *ergo* that is far outside any normal fluctua-
tion from the predictable frequency. The incidence of the word is only
once every 2940 words, which is a frequency lower than the mean by no
less than 1448%. Whereas the frequency of *enim* in the *Dialogues*-
narrative deviates from the Gregorian norm by a factor of 7, in the case
of *ergo* we find that the word occurs 14 times more rarely in that text than
in normal Gregorian usage.

All arguments drawn from statistical patterns require critical scrutiny
to see whether they may be affected by possible statistical biases. I would
point out a factor that may affect my argument drawn from the comparative frequencies of *enim* and *ergo*. I will call it "the inference factor".
Both those conjunctions imply a logical progression of thought, which
would naturally be found more often in theological and didactic writings
than in a work of a popular and narrative character, such as the *Dialogues*.
Thus it would be natural to find Gregory using those two conjunctions
more frequently in his main theological works, where the *genre* is that of
reasoned exposition and he is adducing Scripture texts and drawing in-
ferences from them. A partial answer to this objection is to point out
(from Tables 4 and 5) that in Gregory's *Homilies on the Gospels*—which
though still "theological" in approach are more "popular" in
expression—the frequency of the two conjunctions shows no significant
divergence from that in the other Gregorian treatises. Indeed the frequency of *ergo* there is greater even than in the *Moralia*. This answer,
however, requires some modification. It may be objected that within the

TABLE 5

Occurrences of *ergo* in the Gregorian corpus

(a) Title of work	(b) Total wordage	(c) Number of occurrences of *ergo*.	(d) (b) ÷ (c) to show frequency of *ergo* (i.e. number of words per occurrence of *ergo*.)	(e) Percentage variation of (d) from mean frequency of *ergo* in the 6 works.
Moralia	483,569	2031	238	— 17%
Homilies on Ezekiel	112,035	538	208	— 2%
Homilies on the Gospels	81,847	540	152	+ 25%
Regula Pastoralis	40,638	119	341	— 68%
In 1 Regum	180,165	1423	127	+ 37%
In Cantica Canticorum	7,483	48	156	+ 23%
Totals for the above 6 works together	905,737	4699	(mean frequency) 203	(standard deviation 26%[48])
Registrum	211,341	489	432	— 113%
Dialogues-IGPs	12,944	16	809	— 398%
Dialogues-main narrative	41,171	14	2940	— 1448%

[48] The standard deviation, here expressed as a percentage of the mean frequency, is 53.

Gospel *Homilies* a somewhat lower incidence of *enim* and *ergo* can be detected in the occasional narrative passages than in the main body of the text. Indeed a sample count of their incidence in three homilies containing narratives (38, 39 and 40) has shown that in 24 columns of the *PL* text there are 44 occurrences of *ergo* and 49 of *enim* in the main didactic body of the sermons, whereas in 5 columns of narrative passages the occurrences of those two conjunctions are 5 and 4 respectively. These figures reveal a frequency of the two conjunctions twice as great in the main didactic text as in the narrative *exempla*. While duly noting that this proportion is less than that recorded for the *Homilies* as a whole, we must remark that it is still very far from the proportions recorded in Tables 4 and 5, which show that in the six main Gregorian works *enim* and *ergo* occur respectively 7 and 14 times more frequently than in the *Dialogues*-narrative. In any case the argument drawn from those few narrative passages in the *Homilies* is a tenuous one. The wordage involved is much too exiguous to form the base for a reliable statistical survey.

I agree that "the inference factor" should be taken into account when drawing conclusions from the comparative statistics of *enim* and *ergo* in Tables 4 and 5. (The greater rarity of the probative conjunction *ergo* in the *Dialogues*-narrative, even compared with that of *enim*, may to some extent reflect that factor.) But the striking overall contrast between the *Dialogues*-narrative and the six main Gregorian works, in usage of the two conjunctions, which is demonstrated from a very large statistical base, cannot be explained away by appeal to that factor. (In any case, it is too facile to suppose that "the inference factor" would be largely lacking in the *Dialogues*-narrative. That work also has a didactic intent: indeed in Book IV the author strives to prove his theme by reason.) Moreover, I would point out that those two commonplace words occur naturally in all *genres* of writing in the Latin of that age. Often they are incidental insertions to smooth the flow of the discourse, rather than structural pivots to mark the stages of logical demonstration. Examination of the places at which the Dialogist does use them shows that they fit easily into his narrative of events and his comments thereon, and could easily have been used in a hundred other similar places—if his subconscious word-preferences had been otherwise. The subconscious word-choices of Gregory himself, on the other hand, included a marked tendency to very frequent use of both *enim* and *ergo*. The Dialogist did have alternative preferences in his usage of linking conjunctions. Whereas he used *ergo* only 14 times, he used the equivalent *igitur* 40 times (a frequency of once every 1029 words). Indeed, when he reproduced in his text the genuine Gregorian narrative of the edifying death of the poor woman Romula, taken from the *Homilies on the Gospels*, he twice substituted the word *igitur* for the original *ergo*.[49]

Other traits of vocabulary

The *Thesaurus Gregorii Magni* of CETEDOC also provides, in addition to the main concordance, an alphabetical list, arranged according to the reverse order of letters, of every word in the Gregorian corpus, with an index showing its distribution in the individual works. This useful resource enables one to study the statistical patterns not only of suffixes but also, through verb terminations, of the usage of tenses and moods. The Dialogist uses with greater frequency imperfect and pluperfect subjunctives like *haberet, fuisset, potuisset* and *debuisset*. For example, he uses *fuisset* some 50 times; which, on the assumption of the same Gregorian authorship, would give a statistical probability in the other seven Gregorian works of about 1,350 occurrences. In fact this verb-form occurs in them only 130 times—that is, ten times less frequently than the projected probability. In the IGPs, smaller than the *Dialogues*-narrative in the ratio of 1:3, *fuisset* occurs only 3 times; *esset* occurs there only 8 times, against 74 occurrences in the rest of the *Dialogues*. On the other side, comparative scrutiny shows some patterns of rarity in the Dialogist's preferred verb-usages. His use of the present indicative passive, for instance, is proportionately lower.

The author of the *Dialogues* has the obtrusive habit, as A. de Vogüé has pointed out, of using stilted phrases of "reference back", like a lawyer's clerk. This involves repeated use of the identifying demonstrative *idem* (*isdem*) in all its cases (e.g. *idem presbyter in eodem loco*" — "the same priest in the same place": IV.57.3). Comparison of the large number of occurrences shows that forms of *idem* are more numerous, proportionately, in both the *Dialogues*-narrative and in the *Registrum* than in Gregory's six personally edited works. The clerkish affinity between those two works is readily understandable when both are seen as reflecting the linguistic habits of *scriniarii*.[50] The Dialogist's usage of *idem*-forms, which is con-

---

[49] Cf. Homily 40.11 and *Dialogues* IV.16.4 and 7. Gregory's repeated "*Nocte ergo ...*" is in both instances changed to "*Nocte igitur ...*" by the Dialogist.

[50] On p. 428n above, and again on p. 635 and 636n, I referred to the series of four stories of preternatural events connected with St Andrew's monastery in Rome, which were appended to a letter of Gregory (XI.26) to a noble benefactress Rusticiana in Constantinople. Those stories are prefaced with a remark which attributes them to "the abbot and prior of the monastery", and I suggested that this section of the letter reflected, not Gregory's own literary style, but that of the monastic relators, as edited by the papal secretary responsible for the despatch of the letter. An indication that this was so can be seen in the obtrusively frequent use, in that section of the letter, of "the same" as a

siderably more frequent *pro rata* than that of the *Registrum*, is in the order of five times more frequent than that found in the six Gregorian writings.[51] Another tell-tale mark of notarial style is reference to an antecedent by use of the adjective *praedictus-a-um*—"the aforesaid". In the *Dialogues*-narrative it occurs 51 times, in the *Registrum* 333 times, but in all the other six works together it occurs only 27 times. Thus the Dialogist's use of this adjective of "reference back" is proportionately about 415 times more frequent than that of Gregory in those six works.[52] Also relevant here is the contrast between the *Dialogues* and the *Registrum*, on the one hand, and all Gregory's personal writings, on the other, in the use of "direct" terms to denote the different categories in the Church, as against Gregory's own habitual use of non-technical and "veiled" terms.[53]

Statistical comparison reveals other affinities between the *Dialogues*-narrative and the *Registrum*. Several words which are proportionately rare in Gregory's six personal works are found with greater frequency in those two texts—though in no consistent pattern. I note the following examples, while recalling that the Dialogist's text amount to only 4.5% of the total wordage of the Gregorian corpus, and the *Registrum* to 18%: *arrianus* (Dialogist's uses 17, *Registrum* 3, others nil); *cella* (*Dial.* 35, *Regist.* 14, others 2); *defunctus* (*Dial.* 16, *Regist.* 48, others 1); *diutius* (*Dial.* 12, *Regist.* 20, others 36); *illic* (*Dial.* 67, *Regist.* 356, others 310); *innotuit* (*Dial.* 13, *Regist.* 25, others 60); *obitus* (*Dial.* 8, *Regist.* 28, others 3); *biennium* (*Dial.* 4, *Regist.* 6, others 1); *reverendissimus* (*Dial.* 10, *Regist.* 90, others 2).

While there is closer affinity between the vocabulary of the Dialogist and that of the *Registrum*, there are also some striking differences. For instance, from Table 1 it can be seen that forms of the word *unitas* do not occur at all in the *Dialogues*-narrative. Nevertheless, out of their 182 occurrences in the whole of the Gregorian corpus, no less than 87 (or 48%) are found in the *Registrum*. Again, although the two works have in common an exceptional frequency of the clerkish adjective *praedictus* (cf.

---

phrase of reference back (e.g. "*de eodem pretio*", "*in eisdem tenebrosis latibulis*", "*ex eodem miraculo*"). Gregory's own usage of *idem*-forms to refer back to an antecedent follows normal frequency, and is not repetitively obtrusive, as in the clerkish usage of the chancery—and still more in the later usage of the Dialogist himself.

[51] In the *Homilies on Ezekiel*, for instance, about one word in 460 is a form of *idem*; in the *Moralia* the proportion is one in about 680; but in the *Dialogues*-narrative it is one in 102.

[52] Another contrast may be observed in the usage of the genitive relative pronoun *cuius* to begin a sentence. In Gregory's own works this usage occurs about once every 8300 words; in the *Dialogues*-narrative it occurs much more frequently—once every 1605 words.

[53] See A. de Vogüé's observations on this point, *SC* 251, pp. 80-1; and R. Gillet, *loc. cit.* (in *Théologie* no. 49).

Table 3), the very similar alternative *antedictus*, which occurs 57 times in the *Registrum*, is found only once in the *Dialogues*-narrative and nowhere else in the Gregorian corpus.

The Dialogist had a flexible command of the Latin of his day and a fairly widely ranging vocabulary. In her study of *The Late Latin Vocabulary of the Dialogues of St Gregory the Great*,[54] Sister A. J. Kinnirey counted 305 distinctively Late Latin words in the *Dialogues*, including 55 nouns, 25 adjectives, 19 adverbs and 20 verbs which she did not find in the *Registrum*. She also counted 29 words of Greek origin. She makes an incidental comment which has its interest in our quest of the elusive Dialogist: "The *Dialogues* may be said to reflect a monastic *Sonder-sprache*".[55] Another researcher, Sister R. M. Hauber, looked at the Late Latin vocabulary of the *Moralia*.[56] She noted there a very few post-classical words which are also found in the *Dialogues*, such as *tortitudo, conspersio* and *conviator*. She also showed that the *Dialogues* does not approach the richness of Gregory's vocabulary in the *Moralia*. Out of some 1,400 words used in Late Latin and found in the *Moralia*, she found that little more than a third occur in either the *Dialogues* or the *Registrum*. Of 646 words of recent coinage used by Gregory in the *Moralia* only 264 (or about two-fifths) are found in those two works taken together.[57]

To counter my arguments showing the linguistic and stylistic disparity between the *Dialogues* and Gregory's acknowledged works, those who defend his authorship of the *Dialogues* will naturally object that there are nevertheless not a few phrases, allusions and sentiments which seem to be clearly parallel to similar elements in the *Moralia* and other writings of the great pope. Therefore, they would argue, the evidence of dissimilarity is offset by evidence of similarity. This objection falls almost entirely wide of the mark since it fails to distinguish between the two strands in the *Dialogues*—the IGPs and the main narrative. By concentrating on the former strand, which is less than a quarter of the total text, it is easy to find a genuine Gregorian flavour in the *Dialogues*. Nevertheless one must also acknowledge the presence of some isolated phrases and linguistic features even in the main non-IGP narrative which do seem to be distinctively Gregorian in character. The explanation of those features is to be found, once again, in the astuteness and literary duplicity of the Dialogist, of which we have seen so many instances in previous chapters.

---

[54] Washington DC, 1935.

[55] *Ibid.* p. 124.

[56] *The Late Latin Vocabulary of the Moralia of St Gregory the Great. A morphological and semasiological study*, Washington DC, 1938.

[57] *Ibid.*, pp. 129-30, 135.

He had evidently read Gregory's writings assiduously, and he sought here and there to echo in his own narrative words and phrases of the great pope whose name he was borrowing.[58] I pointed out on an earlier[59] page that, in addition to the self-contained doctrinal passages which are the borrowed IGPs, we find occasionally in his own narrative what seem to be verbatim snatches of Gregorian expressions, probably taken from the same unused store in the *scrinium* from which most of his excerpts were drawn. Once or twice, it seems, he even succeeds in imitating (or at least adapting) an elegant turn of Gregory's distinctive style. An inverted construction singled out by the Maurists from *Dialogues* II.1.2[60] is a notable instance. Now and again we can discover, in a published work of Gregory, the source of an isolated phrase appropriated by the Dialogist: for instance, the phrase *"flere magis libet quam aliquid dicere"*, picked out from *Homilies on the Gospels* 33.1 and incongruously put into the mouth of Peter the Deacon in III.1.9.

Orthography and morphology

The controverted question of the original spelling and morphology of the *Dialogues* text is also relevant to our discussion. In a study published in 1904-5, A. Sepulcri[61] put forward reasons for concluding that the Latin word-forms written in the secretariate of Gregory and edited by the pope himself were surprisingly debased. Surveying the manuscript evidence of the orthography of the three principal writers in Latin in the second half of the sixth century, Gregory of Tours, Venantius Fortunatus and Pope Gregory I, he judged that in the Latin forms of the first two authors "the echo of the classical tradition was not extinguished", but that in the case of Gregory I the standard was *"molto mediocre"*.[62]

Sepulcri based this conclusion almost entirely on five early MSS of the *Dialogues*, with only incidental reference to MSS of the *Regula Pastoralis*

---

[58] Some examples from the *Dialogues*, which echo phrases in Gregory's theological works, are the following: *"nosse velim"*; *"pensandum ergo quantum, etc."*; *"mira res valde"*; *"in quanto culmine"*; *"ut astruis, ita est"*; *"neque hoc silendum puto"*; *"quo ordine"*; *"manus locutionis"*; *"aliis ad adiutorium, aliis vero ad testimonium"*; *"malignus spiritus"*; *"innotescere"*, in the sense of "to show forth". Fr Marc Doucet has made a collection of a number of instances pointing to roots in the *Moralia* for phrases in the *Dialogues*. He sagely comments (in a study paper kindly communicated to me): *"Enracinement n'est pas authenticité. En ce sens, le problème de départ reste entier"*.

[59] At the end of Chapter 13 (pp. 439-40), where I cited some examples.

[60] "... *quatenus* ... *omnes agnoscerent, Benedictus puer conversationis gratiam a quanta perfectione coepisset.*" This the Maurists observantly equate with other examples of the stylistic inversion favoured by Gregory, *"quodam praepostero vocabulorum contextu"* (*PL* 79.11).

[61] *"Le alterazioni fonetiche e morfologiche nel latino di Gregorio Magno e del suo tempo"*, in *Studi Medievali* (Turin), 1, pp. 171-235.

[62] *Ibid.* p. 174.

and the *Homilies on Ezekiel*. He found that those manuscripts of the *Dialogues* (the earliest of them surviving from the later eighth century) showed phonetic and morphological characteristics, in spelling, word-formation, case-endings, etc., which were notably deviant from classical forms. Because their linguistic barbarisms followed consistent patterns, Sepulcri concluded that their common debasement must be traced back to the original archetype of the work. The *Dialogues* were clearly a painstaking composition, which must have been carefully revised by the author. Hence Sepulcri's conclusions laid responsibility for the orthographical debasement at the door of Pope Gregory himself. Even though the original archetype would not have been an autograph from the pope's own hands, he would necessarily have edited it personally and authorized it for publication, according to his known meticulous practice, attested in the case of his other writings. This crude word-formation in the earliest MSS of the *Dialogues* had, before Sepulcri drew attention to it, been unremarked, since scribes and editors in later centuries had corrected the manuscript spelling and morphology in order to reduce the text to the forms of classical Latin.

In his edition of the *Dialogues*,[63] U. Moricca accepted Sepulcri's findings and developed them further, paying particular attention to the two oldest MSS, the Ambrosian and the Veronese. The latter was copied by an unlearned scribe who simply wrote out the vulgar forms in the exemplar before him. The scribe who penned the Ambrosian MS was more aware of classical forms, and often corrected the barbarisms that he found. Like Sepulcri, Moricca argued that the consistency with which the early copyists faithfully reproduced the same non-classical spelling of Latin words in many different occurrences indicated that those vulgar forms were not merely their own but went back to a common source. He himself sought to convey what he took to be the evidence of the early MSS by printing in his own critical edition many of the non-classical spellings and grammatical usages. Thus he attempted to represent the original condition of the text.[64] This disconcerting feature of his edition was a main reason for its being eventually set aside.

Other authors reacted, with some indignation, against the conclusions of Sepulcri and Moricca. Before Sepulcri wrote, L. M. Hartmann had already judged that Gregory's own orthography was correct. He based this judgement mainly on two early MSS of the *Regula Pastoralis*, "which, although they are not autographs, undoubtedly do not differ much from

---

[63] Rome 1924.

[64] Out of countless possible examples of such vulgar forms, attested by the early MSS and printed by Moricca, I cite a single specimen here: the misuse of the accusative case in place of the nominative in the phrase "*ad portam quae vocatur auream*" (*Dialogues* III.2.3).

the original exemplar—indeed one may conjecture that they were copied from one of those codices which the author himself sent to Gaul".[65] Some aberrant word-forms were inscribed in that very early Gregorian text, but Hartmann inferred that these were merely copyist's errors, because "in those ancient codices a contemporary corrector consistently put right almost all the mistakes which had crept in through the negligence of an unskilled scribe". Hence, Hartmann concluded, it can be said of Gregory himself that "in orthography he departed but little from the rules of the grammarians".

A. de Vogüé criticizes Sepulcri and Moricca for attributing "too easi-ly" to St Gregory himself the phonetic and morphological vagaries of the earliest surviving manuscripts of the *Dialogues*.[66] He also notes frequent errors made by Moricca in his edition of the text, many of which stemmed from his attempt to reconstruct the original word-forms of the primitive text. In his own edition Fr de Vogüé habitually ignores or-thographical distortions in that manuscript tradition, unless they are rele-vant to the sense of the words.[67] D. Norberg, however, was impressed by Sepulcri's criticisms of Hartmann's conclusions and by the arguments brought to show that the oldest manuscripts of the *Dialogues* descended from a common archetype of consistently uncultured word-formation. Norberg found the same features in the oldest MSS of the Gregorian let-ters, but acknowledged that any firm conclusions about the original or-thography of those letters were precluded by the late date at which the *Registrum* was first transcribed (i.e. at the end of the eighth century).[68] A number of scholars today continue to see force in the arguments of Sepulcri and Moricca about the earliest orthography of the *Dialogues*.[69]

I suggest that both sides in this dispute may be right after all. Hart-mann and Vogüé reasonably decline to attribute the degenerate or-thography of the earliest MSS of the *Dialogues* to Gregory himself. But equally Sepulcri and Moricca, and their more recent supporters, have strong probability on their side when they infer that the consistently debased word-formation of those MSS stemmed from their original ar-chetype. The reconciliation of the two opposing views may well lie in ap-

---

[65] Hartmann, in his discussion of "*Orthographica*", prefaced to Vol. II of the *MGH* edi-tion of Gregory's *Registrum*, Berlin 1899, pp. XXXII-XXXIII. His detailed study of the early seventh-century *Codex Trecensis* 504 was given in an article, "*Über die Orthographie Papst Gregors I*", in *Neues Archiv der Gesellschaft für ält-deutsche Geschichtskunde*, XV, 1890, pp. 527 seq.

[66] *SC* 251, p. 83, note 166, and pp. 168-9.

[67] *SC* 251, p. 175.

[68] *In Registrum*, pp. 19-21.

[69] E.g. F. Gastaldelli, "*Per un profilo letterario di San Gregorio Magno*", in *Salesianum* 3, 1964, pp. 456-7; and M. Van Uytfanghe, in a contribution to the Chantilly conference on St Gregory the Great in 1982.

preciating that the *Dialogues*, on which Sepulcri's case was almost entirely based, did not originate in the age of Gregory the Great. The pattern of the vulgar word-forms which Hartmann rejected as incompatible with what we know of the culture and scriptorial standards of Gregory's circle, and in particular with the pope's own careful editing of his writings, is not puzzling if the *Dialogues* were the work of a less literate author and originated nearly a hundred years after the usually assumed date, in an age when low standards of orthography and morphology had become general.

The intended level of the Dialogues

Many authors have explained the marked stylistic differences between the *Dialogues* and the other Gregorian writings as due to a deliberate decision on Pope Gregory's part to sacrifice his habitual literary standards and to descend to a popular level. His motive, it is said, was to bring edification to simple folk as well as to the cultured class to whom all his other works were directed. Thus W. Ullmann writes: "though his Latinity as expressed in his official letters to the imperial government in Constantinople was in no wise below the standard of his great predecessors in office, such as Leo I, he nevertheless was quite capable of descending to an uncouth Latin when it was necessary to reach the semi-literate lower clerical sections in distant regions".[70] Many others have written in a similar vein about Gregory's motive for thus descending to an uncouth style.[71] Indeed, it is commonly held that in writing the *Dialogues* Gregory intended to reach not merely "the semi-literate lower clerical sections" but through them the mass of the people, townsfolk and rustics. The book was, says P. Batiffol, "a popular work, and intentionally popular".[72] C. Dagens considers that it was aimed at "believers still close to paganism".[73]

But *were* such simple and uncultured folk the readers actually envisaged by the author of the *Dialogues*? Against the commonly held view that he adopted an uncultured style in order to reach the lower orders of society, some more recent authors have argued on the contrary that his book was intended for a cultured readership, and that it reveals careful attention to literary technique.[74] More cogently than any other, A. de Vogüé

---

[70] *A Short History of the Papacy in the Middle Ages*, London 1972, p. 51.

[71] See especially E. Auerbach, *op. cit.*, pp. 72-7.

[72] *Op. cit.* p. 181. "The *Dialogues*", he adds, "were the *City of God* rewritten for the simple".

[73] *Op. cit.* p. 230.

[74] Thus F. Tateo, *op. cit.*; and A. Vitale Brovarone, *op. cit.*, pp. 95-173. Both these authors, it should be noted, base their arguments on sections of the *Dialogues* that are

has argued that in writing the *Dialogues* "Gregory had principally in mind a religious and social elite". He noted passages in which there are explicit lessons for priests and clerics, indeed for prelates, as also for "nobles". He also brings out the author's disparaging attitude to rustics and indeed his pessimistic view on the prospects for salvation of layfolk generally. This, Vogüé observes, would hardly commend the *Dialogues* to the people, or give them spiritual encouragement. Accordingly he rejects the generally-held view on the intended scope of the book:

> The popular character which is attributed to the *Dialogues* is, then, largely illusory. If by "the people" one understands the Christian layfolk, or the lower social classes, or persons without education, in each case one is obliged to recognize that the work is adapted just as well, if not better, to the opposite sector of society—that is to say, to the élite of consecrated persons, of notables and of educated minds.[75]

This perception of the intention of the author of the *Dialogues* is a timely corrective to the usual assumptions, and further highlights the problematic character of his book. Far from intending to sacrifice literary elegance, he clearly had pretensions to it. He also took care to interpret rustic terms for his readers, and was concerned lest in repeating his informants' words their "rustic idiom" should appear unfitted to his "*stilus scribentis*".[76] In Chapter 22 I shall argue that the Dialogist had principally in mind, as his prospective readers, those whom I see as his own wider "peer-group"—that is, the *scrinarii* and ecclesiastical officials, the numerous class of middle-ranking clerics, the curial administrators, even the *mansionarii* or sacristans, as well as the communities of monks and the book-buyers from north of the Alps. To demonstrate, however, that the *Dialogues* were not aimed at a "vulgar" readership but at a religious and social elite, is not to rehabilitate the actual language and style of the narrative. Its uncouthness and the distinctively lower level of its Latinity from that of Gregory's other writings cannot plausibly be denied, as most commentators recognize. Those who maintain the contrary about the style of the *Dialogues* can only do so by restricting their attention to that extraneous and minor component of the book that is constituted by the IGPs.

IGPs. F. Tateo does observe that the narrative sections show distinctive linguistic differences: in them the use of alliteration is much more frequent, and "the use of the rhetorical *ornatus*" deficient (*op. cit.*, p. 110). V. Diglio was another who judged that the Latin of the *Dialogues* was "classical" and directed to "*uomini da tavolino*" (*La bassa latinità e Gregorio Magno*, Benevento 1912).

[75] *SC* 251, p. 42; see also pp. 37-40, 43, 83.
[76] I. Prologue, 10.

We are left, then, with another paradox. If the book was not, after all, intended to be a "popular" work, why should Gregory have chosen to sacrifice his normal grace of style when writing it and to adopt a lower and often uncouth Latinity? The imaginative, non-Scriptural and naive character of the narrative has usually been explained as a pedagogical quality intended to attract and edify the untutored minds of simple folk. But if the book was aimed at a religious and social élite, what becomes of its supposed pedagogical aim and pastoral aptness for reaching the lower orders of society?

PART FOUR

THE DIALOGIST AND HIS LEGACY

CHAPTER TWENTY TWO

A PROFILE OF THE DIALOGIST: THE HISTORICAL SETTING OF HIS LIFE; HIS STATION, SOURCES, EXPERIENCE AND CHARACTER

A mass of external and internal evidence, surveyed in Parts Two and Three of this book, converges to support the conclusion that the *Dialogues* were not written by Pope Gregory I. Now it is time to turn our attention more specifically to the real author, and to bring together the scattered clues that we possess concerning his personality, life and activity. What can we know, or infer with probability, about the Dialogist himself? At what time did he live and write his book? From what milieu did he come? What was his social and cultural background, what were his interests and past experience? What can we say about his talents and distinctive traits, about his sources, aims and methods in writing, and about his achievement in his own day?

The historical setting of the Dialogist's life

We have seen that there is an eloquent silence about the very existence of the *Dialogues*, lasting from the lifetime of St Gregory himself until the end of the ninth decade of the seventh century. This argument provides a first pointer to the probable age in which the Dialogist was active. It does not by itself exclude the possibility that he wrote his book in the earlier years of the seventh century, but did not make it public; and that his manuscript was not brought to light, copied and circulated until long afterwards. However, not only the circumstances of the book's emergence but other weighty arguments tell against such a theory. We shall see that there are good reasons to infer that the *Dialogues* were not only first published in the last part of the seventh century but were also composed not long before that date.

We saw in Chapter 4 that sources, both in Gregory's lifetime and in the subsequent decades, that would surely be expected to reveal knowledge of the book, if it existed in that age, do not do so. In Chapters 5-8 we also considered several specific claims that it was known earlier in the seventh century, and have seen them to be unfounded. I may mention here in passing one objection that will possibly be made against this striking argument from silence. From some phrases in the *Liber Pontificalis* it has been inferred that after Gregory's death there was a reaction against his memory on the part of the Roman clergy, who resented his employment of monks in the papal curia and the diminution of their own privileges.[1] Accordingly, it may be objected, it is not surprising if a Gregorian writing remained in eclipse at that time. I answer that even if such a factor were operative in Rome (and in any case whatever anti-Gregorian feeling there may have been was limited and short-lived) it would not apply to the rest of Christendom. We know how avidly the works of St Gregory were copied and sought throughout the seventh century, especially in Spain and England.[2] Tajo of Saragossa was deputed by a national council of the Visigothic kingdom to journey to Rome in search of Gregorian writings. Through him the *Dialogues* would surely have become known in Spain if the book had existed at that time. The English were even more devoted to the legacy of their Father in the Faith. We have ample record of the eager book-questing pilgrimages of Anglo-Saxon churchmen to Rome in the second half of the century. From even earlier, there is a letter of Pope Honorius I, written about 630, to the pious and powerful King Edwin of Northumbria, exhorting him "to be frequently occupied in the reading of your teacher and my master, Gregory of apostolic memory".[3]

If the *Dialogues*, a work bearing the name of St Gregory and so impressive, diverting and autobiographical, had been extant in Rome throughout the seventh century, it is inconceivable that it would have remained unremarked and undivulged. Even at the commercial level, the *librarii* or copyists who supplied the demand from north of the Alps for patristic texts, and who busily transcribed the *Moralia*, *Homilies* and *Regula Pastoralis* of Gregory, would have been well aware how lucratively marketable would be another Gregorian work of such great interest.

In Chapter 9 I argued that if the *Dialogues* had already been known in Rome in the years 668-670, when Archbishop Theodore and his learned associate Abbot Hadrian arrived in England from the Eternal City and founded the school of Canterbury, they would surely have made the book known to their pupils, who included Aldhelm; whereas the indications are that it did not come into Aldhelm's hands until considerably later.[4] So too in Chapter 11 I pointed out the significance of the fact that when Hadrian introduced the liturgical cycle of the Neapolitan church into

---

[1] Cf. P. Llewellyn, "The Roman Church in the 7th Century; the Legacy of Gregory I", in *JEH* 25, 1974.

[2] See Chapters 7 and 9 above pp. 112-8, 170.

[3] Epistola VI; *PL* 80.476.

[4] Also significant here is the silence of the redactor of the notice devoted to Gregory I in the Cononian Abridgement of the *LP*. Writing at a date after 687 he still attests the omission of the *Dialogues* from the list of Gregory's writings.

England, with a commemoration of saints of Campania—including two from Cassino itself—the name of the wonder-working abbot of Cassino, St Benedict, was not among those commemorated. Benedict would surely have been the most famous of the saints of that region if Book II of the *Dialogues* had been publicly known at that time. As we have seen, the first trace of liturgical commemoration of or devotion to St Benedict does not appear until the early years of the eighth century.

At almost exactly the same time that the text of the *Dialogues* is first explicitly cited by Aldhelm of Malmesbury, we find implicit citations from it in a work of Julian of Toledo, dateable to 688-9. Soon after those first two documentary proofs of the book's existence there follow borrowings from it in the writings of Adamnan of Iona and Defensor of Ligugé. Thereafter the documentary witness to the book's circulation, including the evidence of the earliest manuscript fragments, multiplies. All this serves to confirm that it surfaced outside Italy, with relative suddenness, about a dozen years before the end of the seventh century, and that copies of it were diffused fairly rapidly in western Europe—in England, Spain, Scotland, Burgundy and Aquitaine. If the first codices reached England and Spain in the 'eighties, one must date the production of the work some time earlier, to allow time for its diffusion. For the reasons stated, and for others still to be explained in this chapter, I see a date around 670 as the *terminus ante quem non* for its first becoming available in Rome. Its first divulgation from that point of origin may be placed within the years from about 671 to 686, with the probabilities pointing to the later part of that period. Given the frequent traffic of English scholars and pilgrims to and from Rome, it is unlikely that so attractive a book, by the great pope whom the English honoured as their own, should have remained unknown in England for several years after it had become known in Rome. However, to show the approximate date of its first emergence into the light still does not prove that it had been composed only a short time before that date. We must allow for the possibility that the author had completed it some years previously and bided his time before bringing it into the open. It is in any case a carefully contrived book, the preparation and composition of which may well have taken a considerable time.

There are several other historical pointers which serve to show us the period in which the Dialogist was active. Although in his writing he was astute in covering his traces, and took pains to preserve the consistency of his convention which situated his recital in the fourth year of St Gregory's pontificate, some vital clues yet escape from his pages. I recall in the first place the evidence we considered in the second part of Chapter 18, which argues that he incautiously used literary sources that originated later than the lifetime of St Gregory. Of cardinal importance are the indications that his text was posterior to, and even dependent on, some of the legendary *Gesta Martyrum* of the duchy of Rome that were composed during the seventh century. These include not only writings that can be dated to about the first quarter of that century (in particular the *Passio Donati*, to which he expressly refers, and the *Gesta Felicis*), but also others that originated in the second and third quarters. It is particularly significant that his text has verbatim correspondence with the *Gesta Severii*, which dates from the middle years of the seventh century yet which can be seen in one passage to present a text more original than that of the *Dialogues*. Likewise there are indications that his writing was contemporary with and indebted to the ramified *Gesta* of The Twelve Syrians, a legendary saga which can be dated to the second half of the seventh century and which is attributed by Dufourcq to a writer in the pontifical administration. We have seen, too, that echoes of other post-Gregorian writings can be detected in the Dialogist's pages, and that in all probability he knew and used anecdotes told in the *Pratum Spirituale* of John Moschus and in the *Vita Burgundofarae* of Jonas of Bobbio. Both these works date from the seventh century—the latter from after 642.

In Chapter 20 we saw that the *Dialogues* reflect a social, cultural and political situation in Italy that accords better with the middle or later years of the seventh century than with its beginning. Here I would draw attention to two further considerations which may also serve to illuminate the author's historical background. First, his Italian religious chauvinism, with its implied reaction against prevalent eastern influence in the peninsula, is better understood in the light of what we know of the hellenization of church life in seventh-century Rome, and of Byzantine relations with Italy in that period. Secondly, it is interesting to reflect on the Dialogist's attitude to the Lombards in the light of what we know of the fluctuations in Lombard domination in the peninsula during that century. I will discuss each of these two topics in turn.

Italian religious chauvinism

Assertion of a specifically Italian religious loyalty, as I pointed out in Chapter 20, is not something that we find in the writings of Gregory the Great. "God's consul", as his epitaph described him, embraced the whole Christian world in his pastoral concern. The Dialogist's emphatic claim—both in the title of his book and explicitly in I Prologue, 7-9—that Italy was a land of spiritual heroes, was something new in ecclesiastical literature. The Gregory of the *Dialogues* tells the surprised Peter that he has a superabundant store of information about the wonder-working saints of their native land, and throughout the book his hagiographical perspective remains almost exclusively Italian. When he does introduce a solitary thaumaturge of non-Italian origin, the holy stranger Isaac who came to Spoleto from Syria, he feels the need to excuse his rehearsal of the prowess of a foreign saint: "Now this venerable Isaac was not born in Italy; but I will narrate the miracles he performed while dwelling in Italy" (III.14.1).

As we saw in Chapter 18, the Dialogist was well acquainted with the hagiographical traditions of other lands, particularly those of the mainstream of legendary piety which had originated in the eastern Church and flowed westwards, and also those of Gaul. The Christians of Gaul had already asserted their own regional religious patriotism in the glorification of St Martin of Tours by Sulpicius Severus, and in the writings of St Gregory of Tours and others. The Dialogist's assertion, indeed his creation, of a great hagiographical legend for the Italian peninsula can be seen as a reaction especially against the predominance of eastern cultural influence in the Church of Rome, which reached remarkable proportions during the seventh century. While imperial administrative control of Italy waned, the religious and cultural invasion from the Byzantine world during that century is well documented,[5] and has become increasingly clear in recent research. As J. M. Wallace-Hadrill remarks, "It is not going too far to say that Rome was hellenized afresh between 600 and 750".[6] During the period no less than thirteen of the popes were Greek-speaking easterners. Several factors accounted for this hellenizing wave which flooded anew into Rome and Italy in the century following the pontificate of Gregory I. It was a time of accelerating decline in Roman and Italian culture, under the pressure of Lombard barbarism and the continuing break-up of the old order. Constantinople and the heartland of the Empire in the East was the beacon of Christian civilization and learning. Seventy-five years after the death of Gregory the Great a Roman pontiff, Agatho, sent to the imperial capital a sad acknowledgement of the level of theological and cultural inferiority to which his Church had by then descended.[7]

From the fourth decade of the seventh century onwards a new factor further stimulated the influx of clerics and monks from the East into Rome and southern Italy: namely, the meteoric rise of Islam and the conquest by the Arab armies of the ancient Christian provinces of the eastern Mediterranean and North Africa. At the same time there was sporadic Byzantine intervention in the affairs of Italy, culminating in the dramatic

---

[5] C. Diehl, op. cit., pp. 251-66: "L'hellenisme dans l'Église".
[6] The Barbarian West, 400-1000, London 1952, p. 64.
[7] Text in P. Jaffe, Regesta pontificum, 2109.

arrest, deposition and harsh maltreatment of Pope St Martin I by the imperial authorities in 653. The exarchate of Ravenna, though in decline, was made an instrument for this hellenization of Italy. In 664 the Emperor Constans II himself came to campaign in Italy with an army of 20,000 men, and paid a state visit to old Rome. Although Byzantine influence in Italy waned thereafter in the political and administrative sphere, it continued to increase in the cultural sphere.

As Latin monasticism declined in the Italian peninsula, Greek-speaking monastic foundations arose and flourished, especially in Rome, southern Italy and Sicily. Greek art and the cult of eastern saints began to dominate the devotional life of the Eternal City, as still-surviving church decoration shows. The importation of eastern art-forms and techniques was further promoted by refugees from the Arab invasions.[8] This prevalence of Byzantine iconography in seventh-century Rome reflected the popularity of literary hagiography from the East, which the Greek-speaking monks and clerics popularized in Italy, and which can be seen to have powerfully influenced the authors of the contemporary legendary *Gesta* of the duchy of Rome. This was the background against which the Dialogist was writing his own hagiographical collection, in a spirit of sturdy Italian reaction against that tide of foreign devotion. In this respect he stands out in distinction from his fellow legend-spinners in that age, the authors of the *Gesta Martyrum* of the duchy of Rome. In writing their tales they accepted the current presupposition of superior eastern sanctity; but he would not. He would show the proud ecclesiastical immigrants and his own diffident fellow-countrymen that Italy also could boast of a multitude of saintly thaumaturges. To rival and even to excel St Anthony of Egypt (and likewise St Martin of Gaul) he would promote for Italy the figure of the great wonder-working abbot St Benedict, and of many other saints such as Libertinus, Equitius, Nonnosus, Anastasius, Boniface, Fortunatus, Sabinus, Cerbonius, Euthicius, Florentius and Sanctulus.

For all that, his own literary enterprise was influenced to a not insignificant extent by the thought-forms of the eastern hagiographers. In order to exalt the spiritual renown of his own land and Church he borrowed models from the rich tradition of *Lives* of the Fathers of the East.[9] Furthermore, his narrative reflects the eastern mystique of the "holy man". Peter Brown has pointed out the special position, prestige and social function of the living spiritual hero in the Greek-speaking world of

---

[8] P. Llewellyn, *op. cit.* (1971), pp. 197-8.

[9] "The picture of Italian monasticism which emerges from the *Dialogues* strongly suggests that Gregory had in mind a corpus of material emanating in Eastern Christendom" (J. Petersen, *op. cit.*, p. 154).

Late Antiquity.[10] He shows that this charismatic phenomenon was distinctive of the eastern Church, and he remarks that (in the special sense in which he is using the term), "No holy man was active in Dark Age Rome".[11] In the Gregorian age the Roman Church—including St Gregory himself—had still looked rather to the sanctity of the relics of the Apostles and of other saints as a source of present spiritual power. It had not yet followed eastern Christendom (and Gaul) in exaltation of the cult of living or recent charismatic personalities. For the real Gregory—and for some of the Dialogist's contemporaries, whom he pillories in his story of the detractors of Equitius in I.4.11-12—the faithful were not to look for religious leadership from such extra-canonical holy men, but from the ecclesiastical rulers vested with apostolic authority, who exercised the *culmen regiminis*. The Dialogist, on the other hand, depicts as idealized spiritual leaders his charismatic Fathers of Italy, who have a sacredness and effectiveness independent of canonical commission. They are presented as the wielders of prodigious power in their contemporary world, who emerge victorious over all adversity and provide a dramatic spectacle for the admiration of the ordinary faithful. In the Italian country setting that he evokes they have the same aura and supernatural immediacy as the holy men who awed, fascinated and inspired the communities of eastern Christendom.[12] Here we have another indication that the religious thought-world of the Dialogist reflects that of the hellenizers of the seventh century, even when he asserts his peninsular loyalty.

It was not merely in the devotional and ecclesiastical sphere that native-born Romans and Italians were reacting against Byzantine influence during that period. The development of Italian political resentment, leading at times to military resistance, can be traced from the third decade of the seventh century onwards. It was inflamed by the Emperor's persecution of Pope Martin I,[13] and it increased in intensity and effec-

---

[10] "The rise and function of the holy man in Late Antiquity", in *The Journal of Roman Studies*, 61, 1971, pp. 80-101.

[11] *Ibid.* p. 100.

[12] One of the main merits of Dr Petersen's recent study is in bringing out the affinity of the *Dialogues* to the contemporary climate and traditions of *Eastern* hagiography. (See especially her sixth chapter and pp. 116-7.) For instance, she stresses the striking parallels between stories in the *Dialogues* and in the *Historia religiosa* of Theodoret (*ibid.*, pp. 181-6). The real Gregory could not have read Theodoret's work; nor, as we have seen, does he evince the slightest interest in such sources. But the Dialogist, writing in the newly re-hellenized City of seventh-century Rome, would have picked up those, and many other stories of Eastern provenance, from contact with the many monks of Greek origin who now swarmed in the City.

[13] Then, for the first time, as Bertolini observes, "Rome was prepared for even a political breach with Byzantium and its sovereign" (*"Riflessi politici delle controversie con Bisancio nelle vicende del secolo VII in Italia"*, in the symposium *Caratteri del secolo VII in Occidente*, Spoleto 1958, p. 744.)

tiveness later in the century.[14] Against this backcloth of nascent Roman and Italian regional patriotism in the political and social sphere, the Dialogist's literary enterprise of religious chauvinism fits well. It should again be remarked that in his pages, although there is occasional mention of long-ago journeys by ecclesiastics from Italy to Constantinople (in particular, the account in III.2.3 of a miracle performed by Pope John when making a ceremonial entry into that city), there is virtually complete silence about imperial authority and imperial institutions, which loom so large in the *Registrum* of Gregory the Great.

Clues from Lombard history

Lombard history may also afford us some clues to the period of the Dialogist's activity. As I pointed out in Chapter 5, the Lombards are the villains of the *Dialogues*. The author writes with consistent animosity of them and their bloodthirsty wickedness—"... *sicut sunt nimiae crudelitatis*" (III.37.13). S. Boesch Gajano shows well that, although he relates stories of the perfidy and cruelty of both the Goths and the Lombards, there is a significant difference in his attitude to those two races of barbarian invaders of Italy. His stories about the Goths have as a sequel a kind of entrance of the reluctant barbarians into the religious world that he describes: "in the end they are inserted and involved in that very religious reality that they seek to destroy or ridicule, often coming even to see the error of their ways".[15] For the Lombards there is no such mitigation in the judgement of the author of the *Dialogues*: "They are completely extrinsic to the world he describes". The miracles of his saintly heroes terrify the Lombards, thwart them, put them to flight, but (with a single exception in III.37.17) have no positive effect on them. Those miraculous signs do not induce the cruel barbarians to conversion, repentance or moderation: "spiritually insensible to sanctity, they only experience its punitive power".[16] The reason for this difference in the author's attitude to the two tribes of barbarian invaders, as Boesch Gajano justly observes, is to be found in the fact that the Goths were more remote in history, defeated and departed, or with their residual elements assimilated into the Italian population; whereas the Lombards were a present and ever active enemy, a hostile occupying power still oppressing the native people and institutions of the land.

---

[14] Cf. Diehl, *op. cit.*, pp. 401-11. The first serious insurrection of Italy against Byzantine suzerainty came in 692 (*ibid.* p. 360).

[15] *Op. cit.*, "*Dislivelli*", p. 400.

[16] *Ibid.* p. 401. Boesch Gajano remarks that C. Dagens (*Saint Grégoire*, pp. 307-9) did not appreciate this difference of attitude to the two races of invaders.

The Lombards first descended on northern Italy in 568. Their marauding bands established their "duchies" in central and southern Italy about twenty years before 593, the ostensible date of the Gregorian *Dialogues*. A horror-story such as that told in III.28, of the slaughter of 400 Christian rustics who refused to adore a goat's head immolated to the devil by the Lombards, hardly belongs to the realm of history. But it evidently reflects the author's loathing for the Lombards and their very real barbarity. He was therefore writing at a time when bitter memories and fears of Lombard savagery was still alive in Italian minds and hearts, and had not faded into past history like the brutality of the Goths. It is usually assumed that the accounts of the Lombards' cruelty in the *Dialogues* must reflect events of the first period of their conquest, in the later sixth century, but we shall see that such an assumption is too facile. From the later history of the Lombards in Italy, it can be realized that the Dialogist's attitude to them concords aptly with the situation in the middle decades or third quarter of the seventh century.[17]

In the last years of his pontificate Gregory the Great achieved an uneasy peace with the Lombard kingdom, which continued after his death. The pro-Catholic policy of Queen Theodelinda and King Adaloald, and the tolerance of the court of Pavia, meant that the first quarter of the seventh century was, relatively speaking, a period of unwonted religious and social peace for the peninsula. The mitigating effect on the Arian Lombard duchies of Spoleto and Benevento was, however, only indirect and limited.[18] There followed a harsh return to repression of the Italian population and renewed attacks on the Exarchate and on the Roman territory during the reigns of the Arian kings Arioald (625-636) and Rothari (636-652). In those years, writes Bognetti, "It was worse for Tuscia, Spoleto and Benevento, which were obliged, as far as we know, to endure a period of the most radical "Germanization" of the population, which was not alleviated by the slightest possibility of action on behalf of the Catholics".[19] This period may well have been that of the Dialogist's youth. It would have left him with memories of those turbulent times, when the fierce soldiers of the Lombard duchies, some of them Arians, some still pagans, were laying an iron heel on the necks of the people of central and southern Italy.

During Rothari's reign the conquering Germanic race re-emphasized their sense of national identity and their domination over the native inhabitants. For the first time a king of the Lombards exercised effective

---

[17] In what follows I refer to the massive researches of G. Bognetti, *L'Età Longobarda*, 4 volumes, Milan 1966-1968.

[18] Bognetti, I, p. 162; III, p. 326.

[19] *Op. cit.*, III, p. 327; cf. I, pp. 164-5.

power over all the territories occupied by them between the Alps and the gulf of Taranto. Arianism was reasserted against the native Catholicism of the Italians. For all his Arian resolution, however, Rothari sought order and stability in his realm. Under his firm rule Arian bishoprics were everywhere established, but restoration of the Catholic bishoprics, which had been practically suppressed in many regions since the first Lombard conquests, also became possible. Paul Warnefrid later recorded that during Rothari's reign there were two bishops, one Catholic and the other Arian, in almost all the towns of the Lombard territories.[20] This period of vigorous but mitigated resurgence of Arianism, during which the region around Spoleto was thoroughly Lombardized,[21] may be the background for the story told by the Dialogist in III.29.1-4. It tells how an aggressive Arian bishop, at the head of a band of followers, attempted to seize by force one of the Catholic churches in Spoleto, but was deterred by a miracle. Although this episode is anachronistically placed in the pontificate of Gregory I, it accords well with the religious climate of Rothari's age.

After Rothari's systematic restoration of Arianism as the dominant religion of his realm, and the brief reign of his successor Rodoald, also an Arian, there came a swing of the pendulum with the accession to the Lombard throne in 653 of the Catholic king Aripert I. During his reign of nearly ten years he disestablished Arianism and favoured Catholicism. Then followed the last and major period of oppression under the Arianizing king Grimoald (662-671), who drove Aripert from the throne. He was a barbarian chief as ruthless as any of those in the first period of the Lombard invasion of Italy.[22] Before seizing the throne of Pavia with the help of the Lombards of Spoleto and Tuscia, he had been (since 657) Duke of Benevento, and had brought renewed strife and tribulation to the southern part of the peninsula. In his ducal palace he (and his son Romoald) had "adored the pagan viper".[23] As king, Grimoald again united all the Lombard dominions under a strong centralized rule. His campaigns against the Byzantine Emperor and the Franks harried the land. His rule was often a reign of terror for the subject Catholic population. We know details of one of his atrocities, a massacre in the baptistery at Forimpopoli, carried out in revenge for opposition from that town during one of his military expeditions in the south. Surprising the Catholic deacons as they stood baptizing during the paschal ceremonies,

---

[20] *Historia Langobardorum* IV.42; *MGH* ed. p. 134.
[21] Bognetti, III, p. 490.
[22] Bognetti, I, p. 166.
[23] *Ibid.* I, p. 204; II, p. 335.

he slew all without mercy.[24] If such things were done by direct command of the Lombard king himself, the stories in the *Dialogues* of atrocities committed by indisciplined bands of Lombard marauders would still have been grimly topical in the third quarter of the seventh century.

The recrudescence of Lombard barbarity under Grimoald between 662 and 671 may well have provided the proximate background to the writing of the *Dialogues*. The author would have been in his prime during those years. If he was preparing and writing his book about that time, or a few years later, he would have vividly in his mind the recent events of Grimoald's ruthless regime, and a deep-seated Italian resentment to give force to his bitter tales of Lombard savagery in a previous age. What Bognetti describes[25] as the "barbarian restoration" under Grimoald was brought to an end when in 671 the pro-Catholic king Perctarit ascended the Lombard throne.[26] This time the reversal of the political and religious situation was to have permanent effect. The definitive conversion of the Lombard chiefs and people to Catholicism was not achieved suddenly, however, but was still to be a gradual and irregular process.[27] Native Italian hatred of the conquerors was slow to die down. Even though Perctarit's reign (671-688) ushered in a new age, the old animosities, especially in the Lombard duchies of central and southern Italy, still fed on the grim memories of the recent past. The *Dialogues*, written probably during Perctarit's reign, still reflect those animosities.

The Dialogist's station in life

What can we deduce about the Dialogist's status and station in life? In previous chapters I have pointed out many features of his work which suggest that he was a clerical functionary in the Roman curia. The signs are that he was a *scriniarius*, employed in the Lateran secretariate which was responsible for the papal letters and other official documents, for the book-production bureau, and for the care of the library and archives of the Roman Church. In that department worked the *notarii*, *chartularii* and *librarii*, and other lesser scribes and clerical apprentices. I have discussed in Chapters 12 and 21 the Dialogist's clerkish traits—especially what Fr de Vogüé calls his "*style de notaire*",[28] which shows especially in his excessive use of terms referring back to grammatical antecedents, such as "the aforesaid", "the same", "the above-mentioned", etc. It is the style

---

[24] *Ibid.* II, p. 343.
[25] *Ibid.* II, p. 344.
[26] Bognetti, I, pp. 166 seq.; II, pp. 345-6.
[27] *Ibid.* II, pp. 199-200, 205.
[28] *SC* 251, pp. 81-2.

of a scribe trained to make clear, with stilted precision, just who and what are being referred to. In Chapter 21 I pointed to other features of vocabulary and style in the *Dialogues* which likewise suggest that the author was schooled in secretarial habits. The Dialogist brings into his book references to *scriniarii* and notaries—perhaps as titbits of interest for his colleagues! The venerable Anastasius was a notary of the Roman Church before he "abandoned the *scrinium* for a monastery" (I.7.1). Contrariwise, *"Exhilaratus noster"* was a *conversus* before he became a notary of the Roman Church (cf. II.18). A notary features both as scribe and actor in the story of the prodigious restraining of the river Po by Bishop Sabinus (III.10.3). An *honestus notarius* named Deusdedit who drew up an official document for the real Gregory seems to be represented in *Dialogues* IV.32.1 as *honestus senex Deusdedit* who there becomes an intimate friend and informant of the pope.[29] In I.4.12 the author gives us a glimpse of scribes at work at their desks. The *defensor* Julian arrives at a monastery seeking to arrest Equitius; the holy man is absent, but the Roman official "finds the copyists busy writing"—*antiquarios scribentes repperit"*—and asks them for information about their abbot.

We have seen that the *Dialogues* have a strongly monastic colouring. The author has a distinctive preoccupation with holy abbots and hermits, and with events in monasteries. No doubt he expected many of his readers to be monks, and he was catering for their tastes. Was he himself a monk? Did he perhaps, like his two characters, Anastasius, the notary turned monk, and *Exhilaratus noster*, the *conversus* turned notary, have experience of both the cloister and the *scrinium*? During the seventh century monastic influence in the Roman Church had ebbed and flowed. There are signs, as we have noted, of an anti-monastic reaction at the beginning of the century on the part of the clerical order, who resented what they saw as an erosion of their privileges. There followed a see-saw of rival interests.[30] After the pro-monastic pontificate of Honorius I (625-638), the clergy firmly secured their control of the ecclesiastical establishment, and by the end of the century "the monasteries had been absorbed into the orbit of the clerical administration".[31] The number of cenobitical communities in the City, and of their inmates, continued to increase, swelled by the flood of refugees both from the eastern provinces of the Empire and from the devastated countryside of Italy. While the institutional power of the monks decreased, esteem for the monastic ethos did not. The *Dialogues* may be seen to reflect the pervasive influence of monastic piety in seventh-century Italy. The eager thirst for hagiographical

---

[29] Cf. Ewald-Hartmann, II, p. 438 and Vogüé, *SC* 265, p. 107.
[30] Cf. J. Richards, *op. cit*, pp. 80-4.
[31] *Ibid.* p. 83.

wonder-stories about monks, which for those accustomed to the prevalent hagiography of Greek origin was catered for by such works as the *Spiritual Meadow* of John Moschus, at length received a novel satisfaction in the *Dialogues*, a Latin work relating wonderful things about Italian abbots and monasteries.

Two pontificates have a special interest in our quest for the time of origin of the *Dialogues*: those of Pope Vitalian (657-672) and of Pope Adeodatus II (672-676). Those nineteen years may well have been the period during which the Dialogist was reaching maturity in the papal service; during its later part he may already have embarked upon his imaginative literary project. Vitalian was a friend and promoter of monks, and Adeodatus was himself a monk—the first monastic pope of the seventh century. The atmosphere of the Roman curia during those two pontificates would have been propitious for a curial official who was either a monk or at least a familiar friend of and visitor to the monastic communities of the City and surrounding regions. Moreover both those two popes were natives of the duchy of Rome. Although both were well affected towards the Greek-speaking monks and ecclesiastics who were becoming ever more numerous and influential in Rome, they were also a focus for Italian and western loyalties. Vitalian, "one of the greatest of the popes",[32] was a native of Campania, and a friend and admirer of the learned abbot Hadrian. The phrase describing Pope Adeodatus in the *Liber Pontificalis* says much: "*natione Romanus, ex monachis*".[33] It is not difficult to visualize the Dialogist, with his clearly expressed monastic sympathies and Italian patriotism, as finding a congenial place in the Roman curia during those years.

There is, nevertheless, no clear proof that the author of the *Dialogues* was himself a monk. Undoubtedly he had monastic readers in view for his narrative, but he also had in view readers of other classes and conditions, especially from among the clerics and lay officials of the ecclesiastical establishment. We saw in Chapter 21 that the question of the readership for which the *Dialogues* were intended has been put on a new footing in recent years. The older assumption that the author, supposedly St Gregory, wrote at a popular level, with the main pedagogical intent of bringing a message of edification to the multitude of simple faithful, is now discredited. The literary ambitions, interests and prejudices of the author of the *Dialogues* were not populist but élitist. It was especially for an ecclesiastical caste that he was writing. The hypothesis that he was himself a functionary in the Church establishment fits very well with the character of his book.

[32] Bognetti, IV, p. 283.
[33] Duchesne, *op. cit.*, I, p. 346.

He despises the rustics and has scant interest in the common herd of townsfolk—traders, artisans and servants. On the other hand, he stresses the "venerability" of the middle and higher ranks of the clerical order, and also the dignity of secular notables, with an obsequiousness that Fr de Vogüé finds heavy and monotonous.[34] For all that, he can be critical of the arrogance of those of superior rank. We gain a glimpse of resentment of aristocratic privilege in a passing but revealing remark in III.23.2: "In some people nobility of birth is wont to bring forth baseness of mind".[35] He dislikes officials who flaunt their authority, like the haughty *defensor* Julian and the Roman ecclesiastics whose favour Julian curried. While the greater number of his heroes of spiritual power are abbots and bishops, his pages also contain much that is of special interest to other ranks in the Church's service: to the priests, deacons, subdeacons, *defensores*, notaries, *scriniarii* and even to those humbler functionaries, the *mansionarii* and *custodes*, who were responsible for the material care of the churches. Three of those sacristans are among his thaumaturges.

The Dialogist's sources and experience

Further light on the personality and career of the Dialogist can be gained by studying his text for traces of the sources he used, and especially for indications of his own sphere of activity and experience. His literary borrowings from the luxuriant growth of legendary hagiography have already been discussed in Chapter 18. Clearly he was steeped in that *genre* of literature (which the real Gregory was not) and it was his preferred field of interest. Chief among his other written sources, as we have seen in previous chapters, were the writings of St Gregory, especially the *Homilies on the Gospels*. He also knew well the archive file in which the letters of Gregory I were preserved. In previous pages I have noted many indications of such knowledge. A couple of further instances may be cited here. In two of Gregory's administrative letters from the year 599 there is the formal phrase "*abbas monasterii quod a Liberio quondam patricio in Campaniae partibus ... constructum*".[36] The identical phrase is gratuitously brought by the Dialogist into an anecdote in II.35.1.[37] He makes it refer to an abbot Servandus, who was also a deacon.

---

[34] *SC* 251, p. 82.

[35] "*... nonnullis solet nobilitas generis parere ignobilitatem mentis ...*"

[36] Ep. IX, 162 and 164; Ewald-Hartmann II, pp. 162-3. In these letters the abbot referred to is Theodosius.

[37] Ironically, while he has copied this phrase from those two Gregorian letters and put it into Gregory's own mouth, in order to give a touch of verisimilitude to his narration, that clause in the letters would not have been originally written by Gregory himself. In

The Dialogist has pat to his pen traditional formulas of the papal chancery. In I.8.1, when telling the story of supernatural portents which preceded the death of the former notary Anastasius, he makes Gregory, in describing the man, solemnly refer to his own sacred dignity as Roman Pontiff by use of a stereotyped official formula. Anastasius, he said, "was a notary of the holy Roman Church, to which, by the authority of God, I minister"—"*sanctae Romanae ecclesiae, cui Deo auctore deservio, notarius fuit*". The phrase used was a standard formula of the papal secretariate before and after the time of Gregory I. As Dobschütz notes, it is found in a stylized form ("*sanctae Romanae cui Deo auctore deservimus ecclesiae*") in the oldest part of the *Liber Diurnus*, and also in a letter of Gregory II or Gregory III.[38] M. B. Dunn finds that in the Gregorian *Registrum* such usage of the phrase "*Deo auctore*" occurs sixty-four times, and other similar phrases a further 131 times.[39]

From attention to the dates of the Indiction years given in the archive of Gregory's letters the Dialogist was able, for the most part, to observe chronological consistency in relating his narrative to the events of Gregory's lifetime. He would also have had access to the biographical notices of the sixth-century popes preserved in the Lateran *scrinium*, in the record which we call the *Liber Pontificalis*. From this source he probably took his references to the journeys of Popes John and Agapitus to Constantinople (III 2.1 and 3.1).[40]

In II.36 the Dialogist refers to a rule for monks admirably written by the holy abbot Benedict of Cassino. We know that around the year 625 a hitherto unknown *Regula sancti Benedicti* was introduced into Gaul by Venerandus, patron of a monastery at Altaripa, and that in later decades it was in use in some Merovingian monasteries in conjunction with the rule of Columban.[41] There is no trace of its observance in Italy during the seventh century. How did the Dialogist know of its existence? I suggest that from his employment in the Lateran *scrinium*, which also contained the library of the Roman See, he had knowledge of a codex of a monastic rule bearing the name of Benedict, which was in that library.

---

the light of Professor D. Norberg's findings we can recognize it as a typical turn of curial terminology, of the kind found *passim* in the routine administrative letters sent from Pope Gregory's chancery. The two letters in which it occurs are clearly of the formalized and impersonal type which were composed by the papal secretaries.

[38] *Op. cit.* p. 234. He cites eight instances from Sickel's edition of the *Liber Diurnus*. cf. Ewald-Hartmann, II, p. 468.

[39] *The Style of the Letters of St Gregory the Great*, Washington 1931, pp. 63-4. In a very close parallel to *Dialogues* I.8.1, the full phrase is linked with reference to a notary in an administrative letter from Gregory's curia in July 591: *Ep.* I.63 (Ewald-Hartmann, I, p. 85, line 1).

[40] Cf. *Dialogues* III.2.1 and 3.1; *LP* (Duchesne), I, pp. 275-6 and 287-8.

[41] See Chapter 11 above, pp. 221-47.

(That he had seen the *Regula Benedicti* is suggested by a possible echo of its phrasing in his fourth book.[42]) That codex may well have been the archetype from which earlier in the century Venerandus had obtained his copy of the document that he described as "the rule of holy Benedict a Roman abbot". We know that in the middle and second half of the century copies of the *RB* were in use in Francia. It is quite likely that the Roman *librarii* who supplied the needs of the book-questors from north of the Alps found that this monastic rule was one of the texts for which there was an increasing market. Thus the MS model in the *scrinium* would have become fairly well known to the personnel of that office. One may even surmise that it was this quickening interest in the *RB*, leading to requests for information about its otherwise unknown author, that prompted the Dialogist to supply the missing biography of the holy abbot Benedict in Book II of the *Dialogues*. (It may also have been the selfsame Lateran codex of the Benedictine rule, known to the Dialogist in the second half of the seventh century, that was donated by Pope Zachary to the newly refounded abbey and shrine of St Benedict at Montecassino in the middle of the eighth century.)

We may also infer that the Dialogist made some use of oral folk-traditions going back to the age of the Ostrogoths. This factor must not be exaggerated, however; such "sources" had a very minor part in the composition of a fictional work spun from the author's fertile imagination, with the aid of earlier literary models. We cannot discern a kernel of solid history underlying the legendary chaff in the *Dialogues*, any more than we can in the case of the contemporary Roman *Gesta Martyrum* with which the book is so closely akin in *genre*.[43] The Dialogist takes care to excuse himself to his possibly fastidious readers for repeating unpolished reports. In a couple of instances he reproduces rustic terms with a gloss on their meaning; in other instances, he explains, he has had to edit the stories from his plebeian sources because "*haec rusticano usu prolata stilus scribentis non apte susciperet*" (I, Prologue 10).

Several authors have drawn attention to surprising traces of pre-Christian folklore and popular superstitions in the *Dialogues*. A pioneer in this field was J. Laporte, who wrote a monograph entitled *St Benoît et*

---

[42] Cf. *Dialogues* IV.57.11: "*Nullus ex fratribus se ad eum ... iungat, nec sermonem ...*"; and *RB* 25.2: "*Nullus ei fratrum ... iungatur ... nec in colloquio ...*".

[43] Justly may we apply to the *Dialogues* the description which H. Delehaye wrote of those apocryphal *Gesta* and *Passiones*: "*Ce sont des compositions de caractère livresque, et nullement une sorte de codification des traditions répandues dans la foule ... des récits artificiels, qu'il faut se figurer péniblement écrits dans une cellule, à la lueur d'une lampe fumeuse, sur de vagues réminiscences, developpées d'après les procédés d'une rhétorique vulgaire*" (*Le Légendier*, p. 15).

le paganisme.[44] He found echoes of pagan and magical conceptions here and there in the narrative: for instance, in the ring-dance of the seven naked maidens in II.8.4. S. Boesch Gajano accepts that such vestiges of pagan folklore are discernible in Gregory's *Dialogues*, but she claims it as a merit of the great pope that he deliberately drew out those obscure rural traditions to give them what she calls *"il crisma della veridicità e dell' ufficialità"*. Her claim seems to be special pleading to explain a disconcerting phenomenon: "he knew how to recapture within the official Church ... a reality which was Christian in name but often in fact withdrawn from ecclesiastical control, and which was exposed, especially in the countryside, to very diverse influences. The apparently superstitious accounts, the apparently contradictory 'popular' beliefs are integrated, through the *Dialogues*, in Gregory's spirituality".[45] Implausible as it undoubtedly is to attribute to St Gregory the Great any concern to use, in such a cryptic fashion, elements of pagan belief and magical lore, nevertheless the traces of such conceptions in the *Dialogues* afford another indication of the pseudonymous author's acquaintance with the cruder folk-religion of rural Italy.

Clues from the Dialogist's topography

"One can say that, essentially, it is the legend of the duchy of Rome that the *Dialogues* express".[46] From many indications it seems very probable that the Dialogist had first-hand knowledge of the rural localities that he mentions. Indeed one may infer that he had a particular connection with the hill country of Tuscia, Valeria (Umbria), Sabina and Samnium.[47] A significant number of his stories are placed in those regions, which provide the centre of gravity for Books I and III of his work. Was he himself a native of one of those rural provinces? It is quite possible.[48] Alternatively, he could have gained his local knowledge of it (and also of the upper valley of the Aniene and of Campania, shown in Book II) from experience as a clerical official employed in administrative journeys to

---

[44] First circulated from the Abbey of Saint Wandrille, 1963, *pro manuscripto*; then re-edited in *Études Ligériennes d'histoire et d'archéologie médiévales*, ed. R. Louis, Auxerre, 1975, pp. 233-46.

[45] *Op. cit.*, ("*Dislivelli*"), p. 407.

[46] Dufourcq, *op. cit.* III, p. 288.

[47] See maps appended to Lanzoni's *Diocesi*, and to *SC* 251; also Petersen's Map 1, *op. cit.*, p. XXII. In III.26, relating the power and sanctity of the Samnite hermit Menas, the Dialogist claims: "I have almost as many witnesses to attest his way of life as there are people who know the province of Samnium".

[48] Martin I, pope from 649 to 653, was born at Todi in Umbria. The middle years of the seventh century would have been a propitious time for young recruits to the papal service who were natives of that region.

the papal patrimonies or to the rural domains possessed by individual Roman churches.

Even after a century of Lombard occupation of large tracts of Italy, considerable sectors of the once vast patrimonies of the Roman Church survived in central Italy and in the region south-east of Rome. They were, most relevantly, the *patrimonium Tusciae*,[49] the *patrimonium Sabinum et Carseolanum* and the *patrimonium Appiae*, with some remaining parts of the *patrimonium Campaniae*, although the latter had been much reduced by encroachments of the Lombard duchy of Benevento.[50] Spoleto and its surrounding region was the seat of Lombard power in central Italy. In the first age of the Lombard occupation it was held by the fierce duke Faraold. Before and during the pontificate of Gregory I most of the Catholic bishops had been expelled from their sees and their flocks sorely oppressed. After the truce of 598 and in the period of relative peace under the pro-Catholic Lombard monarchy in the first quarter of the seventh century, a *modus vivendi* was arrived at in central Italy. Church life revived[51] even in the territories harassed by the Lombards of Spoleto. During the seventh century, especially through the vigilance and energy of the Exarch Isaac of Ravenna in the third and fourth decades, the corridor of imperial territory running diagonally across Italy from Ravenna to Rome and Campania remained a cohesive political entity, though flanked and eroded by Lombard states and strongholds.[52] The setting of the Dialogist's stories in that corridor fits well into what we know of the untidy territorial and political situation, in which Lombard "frightfulness" was still a recurring reality, but in which church life in the decayed towns and their surrounding countryside kept some degree of continuity. With that unsettled and remote society we sense that the Dialogist had familiarity and affinity. Though his interests were not directly secular, his pages give us vivid glimpses of the Italian countryside, and of that rough-and-ready world of peasants, travellers, servants, soldiers, robbers and others, seen from the viewpoint of monks and clerics. It was that world which provided the backcloth for his tales of the prodigies of abbots, bishops and other holy men; on it he also projected his tales reflecting folk-tradition from the time of the Goths.

One fascinating chapter of the *Dialogues* (I.4) may reflect the distaste of the provincial countryman for the bureaucracy of the City. As S.

---

[49] Dufourcq notes "a curious expansion of the Tuscian patrimony in the course of the seventh century" (*op. cit.* III, p. 314).

[50] Bertolini, *op. cit.* (1941), pp. 264.

[51] *Ibid.* pp. 295-6.

[52] P. Llewellyn *op. cit.*, pp. 144-5. Ravenna features in three of the Dialogist's stories. The geography of the duchy of Rome is delineated by C. Diehl, *op. cit.*, pp. 63-8. See also Map 2 in Petersen, *op. cit.*, p. XXIII.

Boesch Gajano points out, the author there presents Rome not only as the seat of pontifical authority, "but also as that of an adulatory and malign clergy, who throw doubt on a [provincial] saint and induce the pontiff to an unjust action".[53] She also observes that while the book of the *Dialogues* shares certain basic characteristics with the almost contemporary legends in the Roman *Gesta Martyrum*, there is a difference in the setting of the stories. In the *Gesta* the background is urban; in the *Dialogues* it is not. Even when the episodes take place in towns, she remarks, they are not characterized *"urbanicamente"*, that is, not presented in the setting of urban society.

The Dialogist seems to have visited the hills and valleys around Subiaco, in which he situated the earlier monastic experiences of St Benedict. Likewise he knew the district where Latium Adiectum joined Campania, which was the setting of Benedict's foundation and later life at Cassino. Travelling along the Via Latina, he would have seen the mountain cone of Montecassino and the ruined monastic *cellula* on the summit, and would have heard the countryfolk tell how the Lombards had destroyed it in times past. There may have been a genuine tradition of the escape of the monks from that barbarian raid, which he echoed in II.17 of his book.[54] The Dialogist says that what Benedict found and pulled down on the mountain top when he first arrived there was a temple of Apollo. In his eighth-century poem Mark of Montecassino, on the other hand, said that the god worshipped there had been "foul Jove". His statement has been proved more accurate than the Dialogist's by the discovery in 1880 of a second-century inscription on the site referring to the *aedem Iovis*.[55]

It is noteworthy that the Dialogist betrays no personal knowledge of the topography of Sicily. He has no wonder-stories about that island to match those he tells of happenings in the peninsula itself. This contrasts with Pope Gregory's intense personal concern for Sicily and its people. No other region claimed a greater share of his pastoral care. As well as the important Sicilian patrimony of the Roman Church, Gregory himself had family estates in the island and founded monasteries there. Had he written the *Dialogues*, we should surely expect some reflection of this

---

[53] *Op. cit.* ("*La proposta agiografica*"), p. 635.

[54] Much has been written about the problem of exactly dating that first destruction of Montecassino. Paul Warnefrid, historian of the Lombards, puts it in the early years of the seventh century. (cf. *Hist. Lang.* VI.40.) His dating is not a casual remark, but fits in with his wider chronological frame of events, which is not without external corroboration. His statement is usually dismissed as a blunder, since the destruction is mentioned in Gregory's *Dialogues*, supposedly written in 593. But perhaps Paul was right after all in this instance.

[55] Cf. J. Chapman, *op. cit.* p. 173; Vogüé, *SC* 260, p. 167, note 10.

Sicilian dimension. The virtual neglect of Sicily in the *Dialogues* perhaps reflects the difficult situation in the second half of the seventh century. From the time that the Emperor Constans landed in Italy in 664 Sicily became a main Byzantine base. The papal patrimony there suffered from the harsh imperial presence. In those circumstances it would not be surprising if a functionary in the papal curia had little direct contact with that island.

The Fathers of Italy, to whose wondrous deeds the Dialogist initially promised to devote his book, are found to be almost all rural saints and thaumaturges dwelling in *loci minores* remote from Rome. His narrative does eventually include events in the Eternal City, but his Fathers do not dwell there. Some Roman episodes are introduced as Book III progresses, and the phenomena of Book IV are mainly related from a vantage point in Rome. St Peter's basilica has a special place in his story (cf. his remark in III.25.3). Thus, while the Dialogist's narrative is primarily concerned with saints and wonders outside Rome, it also reflects his personal experience of ecclesiastical life in the City itself. If he could not write of that life with the vision and pastoral earnestness of Pope Gregory, he did at least write of it from his more lowly viewpoint with the familiarity that came from personal involvement in it.

The Dialogist and his peers in the Roman secretariate

In Chapter 18 we saw that, despite the criticisms to which it gave rise, the study of A. Dufourcq on the legendary *Gesta Martyrum* of the City and duchy of Rome has many elements of permanent value. Among these (as S. Boesch Gajano acknowledges[56]) is the comparison he makes to situate the *Dialogues* within the wider movement of legendary hagiography that originated during the later sixth century and continued during the seventh. Dufourcq concluded that both the legend of the *Dialogues* and that of the *Gesta* have "the same date, the same local roots and the same character".[57] He inferred that "middle ranking Roman clergy" were involved in the authorship of the legendary *Gesta*. He observed that there is a close connection, indeed a solidarity, between martyrological legends of the duchy of Rome and those of the City itself. He goes on, in a passage which has clear relevance to our quest of the elusive Dialogist, to recognize the influence of legend-making in the City on the composition of the legends of rural parts of Italy:

---

[56] She praises the good points of Dufourcq's work in her article ("*La proposta agiografica*"), p. 657, note 173.

[57] "... *l'une et l'autre ont même date, mêmes racines locales, même caractère édifiant.*" (*op. cit.* III, pp. 292-3).

And there is nothing surprising in that, given that it was Roman clerics who composed some of our texts. The Roman churches possessed domains in diverse regions of Italy. The clerics who were responsible for their administration came to learn the legends that were related there; they edited them on the model of the Roman legends. Rome was the religious metropolis and the military capital. Its influence could not fail to be felt— we can discern its traces.[58]

Whether the Dialogist was a Roman cleric who in the course of administrative journeys gained contact with the legends of the hinterland to the north and south-east of the City, or whether he was a provincial who brought knowledge of his regional traditions with him when he entered the curial service in Rome, he can be recognized as one of a "school" of clerical writers of religious fiction who busily plied their pens in seventh-century Rome. Dufourcq observes that, for the authors who belonged to what he calls "the Gregorian legendary movement", there was "a tendency to dissociate the idea of a martyr and the idea of a saint", and he cites examples of venerated saints who were no longer represented as martyrs (such as John Penariensis and Laurence of Spoleto). He notes in particular the indirect influence on this Italian hagiography of the religious settlement of Rothari in the mid-seventh century, with the restoration of the Catholic bishoprics in the previously unsettled regions.[59]

In this perspective my profile of the Dialogist, writing his work of religious fiction at a Roman desk in the later seventh century, cannot be dismissed as a gratuitous and unlikely hypothesis. Although there remains obscurity about the dating of the individual legendary *Gesta* and *Passiones*, and although the period of their production lasted from the fifth to the late seventh century, it is now accepted that (as Dufourcq argued) their writers did constitute a continuing and distinctive "school".[60] There must undoubtedly have been an eager demand for this type of literature, which the legend-spinners applied themselves to meet. While Dufourcq was mistaken about both the identity of the author and the date of origin of the *Dialogues*, he rightly placed the author in the company of the contemporary writers of the *Gesta*, and established the close relationship between his work and theirs. St Gregory, he writes (and here I

---

[58] *Ibid.* III, p. 283.

[59] *Ibid.*, pp. 283-5.

[60] Cf. Lanzoni, *op. cit.*, pp. 31-50. Likewise H. Delehaye: "*Ce qui est incontestable, c'est que les auteurs des légendes romaines appartiennent à une même ecole, que leur psychologie, leur morale, leur érudition sont au même niveau, que leur littérature sort du même milieu; qu'ils ont même une phraséologie caractéristique ...*" (*Le Légendier*, p. 12; cf. also his *Les Passions des martyrs*, pp. 236-64.) G. Lucchesi likewise points out that those fictional accounts of Umbro-Tuscan and Roman saints were all written by writers of one recognizable school (*BS* IV, col. 778).

would substitute "The Dialogist"), "*n'est que l'émule illustre de cent écrivains obscurs*".[61] If, in this context, the work of the Dialogist no longer appears as an isolated phenomenon, he may still be recognized as the most talented and successful legend-spinner of them all. The contemporary authors of the *Gesta*, like the Dialogist, constantly insisted on the veracity of their legendary narrations, and piled up testimonies to authenticate them. Some of them, like him, even ascribed their fictions to illustrious authors.[62] He not only excelled them in the scale and design of his writing, but his achievement was incomparably greater than theirs because he succeeded in passing off his literary creation as the work of Gregory the Great.

The Dialogist would have been working in the Roman secretariate at the same time as a curial official called Gregory, who, after being trained from an early age in the papal household of the Lateran, rose to become one of the seven subdeacons, and was later *sacellarius* or paymaster of the Roman Church. When the work of the *scrinium* was divided into two departments by Pope Sergius I (687-701), he was made first curator of the pontifical library. This Gregory eventually became pope himself, in 715, as Gregory II—the first Roman to be bishop of Rome after a succession of seven Greek popes. When Aldhelm of Malmesbury was in Rome between 688 and 693, acquiring codices for the monks in England from the book-production bureau in the papal secretariate, he would probably have met Gregory the librarian—and perhaps also (who knows?) the Dialogist. We know that Aldhelm acquired and devoutly studied the legendary literature of the *Gesta Martyrum* of Rome, from which he borrowed numerous elements for his writings *De virginitate*.[63] He is an early witness to the wider circulation of those apocryphal Acts. Significantly, he is also the first witness to signal the existence of the Gregorian *Dialogues*, the text of which he may even have acquired on his book-questing visit to the court of Pope Sergius.

The *Liber Pontificalis* describes Gregory II as *facundus loquela*.[64] He was devoted to the memory and example of his predecessor and namesake Gregory the Great. He was also the principal patron of the new devotion to the major saint of the *Dialogues*, St Benedict of Montecassino, which he kindled as soon as he became pope. It was during his pontificate that the Gregorian *Dialogues* began to exercise the great influence that was

---

[61] *Op. cit.*, III, Preface.

[62] For instance, at least five fantastic *Passiones* were put out under the name of St Ambrose (Lanzoni, *op. cit.*, p. 36).

[63] Cf. B. de Gaiffier, *Études critiques d'hagiographie et d'iconologie*, Brussels 1967, pp. 71-2; and Dufourcq, *op. cit.*, I, p. 394. See also pp. 168-9 above.

[64] Duchesne, I, p. 396.

eventually to lead to the exaltation of the *Regula Benedicti* as the sole rule for western monks. Someone may wonder whether Gregory II, former official of the papal *scrinium* and first curator of the Apostolic Library, was not perhaps the same person as the Dialogist. The identification may seem tempting. In both men there was a strong interest in and devotion to St Gregory and his writings. Both, reacting against the predominating Greek influence, showed a native religious patriotism. The Dialogist, like Gregory the librarian and future pope, was *facundus loquela*. There were very few men of any talent in the service of the Roman Church in the late seventh century, as Pope Agatho lamented when writing to the Emperor and the eastern theologians at the time of the Trullan Council of 680-681.

Nevertheless, although the identification of Gregory the librarian with the Dialogist may seem at first sight to have some plausibility, it does not survive serious scrutiny. When Gregory II was elected pope in 715 he was doubtless still in full vigour. He lived until 731. These dates suggest that he was not born before the middle of the seventh century, and probably later. I see it as much more likely that the Dialogist was of an older generation, and that he had already had considerable experience in the papal service by the time he came to write his book. If he had been born after the middle of the century he would have been a precociously talented author to be able to compose the *Dialogues* about the end of the pontificate of Pope Adeodatus II (that is, around 676). On the supposition that the date of the composition of the *Dialogues* was as late as about 680-685, this objection concerning his age would have less force. But further—and this objection seems decisive—Gregory II was an able theologian, *"divinae scripturae eruditus"*, whose learning impressed the Emperor Justinian II and his advisors when as deacon he accompanied Pope Constantine to Constantinople in 710, and who was esteemed for his pronouncement in the later Iconoclast controversy.[65] The Dialogist, on the other hand, was not a theologian nor "learned in the Scriptures". His interests and talents were not in speculative theology or Scriptural exposition, but lay in the field of creative imagination. Avid collector and relator of prodigious tales, his own favourite thought-world was that of folk-religion and preternatural phenomena. In talent and religious outlook he appears well below the level of the man who became Pope Gregory II. Moreover, as we have observed, the Dialogist seems to have

---

[65] H. K. Mann, *Lives of the Popes in the Early Middle Ages*, I/2, pp. 141-4. There is, of course, a strong improbability that a man of such theological seriousness would have deliberately fabricated a book of spurious saints' lives and put it out as the work of Gregory the Great. One may suppose that he came to accept the *Dialogues* at their face value.

sprung from the lower ranks of ecclesiastical society; Gregory II was a patrician who, like his model Gregory the Great, turned his paternal mansion into a monastery. Nevertheless the dates and circumstances that we have been considering imply that the two members of the Lateran secretariate must have been known to one another. One can only speculate on the influence exercised by the Dialogist on his younger colleague, who, as pope, was to become a principal promoter of the *Dialogues* and of the Benedictine monasticism which owed its eventual predominance to that book.

It may be seen as significant that the earliest known testimonies to the existence and acceptance of the *Dialogues* (and to knowledge and cult of St Benedict) came from lands far distant from Rome—principally from England. During the quarter of a century between the first indications of its emergence into the light (in the writings of Aldhelm of Malmesbury and Julian of Toledo) and the beginning of the pontificate of Gregory II in 715, we find no trace of it in its Italian homeland. It may well be that the newly-emerged book *De miraculis patrum italicorum* was slow to gain acceptance as a genuine Gregorian work in Rome itself. The Romans would have been more critically aware of the novelty of this ostensibly Gregorian work than the eager readers and seekers of Roman books in the newly-Christianized kingdoms of northern Europe.[66] The Roman Church had not yet abandoned its official attitude of reserve to the wave of legendary hagiography and spurious *Gesta* that had flooded in during the two previous centuries. We cannot know whether the Dialogist himself lived long enough to witness the success and influence of his book. Perhaps a new generation had to grow up before it gained established authority in Rome itself. At all events, from the time of the pontificate of Gregory II it was launched on its course of literary fame and religious influence which has continued for nearly thirteen centuries.

---

[66] Hence the importance of the "Letter to Maximian" (see Chapter 5 above). Personnel in the papal secretariate (such as the future Pope Gregory II) could be reassured of the authenticity of the *Dialogues* by that persuasive "evidence", inserted into the register of the correspondence of Gregory I.

CHAPTER TWENTY THREE

IN CONCLUSION

I emphasized at the outset of this study that the case I am presenting rests on a combination of many arguments. Some of them, taken singly, indicate probabilities rather than certainties. Many are solidly probative even in themselves. It is, I submit, the coherence and convergence of all of them together that give to the total case its massive unity and force and establish the conclusion beyond reasonable doubt. It may even seem to some readers, who have perseveringly followed all the ramifications of my discussion and weighed the superabundant evidence presented in these pages, that I have needlessly multiplied my proofs, and that my argument is prolonged to an extent that in current idiom would be called "overkill". None the less, I have felt it necessary to marshal a very large number of concerted arguments, since the opinion I am refuting is rooted in thirteen centuries of tradition and is universally assumed to be well established.

The humanist and Protestant historians who challenged the authenticity of the *Dialogues* in the sixteenth and seventeenth centuries were right in their basic judgement, but they could not win the debate at that time because they were not able to pursue their demonstration in sufficient depth, and lacked the fuller scholarly resources available to us today. I do not claim that in my book all pertinent proofs of the spuriousness of the *Dialogues* have been exhaustively presented. There is much fruitful research still to be done to exploit the lines of investigation that I have opened up. In particular, it is evident that my computer-based survey is a pioneer exploration of the data, and that much more detailed work could be done in that specialized field.

It has been well said: "No century appears more obscure in the history of Christianity than that which extends from the death of Gregory the Great to the time of Gregory II".[1] It is in that dark post-Gregorian age that I have located the origin and emergence of the *Dialogues*. My hope is that my work will provide stepping stones for other researchers to explore further. I have found in my own long investigation of the *Dialogues* that the more I have probed, compared, questioned and challenged the

---

[1] G. le Bras "*L'Église romaine et les grandes églises occidentales après la mort de Grégoire le Grand*", in *Caratteri del secolo VII in Occidente* (*Settimane di Studi sull' Alto Medioevo*, no 5), Spoleto 1958, p. 184.

sources, the more discoveries I have made of the Dialogist's counterfeits, and the more discrepancies have become apparent between the ostensible claims of the *Dialogues* and the actual historical and literary data. Undoubtedly there are further discoveries still to be made, many other pieces to be fitted into this fascinating mosaic.

I have signalled the first appearance of the *Dialogues* in recorded history at the end of the ninth decade of the seventh century, with the explicit mention of the book and the assertion of its Gregorian authorship by Aldhelm of Malmesbury. Coupled with his testimony is that of Julian of Toledo, and shortly afterwards the testimonies of Adamnan of Iona and Defensor of Ligugé, all of whom implicitly attest knowledge of the book by reproducing phrases from it. But is not my case vulnerable to possible historical disproof? What if future research should discover, in some still latent document from that century, a testimony earlier than those of Aldhelm and Julian? Such a hypothetical possibility cannot, of course, be excluded *a priori*. At all events, there stands the weight of evidence presented in my preceding chapters, which indicates positively that the book was still unknown until well into the last quarter of the seventh century, and that the author's active lifetime lay later rather than earlier in that century. My internal critique of the text shows that it bears the stamp of an author other than Pope Gregory the Great; while my study of the external data shows that it was unknown in the age of Gregory himself and for a considerable time afterwards. That is the substance of my case. I further point out that the available historical evidence points to the book's date of origin, or at least of publication, late in the seventh century. But even if it could be shown that the *Dialogues* were in existence some decades before the date that I have proposed as its probable *terminus post quem*, my case would not be substantially affected.

To prove a negative is indeed a formidable task in historical research. Is it not temerarious to present a sweeping argument from silence which could be invalidated by a single documentary testimony to the contrary? That is, if in one single instance it could be demonstrated that an author or document attested knowledge of the existence of the *Dialogues* during the age of Gregory himself, my case would be seriously weakened, at least in so far as it asserts the tardy emergence of the book. Or even if a single instance could be adduced to demonstrate knowledge of the *Dialogues* at least in the first half or middle of the seventh century, my historical argument, though not invalidated, would still need to be recast. A most striking feature of my 35-year-long investigation, however, has been the realization that not a single such instance has been demonstrated, either in Gregory's own age or for nearly a century afterwards. A number of instances have indeed been alleged, but not one of them survives close examination. On the traditional assumption of the Gregorian authorship of the *Dialogues*, it is surely extraordinary that out of a vast range of documentary remains from a period of around a hundred years, no proven reference can be found to a book supposed to have been universally renowned and which would have aroused the widest interest throughout Christendom. Furthermore, sources (in particular, the lists of Gregory's writings in the *Liber Pontificalis* and in Isidore's *De viris illustribus*) that one would naturally expect to refer to the Gregorian *Dialogues*, if extant, omit mention of the supposedly famous work. No doubt much ink will be spilt in attempting to restore the credit of the traditional testimonies alleged from the anthologies of Paterius and Tajo, or from sources such as the *Vitas Patrum Emeritensium* and the *Vita Fructuosi*. When rigorously scrutinized, those time-honoured ''proofs'' of early awareness of the *Dialogues* are found to be no more surely probative than the celebrated passage from the *De viris illustribus* of Ildephonsus of Toledo, which was long held up as the earliest explicit testimony to the Gregorian authorship of the *Dialogues*. That major exhibit of the traditional apologetic has only recently been exposed as a mediaeval interpolation. I have shown that the other allegedly early testimonies likewise fail to survive critical probing.

I put this hypothetical question: suppose that the *Dialogues* had remained unknown until modern times, and that a manuscript of the text surviving from the early Middle Ages were brought to light by chance. Even though the narrative purported to be written by Pope Gregory, would it be generally accepted by the learned world as genuinely his? The obvious answer, surely, is that it would not. Scholars would see as a primary objection to its authenticity the fact that no historical chain of attribution, reaching back to Gregory's age, attested its origin. Furthermore they would regard the text itself as highly suspect. Sharp-eyed critics would point out the manifest differences in style and vocabulary between this tardily discovered document and Gregory's known writings. They would mark in it many unGregorian characteristics in thought, religious attitude and historical assertion, which they would see as signs of the hand of a literary forger. Some would note, indeed, the presence in the text of certain passages, markedly diverse from the rest of the narrative, in which they would recognize the ring of Gregory's own style and thought, and they would doubtless conclude that some genuine Gregorian fragments had somehow been inserted into the pseudepigraphal work. That hypothetical scenario, I submit, illustrates what is actually the case. It is mainly because it is generally but mistakenly assumed that a historical chain of attribution, attesting the origin of the *Dialogues*, reaches back to the age of Gregory himself that his author-

ship of the work is taken for granted. Once that assumption is overthrown a vital premise is invalidated and the onus of proof is shifted. As
in my hypothetical case, once the alleged pedigree of the *Dialogues* is
discredited and it is realized that the *Dialogues* were not known in the age
of Gregory the Great, one would expect scholarly criticism to recognize
as highly suspect the many unGregorian characteristics of the text itself.
To show that the book of the *Dialogues* emerged only belatedly into the
light is to remove the traditional and uncritical presumption in favour of
its Gregorian origin and to expose its contents to unclouded scrutiny.
Then the deep and ever-recurring unease felt by so many readers in the
past—and still today—when confronted with this disconcerting work,
which contrasts so incongruously with both the spirit and the letter of the
rest of the Gregorian corpus, need no longer be stifled by conformism to
received literary orthodoxy.

If the conclusions of my investigation are accepted, what consequences
will follow in the field of early mediaeval studies and of Gregorian studies
in particular? It is not too much to say that the historiography relating
to Gregory the Great and his age will need substantial revision. His
biography will have to be rewritten, and his personality and his place in
Christian history reassessed. The chronology of his writings—in particular, the dating of his *Homilies on the Gospels*—will be open to recon-
sideration. Furthermore there is hardly any work which has been written
about the history, religion and Latin literature of the early Middle Ages
which will not stand in need of some correction. The book of the
Gregorian *Dialogues* has been treated as a primary document in all those
fields of study; if it is exposed as a pseudepigraphal work from a later date
an imposing fabric of historical conclusions must be partially dismantled
and reconstructed. I foresee that the picture of Pope Gregory I as the
Pater superstitionis and the founding father of *Vulgärkatholizismus*, so
graphically painted by the Liberal Protestant historians because of the
assumed Gregorian authorship of the *Dialogues*, will have to be abandoned. Likewise there will be no need to postulate a strange mental
dichotomy in Gregory, and to represent him, on the one hand, as a wise
master of biblical, mystical and pastoral theology and as a far-sighted ecclesiastical statesman of consummate prudence, and, on the other hand,
as a gullible seeker after and relator of bizarre wonder-stories, who
shared the crude fancies of rural folk-religion.

Our own century has seen a renaissance in Gregorian studies.
Previous generations had acknowledged Gregory's greatness as a wise
ruler of the Church in an age of crisis. In our day there has come a new
appraisal of his towering stature as a master of the spiritual life whose in-

fluence was formative and permanent.[2] Since his writings were not systematic treatises, but mainly diffuse commentaries giving his profound reflections on Holy Scripture and on spiritual experience, he was less accessible to the mentality of centuries in which theology had become set in scholastic categories. Our own age, reacting against undue systematization of the Christian mystery, has come to a deeper appreciation of the experiential wisdom and pastoral genius of the fourth great Doctor of the Western Church. "It appears", writes Dom J. Leclercq, "that in the analysis of Christian experience, nothing essential has been added to that of St Gregory."[3] Elsewhere he writes: "All the streams of holiness and doctrine by which the Church had lived of old flowed into Gregory: the riches of the Bible, the liturgy, the Latin and some of the Eastern Fathers. By his synthesis of them, these treasures were passed on ... He was to be the spiritual father of the Middle Ages in the West."[4] The more the true spiritual greatness of St Gregory has been realized anew in the present century, the more the problem of the *Dialogues* has become obtrusive and embarrassing. How could such an inspired yet humble master of divine wisdom be also the author of that extraordinary farrago of preposterous tales, which seem to reflect a debased level of religious sensitivity? The paradox will not go away simply because some scholars ignore it, or even deny its existence. Ever and again it confronts those who come to share the spiritual vision of St Gregory through his contemplative treatises.

Those who defend the traditional ascription of the *Dialogues* have had to find some explanation for that apparent dichotomy in St Gregory's spiritual and intellectual make-up. To excuse him for writing the *Dialogues* they have developed a variety of pleas. If St Athanasius, St Jerome and St Augustine[5] could regale their readers with far-fetched tales, they retort, why not St Gregory also? Or, alternatively, they deny the naivety of the stories in the *Dialogues*, and suggest that they were a form of symbolic pedagogy on the part of a great pastor, conveying a "supra-historical" religious message. The problem is particularly acute for those commentators on the *Dialogues* who now frankly admit that the

---

[2] In his *Exégèse Médiévale* H. de Lubac documented the pervasive influence of St Gregory in the theology and spirituality of what he aptly called "the Gregorian Middle Ages" (*op. cit.*, Paris 1959, pp. 538-48.) As J. Leclercq put it: "*Tous, en effet, l'avaient lu et vivaient de lui*" (*Initiation aux auteurs monastiques du Moyen Age. L'amour des lettres et le désir de Dieu*, Paris 1957, p. 31.)

[3] *Op. cit.*, p. 39.

[4] In *The Spirituality of the Middle Ages*, edited by J. Leclercq, F. Vandenbroucke and L. Bouyer, English trans., London 1968, pp. 29-30. On Gregory's mastery in the teaching of mystical theology, see also Dom R. Gillet's introduction to *Morales sur Job*, SC 32b, Paris 1950, pp. 81-109.

[5] In his old age.

author himself fabricated miracle-stories for inclusion in his book, using earlier hagiographical models for the composition of his fictions, while constantly declaring that he had learned those true facts from first-hand witnesses. To explain this disquietingly devious procedure on the part of St Gregory, they plead that he must not be judged according to narrow "Anglo-Saxon moralistic principles of literal veracity". Such anachronistic censures, it is urged, are not applicable to the remote thought-world of ancient hagiography. I reply that what is at issue here is not the mentality or conception of veracity of ancient hagiographers in general, but of Pope Gregory I as we know him from his undisputed writings. It is the stark contrast between the Gregory whom we know from those writings and the Gregory of the *Dialogues* that is at the root of the problem, and of the ever-recurring disquiet felt by not a few sensitive admirers of the great pope. The *genre* of fantastic hagiography, in which the author of the *Dialogues* delighted, was certainly current in antiquity; but it was foreign to the spirituality of Gregory himself.

Scholars who have devoted long study to the contents of the *Dialogues* while accepting unquestioningly the traditional authorship of the book, have been constrained, almost inevitably, to form an estimate of St Gregory's mentality and character that does him an injustice. They have had to come to terms with the disconcerting nature of the narrative while still seeking to vindicate religious value for it. They have had to admit naive credulity and (worse) deviousness and dissembling on the part of its illustrious author, while still extolling his greatness of soul and depth of insight. They have thus been led on to attribute to him a religious psychology which is alien not only to the spiritual insight of other contemplative saints and masters of prayer, but to that of Gregory himself in his theological writings. There is no further need for these uneasy apologias. Once the traditional assumption of the Gregorian authorship of the *Dialogues* has been exposed as unfounded, the real Gregory can be seen as he truly was: not as a spiritual and cultural schizophrenic, not as a strange mixture of greatness and puerility of soul, but as a man of transparent integrity, of extraordinary mental acuity and of unitary vision of reality, as a master of faith and religious experience whom all Christians can honour, without the reservations which so many have felt obliged to make.

Where my conclusions are accepted, many other consequences will be seen to follow. Much fictitious "history", taken from the pages of the *Dialogues*, about saints and sites of sixth-century Italy and about the state of the Church and its institutions before and during the pontificate of Gregory I, will have to be discarded. The calendars of saints to which so many of the legendary heroes of the *Dialogues* were admitted, especially during the sixteenth century, should be critically expurgated. Even the place in history of the great patriarch of Western monasticism, St Benedict, will require a fresh objective appraisal. There will be repercussions too, in the study of the origins and early dissemination of the *Regula Benedicti*. Account will have to be taken of the new light thrown on the tardy but rapid rise to pre-eminence of Benedictine monasticism in the eighth century, in the wake of the recent emergence of the *Dialogues*.

In the writing of the history of early Lombard Italy it has been assumed that the *Dialogues* offered firm points of reference. This assumption, too, must be set aside when it is recognized that the book reflects a historical situation nearly a century later than Gregory's lifetime. I am aware that my findings in the matter of the *Vitas Patrum Emeritensium* and associated texts go counter to assumptions widely accepted by historiographers of early mediaeval Spain. There will be many who will stoutly oppose the view (which, however, I am not the first to advance) that the *VPE* dates from after the Moorish conquest of Spain. My case concerning the *Dialogues* does not stand or fall with that post-conquest dating. There are scholars of repute who allow at least that the *VPE* may date from the last decades of the seventh century. Their dating is reconcilable with my main conclusions: so that if my further argument for a still later date is unpalatable, it need not stand in the way of acceptance of my dating of the *Dialogues*. I must, however, qualify as completely unproved the still widely-held theory first proposed by Tamayo de Vargas, which assigns a date of origin for the *VPE* before the middle of the seventh century. This correction of the dating of the *VPE*, and discounting of its value as a source, will have implications for the historiography of Visigothic Spain. The origin and status of the *Vita Fructuosi* will likewise have to be reconsidered.

In the theological sphere, the early development of the doctrine of Purgatory will need to be re-examined. The grossly realistic anecdotes in the *Dialogues* about souls found imprisoned in torrid places of torment, and likewise the story of the sinful monk freed from penal fire by a trental of Masses, were supposed to be vouched for by the authority of the great pope and Doctor of the Church. Accordingly they had a considerable influence on the manner in which the doctrine of Purgatory, and the practice of Mass-suffrages for the souls detained there, were developed in the mediaeval Church. That practice, and the corresponding conception of Purgatory which is still current, require critical questioning. It can no longer be claimed that belief in the special efficacy of a numerical series of Masses offered for deceased souls, which was thus firmly established in popular devotion and clerical practice, was sanctioned by St Gregory's great authority. Although the Roman Catholic doctrine of Purgatory itself does not depend on the *Dialogues*, the way in which it has been interpreted, and the pathetic emphasis which it has been given in popular piety, owe not a little to the circumstantial accounts supposedly related by St Gregory in the fourth book of the *Dialogues*.

So too the notions about demonology which prevailed in later Christendom, and permeated the religious psychology not only of mediaeval Catholics but of Protestants later, were influenced by the tales from the *Dialogues* about the devils' activity even in the small vicissitudes of life. Responsibility for the prevalence of those notions can no longer be laid at the door of Gregory the Great. The sober and sombre Gregorian teaching about the powers of evil can now be restored. When tracing the march of the *Dialogues* through the centuries, G. Dufner[6] remarked on the need for a detailed study to bring out the influence that the Gregorian *Dialogues* exercised on the socio-religious concepts of the mediaeval world. The need is still there, and the influence was undoubtedly great; but it will have to be recognized that it was not a genuinely Gregorian influence.

It is time for ecclesiastical historians to make a new appraisal of the controversial judgement of Adolf Harnack and many other Protestant scholars, who saw in the *Dialogues* of Pope Gregory I a chief source of *Vulgärkatholizismus* and of a coarsening of mediaeval religious sensibility. The sub-Christian character of the *Dialogues*-narrative should be frankly admitted, as also the considerable influence of the book in later centuries. The Liberal Protestant critics were right in their assessment of the character of the book, but wrong in accepting its attribution to one of the greatest popes and doctors of the Roman Church. Their adverse judgement of popular Catholicism as a whole was exaggerated; nevertheless it must be admitted that in so far as the *Dialogues* exercised a baneful influence on Christian sensibility in later centuries, it was to a large extent due to the universal assumption that the book bore the authority of St Gregory the Great. By the Dialogist's successful pseudepigraphy, the stamp of official approval was illegitimately conferred on a near-superstitious mentality which placed greater stress on the marvellous and sensational in religion than on the everyday call to lead the life of Christian virtue in response to God's grace—which had been the constant theme of St Gregory's own teaching. For the author of the *Dialogues*, as Harnack rightly objected, "miracle was the distinguishing mark of the religious". From the colourful fantasies of the *Dialogues* mediaeval Christians would draw, not the central lessons of the Gospel and of its demands on men, but an undemanding delight in legendary religion and an eager thirst for supernatural phenomena.

---

[6] *Op. cit.*, p. 211.

In the course of these pages I have used not a few pejorative terms when referring to the person and work of the fabricator of the *Dialogues*. I have called him dissembler, pseudepigrapher and forger. I have referred to his cunning and deceit, and spoken of his writing as spurious and counterfeit. These emotive-sounding terms are objectively applicable, but they do not imply on my part indignant censure of the far-off anonymous author. After 35 years of acquaintance with his work and his wiles, I seem to know him very well, and would even claim a privileged knowledge of his character and his foibles. Whatever I have to say about his literary forgeries, I do not mean to brand him as a sinister imposter. From long familiarity with his ways I look upon him as an old if eccentric acquaintance. I appreciate with what devotion and painstaking application he conned and culled the writings of St Gregory. Perhaps he even chose to subordinate his own talents, and to sacrifice his own hope of fame, to his desire to pay to the great pope the tribute of literary impersonation. The pseudepigrapher who placed his own writings under the mantle of a great name, in order to ennoble them and to commend them to posterity, is a well-known figure in the literary history of the ancient and early-mediaeval world. The Dialogist, alias Pseudo-Gregory, is in the company of the unknown authors who wrote the Jewish and early Christian apocrypha, and of later celebrated Christian pseudepigraphers like Pseudo-Athanasius, Pseudo-Macarius, Pseudo-Ambrose, Pseudo-Jerome and Pseudo-Dionysius the Areopagite. His imposture, surviving to the present day, has been more successful than theirs. Moreover, he had the considerable advantage of having access to a store of genuine literary remains of the author whose *persona* he adopted, and was able to weave them into the fabric of his composition in order to give it exceptional verisimilitude.

To understand the Dialogist better, then, we may refrain from judging him by our own canons of historicity, literary propriety and religious seriousness. The mentality of a legend-spinner in that age was neither that of a trickster nor of an evangelist, but rather that of a pious romancer.[7] In the balance sheet of Christian history we cannot, indeed, fail to take account of the debasement of religious sensibility for which the Dialogist has been unwittingly responsible. We have seen that his success in fathering his book of bizarre miracle-stories on Pope St Gregory the Great had the effect of legitimating the *genre* of religious sensationalism in the mediaeval Church. One may also reflect, more indulgently, that his inventive talent and quaint tales brought entertain-

---

[7] Lanzoni makes a tolerant *apologia* for the writers of fictitious hagiography in that age: *op. cit.*, p. 39.

ment to countless readers and hearers, lettered and unlettered. At all events, his literary artifice has had one major beneficial effect: it has preserved for posterity not a few gems of genuine Gregorian wisdom (the "IGPs") which might otherwise not have survived.

Almost inevitably, in a work of such complexity which ranges over the whole field of the cultural and religious history of Late Antiquity and the early Middle Ages, there will be errors and omissions in my book which will call for correction. But while welcoming any such corrections, I would urge that they be seen in proportion. To point out flaws and misapprehensions in presentation of the facts and in particular lines of reasoning will not avail to overthrow the whole case while its main structure, compacted of a multitude of firm arguments mutually corroborating one another, remains intact. I hope that a dust-storm of controversy about individual issues will not be allowed to obscure the massive solidity of that case.

I anticipate, indeed, spirited opposition to my whole enterprise and to its conclusions. This is a field in which emotions and traditional loyalties run deep. I must expect something of the obloquy that Abbot Benedict Haeften heaped upon the heads of those who challenged the authenticity of the *Dialogues* in the sixteenth and seventeenth centuries. Present-day critics may be provoked to apply to me what he said of Coccius: "*Affectata enim, ne dicam maligna, est haec Huldrici Coccii dubitatio*".[8] I am content to look beyond the immediate squalls of controversy to a longer and calmer perspective.

"*Habent sua fata libelli*". The fortunes of the book entitled *The Dialogues of Pope Gregory concerning the Miracles of the Fathers of Italy*, which first emerged from obscure beginnings thirteen hundred years ago, have through the centuries become interwoven with the piety and history of Christendom. What is its further destiny? Although I am convinced that the evidence I have presented exposes it as a counterfeit, I fully realize how great is the weight of tradition, and of "received orthodoxy" in literary and historical scholarship, that stands in the way of early acceptance of my findings. That is why I still foresee a period of controversy, of uncertain length, before it can be generally admitted that the so-called Gregorian *Dialogues* were not written by Pope St Gregory the Great. If I do not live to see that final turn in the *fata* of this famous *libellus*, I venture a confident prediction that it will eventually come about.

---

[8] *S. Benedictus illustratus*, Antwerp 1644, p. 7.

BIBLIOGRAPHY

PRIMARY SOURCES

Adamnan of Iona. *Adomnan's Life of Columba*, ed. A. and M. Anderson, London 1961.

Aldhelm of Malmesbury. *Opera*, ed. R. Ehwald, *MGH* Berlin 1919.

Bede. *Opera*, ed. Migne, *PL* 90-95. *Historia Ecclesiastica, Historia Abbatum*, etc., ed. C. Plummer, 2 vols., Oxford 1896, reprinted 1946. *Ecclesiastical History*, ed. B. Colgrave and R. Mynors, Oxford 1969.

Cassian. *Opera*, ed. M. Petschenig, 2 vols., *CSEL* 13, 17 (1886, 1888). *Collationes*, ed. E. Pichery, *SC* 42, 54, 64, reprinted 1966, 1971.

Codices latini antiquiores, ed. E. Lowe, 7 vols. and *Supplement*, Oxford 1934-71.

Columba of Iona. *Columbani Epistolae*, ed. Migne, *PL* 80.

Concilia Galliae AD 511-695, ed. C. de Clercq, *CCL* 148A (1963).

Defensor of Ligugé. *Defensoris Locogiacensis Liber Scintillarum*, ed. H. Rochais, *CCL* 117 (1957).

Diplomata, chartae et instrumenta aetatis Merovingicae, ed. J. Pardessus, 2 vols., Paris 1843-9.

Gregory of Tours. *Opera*, ed. W. Arndt and B. Krusch, *MGH* Hanover 1884. Ed. Migne, *PL* 71.

Gregory the Great.

    Dialogues, ed. A. de Vogüé, Books I-III, *SC* 254 (1978), 260 (1979); Book IV, *SC* 265 (1980); ed. U. Moricca, *Fonti per la Storia d'Italia* 57, Rome 1924.

    Moralia in Iob, ed. M. Adriaen, Books I-XXII, *CCL* 143, 143A (1979); ed. R. Gillet, A. de Gaudemaris, A. Bocognano, Books I-XVI, *SC* 32B, 212, 221 (1974-5); ed. Migne, *PL* 75-76.

    Homiliae in Evangelia, ed. Migne, *PL* 76.

    Homiliae in Hiezechielem, ed. M. Adriaen, *CCL* 142 (1971).

    Regula Pastoralis, ed. Migne. *PL* 77.

    In Cantica Canticorum, In librum primum Regum, ed. P. Verbraken, *CCL* 144 (1963).

    Letters: Registrum Epistolarum, ed. P. Ewald and L. Hartmann, 2 vols., *MGH* Berlin 1891, 1899. *Registrum Epistularum*, ed. D. Norberg, *CCL* 140, 140A (1982).

Historia monachorum in Aegypto, Latin version of T. Rufinus, ed. Migne, *PL* 21.

Ildephonsus of Toledo. *El 'De Viris Illustribus' de Ildefonso de Toledo: estudio y edición crítica*, ed. C. Codoñer Merino, Salamanca 1972.

Isidore of Seville. *Opera omnia*, ed. F. Arévalo, 7 vols., Rome 1797-1803. Ed. of A. Lorenzana reprinted by Migne, *PL* 81-84. *De viris illustribus*, ed. C. Codoñer Merino, Salamanca 1964. *Etymologiae*, ed. W. Lindsay, 2 vols., Oxford 1911.

Jonas of Bobbio. *Vita Columbani*, *etc.*, ed. B. Krusch, Hanover and Leipzig, 1905. ed. Migne, *PL* 87.

Julian of Toledo. *Prognosticon futuri saeculi*, *etc.*, ed. J. Hillgarth, *CCL* 115 (1976).

Liber Pontificalis ed. L. Duchesne, Vol. I (1886); 2nd ed., with revisions by C. Vogel in supplementary volume, Paris 1955-7; ed. T. Mommsen, *Gesta Pontificum Romanorum* I/1, (to AD 715), *MGH* Berlin 1898.

Martyrologium Hieronymianum ad fidem codicum, ed. J. De Rossi and L. Duchesne, in *AA. SS.*, November II/1, Brussels 1894.

Moschus, John. *Pratum Spirituale*, French ed. M. J. Roüet de Journel, *SC* 12 (1946). Unreliable Greek text in *PG* 87. New critical edition by P. Pattenden in preparation.

Paterius. *Liber Testimoniorum*, ed. R. Vander Plaetse, *CCL* 145A (*sub prelio*).

Paul Warnefrid. *Historia Langobardorum*, ed. G. Waitz, *MGH* Hanover 1878; ed. Migne, *PL* 95.

Regula Benedicti, ed. A. de Vogüé and J. Neufville, *La Règle de saint Benoît*; text in *SC* 181, 182 (1972).

Regula Magistri, ed. A. de Vogüé, *La Règle du Maître*, SC 105, 106 (1964).

Sanctuarium (*passiones* collected by B. Mombritius), modern ed. Paris 1919.

Sulpicius Severus. *Vita Martini*, ed. J. Fontaine, *SC* 133 (1967). *Dialogi*, ed. C. Halm, *CSEL* 1, 152 (1866).

Vita Fructuosi, ed. F. Nock, *The Vita Sancti Fructuosi*, Washington 1946; ed. M. Díaz, *La Vida de San Frutuoso de Braga, Estudio y edición crítica*, Braga 1974.

Vita Sancti Bonifatii, ed. W. Levison, Hanover 1905.

Vitae Patrum — Vitae Seniorum, ed. Migne, *PL* 73.

Vitas Patrum Emeritensium: ed. C. De Smedt in *AA. SS.* 63, November 1, Paris 1887; published separately, *Anonymi libellus*, Brussels 1884; ed. J. Garvin, Washington 1946; ed. Migne, *PL* 80.

SECONDARY SOURCES

(Works mentioned a number of times)

Aherne, C. *Valerius of Bierzo*, Washington 1949.

Auerbach, E. *Literatursprache und Publikum in der lateinischen Spätantike und im Mittelalter*, Bern 1958.

Batiffol, P. *St Gregory the Great* (trans.), London 1929.

Bertolini, O. *Roma di fronte a Bisanzio e ai Longobardi*, Rome 1941.

Boesch Gajano, S. '*Dislivelli culturali e mediazioni ecclesiastiche nei Dialoghi di Gregorio Magno*', in *Quaderni Storici* 41, 1979, pp. 398-415. '*La proposta agiografica dei Dialoghi di Gregorio Magno*', in *Studi Medievali* (3rd series) 21, 1980.

Bognetti, G. *L'Età Longobarda*, 4 vols., Milan 1966-8.

Brazzel, K. *The Clausulae in the Works of Saint Gregory the Great*, Washington 1939.

Brechter, S. '*War Gregor der Grosse Abt vor seiner Erhebung zum Papst?*', in *SMGBO* 57, 1939, pp. 209-24. '*Montecassinos erste Zerstörung*', in *SMGBO* 56, 1938, pp. 109-50.

Brunhölzl, F. *Geschichte der lateinischen Literatur des Mittelalters*, Vol. I, Munich 1975.

Bruys, F. *Histoire des Papes*, La Haye 1732.

Cave, W. *Scriptorum ecclesiasticorum historia literaria*, London 1688.

Ceillier, R. *Histoire générale des auteurs sacrés et ecclésiastiques*, Vol. XVII, Paris 1750.

Chapman, J. '*À propos des martyrologes*', in *Rev. Bén.* 20, 1903, pp. 285-313. *St Benedict and the Sixth Century*, London 1929.

Cooke, R. *Censura quorundam scriptorum*, London 1614.

Cremascoli, G. *Novissima hominis nei Dialoghi di Gregorio Magno*, Bologna 1979.

D'Achéry, L. *Acta Sanctorum Ordinis S. Benedicti*, Paris 1688.

Dagens, C. *Saint Grégoire le Grand: culture et expérience chrétiennes*, Paris 1977.

Delehaye, H. *Sanctus: essai sur le culte des saints dans l'antiquité*, Brussels 1927. *Les Légendes hagiographiques*, Brussels 1905. *Étude sur le légendier romain*, Brussels 1936.

Deshusses, J. and Hourlier, J. '*Saint Benoît dans les livres liturgiques*', in *SM* 21, 1979, pp. 143-204.

Díaz y Díaz, M. *De Isidoro al Siglo XI*, Barcelona 1956. *Index scriptorum latinorum medii aevi Hispanorum*, 2nd ed., Madrid 1959. '*La Compilación hagiografica de Valerio de Bierzo*', in *Hispania Sacra* 4, 1931, pp. 3-25.

Diehl, C. *Études sur l'administration byzantine dans l'Exarchat de Ravenne (568-751)*, Paris 1888.

Dobschütz, E. von. *Das Decretum Gelasianum*, Leipzig 1912.

Du Pin, Ellies. *Nouvelle bibliothèque des auteurs ecclésiastiques*, Vol. V, Paris 1691.

Dudden, F. *Gregory the Great: his Place in History and Thought*, 2 vols., London 1905.

Dufner, G. *Die Dialoge Gregors der Grossen im Wandel der Zeiten und Sprachen*, Padua 1968.

Dufourcq, A. *Étude sur les Gesta Martyrum romains*, Paris, Vol., I, 1900; Vols. II-III, 1907; Vol. IV, 1910.

Dzialowski, G. von. *Isidor und Ildefons als Literaturhistoriker*, Munster 1898.

Ebert, A. *Geschichte der christliche-lateinischen Literatur*, Vol. I, Leipzig 1894.

Étaix, R. '*Le Liber Testimoniorum de Paterius*', in *RSR* 32, 1958, pp. 66-78.
Ferrari, G. *Early Roman Monasteries ... from the V through X Century*, Rome 1957.
Fliche, A. and Martin, V. *Histoire de l'Église*, Vol. IV, Paris 1945.
Froger, J. '*La Règle du Maître et les sources du monachisme bénédictin*', in *Revue d'Ascétique et de Mystique* 30, 1954, pp. 275-88.
Funk, J. (ed. and trans.) *Gregor der Grosse vier Bücher Dialoge*, Munich 1933.
Geary, P. *Sacra Furta. Theft of Relics in the Central Middle Ages*, Princeton 1978.
Gillet, R. '*Grégoire le Grand*', in *Dictionnaire de Spiritualité* VI (1967), cols. 872-910. Introduction to translation of *Moralia* of St Gregory in *SC* 32 (*Morales sur Job*), pp. 81-109. '*Spiritualité et place du moine dans l'Église selon saint Grégoire le Grand*' in *Théologie de la Vie monastique*, Paris 1961, pp. 323-52.
Goffart, W. *The Le Mans Forgeries*, Cambridge, Mass., 1966.
Gregorovius, F. *A History of the City of Rome in the Middle Ages* (trans.), Vol. II, London 1894.
Hallinger, K. '*Papst Gregor der Grosse und der heiliger Benedikt*', in *SA* 42, 1957, pp. 231-319. '*Römische Voraussetzungen der bonifatianischen Wirksamkeit in Frankenreich*', in symposium, *Sankt Bonifatius*, Fulda 1954.
Harnack, A. *Lehrbuch der Dogmengeschichte*, Vol. III (3rd ed.), Freiburg-im-Breisgau 1897.
Hauck, A. *Kirchengeschichte Deutschlands*, Vol. I (8th ed.), Leipzig-Berlin 1954.
Holdsworth, C. 'St Boniface the Monk', in *The Greatest Englishman*, ed. T. Reuter (*q.v.*).
Hunter Blair, P. *The World of Bede*, London 1970.
Kinnirey, A. *The Late Latin Vocabulary of the Dialogues of St Gregory the Great*, Washington 1935.
Lanzoni, F. *Le Origini delle Diocesi antiche d'Italia*, Rome 1923.
Lau, G. *Gregor I der Grosse nach seinem Leben und seiner Lehre*, Leipzig 1845.
Le Culte et les reliques de saint Benoît et de sainte Scholastique, by various authors, *SM* 21, 1979.
Le Goff, J. *La Naissance du Purgatoire*, Gallimard 1981.
Llewellyn, P. *Rome in the Dark Ages*, London 1970. 'The Roman Church in the 7th Century; the Legacy of Gregory I', in *JEH* 25, 1974.
Mabillon, J. *Annales Ordinis S. Benedicti*, Vol. I, Paris ed. 1723.
Mähler, M. '*Evocations bibliques et hagiographiques dans la Vie de saint Benoît par saint Grégoire*', in *Rev. Bén.* 83, 1973, pp. 398-429.
Malnory, A. *Quid Luxovienses monachi ... ad regulam monasteriorum ... contulerint*, Paris 1894.
Manitius, M. *Geschichte der lateinischen Literatur des Mittelalters*, Vol. I, Munich 1911.
Masdeu, J. de. *Historia Crítica de España y de la Cultura Española*, Vol. XIII, Madrid 1794.
Maya Sanchez, A. '*La Versión Primitiva de la Vita Fructuosi*', in *Habis* 9, 1978, pp. 169-96.
McClain, J. *The Doctrine of Heaven in the Writings of St Gregory the Great*, Washington 1956.
Mélanges Colombaniens. Actes du Congrès International de Luxeuil 1950, Paris 1950.
Merdrignac, B. *La Première Vie de saint Samson*, in *Britannia Christiana* 1986.
Meyvaert, P. 'The Date of Gregory the Great's Commentaries on the *Canticle* and on *Kings*', in *Sacris Erudiri* 23, 1978-9.
Mundó, A. '*L'Authenticité de la Regula Sancti Benedicti*', in *SA* 42, 1957, pp. 114-26.
Murray, P. '*The Miracles of St Benedict: may we doubt them?*', in *Hallel* 11, 1983, pp. 64-8.
Norberg, D. *In Registrum Gregorii Magni studia critica*, Uppsala 1937.
O'Carroll, J. 'Monastic Rules in Merovingian Gaul', in *Studies* 42, 1953, pp. 407-19.
Penco, G. *Storia del Monachesimo in Italia*, Rome 1960. '*La prima diffusione della Regula di San Benedetto*', in *SA* 42, 1957, pp. 321-45.
Petersen, J. *The Dialogues of Gregory the Great in their Late Antique Cultural Background*, Toronto 1984.
Pfeilschifter, G. *Die authentische Ausgabe des 40 Evangelienhomilien Gregors des Grossen*, Munich 1900 (reprinted 1970).
Porcel, O. *La Doctrina Monástica de San Gregorio Magno y la 'Regula Monachorum'*, Madrid 1950 and Washington 1951.
Prinz, F. *Frühes Mönchtum in Frankenreich*, Munich 1965.
Quentin, H. *Les Martyrologes historiques du moyen âge*, Paris 1908.
Reuter, T. *The Greatest Englishman. Essays on St Boniface*, Exeter 1980.

Richards, J. *Consul of God*, London 1980.

Rivetus, A. *Critici sacri specimen*, Leipzig (?) 1612; augmented ed., Geneva 1642.

Rossi, J. De. '*De scrinio et bibliotheca sedis apostolicae saeculo septimo*', in the preface to his *Codices palatini bibliothecae Vaticanae*, Rome 1886.

Schmitz, P. *Histoire de l'ordre de saint Benoît*, Vol. I, Maredsous 1948.

Schrörs, H. '*Das Charakterbild des heiligen Benedikt von Nursia und seine Quellen*', in *ZkT* 42, 1921, pp. 169-207.

Sepulcri, A. '*Le Alterazioni fonetiche e morfologiche nel latino di Gregorio Magno*', in *Studi Medievali* 1, 1904.

Talbot, C. *The Anglo-Saxon Missionaries in Germany*, London 1954.

Tateo, F. '*La Struttura dei Dialoghi di Gregorio Magno*', in *Vetera Christiana* 2, 1965, pp. 101-27.

Tausch, H. *Benediktinisches Mönchtum in Österreich*, Vienna 1949.

Traube, L. *Textgeschichte der Regula S. Benedicti*, in *Abhandlungen der bayerischen Akademie* XXV, 2, Munich 1911.

Vogüé, A. de. '*Les vues de Grégoire le Grand sur la vie religieuse dans son commentaire des Rois*', in *SM* 20, 1979. *Vie de saint Benoît*, Bégrolles-en-Mauges 1982. '*Le pape qui persécuta saint Equitius: essai d'identification*', in *AB* 100, 1982. (See also editions listed under Primary Sources.)

Wallace-Hadrill, J. *Early Mediaeval History*, Oxford 1975. *The Frankish Church*, Oxford 1983.

Wasselynck, R. '*Les Compilations des "Moralia in Job" du VIIe au XIIe siècle*', in *Recherches de théologie ancienne et médiévale* 29, 1962.

Wilmart, A. '*Le Recueil Grégorien de Paterius*', in *Rev. Bén.* 1927, pp. 81-104.

Zibermayr, I. *Noricum, Bayern und Österreich*, Munich-Berlin 1944.

Zimmermann, A. *Kalendarium Benedictinum*, Vol. I, Mettern 1933.

INDEX NOMINUM

INDEX RERUM

"Council of nobles" in Gregory's Rome   26, 549, 683
Critical reappraisal of early Benedictine history   16, 189-97
Cult of St Benedict, non-existent before eighth century   16, 251-61, 281n
Cursing, malice of   499-500

Date of composition of *Dialogues*   29, 722-4 and *passim*
Dating of St Gregory's *Homilies on the Gospels*   83-5, 748
Dating of *Vita Fructuosi*   156-62, 751
Dating of *Vitas Patrum Emeritensium*   131-7, 142-9, 152-4, 160, 162, 751
Dearth of thaumaturges in Rome   678
Deathbed visions   108-9, 541-5, 557-8, 565-6, 636, 658
Demonology of *Dialogues*   23, 43, 480, 505-7, 588, 650-2, 752
Dialogist's sources and experience   734-7
Dialogist's station in life   29-30, 731-4, 740-4
Disciples of St Benedict unknown in seventh century   248-50
Disciples of St Columban well known in seventh century   249-50, 255-6
Divine chastisement of the just   539-42
Donation of Constantine   31, 33
Doublets in Gregorian writings   418, 437, 451, 457, 474-5, 479, 481, 576-7 and *passim*
Drafting of Gregorian letters   689-90
Dreams, discernment of   527, 568-72
Dwelling with oneself   470-4, 657

Earlist mention of *VPE*   152
Earliest MSS of *Dialogues*   179-85
Earliest observance of *Regula Benedicti*   188-92, 201, 204, 221-8, 231, 233, 239, 250
Early Benedictine monasticism   16-8, 186-295
Ecclesial perspective, differences in   652-3
enim, frequency of   27, 703-8
ergo, frequency of   27-8, 703-9
Eschatology of *Dialogues*   23, 43, 503, 521-3, 526, 550-4, 561, 643-50. See also Hell
    and Purgatory
Exaggerated concern for authentification of tales   25, 580, 590, 596-7, 605, 607,
    639-43, 674-6, 742
exempla in Gregorian usage   444-6, 465, 507, 527-8, 577

Faith and unbelief   530-1
falcastrum, etymology of   627
False Chroniclers   135, 138
First destruction of Montecassino   61, 225, 228, 242, 251, 277, 739n
First emergence of *Dialogues* into light of history   15, 163-78, 722-3
First liturgical mention of St Benedict   16, 258-9
Formal clausulae in Gregory's works   26-7, 688-91
Four hundred peasants, supposed martyrdom of   24, 62, 511, 668-9

Grammatical phenomena   26, 691-3
Greek hagiography   104-5, 109-10, 293, 623-4, 726-7, 733
Gregory's knowledge of hagiographical literature   21-2, 597-603
Gregory's methods of composition   92-3, 411-9, 431, 437-8

Hadrianic Register   79, 124-7
Hagiographical borrowings   21-2, 497, 580-627 and *passim*
Haplography   560
Hell   177, 503, 526, 544, 550-1, 553-4, 562-5, 581, 594, 644
Heuristic exegesis   479, 550, 629
Historical discrepancies   659-83 and *passim*